Testing Object-Oriented Software

Testing Object-Oriented Software

David C. Kung
Pei Hsia
Jerry Gao

IEEE
COMPUTER
SOCIETY

Los Alamitos, California

Washington • Brussels • Tokyo

Library of Congress Cataloging-in-Publication Data

Kung, David C.
  Testing object-oriented software / David C. Kung, Pei Hsia, Jerry Gao.
      p.   cm.
  Includes bibliographical references.
  ISBN 0-8186-8520-4
    1. Object-oriented programming (Computer science)   2. Computer software—Testing.
  I. Hsia, Pei.   II. Gao, Jerry.   III. Title.
  QA76.64.K86   1998
  005.1 ' 17—dc21   98-18855
                                                                              CIP

IEEE Computer Society Press Order Number BP08520
Library of Congress Number 98-18855
ISBN 0-8186-8520-4

Additional copies can be ordered from

IEEE Computer Society Press
Customer Service Center
10662 Los Vaqueros Circle
P.O. Box 3014
Los Alamitos, CA 90720-1314
Tel: (714) 821-8380
Fax: (714) 821-4641
Email: cs.books@computer.org

IEEE Service Center
445 Hoes Lane
P.O. Box 1331
Piscataway, NJ 08855-1331
Tel: (732) 981-1393
Fax: (732) 981-9667
mis.custserv@computer.org

IEEE Computer Society
Watanabe Building
1-4-2 Minami-Aoyama
Minato-ku, Tokyo 107-0062
JAPAN
Tel: +81-3-3408-3118
Fax: +81-3-3408-3553
tokyo.ofc@computer.org

Publisher: Matt Loeb
Technical Editor: Pradip Srimani
Project Editor: Cheryl Baltes
Advertising/Promotions: Tom Fink
Production Editor: Lisa O'Conner
Cover Design: Joel Bruce

Printed in the United States of America

Contents

Preface

The object-oriented (OO) paradigm adopts a more natural view of the application domain as consisting of objects, their behaviors, and their interactions. It provides a better understanding of requirements in terms of identifying and specifying the objects, their behaviors, the services provided by objects, object interactions, and the constraints. Furthermore, the seamless transition into OO design and programming facilitates design verification, code review, and maintenance. It is widely accepted that the OO paradigm will significantly increase software reusability, extendibility, interoperability, and reliability.

Software testing is an important software quality assurance activity to ensure that the benefits of OO programming will be realized. The objective of software testing is to uncover as many errors as possible with a minimum cost. A successful test should show that a program contains bugs rather than showing that the program works. Since software testing consumes 40–80 percent of the development costs, how to reduce its cost and improve its quality has always been a big challenge to the software engineering community.

During the last two decades, many software testing strategies, methods, and reliability models have been proposed. These include formal code review, equivalence partitioning, boundary value analysis, cause-effect analysis, basis path testing, control structure testing, mutation testing, and symbolic execution. Most of them were designed based on the traditional function-oriented paradigm. They have been found to be inadequate for testing OO systems.

OO software testing has to deal with new problems introduced by the powerful new features of OO languages. OO features (such as encapsulation, inheritance, polymorphism, and dynamic binding) provide visible benefits in software design and programming. However, these new features also raise challenging problems in the software testing and maintenance phases [wild92a] [lejt92a] [bind94a]. *Encapsulation* means modeling and storing with an object the attributes and the operations an object is capable of performing. The interaction between two or more objects becomes implicit in the code. This makes it difficult to understand object interactions and prepare test cases to test such interactions [leto86a]. *Inheritance* means properties defined for a class are inherited by its subclasses, unless it is otherwise stated. However, a method that is tested to be "correct" in the context of the base class does not guarantee that it will work "correctly" in the context of the derived class [perr90a]. *Polymorphism* means the ability to assume more than one form, both in terms of data and operations. That is, an attribute of an object may refer to more than one type of data, and an operation may have more than one implementation. *Dynamic binding* means code that implements an operation is unknown until run time. These features make testing more difficult because the exact data type and implementation cannot be determined statically, and the control flow of the OO program is less transparent [smit90a].

Currently, most software development organizations are still in the process of observing and/or transitioning to the OO paradigm. It is anticipated that OO software testing will receive much attention. More and more organizations will seek OO testing methods and techniques in the near future as more C++ and Java programs are developed.

The audience of this book includes OO program testers, OO program developers, OO software project managers, and OO researchers who have something to do with OO testing. OO software testers will learn OO software testing problems, various test methods and other aspects of OO development. Software developers usually conduct unit testing of the code they developed. The Unit Testing and Integration Testing chapter will be useful for OO developers. In addition, the Specification and Verification chapter contains an article on design for testability in which a set of design metrics is proposed. Reading this article, OO developers can learn about what should be considered during the design phase to produce a program with good testability.

The book can also be used for a graduate course in software engineering, preferably a special topic or seminar course on OO software testing. In fact, most of the articles in this book were used in a graduate level special topic course taught by one of the editors.

The book begins with a chapter on OO software testing problems to expose the reader to the differences between testing a conventional program and testing an OO program and focuses on the difficulties or challenges a tester would face when testing an OO program. This chapter also helps the reader to understand some subtle issues of OO programming.

Software verification is a software quality assurance activity closely related to software testing. Software verification checks for inconsistencies in a specification or code, for example, what should be checked when adding a subclass to a super class and what are valid invocation sequences of the methods of a class. Solutions to these problems are answered in the Specification and Verification chapter.

The Unit Testing and Integration Testing chapter addresses OO testing techniques. In conventional programming, the basic program unit for unit testing is usually a function, or a module. Is this still valid and effective for OO testing? If not, what is the unit? How should OO unit testing be conducted? This chapter offers some ideas and methods. Integration testing is a crucial phase in software testing in which the components of a software system are integrated and tested according to a certain integration strategy. In conventional programming, integration testing can be carried out either bottom-up, top-down, or a combination of the methods. Depending on the design approach that is used, these integration testing strategies may still be used. That is, the design approach must generate a module structure chart that shows a lattice structure of module invocation relationships. Based on this structure, the conventional integration testing strategies can be applied as usual. In this chapter, however, an OO program integration testing strategy is described.

Regression testing refers to retesting a program after modifications are made to ensure that the program still performs correctly according to its requirements. One simple approach to regression testing is to retest everything whenever a program is modified. However, this approach is not economical since the modification my affect only a small portion of a large program. In the Regression Testing chapter, we present to the reader approaches that can drastically reduce the regression test costs. One approach is to identify classes that are affected by the modification and retest only these classes. Another approach allows the regression tester to select from an existing set of test cases those that will cause the modified program to produce different output. This will further reduce the regression test costs, and will do so to a significant degree, because the tester only needs to focus on the test cases that will produce different results.

One significant difference between conventional program testing and OO software testing is object state testing [kung94c]. In conventional programming, state dependent behaviors are usually found in embedded systems in which the environment of the software system generates stimuli to the software that responds to the stimuli by executing appropriate actions. The software system may generate certain output to the environment as responses to the stimuli. In OO programming, many objects may have state dependent behaviors and these objects may interact with each other intimately. For example, if the engine is in the "on" state, and the transmission is in the "forward" state, then releasing the brake will cause the car to move forward. If the transmission is in the "park" state, then the car will not move when the brake pedal is released. The Object State Testing chapter presents methods for testing object state dependent behaviors. One of the methods uses a reverse engineering approach to recover the state dependent behavior of an object from code. The article also describes a method for testing the interactions between the objects through their state dependent behavior. Another method proposes to use a state equivalence checker to determine whether two sequences of method invocations will result in the same state as expected. The first method is white-box object state testing. The tester derives test cases from the internal logic of the software and ensures that all statements are tested to a certain extent. For example, 80 percent or 100 percent of the statements are tested at least once. The second method is black-box object state testing, in which test cases are derived from requirements to ensure that the software correctly implements the requirements. Clearly, these two methods are complementary: one ensures that all of the requirements are fulfilled and the other ensures that the desired percentage of code is tested at least once.

After the general philosophy, principles, and OO testing methods, the Test Methodology chapter describes the steps for conducting OO testing. One methodology proposes to integrate the development process with the OO testing process. That is, during the OO development phases, verification and validation of the development products are performed and appropriate testing plans and test procedures are generated. Another methodology deals with testing a class inheritance hierarchy. This methodology recognizes the dependencies of the derived classes of the base classes and proposes a detailed procedure to test the classes in the hierarchy by reusing the test information of the based classes.

OO testing is tedious and time consuming. Tool support is important and necessary. Therefore, the last chapter presents some OO test tools and systems. We hope that more OO testing tools and systems will be developed in the near future and will be available in the commercial market.

This book is organized in such a way that it introduces the reader first to OO testing problems, then general discussions on OO software verification, followed by OO unit testing, integration testing, regression testing, object state testing methods, and finally OO testing methodologies and tool support. We believe that this organizational scheme covers both the overall aspects and the detailed aspects of OO software testing.

Each chapter begins with an editorial introduction and comments on the papers selected. It covers the motivation for selecting the papers, what the reader should look for when reading the papers, and insight and integration of the papers to provide the reader an integrated view of the section. We hope the introductions will help the reader understand the papers.

References

[leto86a] S. Letovski and E. Soloway, "Delocalized Plans and Program Comprehension," *IEEE Software*, Vol. 3, No. 3, May 1986, pp. 41–49.

[perr90a] D.E. Perry and G.E. Kaiser, "Adequate Testing and Object-Oriented Programming," *J. Object-Oriented Programming*, Vol. 2, Jan.-Feb. 1990, pp. 13–19.

[smit90a] M.D. Smith and D.J. Robson, "Object-Oriented Programming—The Problems of Validation," *Proc. IEEE Conf. Software Maintenance*, IEEE Computer Society Press, Los Alamitos, Calif., 1990, pp. 272–281.

[wild92a] N. Wilde and R. Huitt, "Maintenance Support for Object-Oriented Programs," *IEEE Trans. Software Eng.*, Vol. 18, No. 12, Dec. 1992, pp. 1038–1044.

[lejt92a] M. Lejter, S. Meyers, and S.P. Reiss, "Support for Maintaining Object-Oriented Programs," *IEEE Trans. Software Eng.*, Vol. 18, No. 12, Dec. 1992, pp. 1045–1052.

[kung94c] D. Kung, et al, "On Object State Testing," *Proc. COMPSAC '94*, IEEE Computer Society Press, Los Alamitos, Calif., 1994, pp. 222–227.

[bind94a] R. Binder (Guest Editor), "Object-Oriented Software Testing," *Comm. ACM,* Vol. 37, No. 9, Sept. 1994, pp. 28–29.

Chapter 1

OO Testing Problems

The OO paradigm enjoys increasing acceptance in the software industry, due to its visible benefits in analysis, design, and coding. Numerous software development organizations have adopted OO as the development paradigm. However, the conventional software testing and maintenance methods are not adequate for OO programs [harr91a] [kung93b] [kung93b] [perr90a] [smit90a], because they do not address the testing and maintenance problems associated with the OO features. It can be anticipated that as more OO software is developed testing and maintaining OO programs will become a real challenge.

The papers in this chapter present to the reader the OO testing problems from different angles. The first paper [perr90a], by D.E. Perry and G.E. Kaiser, discusses the problems from a theoretical point of view. It revisits some of the test adequacy axioms originally proposed by Weyuker [weyu86a] [weyu88a]:

- **Antiextensionality**. If two programs compute the same function (that is, they are semantically close), a test set adequate for one is not necessarily adequate for the other.

- **General Multiple Change**. When two programs are syntactically similar (that is, one can be obtained from the other by changing constants and/or relational/arithmetic operators) they usually require different test sets.

- **Antidecomposition**. Testing a program in the context of an enclosing program may be adequate with respect to that enclosing program, but not necessarily adequate for other uses of the component.

- **Anticomposition.** Adequately testing each individual program component in isolation does not necessarily suffice to adequately test the the entire program. Composing two program components results in interaction that cannot arise in isolation.

The paper then derives a surprising conclusion which is opposite to what we used to believe. That is, we often think that an inherited method can be used without testing if it has been tested in the context of the based class. However, Perry and Kaiser's paper points out that it is not always the case. They point out that (1) when a subclass or superclass is added to a class, the inherited methods must be retested in this newly formed context; (2) even if the overriding and overridden methods are semantically similar, there is a need to retest the classes in the context of overriding and overridden methods; and (3) if the order of specification of superclasses of a subclass is changed, the subclass must be retested even though only syntactic changes are made.

The second paper [smit90a], by Smith et al., considers problems involved in testing classes, abstract classes, message passing, concurrency, inheritance, polymorphism, and template classes. For example, these authors discuss how to test a class, an abstract class, or a template class. Another problem is the concept of control flow through a conventional program does not map readily to an OO program. Flow of control in OO programs may be thought of as message passing from one object to another, causing the receiving object to perform some operation, be it an examination or alteration, of its state. In order to test such programs, when there is no conceptual input/process/output, it is probably more appropriate to specify how the object's state will change under certain conditions. If one object sends two messages to two other objects, the two can respond concurrently. The complexity of testing such systems, considering the possible time-dependent interactions between objects, is potentially greater than that for normal sequential OO programs.

Smith et al. [smit90a], classify inheritance into restrictive, nonrestrictive and repeated inheritance, and multiple and simple inheritance. *Simple inheritance* means inheriting from only one parent class while *multiple inheritance* occurs when a child class inherits from two or more parent classes. *Strict inheritance* occurs when the child class takes all the features from the parent class. *Nonstrict inheritance* occurs when some of the features from the parent class are not present or are renamed in the child class. This can occur in the simple case by omission, or through multiple or repeated inheritance. *Repeated inheritance* occurs when a child class derives from the same parent class more than once. This occurs when a class inherits from two other classes that inherit from a common parent. Table 1 summarizes the implications of these inheritances to testing.

Table 1. Implications of various inheritances.

	Simple	Multiple
Strict	• Can reuse parent class's test cases • Require new test cases for added features.	• May invoke the wrong inherited feature when two parents use identical names for that feature • Complexity increases because the inheritancehierarchy becomes a lattice rather than a tree • Causes undesirable interactions in the child class
Nonstrict	Runtime error could occur when the redefined feature is invoked in the context of the superclass for an object of the subclass	
Repeated	Unclear whether parent test cases can be reused to test the child class	

The third paper [wild92a], written by Wilde and Huit, addresses problems in maintaining an OO system and proposes potential solutions to these problems. These include problems of dynamic binding, object dependencies, dispersed program structure, control of polymorphism, high-level understanding, and detailed code understanding. In fact, all of these are problems in the testing and regression testing processes and this is the reason that we include this paper. For example, dynamic binding implies that the code that implements a given function is unknown until run time. Therefore, static analysis cannot be used to precisely identify the dependencies in the program. Hence, it is difficult for a tester to prepare test stubs as well as identifying the change impact in regression testing.

The dependencies occurring in conventional systems are:

* data dependencies between variables;
* calling dependencies between modules;
* functional dependencies between a module and the variables it computes;
* definitional dependencies between a variable and its type.

OO systems have additional dependencies:

* class-to-class dependencies;
* class-to-method dependencies;
* class-to-message dependencies;
* class-to-variable dependencies;
* method-to-variable dependencies;
* method-to-message dependencies; and
* method-to-method dependencies.

Environments for maintaining object-oriented programs need to provide ways of browsing these different kinds of relationships. The multidimensional nature of interconnections will make it very difficult to use listing or text-screen-based systems for program understanding.

Although all three papers address OO test problems, we can see that their emphases are different. Perry and Kaiser's paper [perr90a] emphasizes retesting inherited methods in the context of the derived class, based on Weyuker's test adequacy axioms. Smith and Robson's paper [smit90a] emphasizes the practical difficulties in testing OO programs. Wilde and Huitt's paper [wilde92] emphasizes the complexity, dependency, and understanding problems relating to testing and maintaining OO programs. We believe that the these papers together provide a more or less complete picture (except object state testing which will be addressed in Chapter 5) of the problems and difficulties involved in OO software testing.

References

[harr92a] M.J. Harrold, J.D. McGregor, and K.J. Fitzpatrick, "Incremental Testing of Object-Oriented Class Structure," *Proc. 14th Int'l Conf. Software Eng.*, IEEE Computer Society Press, Los Alamitos, Calif., 1992, pp. 68–80.

[kung93b] D. Kung, et al., "Design Recovery for Software Testing of Object-Oriented Programs," *Proc. Working Conf. Reverse Engineering,* IEEE Computer Society Press, Los Alamitos, Calif., 1993, pp. 202–211.

[perr90a] D.E. Perry and G.E. Kaiser, "Adequate Testing and Object-Oriented Programming,'" *J. Object-Oriented Programming*, Vol. 2, Jan.-Feb. 1990, pp. 13–19.

[smit90a] M.D. Smith and D.J. Robson, "Object-Oriented Programming—The Problems of Validation," *Proc. IEEE Conf. Software Maintenance*, IEEE Computer Society Press, Los Alamitos, Calif., 1990, pp. 272–281.

[weyu86a] E.J. Weyuker, "Axiomatizing Software Test Data Adequacy," *IEEE Trans. Software Eng.,* Vol. SE-12, No. 12, 1986, pp. 1128–1138.

[weyu88a] E.J. Weyuker, "The Evaluation of Program-Based Software Test Data Adequacy Criteria," *Comm. ACM,* Vol. 31, No. 6, 1988, pp. 668–675.

[wild92a] N. Wilde and R. Huitt, "Maintenance Support for Object-Oriented Programs," *IEEE Trans. Software Eng.,* Vol. 18, No. 12, Dec. 1992, pp. 1038–1044.

Adequate Testing and Object-Oriented Programming

By Dewayne E. Perry and Gail E. Kaiser

Introduction

Brooks, in his paper "No Silver Bullet: Essence and Accidents of Software Engineering" [3], states:

> Many students of the art hold out more hope for object-oriented programming than for any of the other technical fads of the day. I am among them.

We are among them as well. However, we have uncovered a flaw in the general wisdom about object-oriented languages—that "proven" (that is, well-understood, well-tested, and well-used) classes can be reused as superclasses without retesting the inherited code. On the contrary, inherited methods must be retested in most contexts of reuse in order to meet the standards of adequate testing. In this article, we prove this result by applying test adequacy axioms to certain major features of object-oriented languages—in particular, encapsulation in classes, overriding of inherited methods, and multiple inheritance which pose various difficulties for adequately testing a program. Note that our results do not indicate that there is a flaw in the general wisdom that classes promote reuse (which they in fact do), but that some of the attendant assumptions about reuse are mistaken (that is, those concerning testing.)

Our past work in object-oriented languages has been concerned with multiple inheritance and issues of granularity as they support reuse [10, 11]. Independently, we have developed several technologies for change management in large systems [12, 14, 20] and recently have been investigating the problems of testing as a component of the change process [13], especially the issues of integration and regression testing. When we began to apply our testing approach to object-oriented programs, we expected that retesting object-oriented programs after changes would be easier than retesting equivalent programs written in conventional languages. Our results, however, have brought this thesis into doubt. Testing object-oriented programs may still turn out to be easier than testing conventional-language programs, but there are certain pitfalls that must be avoided.

First we explain the concepts of specification-and program-based testing, and describe criteria for *adequate testing*. Next, we list a set of axioms for test data adequacy developed in the testing community for program-based testing. We then apply the adequacy axioms to three features common to many object-oriented programming languages, and show why the axioms may require inherited code to be retested.

Author's Addresses: D.E. Perry, AT&T Bell Laboratories, Murray Hill, NJ 07974. G.E. Kaiser, Columbia University, Department of Computer Science, New York, NY 10027.

Testing

By definition, a program is deemed to be *adequately tested* if it has been covered according to the selected criteria. The principle choice is between two divergent forms of test case coverage reported by Howden [9]: specification-based and program-based testing.

Specification-based (or "black-box") testing is what most programmers have in mind when they set out to test their programs. The goal is to determine whether the program meets its functional and non-functional (i.e., performance) specifications. The current state of the practice is informal specification, and thus informal determination of coverage of the specification is the norm. For example, tests can be cross-referenced with portions of the design document [19], and a test management tool can make sure that all parts of the design document are covered. Test adequacy determination has been formalized for only a few special cases of specification-based testing—most notably, mathematical subroutines [23].

In contrast to specification-based testing, *program-based* (or "white-box") testing implies inspection of the source code of the program and selection of test cases that together cover the program, as opposed to its specification. Various criteria have been proposed for determining whether the program has been covered—for example, whether all statements, branches, control flow paths, or data flow paths have been executed. In practice, some intermediate measure such as essential branch coverage [4] or feasible data flow path coverage [5] is most likely to be used, since the number of possibilities might otherwise be infinite or at least infeasibly large. The rationale here is that we should not be confident about the correctness of a program if (reachable) parts of it have never been executed.

The two approaches are orthogonal and complimentary. Specification-based testing is weak with respect to formal adequacy criteria, while program-based testing has been extensively studied [6]. On the one hand, specification-based testing tells us how well it meets the specification, but tells us nothing about what part of the program is executed to meet each part of the specification. On the other hand, program based testing tells us nothing about whether the program meets its intended functionality. Thus, if both approaches are used, program-based testing provides a level of confidence derived from the adequacy criteria that the program has been well tested whereas specification-based testing determines whether in fact the program does what it is supposed to do.

Axioms of Test Data Adequacy

Weyuker in "Axiomatizing Software Test Data Adequacy" [29] develops a general axiomatic theory of test data adequacy and considers various adequacy criteria in the light of these axioms. Recently, in

"Adequate Testing and Object-Oriented Programming" by D.E. Perry and G.E. Kaiser from *J. Object-Oriented Programming*, Jan./Feb. 1990, pp. 13–19. Reprinted by permission of SIGS.

"The Evaluation of Program-Based Software Test Data Adequacy Criteria" [30], Weyuker revises and expands the original set of 8 axioms to 11. The goal of the first paper was to demonstrate that the original axioms are useful in exposing weaknesses in several well-known program-based adequacy criteria. The point of the second paper is to demonstrate the *insufficiency* of the current set of axioms, that is, there are adequacy criteria that meet all eleven axioms but clearly are irrelevant to detecting errors in programs. The contribution of our article is that, by applying these axioms to object-oriented programming, we expose weaknesses in the common intuition that programs using inherited code require less testing than those written using other paradigms.

The first four axioms state:

- **Applicability.** *For every program, there exists an adequate test set.*
- **Non-Exhaustive Applicability.** *There is a program P and test set T such that P is adequately tested by T, and T is not an exhaustive test set.*
- **Monotonicity.** *If T is adequate for P, and T is a subset of T' then T' is adequate for P.*
- **Inadequate Empty Set.** *The empty set is not an adequate test set for any program.*

These (intuitively obvious) axioms apply to all programs independent of which programming language or paradigm is used for implementation, and apply equally to program-based and specification-based testing.

Weyuker's three new axioms are also intuitively obvious.

- **Renaming.** *Let P be a renaming of Q; then T is adequate for P if and only if T is adequate for Q.*
- **Complexity.** *For every n, there is a program P, such that P is adequately tested by a size n test set, but not by any size n-1 test set.*
- **Statement Coverage.** *If T is adequate for P, then T causes every executable statement of P to be executed.*

A program P is a *renaming* of Q if P is identical to Q except that all instances of an identifier x of Q have been replaced in P by an identifier y, where y does not appear in Q, or if there is a set of such renamed identifiers. The first two axioms are applicable to both forms of testing; the third applies only to program-based testing. The concepts of renaming, size of test set, and statement depend on the language paradigm, but this is outside the scope of this article.

Antiextensionality, General Multiple Change, Antidecomposition, and Anticomposition Axioms

We are interested in the four remaining (not so obvious) axioms: the antiextensionality, general multiple change, antidecomposition and anticomposition axioms. These axioms are concerned with testing various parts of a program in relationship to the whole and vice versa, and certain of them apply only to program-based and not to specification-based adequacy criteria. They are, in some sense, negative axioms in that they expose inadequacy rather than guarantee adequacy.

Antiextensionality

If two programs compute the same function (that is, they are semantically close), a test set adequate for one is not necessarily adequate for the other.

There are programs P and Q such that P≡Q, [test set] T is adequate for P, but T is not adequate for Q.

This is probably the most surprising of the axioms, partly because our intuition of what it means to adequately test a program is rooted in specification-based testing. In specification-based testing, adequate testing is a function of covering the specification. Since equivalent programs have, by definition, the same specification [22], any test set that is adequate for one must be adequate for the other. However, in program-based testing, adequate testing is a function of covering the source code. Since equivalent programs may have radically different implementations, there is no reason to expect a test set that, for example, executes all the statements of one implementation will execute all the statements of another implementation.

General Multiple Change

When two programs are syntactically similar (that is, they have the same shape), they usually require different test sets.

There are programs P and Q which are the same shape, and a test set T such that T is adequate for P, but T is not adequate for Q.

Weyuker states: "Two programs are of the *same shape* if one can be transformed into the other by applying the following rules any number of times: (a) Replace relational operator r1 in a predicate with relational operator r2. (b) Replace constant c1 in a predicate or assignment statement with constant c2. (c) Replace arithmetic operator a1 in an assignment statement with arithmetic operator a2." Since an adequate test set for program-based testing may be selected, for example, to force execution of both branches of each conditional statement, new relational operators and/or constants in the predicates may require a different test set to maintain branch coverage. Although this axiom is clearly concerned with the implementation, not the specification, of a program, we could postulate a similar axiom about the syntactic similarity of specifications, as opposed to source code.

Antidecomposition

Testing a program component in the context of an enclosing program may be adequate with respect to that enclosing program, but not necessarily adequate for other uses of the component.

There exists a program P and component Q such that T is adequate for P, T' is the set of vectors of values that variables can assume on entrance to Q for some t of T, and T' is not adequate for Q.

This axiom characterizes a property of adequacy as well as an interesting property of testing—that is, a program can be adequately tested even though it contains unreachable code [31]. But the unreachable code remains untested, adequately or otherwise. The degenerate example is that in which Q is unreachable in P and T' is the null set. By the Inadequate Empty Set axiom of the previous section, T' cannot be adequate for Q. In the more typical case, some part of Q is not reachable in P but is reachable in other contexts; hence, T' will not adequately test Q. While this axiom is written in program-based terms, it is equally applicable to specification-based testing. In particular, the enclosing program P may not utilize all the functionality defined by the specification of Q and thus could not possible test Q adequately.

6

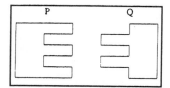

Figure 1.

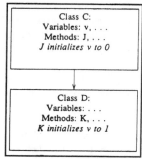

Figure 2.

Anticomposition

Adequately testing each individual program component in isolation does not necessarily suffice to adequately test the entire program. Composing two program components results in interaction that cannot arise in isolation.

> *There exist programs P and Q, and test set T, such that T is adequate for P, and the set of vectors of values that variables can assume on entrance to Q for inputs in T is adequate for Q, but T is not adequate for P;Q. [P;Q is the composition of P and Q.]*

This axiom is counter-intuitive if we limit our thinking to *sequential* composition of P and Q. Consider instead the composition illustrated in Figure 1, which can be interpreted as either P calls Q multiple times or P and Q are mutually recursive. In either case, one has the opportunity to modify the context seen by the other in a more complex manner than could be done using stubs during testing of individual components in isolation.

If the composition of P and Q is in fact sequential, then the axiom is still true—just less useful. The proof is by a simple combinatorics argument: if p is the set of paths through P and q is the set of paths through Q, then the set of paths through P;Q may be as large as p * q, depending on the form of composition and on reachability as considered by the previous axiom. However, T applied to P;Q generates at most p paths. A larger test set may be needed to induce the full set of paths. This is an issue for specification-based as well as program-based testing when the specification captures only what the program is supposed to do and behavior outside the scope of the specification may be benign in one context, but cause problems in another.

Encapsulation in Classes

In this and the following two sections, we consider only abstractions of encapsulation, overriding of inherited methods and multiple inheritance, respectively, rather than concern ourselves with the details of specific object-oriented languages, such as Smalltalk-80 [7], Flavors [18], CommonLoops [1] and C++ [28].

Encapsulation is a technique for enforcing information hiding, where the interface and implementation of a program unit are syntactically separated. This enables the programmer to hide design decisions within the implementation, and to narrow the possible interdependencies with other components by means of the interface. Encapsulation encourages program modularity, isolates separately developed program units, and restricts the implications of changes. In particular, if a programmer changes the implementation of a unit, leaving the interface the same, other units should be unaffected by those changes. Our initial intuition, grounded in specification-based testing, is that we should be able to limit testing to just the modified unit. However, the **anticomposition** axiom reminds us of the necessity

of retesting every dependent unit as well, because a program that has been adequately tested in isolation may not be adequately tested in combination. This means that integration testing is always necessary in addition to unit testing, regardless of the programming language paradigm.

Fortunately, one ramification of encapsulation for testing is that the dependencies tend to be explicit and obvious. If a programmer changes only the implementation of a unit, he need only retest that unit and any units that explicitly depend on it (call it, use its global variables, etc), as opposed to the entire program. Similarly, if the programmer adds a new unit, he need only test that unit and those existing units that have been modified to use it (plus unmodified existing units that previously used a different unit that is now masked due to a naming conflict).

One would assume that the classes of object-oriented languages would exhibit this behavior, sot hat it would be both necessary and sufficient to retest those classes explicitly dependent on a changed class as well as the modified class itself. We would expect that, when a superclass is modified, it would be necessary to retest all its subclasses since they depend on it in the sense that they inherit its methods. What we don't expect is the result of the **antidecomposition** axiom—that, when we add a new subclass (or modify an existing subclass), we must retest the methods inherited from each of its ancestor superclasses. The use of subclasses adds this unexpected form of dependency because it provides a new context for the inherited components—that is, the dependency is in both directions where we thought it was only in the one direction.

For example, consider a class C with method J; we have adequately tested J with respect to C. We now create a new class D as a subclass D as a subclass of C; D does not replace J but inherits it from C. According to the **antidecomposition** axiom, it is necessary to retest J in the context of class D. There may be new errors when in the context of D, with its enlarged set of methods and instance variables—and perhaps subtly different local *meanings* for instance variables inherited from C. The bug illustrated in Figure 2 (the conflicting assumptions about instance variable v) would not be detected without retesting J in the context of D.

In order to make this example more concrete, consider C to the class WindowManager, D to be the class SunWindowManager, J is the method InitializeScreen, and K is SetScreenBackground. J initializes to a blank screen, while K puts a digitized picture in the background. There are obvious problems if K is invoked first and then J, and vice versa, since other parts of the WindowManager and the SunWindowManager assume initialization in certain ways.

There is one case where adding a new subclass does not require retesting the methods inherited from the superclass in order to meet the adequacy axioms. This is when the new subclass is a pure extension of the superclass, that is, it adds new instance variables and new methods and there are no interactions in either direction between the new instance variables and methods and any inherited instance variables and methods.

At least one object-oriented language has solved this problem in the general case, by prohibiting unexpected dependencies: CommonObjects [25, 26] removes all implicit inheritance—that is, inherited methods must be explicitly invoked. This, in effect, inserts "firewalls" between each superclass and its subclasses, in the same sense that encapsulation inserts firewalls between a class and its clients.

Overriding of Methods

Almost all object-oriented languages permit a subclass to replace an inherited method with a locally defined method with the same name, although some support a subtyping hierarchy that restricts the method to have the same specification [24]. In either case, it is obvious that the overriding subclass has to be retested. What is not so obvious is that a different test set is often needed. This is expressed by the **antiextensionality** axiom: Although the two methods compute semantically close functions, a test set adequate for one is not necessarily adequate for the other.

For example, consider Figure 3 where class C has subclass D, and method M is defined in C but not in D. Say there exists an object O that is an instance of class D, which receives a message containing the method selector M; M applied to O has already been adequately tested. Now we change class D to add its own method M, which is similar to C.M (by "C.M", we mean the method M from superclass C). Obviously, we need to retest class D. Intuitively, we would expect that the old test data would be adequate, but the **antiextensionality** axiom reminds us that it may not be adequate. Thus, we may have to develop new test cases for two reasons. First, remember that program-based testing considers the details of the program formulation, attempting to cover, for example, each statement or branch. The test data would necessarily be at least slightly different for C.M and D.M if the formulation in terms of statements and branches were different; the test data would probably be very different if C.M and D.M used different algorithms. Second, it is very likely that the underlying motivation for overriding a method affects not only the internal structure of the overriding method but its external behavior as well—that is, it changes the functional specification. Hence, in addition to test cases to exercise the different structure of the method, we need to test the different specification of that method.

More concretely, consider C to be the class WindowManager, D to be the class SunWindowManager, C.M to be the method

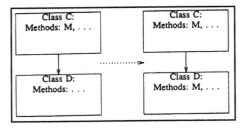

Figure 3.

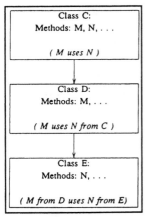

Figure 4.

RefreshDisplay that rewrites an entire bitmapped screen, and D.M to be the method RefreshDisplay that repaints only the "damaged" part of a bitmapped screen. In this case, the specifications as well as the implementations of the two methods might be different, in which case different test sets would be required for specification-based as well as program-based testing.

In the previous section, we treated the two-way dependency between classes and superclasses and explained how the **antidecomposition** axiom requires testing of inherited methods in each inheriting context as well as the defining context. What we did not discuss there was the application of the **antiextensionality** axiom to this additional testing: Different test sets may be needed at every point in the ancestor chain between the class defining the overriding method and its ancestor class defining the overridden method.

In Figure 4, class C has subclass D, which in turn has subclass E; C has methods M and N; D has method M, which uses method N (from C); class E does not have method M but does have method N (overriding the N inherited from C). The antiextensionality axiom reminds us that we need different test data for M with respect to each of the classes C, D, and E. This is obvious with respect to instances of C and D, since they invoke distinct methods M in response to the message M; even if these methods are semantically close, test data adequate for one may not be adequate for the other. This is less obvious with respect to D and E, since they invoke the identical method M. But when we consider that M calls C.N for D whereas it calls E.N for E, it becomes clear that different test sets are required since the formulation and algorithms used by C.N and E.N are likely to be different in functionality as well as structure.

Again, more concretely, let class C be WindowManager where method M is RefreshDisplay and method N is DrawCharacter, using bitmapped fonts; let class D be SunWindowManager where method M is D's replacement for the method RefreshDisplay; and let class E be NeWS where method N is E's replacement for the method DrawCharacter, using Postscript fonts.

Multiple Inheritance

Some, but not all, object-oriented languages support multiple inheritance [2], where each class may have an arbitrary number of superclasses. The so-called "multiple inheritance problem" arises when the same component may be inherited along different ancestor paths.

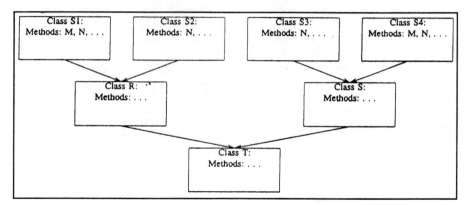

Figure 6.

Solutions to this problem typically define a precedence ordering, which linearized the set of ancestors so that there is a unique selection (or a unique ordering if the semantics of the language are such that all conflicting inherited methods must be invoked) [27]. These solutions, unfortunately, cause very small syntactic changes to have very large semantic consequences. Fortunately, the **general multiple change** axiom reminds us that programs that are syntactically similar usually require different test sets.

In Figure 5, class D lists superclasses C and B, in that order, and the language imposes the precedence ordering C, B. Method M is defined by both C and B, but not by D. Class D is then changed so that the ordering of the superclasses is B and C (meaning that the precedence ordering is B,C). Not only must class D be retested, since it now uses B.M rather than C.M, but most likely a different set of tests must be used. Since C and B are independent, and perhaps developed separately, there is no reason that B.M would be either syntactically or semantically similar to C.M—and even if it were, the **antiextensionality** and **general multiple change** axioms reminds us that even then different test sets may be necessary.

As a concrete realization of this example, let class C be TextWindowManager where method M is RefreshDisplay (that repaints the window from a text description), let class B be GraphicsWindowManager where method M is RefreshDisplay (that repaints the window from a bit-mapped representation), and let class D be SunWindowManager.

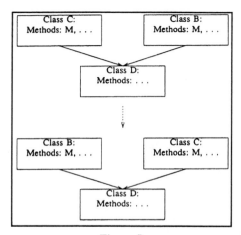

Figure 5.

The example in Figure 6 shows the inherent compounding effects of multiple inheritance. This implication of the **general multiple change** axiom is probably the most significant result of applying the test data adequacy axioms to object-oriented languages, but also the least surprising to the object-oriented languages community. Multiple inheritance is already widely recognized as both a blessing and a curse [15, 16, 17].

Conclusion

Inheritance is one of the primary strengths of object-oriented programming. However, it is precisely because of inheritance that we find problems arising with respect to testing.

- Encapsulation together with inheritance, which intuitively ought to bring a reduction in testing problems, compounds them instead.
- Where non-inheritance languages make the effects of changes explicit, inheritance languages tend to make these implicit and dependent on the various underlying, and complicated, inheritance models.

Brooks concludes his section on object-oriented programming:

> Nevertheless, such advances can do no more than to remove all the accidental difficulties from the expression of the design. The complexity of the design itself is essential, and such attacks make no change whatever in it. An order-of-magnitude gain can be made by object-oriented programming only if the unnecessary type-specification underbrush still in our programming language is itself nine-tenths of the work involved in designing a program product. I doubt it.

While object-oriented programming clears away much of the accidental underbrush of design, we have noted ways in which it adds to the accidental underbrush of change management and testing. We conclude that there is a pressing need for research on testing of object-oriented languages. We have begun work on this in the context of a data-oriented debugger for concurrent object-oriented languages [8] and in the context of semantic analysis (applying the approach of Inscape [21] to C++).

9

Acknowledgments

Professor Kaiser is supported in part by National Science Foundation grants CCR-8858029 and CCR-8802741, in part by grants from AT&T, DEC, IBM, Siemens, Sun, and Xerox, in part by the Center for Advanced Technology and by the Center for Telecommunications Research.

Jim Coplien, Narain Gehani, Jim Krist, and Alex Wolf provided useful criticism and suggestions on earlier version's of this article.

References

[1] Daniel G. Bobrow, Kenneth Kahn, Gregor Kiczales, Larry Masinter, Mark Stefik, and Frank Zdybel, "CommonLoops: Merging Lisp and Object-Oriented Programming," *In:* Object-Oriented Programming Systems, Languages and Applications Conference Proceedings, Portland, OR, September 1986, pp. 17-29.

[2] Alan Borning and Daniel Ingalls, "Multiple Inheritance in Smalltalk-80," *In:* Proceedings of the National Conference on Artificial Intelligence, Pittsburgh, PA, 1982, pp. 234-237.

[3] Frederick P. Brooks, Jr., "No Silver Bullet: Essence and Accidents of Software Engineering," *Computer*, 20(4), April 1987, pp. 10-20.

[4] Takeshi Chusho, "Test Data Selection and Quality Estimation Based on the Concept of Essential Branches for Path Testing," *IEEE Transactions on Software Engineering*, SE-13:5, May 1987, pp. 509-517.

[5] Phyllis G. Frankel and Elaine J. Weyuker, "Data Flow Testing in the Presence of Unexecutable Paths," *In:* Workshop on Software Testing, Banff, Canada, July 1987, pp. 4-13.

[6] David Gelperin and Bill Hetzel, "The Growth of Software Testing," *Communications of the ACM*, 31(6), June 1988, pp. 687-695.

[7] Adele Goldberg and David Robson, *Smalltalk-80: The Language and its Implementation*, Reading, MA: Addison-Wesley, 1983.

[8] Wenwey Hseush and Gail E. Kaiser, "Data Path Debugging: Data-Oriented Debugging for a Concurrent Programming Language," *In:* Proceedings of the ACM SIGPlan/SIGOps Workshop on Parallel and Distributed Debugging, Madison, WI, May 1988, pp. 236-246.

[9] William Howden, *Software Engineering and Technology: Functional Program Testing and Analysis*, New York: McGraw-Hill, 1987.

[10] Gail E. Kaiser and David Garlan, "Melding Software Systems from Reusable Building Blocks," *IEEE Software*, July 1987, pp. 17-24.

[11] Gail K. Kaiser and David Garlan, "MELDing Data Flow and *Object-Oriented Programming,*" *In:* Object-Oriented Programming Systems, Languages, and Applications Conference Proceedings, Kissimmee, FL, October 1987. *SIGPlan Notices*, 22(12) December 1987, pp. 254-267.

[12] Gail E. Kaiser and Dewayne E. Perry, "Workspaces and Experimental Databases: Automated Support for Software Maintenance and Evolution," *In:* Proceedings of the Conference on Software Maintenance, Austin, TX, September 1987, pp. 108-114.

[13] Gail E. Kaiser and Dewayne E. Perry, William M. Schell, "INFUSE: Fusing Integration Test Management with Change Management," *In:* Proceedings of COMPASAC'89—The 13th Annual International Computer Software and Application Conference, Orlando, FL, September 1989, pp. 552-558.

[14] Gail E. Kaiser, Simon M. Kaplan, and Josephine Micallef, "Multiuser, Distributed Language-Based Environments," *IEEE Software*, November 1987, pp. 58-67.

[15] Norman Meyrowitz, *Object-Oriented Programming Systems, Languages and Applications Conference Proceedings*, Portland, OR, September 1986. Special Issue of *SIGPlan Notices*, 21(11), November 1986.

[16] Norman Meyrowitz, *In:* Object-Oriented Programming Systems, Languages and Applications Conference Proceedings, Orlando, FL, October 1987. Special Issue of *SIGPlan Notices*, 22(12), December 1987.

[17] Norman Meyrowitz, *In:* Object-Oriented Programming Systems, Languages and Applications Conference Proceedings, San Diego, CA, September 1988. Special Issue of *SIGPlan Notices*, 23(11), November 1988.

[18] David A. Moon, "Object-Oriented Programming with Flavors," *In:* Object-Oriented Programming Systems, Languages and Applications Conference Proceedings, Portland, OR, September 1986, pp. 1-8.

[19] Thomas J. Ostrand, Ron Sigal, and Elaine Weyuker, "Design for a Tool to Manage Specification-Based Testing," *In:* Workshop on Software Testing, Banff, Canada, July 1987, pp. 41-50.

[20] Dewayne E. Perry and Gail E. Kaiser, "Infuse: A Tool for Automatically Managing and Coordinating Source Changes in Large Systems," *In:* Proceedings of the ACM Fifteenth Annual Computer Science Conference, St.Louis, MO, February 1987, pp. 292-299.

[21] Dewayne E. Perry, "The Inscape Environment," *In:* Proceedings of the 11th International Conference on Software Engineering, Pittsburgh, PA, May 1988, pp. 2-12.

[22] Dewayne E. Perry, "Version Control in the Inscape Environment," *In:* Proceedings of the 9th International Conference on Software Engineering, Monterey, CA, April 1987, pp. 142-149.

[23] Robert P. Roe and John H. Rowland, "Some Theory Concerning Certification of Mathematical Subroutines by Black Box Testing," *IEEE Transactions on Software Engineering*, SE-13:7, July 1987, pp. 761-766.

[24] Craig Schaffert, Topher Cooper, Bruce Bullis, Mike Kilian, and Carrie Wilpot, "An Introduction to Trellis/Owl," *In:* Object-Oriented Programming Systems, Languages and Applications Conference Proceedings, Portland, OR, September 1986, pp.1-8.

[25] Alan Snyder, "CommonObjects: An Overview," *In:* Object-Oriented Programming Workshop Proceedings, Yorktown Heights, NY, June 1986, pp. 19-29.

[26] Alan Snyder, "Inheritance and the Development of Encapsulated Software Components," *In:* Twentieth Hawaii International Conference on System Sciences, Kona, HI, January 1987, Volume II, pp. 227-238.

[27] Mark Stefik and Daniel G. Bobrow, "Object-Oriented Programming: Themes and Variations," *The AI Magazine*, Winter 1985, pp. 40-62.

[28] Bjarne Stroustrup, *The C++ Programming Language*, Reading, MA, Addison-Wesley, 1986.

[29] Elaine J. Weyuker, "Axiomatizing Software Test Data Adequacy," IEEE *Transactions on Software Engineering*, SE-12:12, December 1986, pp. 1128-1138.

[30] Elain J. Weyuker, "The Evaluation of Program-based Software Test Data Adequacy Criteria," *Communications of the ACM*, 31:6, June 1988, pp. 668-675.

[31] Stuart H. Zweban and John S. Gourlay, "On the Adequacy of Weyuker's Test Data Adequacy Axioms," Correspondence, *IEEE Transactions on Software Engineering*, 15:4, April 1989, pp. 496–500.

Object-Oriented Programming—The Problems of Validation

M.D. Smith
D.J. Robson
Centre for Software Maintenance
University of Durham
Durham, DH1 3LE, England
Tel. +44 91 374-2635

Abstract

Current maintenance problems generally involve large systems developed in old languages such as COBOL. This has lead to a great deal of experience in maintenance with these languages. The growing interest in object-oriented programming for development work, however, makes it necessary to examine the applicability of maintenance techniques in this new area.

This paper considers software validation, a process common to both maintenance and development, in the context of systems written in an object-oriented language. The problems in using current testing techniques for object-oriented systems will be shown, with the conclusion that new techniques must be developed.

Introduction

The phrase "object-oriented" has now become the latest buzzword in the computer world. In the maintenance field, many see object-orientation as "The Answer" that yields maintainable code. In order to promote something as being good, it must now be object-oriented. A number of papers provide definitions for what the term "object-oriented" actually means (for example, see 4, 11, 13, 14) and it is not the intention of this paper to restate their work. However, some brief definitions will be given in order to demonstrate more clearly the points made.

The purpose of this paper is to consider the effect that using an object-oriented programming language has on testing the software. The question of whether the language features present in object-oriented programming languages enhance or inhibit the testing process is raised. It also considers whether any new techniques designed for object-oriented programming could be employed to ease the testing process. This in turn will help both developers and maintainers to produce more reliable code.

The content of the rest of this paper is as follows.

1. A brief introduction to object-oriented programming is given summarizing its main features.
2. A number of sections are devoted to considering the ramifications that the main features of object-oriented programming have for software testing.
3. The object-oriented concept as a whole is considered from a reusability anal testing standpoint. Other techniques are initially considered that may be of use to enhance the quality of object-oriented programs.
4. Next a different concept of software testing is introduced, namely that of ensuring that class structure is maintained in a coherent way.
5. Finally, an outline is given of the work being undertaken at Durham to address the problems raised in this paper.

Object-Oriented Programming

Object-oriented programming can be simply described as the description of a task to be performed in terms of the objects that the task involves and the properties of the objects, rather than in terms of procedures operating on data. This is a conceptual shift and its proponents claim that its major advantages are that it permits the writing of easily understood readable code [5] that is also reusable and maintainable [9]. Note that a large number of programming languages which are object-oriented have a great variance in the facilities that they provide for the programmer. Some of these facilities, such as strong type checking, are important for software testing and will be discussed below, even though they are not present in all object-oriented languages.

What is object-oriented programming?

The simple definition of object-oriented programming given above is not sufficient to define the term adequately. This section will provide a more complete version for use in the rest of this paper.

A better definition of an object is as follows: An object is an instantiated entity which has

1. A set of operations to which it responds.
2. A state which is affected by a subset of the operations.

3. The ability to send messages to other objects to invoke operations of those other objects

Note that an object is "instantiated." This is important as it means that a particular object actually represents something e.g. *a* window, *a* square, *a* car, and so on. However, defining object-oriented programming as programming with objects is insufficient. A definition must also include classes defined as follows:

A class is a template which specifies *properties* of an object. Classes have:

1. An interface which details how the public properties of the class are accessed.
2. A class body implementing the code of the operations described in the interface.
3. Instance variables which implement the object's state.

Although classes and objects provide a method of abstraction and encapsulation which is important for software re-use, neither on their own allow easy extensibility. Mechanisms to facilitate this are present in most true object-oriented programming languages, the two most common methods being class buying and class inheritance. Class buying can be thought of as a relationship between two classes, where one class (the consumer) uses or has as part of it, another class (the producer). Class inheritance is the mechanism in which a child class inherits features from its parent class and extends them or restricts them in some way. This relationship can be thought of as *is-a*. That is, the child *is-a* specialization of the parent.

From this description, there are two initial implications for the validation of object-oriented software. Firstly, encapsulation in the form of an object represents a fairly obvious mapping from the world to an abstraction of it. This may aid a programmer's comprehension (seeing a stack object with a public interface describes properties such as push, pop, and top automatically creates an image in a programmer's mind) which may suggest good test cases.

Secondly, note that of the items usual to describe object-oriented programming, only the first "objects" are directly testable. Not in the traditional "test case" input / process / output sense but in the sense that at least there is something instantiated to test.

In the case of classes, the programmer designing the class must think carefully about how it is to be used. Tests must then be derived to test objects instantiated from the class. For inheritance, the problems arise not so much from the fact that there is nothing actually to test, but rather the way in which the class evolves. A programmer may inherit from a class a number of times, creating classes that are variations of the super-class. The main

problem comes from the need to change the superclass as follows:

1. A change to the superclass directly effects the subclasses that inherit from it. It may be that it is difficult to test these subclasses individually and the larger the system of classes is, the more difficult it will be to isolate any error to one class (be it super- or sub-).
2. Tests which may have been developed for the classes may now have to be substantially revised due to the changes filtering over two levels of the system, namely the parent class and the child class.
3. Standard regression testing techniques which analyze dependencies in code may not be applicable due to the possibility of quite radical changes being made as the original superclass is deemed insufficient.

Note, however, that a feature of object-oriented programming, that of the classes being loosely coupled together, is in some ways easier since a class can be individually tested and the errors isolated.

In the following sections. the features of object-oriented programming will be considered in greater detail and the problems of testing will be shown with respect to each feature in turn.

The Problems of Class

The problem of creating a class (be it derived from a parent or not) is that it is not possible to test the class dynamically, only an instantiation of it. Thus the programmer who designs the class must create objects from the class and test those in some manner.

Also, it is best if the class can be both open and closed. Open, in that it is possible to extend it and modify the implementation. Closed, in that the class may be used without fear of needing to modify code which uses it. Unfortunately, this is not always possible so do, as the designer of the class may realize (in particular after a number of classes have been derived from it) that the class can be generalized or that a different class should be chosen. In this case, any tests obtained may need extensive modification (to the parent and child classes). Even if the class interface remains the same and just the implementation is modified (as is held by the open and closed principle—see Meyer [10], p. 23), then tests will need to be carried out to ensure the integrity of the class is maintained.

In creating classes in a system, it is not only concrete classes that require testing, that is classes which actually implement a number of features, but also abstract superclasses. These are classes which are designed for other classes to inherit features from them, but which do not actually implement features themselves. Thus, it is not possible to create an instance of an abstract class. Testing the abstract class is more an action of examining its quality, robustness, and how easy it is to derive classes that can be instantiated from it.

Finally, note that conventional procedural programming languages have a number of different levels for abstraction. For example, consider the following labels for Modula 2:

- Functional/procedural
- local module
- module
- program unit
- program system

In the object-oriented world, there is essentially only one level of abstraction, namely the class. The class maps some concept (be it a physical one or a control idea) into the programmer's world. How the classes are organized is up to the programmer, as there is no ordering or hierarchy Imposed. No studies have been published on the quality of a collection of classes, nor into what level of conceptualization should belong in what level of classes. Arguments have been made recently (namely by Coggins [3]) for the form of class libraries, whether it be as one large tree (as in Smalltalk), or as a collection of smaller trees, but no concrete guidelines have been laid down for good organization that is simple to comprehend. Indeed, in the Eiffel system, for example, there are a number of classes which seem to represent the same idea (that of tree data structures) but the relationship between them is not clear and cannot simply be seen from examining the class interface.

The Problems of Message Passing and Concurrency

How Suitable is "Control Flow" Analysis?

With object-oriented programs, it is not possible to think in terms of conventional static or dynamic testing. In executing an object-oriented program, objects are created, have their state changed in various ways, are examined, and finally are destroyed. The concept of control flow through a conventional program does not map readily to an object-oriented program. Flow of control may be thought of as message passing from one object to another, causing the receiving object to perform some operation, be it an examination or alteration, of its state.

In order to test such code, when there is no conceptual input/process/output, it is probably more appropriate to specify how the object's state will change under certain conditions, perhaps using some terminology similar to Eiffel's pre- and post-conditions.

As messages are passed between objects, some object-oriented systems have taken advantage of this (for example, Actor [6]) and can conceptually be thought of as a number of concurrent units. If one object sends two messages to two other objects, there is no reason why the two cannot occur in parallel. However, the complexity of testing such systems, considering the possible time-dependent interactions between objects, is potentially greater than that for normal sequential object-oriented programs. No work has been done to consider whether approaches developed for testing normal imperative concurrent systems are suitable for object-oriented code and indeed it has been suggested in Kafura and Lee [6] that object-orientedness and concurrency are orthogonal to each other.

Considering either of the concepts of message passing or concurrency when testing a program is similar to analyzing what would be called "control" of a conventional program. That is, analyzing which section of code is executing at what time or for what input.

How Suitable is "Data Flow" Analysis?

The other approach taken in conventional program testing is to use "Data Flow Analysis" to validate code statically. This technique considers definition, usage, and resetting of variables and analyses code for badly formed structures. Much original work was done by Laski [7], later to be generalized by Clarke et al [2] and various extensions have been proposed, for example by Calliss and Cornelius [1]. However, in object-oriented programs, the flow through a program and the subsequent defining and using of variable is much more complex. No study has been published on the use of this approach with object-oriented programs. Thus the applicability of "data flow" approaches is questionable.

The technique may be adaptable by considering the creation and deletion of objects as suitable for some form of data flow anomaly analysis (for example, creation and subsequent immediate deletion without accessing an object would constitute an error).

The Problems of Inheritance

Inheritance as described above allows classes to be described in terms of variations (extensions, restrictions, etc) of other classes. Inheritance is one area which has receive attention for validation, for example see the paper by Perry and Kaiser [12].

Inheritance itself can be divided broadly into two types: strict and non-strict. This and other sub-classifications of inheritance are taken from Collingham [4].

Strict Inheritance

When a class inherits features from another class, it generally is designed as a specialization of the parent class.

For example, the class "Puzzle" in Figure 1 inherits from the class "Toy." The class Puzzle is a specialization or a subset of the class Toy. All the properties of Toy, such as Cost_Suitable_Age_Range, Num_Players, etc. are applicable for the class Puzzle. In addition, the class Puzzle may add features such as Time_To_Solve, Num_Combinations and Difficulty which are specific to that class. This is an example of strict inheritance. Strict inheritance occurs when the child class takes all the features from the parent class (possibly re-implementing some of them, for example a Puzzle is usually for one person) and adds additional features in the specialization. It can be thought of as an "*is-a*" relationship: a Puzzle *is-a* Toy.

As far as testing is concerned, strict inheritance is the easiest form of inheritance. The test cases for the parent class are still suitable for the child class. However, extra cases are required for the added features and to ensure that they do not disrupt the correctness of the original features.

Non-Strict Inheritance

Non-strict inheritance occurs when some of the features from the parent class are not present or are renamed in the child class This can occur in the simple case by omission or through multiple or repeated inheritance. Different complications arise for the tester in each case. Note that non-strict inheritance can be thought of as a "like" relationship. The child class is-like the parent class.

Simple Non-Strict Inheritance occurs when a child class inherits features from one parent class.

Such a situation is shown in Figure 1 between the classes Board_Game and Toy. The class Board Game inherits all the features of the class Toy. It also adds Else features such as Num_Pieces and Strategy_Or_Dice. However, the feature of Num_Players is redefined as Ideal_Num_Players. This is non-strict inheritance since a feature from the parent is no longer available under the same name in the child.

Note that although this allows a more correct representation of the class Board Game, it causes problems in that a run-time error can occur if the Num_Players feature is invoked for a collection of Toys (see below) and one of the Toys is a Board Game. Tests need to be devised to cater for this.

Multiple Inheritance occurs when a child class inherits from two or more parent classes, where the features from both are used to make up the new class.

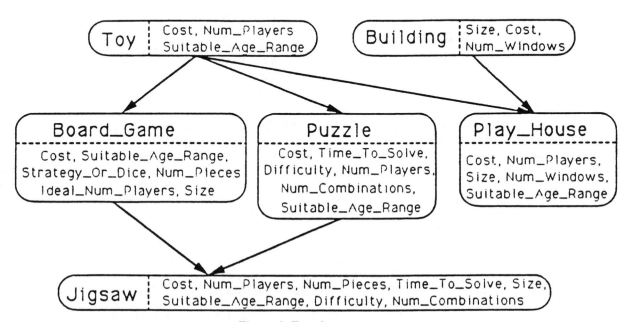

Figure 1. Toy class structure.

14

For example, consider the class Play_House in Figure 1. It inherits from the two classes Toy and Building. Note that it has properties from both its parents, such as suitable_Age_Range (from Toy) and Num_Windows (from Building). Features may also be redefined as in simple non-strict inheritance (such as the Num_Players redefinition in a similar manner to the class Board_Game above). Problems that occur with multiple inheritance are:

1. Two feature names from the two parent classes could be identical. This leads to problems arising from the renaming of the features and the subsequent possible incorrect invocation of the wrong feature.

2. The class structure becomes more complex as it is no longer a simple hierarchical structure but a connected graph. This is more complicated for a programmer to understand and hence more difficult to test.

3. Change to either of the two or more parent classes may cause undesirable interactions in the child class. For example, if initially the two parent classes use different storage methods and then are altered to use the same storage method, errors may arise due to the incomplete testing of the interactions of the storage method.

Repeated Inheritance occurs when a child class derives from the same parent class more than once. Consider again the classes shown in Figure 1. The class Jigsaw inherits from both the class Puzzle (since it has features such as Time_To_Solve) arid the class Board_Game (since it has features such as Num_Pieces). However, this means that it effectively inherits twice from the superclass Toy. This means that a number of routines must be renamed and for some features (such as Cost and Suitable_Age_Range) the duplicates must be removed.

Repeated inheritance is more complicated than multiple inheritance since a number of features are renamed or removed and the possibility of errors from such features are increased. The question as to whether tests for the superclass or both parent classes can be reused and if so what alterations need to be made requires more analysis.

In this section we have described inheritance, by which object-oriented software is reused. However, there is no way for specifically testing the inter-class relationships arising from inheritance, nor is there any mechanism for testing the validity of the inheritance itself.

The Problems of Polymorphism

The word polymorphism means "many forms" and in object-oriented programs can be used in either "object polymorphism" or "feature polymorphism." These two terms were originally defined in [4] to distinguish conceptually between invocation and storage of objects.

Object Polymorphism

Consider the class arrangement as shown in Figure 1. The child classes Board_Game, Puzzle, and Play_House are all directly inherited from the class Toy. One aspect of this inheritance is that the same feature names are recognized by all four classes.[*] For example, consider the following section of code. Note that to avoid arguments over the merits of different object-oriented languages, the examples shown are not written in a particular language. The form object.method (parameter1, ...) implies that the method named method should be invoked for the object object, and the parameters parameter1 ... are to be used.

```
...
object chess is_instance_of Board_Game;
object sliding_block
    is_instance_of Puzzle;
object house is_instance_of Play_House;
object toy_array
    is_instance_of ARRAY [Toy];
...
chess.create(Cost=5,
    Ideal_Num_Players=2,
    Strategy_Or_Dice=Strategy, ...);
Sliding_block.create(Cost=2,
    Num_Players=1,
    Time_To_Solve=15, ...);
house.create(Cost-20,
    Ideal_Num_Players=3,
    Num_Windows=4, ...);
Toy_array.create(size=NumElements);
...
toy_array.put(1,chess);
toy_array.put (2,sliding_block);
toy_array.put (3,house);
...
```

The putting of objects of different but related types into the toy_array demonstrate object polymorphism. That is, an object can be used either as the target of a message or as parameters to a feature invocation, where the type required is either that of the object, or of its parent. Thus in the invocation of toy_array.put the second parameter is an instance of the class Board_Game. It is thus a descendant of the class Toy and is therefore a valid parameter. As Collingham [4] defines it

object polymorphism allows a descendant to take the place of one of its ancestors.

---

[*] Note: The class Jigsaw is also a child of the class Toy and its exclusion form this discussion is to avoid any confusion caused by repeated inheritance. Assigning the value of an object of class Jigsaw to an element of the array Toy_Array is perfectly valid.

This alone causes few problems, except that it is necessary for the programmer to check that the child is only used in place of one of its ancestors and not the other way around. Type checking within the language should catch these errors statically.

Feature Polymorphism

Feature polymorphism can be thought of as the overloading of a feature, much in the same way as overloading in a language such as Ada. It occurs when separate classes have the same feature names (such as Cost and Size in the example) and the particular feature invoked depends upon the class of the object in question. Given the array of toys assigned as above, the following could be used to display the cost of each element of the array:

```
for ElenentNum: =1 to NumElements do
toy_array.get(ElementNum).Cost.print
```

Here, the actual class of each object being sent the Cost message is determined at run time and the appropriate message is sent.

Note that no problems arise for strict inheritance, where the child is a pure specialization of the parent class, adding features to it. Any feature that is present in the parent is also present in the child. However, in non-strict inheritance, where the child may lose a feature of the parent, feature polymorphism allows errors to occur at run-time, since no routine is available in the child class. This would occur if the feature Cost were replaced with Num_Players, which neither chess nor house respond to.

The run-time problems that occur are due to the dynamic (or late) binding of an object to a class. Use of dynamic binding does not imply that a program cannot be type checked. It is, however, more complicated to do and current static analysis tools such as cross referencers are somewhat redundant, since usage of a particular routine on a particular line depends on run-time conditions. In testing, techniques such as symbolic execution become much more complex since actual actions performed depend on run-time conditions in a much more complex way than that determined by normal control-flow constructs in procedural programming languages.

The Problems of Genericity

Genericity is another feature of modern programming languages (not just object-oriented ones) that causes problems in validating software. Genericity is the definition of a class using an unspecified type. The user of the class must specify what particular type is to be used and must ensure any supporting routines for this type exist.

For example, a generic linked list class can exist in which the type of entity which is stored in the list is not specified (it is given as a parameter) until the user of the

class requires it. Then it can be substituted for integer, real, array, linked list etc. provided that the type of variable used is storable in such a structure.

In testing generic code, two problems arise. Firstly, just as classes need to be instantiated before they can be dynamically tested, generic classes need to have the parameter replaced by an actual type. This leads to the problem of choosing a suitable type with which to exchange the parameter. If a simple type is chosen, perhaps the class is not really being correctly tested. The use of some mechanism to specify constraints (if any) on the types which can legally be used instead of the parameter would be advantageous. In actual fact, generic classes are more comparable to abstract super classes than normal classes. That is, by specifying the generic part as a concrete entity, a class is formed from which objects can be instantiated.

Secondly, as with abstract super classes, if changes are made to the generic class then the classes which are derived must be tested for integrity. How regression testing can be used in this way has yet to be considered.

Validation of Reusable Object-Oriented Programs

As the previous sections have shown, the goal of reusability of object-oriented software is impaired by lack of suitable validation techniques for it. How can code be reused if it is not possible to demonstrate the quality of the code being reused? Object-oriented programming has introduced a number of features to support reusability and the need for feature for testing the use of these methods, methods to test inherited, and generic code and methods to maintain regression tests for reused code has been demonstrated.

Some languages provide features which aim to assist in the development of the software and which also aid the testing process. For example, consider the pre- and post-conditions in Eiffel. It is possible for these to be used to suggest test cases; for example they may suggest boundary for a class.

The Quality of Collections of Classes

As object-oriented systems develop, the aim will be to try and establish a large library of classes that can be used by programmers to develop new applications. As class libraries develop and are more widely used, the software will inevitably become more widely tested due to frequent use. However, there are other considerations in having such class libraries that software testing should address.

The aim of software testing is to establish where the code under test can be improved so that its quality is increased. In a similar vein, just producing a collection of classes can actually impair the quality of code that uses them if the programmer is not aware of how to use the classes correctly and in keeping with their initial design. This is particularly crucial for maintenance, since a homogeneous class strcture will be easier to maintain than one which is inconsistent.

Software testing should be extended to include testing for quality and reusability of entire classes, to verify how usable they are for a programmer.

Thus code which uses a consistent method (such as the Demeter method [8] for ensuring a consistent code style) should be testable and show a higher quality than code that has written without use of such a method and written in an ad-hoc manner.

Current Research

The focus of this paper has been to highlight the problems that are present currently with validating object-oriented systems, rather than propose solutions. It is the intention of this section to outline the areas of work that are being undertaken at Durham's Centre for Software Maintenance to address some of these issues.

This paper has shown the progression of complexity from objects through classes to inheritance, so the research is geared towards meeting those needs. In order to form a base for future work, present research is developing an automatic test generation mechanism for objects, based on the static information present in classes. In order to validate any proposed test method, common errors in object-oriented programs are being investigated. This will allow confidence in the system to be assessed.

The assurance in the quality of classes is seen as a by-product of the research and work is being done in assessing currently available class libraries for their quality and robustness. The authors would like to hear from organizations who would like to increase confidence in the classes which they use, in order to provide greater generality of this research.

Future work by co-workers will more fully address the problems of inheritance, building on regression testing expertise at the Centre.

Conclusion

This paper has described a number of the problems of validating software written using an object-oriented programming language. Although the problems outlined do not presently have a solution, it is hopeful that this paper will cause discussion and collaboration that will lead to solutions to these problems before too many mistakes are made.

Acknowledgement

M.D. Smith is supported by a U.K. SERC CASE award in conjunction with British Telecom Research Laboratories, Martlesham Heath, England. The authors would like to thank the anonymous reviewers for their comments on an earlier version of this report, as well as the numerous helpful criticisms given by Barry Cornelius on this work.

References

[1] Callis, F.W. and Cornelius, B.J., "Dynamic Data Flow Analysis of C Programs," *Proc. 21st Hawaii Int'l Conf. System Sciences,* IEEE Computer Society Press, Los Alamitos, Calif., 1988, pp. 518–523.

[2] Clarke, L.A., Podgurski, A., Richardson, D.J., and Zeil, S.J., "A Formal Evaluation of Data Flow Path Selection Criteria," *IEEE Trans. Software Eng.,* Vol. 15, Nov. 1989, pp. 1318–1332.

[3] Coggins, J. M., "Designing C++ Libraries," *1990 USENIX Conf. Proc.,* 1990, pp. 95–35.

[4] Collingham, R.J., "Object-Oriented Programming Languages," Tech. Rep. TR-89/14, Computer Science, Univ. Durham, 1989.

[5] Goldberg, A., "Programmer as Reader," *IEEE Software,* No. 9, 1987, pp. 69–69.

[6] Fafura, D.G. and Lee, K.H., "Inheritance in Actor Based Concurrent Object-Oriented Languages," *The Computer J.,* Vol. 32, Aug. 1989, pp. 297–304.

[7] Laski, J.W. and Korel, B., "A Data Flow Oriented Program Testing Strategy," *IEEE Trans .Software Eng.,* Vol. 9, May 1983, pp 317–351..

[8] Lieberherr K.J. and Riel, A.J., "Demeter: A CASE Study of Software Growth through Parameterized Classes," *IEEE,* 1988, pp. 254–264.

[9] Meyer, B., "Genericity versus Inheritance," *ACM OOPSLA Proc.,* ACM Press, New York, N.Y., 1986, pp. 391–405.

[10] Meyer, B., *Object-Oriented Software Construction,* Prentice-Hall, 1988.

[11] Pascoe, G.A., "Elements of Object-Oriented Programming," *BYTE,* Vol. 11, No. 8, 1986, pp. 139–144.

[12] Perry, D.E. and Kaiser, G.E., "Adequate Testing and Object-Oriented Programming," *J. Object-Oriented Programming,* Vol. 2, Jan/Feb 1990, pp. 13–19.

[13] Stroustrup, B., "What is Object-Oriented Programming?," *IEEE Software,* No. 5, 1988, pp. 10–90.

[14] Wegner, P., "Perspectives on Object-Oriented Programming," Tech. Rep., Brown University, Department of Computer Science, 1986.

Maintenance Support for Object-Oriented Programs

Norman Wilde and Ross Huitt

Abstract—This paper describes some of the difficulties that may be expected in the maintenance of software developed using the new object oriented languages. The concepts of inheritance and of polymorphism provide the great strengths of these languages, but they also introduce difficulties in program analysis and understanding. The paper analyzes problems of dynamic binding, object dependencies, dispersed program structure, control of polymorphism, high-level understanding, and detailed code understanding. Examples are presented based on code from a PC Smalltalk environment and from studies of two systems under development at Bell Communications Research. Recommendations are made for possible tool support, particularly using the concepts of dependency analysis, external dependency graphs, and clustering methodologies.

I. INTRODUCTION

THE SOFTWARE paradigm of object-oriented programming (OOP) has become increasingly popular in recent years. More and more organizations are introducing object-oriented methods and languages into their software development practices. Claimed advantages of OOP include extensive reuse of software objects and easier maintenance through better data encapsulation [1]. Some evidence has begun to appear that these benefits may be achieved in practice [18].

To achieve these gains, object-oriented languages such as C++, Objective C, Smalltalk, and Eiffel have introduced the concepts of an object class inheritance hierarchy and of polymorphism. Each object class may either implement a needed method itself, or else rely on an implementation from one of its superiors in the hierarchy. Different object classes respond to messages having the same name to do similar tasks, even though the code implementing the methods may be quite different for the different classes.

Although maintenance may turn out to be easier for programs written in such languages, it is unlikely that the maintenance burden will completely disappear. Maintenance, in its widest sense of "post deployment software support," is likely to continue to represent a very large fraction of total system costs. Accordingly, the Florida/Purdue Software Engineering Research Center in collaboration with Bell Communications Research (Bellcore) has been studying the im-

Manuscript received April 27, 1992; revised July 23, 1992. This work was supported by Bell Communications Research and the Florida/Purdue Software Engineering Research Center (SERC). SERC is an industry–university research center with support from 13 industrial sponsors, the Florida High Technology and Industry Council, and the National Science Foundation under Grants ECD 861 4385 and ECD 914 6148. Recommended by V. Rajlich.
  N. Wilde is with the Department of Computer Science, University of West Florida, Pensacola, FL 32514.
  R. Huitt is with Bell Communications Research (Bellcore), RRC 1H-206, Piscataway, NJ 08854.
  IEEE Log Number 9204090.

pact of object orientation on the software maintenance task. This study has included discussions with practitioners of object oriented programming at Bellcore and the collection of statistics on several object oriented systems as well as a brief review of some existing commercial object oriented environments.

Inheritance and polymorphism represent complications as well as benefits for the maintenance process. This paper identifies some of the main difficulties that we foresee and describes tool capabilities that would seem to be needed to provide more effective support for the maintenance of object oriented programs. Examples are presented from a PC Smalltalk environment and from two Bellcore systems. We will look for types of tools that can be applied to an existing body of source code; thus there will be no assumption that a particular documentation methodology or CASE tool was used in system development. In any case maintenance programmers have a well-founded distrust of any external documentation not derivable from the code itself. Recommendations for tool support make use of the concepts of dependency analysis, external dependency graphs, and statistical clustering.

II. THE PROBLEM OF DYNAMIC BINDING

Many maintenance tools depend on tracing dependencies within programs. Object-oriented languages such as Smalltalk complicate the tracing process considerably by allowing dynamic binding of messages to specific methods. A given variable may refer to an object of any class so, using polymorphism, the method to be executed when a given message is sent to it will be determined at run time by the class of the object it represents at that instant. Similarly in C++, object pointers and references may refer not only to objects of their declared class but also to descendants of that class. When an operation is performed on the object, a function declared as virtual will dynamically bind to the implementation of the function that is appropriate to the object's underlying class at runtime.

While dynamic binding provides much of the flexibility of object-oriented languages, it may also greatly complicate the tracing of dependencies. Specifically, when a message is sent to a variable holding an object, the actual method implementation that will be called depends on the object's class. Since different implementations will establish different dependencies, static analysis will not always be able to identify precisely the dependencies in the program.

Reprinted from *IEEE Trans. Software Eng.*, Vol. 18, No. 12, Dec. 1992, pp. 1038–1044.

```
Object ‹at:put:›
  ·
  ·
├ Collection
│  ├ Bag ‹at:put:›
│  ├ IndexedCollection
│  │  ├ FixedSizeCollection
│  │  │  ├ Array
│  │  │  │  └ CompiledMethod
│  │  │  ├ Bitmap
│  │  │  ├ ByteArray
│  │  │  ├ Interval ‹at:put:›
│  │  │  └ String ‹at:put:›
│  │  │     └ Symbol ‹at:put:›
│  │  └ OrderedCollection ‹at:put:›
│  │     ├ Process
│  │     └ SortedCollection ‹at:put:›
│  ├ Set ‹at:put:›
│  ├ Dictionary ‹at:put:›
│  │  ├ IdentityDictionary ‹at:put:›
│  │  │  └ MethodDictionary ‹at:put:›
│  │  └ SystemDictionary ‹at:put:›
│  └ SymbolSet
│
├ DisplayObject
│  └ DisplayMedium
│     └ Form ‹at:put:›
│  ·
│  ·
├ MType
│  ·
│  ·
│  └ ListRec ‹at:put:›
│  ·
   ·
```

Fig. 1. Smalltalk/V partial object hierarchy showing at:put: methods.

For example, the Smalltalk/V[1] system provides a large body of reusable object classes organized in a hierarchy as shown in Fig. 1 [5]. Fourteen of these object classes implement the at:put: message, which generally is used to place an object at a particular place within a collection of objects. Encountering an unfamiliar at:put: message while trying to understand a Smalltalk/V program, a maintainer would normally use a cross-reference browser to look at the code being invoked by the message. However, it may be difficult for the maintainer to decide which of the 14 methods must be examined. A more sophisticated tool, such as a program slicer [27], would have even greater difficulty in tracing the data flow of the message since it would not be able to use the maintainer's background knowledge to limit its search to a few object classes.

Broadly speaking there would seem to be four approaches to the problem.

1) Perform a "worst case" analysis in which the possible effects of the message are taken to be the union over all the relationships set up by any of the method implementations. This method might be adequate for C++ programs that use the virtual directive sparingly; it will be less satisfactory for systems such as Fig. 1 that have many implementations of a given message.

[1] Bellcore does not provide comparative analysis or evaluation of products or suppliers. Any mention of products or suppliers in this paper is done where necessary for the sake of scientific accuracy and precision or for background information to a point of technical analysis, or to provide an example of a technology for illustrative purposes, and should not be construed as either positive or negative commentary on that product or vendor. Neither the inclusion of a product or a vendor, nor the omission of a product or vendor, should be interpreted as indicating a position or opinion of that product or vendor on the part of the authors or of Bellcore. Bellcore does not make any purchasing recommendations.

2) Use dynamic analysis, in which the program is run for several test cases with probes inserted to detect the real classes of the objects of interest. The problem, of course, is that the test cases may not detect all the behavior that the program is capable of exhibiting, and thus incorrect conclusions may be drawn.

3) Allow human input to identify the possible classes of objects. We are exploring a design for a more sophisticated Dependency Analysis Tool Set that would allow the user to describe the expected classes of the objects that the program is manipulating. In several cases that we have studied, it would seem that the user can limit the scope of a query to obtain much more focused results. Again, however, the obvious problem is that the human may give the wrong constraints, leading again to incorrect analysis of the system.

4) It may be possible to analyze each message to reduce greatly the number of possible classes for each object. For example some of Graver's work on type analysis of Smalltalk has shown promising results in this area [8]. If types are declared for a relatively small number of objects in the program, the types of many of the remaining objects can be deduced. Even if it is not possible to make a precise determination, it may often be feasible to reduce greatly the number of possibilities.

We would suggest that environments for object-oriented maintenance should provide support for several of these approaches. Debugging environments could usefully store information about the classes of each object that have been encountered at run-time. Analysis tools should be able to make use of such information, as well as human input, to limit the scope of analysis. When no other information is available, tools should default to showing all the potential dependencies in the system using the first approach mentioned above. It may be useful to maintain the distinction between the set of potential relationships and the more limited set of probable relationships found after pruning using one of the mentioned approaches. The first set would be used by tools checking for subtle ripple effects or bugs but the second would probably be sufficient for general program understanding tasks.

III. DEPENDENCIES IN OBJECT-ORIENTED SYSTEMS

A dependency in a software system is, informally, a direct relationship between two entities in the system $X \rightarrow Y$ such that a programmer modifying X must be concerned about possible side effects in Y. Earlier reports ([28]–[30]) analyzed the dependencies in conventional software systems. The main kinds of entity considered were data items (or variables), processing modules, and data types. Dependencies were classified as follows:

- data dependencies between two variables;
- calling dependencies between two modules;
- functional dependencies between a module and the variables it computes;
- definitional dependencies between a variable and its type.

To deal with object oriented languages, we need to add the following kinds of entities:[2]

- object classes;
- methods (which are specific code segments);
- messages (which may be thought of as "names" of methods).

Variables may now represent instances of an object class instead of, or in addition to, conventional data values. Object classes may be thought of as special kinds of types while methods are special kinds of processing module. However the use of polymorphism and hierarchy creates an explosion in the kinds of dependencies that need be considered:

Class-to-Class Dependencies:
— C1 is a direct super class of C2
— C1 is a direct sub class of C2
— C1 inherits from C2
— C1 uses C2 (which may be subclassified as "uses for interface", and "uses for implementation")

Class to Method:
— method M returns object of class C
— C implements method M
— C inherits method M

Class to Message:
— C understands message

Class to Variable:
— V is an instance of class C
— V is a class variable of C
— V is an instance variable of C
— V is defined by class C

Method to Variable:
— V is a parameter for method M
— V is a local variable in method M
— V is imported by M (ie, is a nonlocal variable used in M)
— V is defined by M
— M refers to V

Method to Message:
— message M' is name of method M
— method M sends message M'

Method to Method:
— method M1 invokes method M2
— method M1 overrides M2

Environments for maintaining OOP's need to provide ways of browsing these different kinds of relationships. The multidimensional nature of the interconnections will make it very difficult to use listing or text screen based systems for program understanding. Multi-window displays would seem to be a minimum requirement to display enough information.

IV. THE STRUCTURE OF OOP's

There is a general impression among practitioners that OOP's may tend to be structured rather differently than

---

[2] In the absence of a standard object oriented terminology, we have adopted Smalltalk's terms; in C++ the corresponding terms would be classes, member functions, and member function names.

TABLE I
SIZES OF METHODS IN THREE OBJECT-ORIENTED SYSTEMS

System and Domain	Language	Number of Methods	Median Method Size
Bellcore: Interactive network design aid	C++	1280	1 executable statement
Bellcore: Prototype of noninteractive task planning system	Smalltalk	477	2 noncomment lines
Smalltalk/V: Sample from the environment's class library	Smalltalk	2224	3 noncomment lines

conventional programs. For many tasks very brief methods may be written that simply "pass through" a message to another method with very little processing. Thus a system may consist of a large number of very small modules rather than a relatively smaller number of larger ones.

We know of no large-scale study of the metrics of object-oriented systems. However we have collected data on the three systems shown in Table I [31]. The small sizes of the methods are striking. Although the three systems are for very different problem domains, in all three cases 50% of the methods are less than 2 C++ statements or 4 Smalltalk lines long.

This sample may not, of course, be typical of OOP practices in other systems and languages. However, some of the work on good object oriented programming style would seem to encourage the use of many small methods [11]. The Law of Demeter proposed by Lieberherr and Holland would restrict a method from " . . . retrieving a subpart of an object that lies deep in that object's Part-of hierarchy" [14]. Such prohibited accesses would probably be eliminated by encapsulating the work in specialized methods of the supplier class, with the effect of taking code out of one client method and distributing it through several small methods in the supplier. Lieberherr and his associates have proposed a language of propagation patterns that a programmer could use to reduce the number of methods that need to be constructed [15] and have suggested a way of abstracting out the propagation patterns from existing code to facilitate understanding [26].

If this pattern of a large number of rather small methods does turn out to be typical, there are significant implications for maintenance tool support. The code for any given task would be very widely dispersed [20]. Understanding of a single line of code may require tracing a chain of method invocations through several different object classes and up and down the object hierarchy to find where the work is really getting done (see Fig. 2). Such searching is both time-consuming and error prone. Most existing browsers would have the maintainer walk down the links in the chain one by one, opening a new browse window at each step. However, the result is likely to be a clutter of overlaid windows that adds little to program understanding.

We would suggest that tools for OOP need to address specifically the problem of finding chains of relationships rather than simply cross-referencing the links in a chain. Finding such chains may be complicated by the dynamic

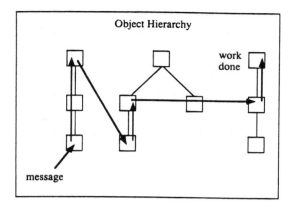

Fig. 2. Typical chain of message invocations.

binding problems discussed in Section II. Also, more interface design work is needed to find better ways of displaying such chains in a comprehensible way without unnecessary clutter. While such displays may be difficult to design, the task of developing them would be considerably eased by the relatively small size of the methods at each link of the chain.

V. HIGH-LEVEL SYSTEM UNDERSTANDING

High level system understanding is chiefly needed when a maintainer is coming to grips with a system for the first time. The maintainer needs some way to sort out the components and perceive the overall architecture of the system. A high-level understanding will give a maintainer a framework to help make sense of the more detailed information acquired as specific maintenance tasks are undertaken.

There is little tool support for high-level system understanding even for conventional (i.e., nonobject oriented) systems. Several researchers have suggested using clustering methods of different kinds to identify system structure (e.g., [2], [17], [10], [24], [25]). However, we know of no generally available tools implementing these ideas.

The module calling hierarchy or structure chart can be generated by several existing tools (e.g., [12]). Calling hierarchies are a useful tool for understanding systems designed using functional decomposition approaches in which the main packaging unit is the processing module (e.g, a function or procedure). In such systems the top level "main module" will likely be a good place to start in system understanding and, if the modules subordinate to it are reasonably cohesive, examining them may give a quick overview of system functions.

But in OOP, the calling hierarchy would be a hierarchy of methods, which has several disadvantages. First, the dynamic binding problem mentioned in Section II may make the hierarchy difficult to compute. Second, there may be no real "main" method in the system [19]. This is one of the facts about object oriented design that beginners tend to find disconcerting. Finally, a hierarchy of methods loses sight of the grouping of methods in objects, which is presumably the most important aspect of the design. An obvious understanding aid would be the object class hierarchy, but because it groups

objects with similar methods, it fails to show how the objects combine to provide the different functional capabilities of the program. For example, in Smalltalk/V the Pane objects work together with Dispatcher objects to provide windows for text editing. But these objects are in different class hierarchies. Helm, Holland, and Gangopodhyay have suggested that object oriented systems should really be described using *contracts* that specify the relationships among such cooperating objects [9].

One possible high-level understanding tool would be a display of the graph of the "Class Uses Class" dependency described in Section III. However the result will be a graph not a hierarchy; graphs are notoriously more difficult to display and comprehend than trees. In a medium scale system with hundreds of object classes the graph may not be particularly comprehensible.

Environments for object-oriented maintenance should probably provide several alternative clustering methods that can be chosen by the user during system exploration. The "Class Uses Class" dependency could provide the links for clustering but some experimentation will be needed to find the most useful methodologies. As suggested by Hutchens and Basili (in [10]) it would probably be necessary to first identify and remove utility classes such as String, Integer, etc. that will have connections to a large number of classes and will thus turn the graph into a spiderweb.

VI. LOCATING SYSTEM FUNCTIONALITY

In the object-oriented paradigm, the location of methods may be more crucial than in conventional programs. The location problem arises partly from the cornucopia of objects and methods offered by systems like Smalltalk. It has been observed that it may be quite difficult to find, for example, the right class to use for a group of objects out of Smalltalk's many different classes of Collection [20]. Another source of the problem is that it may not always be easy to determine which of two or three object classes should be the "host" for a given function. In a library information system, did the designer decide that checking out a book was a method on class Book, class LibraryUser, or class Library?

Thus the maintainer of an OOP may have some difficulty in finding where different functions are carried out, either to reuse them or to modify them. While locating code can also be difficult in conventional programs the dispersion of functionality into different object classes may make the problem more serious for OOP. At a minimum, if the reuse benefits of OOP are to be achieved it must be possible to locate the code to be reused fairly efficiently.

Dynamic analysis may be the best solution. A test case is needed that causes the system to exercise the functionality that is being sought. Debugging environments allow the maintainer to trace or step through the execution of the code, identifying the object classes and methods that are involved. Unfortunately, if little prior information is available to aid in setting breakpoints, it may be necessary to step through a great deal of code to find the code segments of interest.

We would suggest experimenting with statistical analysis of traces of programs. Traces of method invocations could be made of test cases that exercise the functionality in question and compared to traces of other cases where that functionality is expected to be absent. One could imagine a graphic display of the object hierarchy showing only those methods that appear in the first set of traces and not in the second.

VII. UNDERSTANDING POLYMORPHISM

Polymorphism requires consistent use of method names within a system. In theory, a given message name should mean "the same thing" to any object that responds to it. In the example in Fig. 1 the `at:x put:y` message is implemented differently by many different classes, but it should always place the object `y` at the specified location within the receiving collection. The maintainer of such a system knowing what the message means, need not investigate its implementation anew for each implementing class. The use of such *standard protocols* has been identified as one of the strengths of object-oriented methodology [11].

If, however, method naming is not done consistently, subtle errors may be introduced. For example, if a system contains several implementations of the same message with significantly different effects, a maintainer may be misled in interpreting the code and introduce errors when changes are made. Practicing programmers have told us of finding cases of naming confusions; an example from the Smalltalk/V library is given below.

A maintainer who imperfectly understands the naming conventions used by the designers is particularly likely to introduce these kinds of errors, at considerable cost to later maintainers. While problems of inconsistent use of naming conventions are also found in conventional systems, in OOP more reliance is placed on correct naming. In many conventional languages the compiler or linker would complain if two modules had the same name; in OOP such duplicate naming is actively encouraged!

No totally automatic solution would seem to be possible for keeping similar the semantics of similarly named methods. However, some automatic support might be possible using the concept of the *external dependency graph* of each method. External dependency graphs were introduced to represent the effects of execution of a module in a conventional programming language [29]. The graph, which may often be calculated automatically using data flow methods, shows the dependencies between data items that are created by the module.

The different implementations of a message may be categorized into equivalence classes based on their external dependency graphs. As an example consider Smalltalk/Vs 14 implementations of `at:x put:y` shown in Fig. 1. It will be remembered that these methods place the object `y` at location `x` within the receiver. The result of a simplified hand calculation of their external dependency graphs is shown in Fig. 3. As can be seen, there are four equivalence classes of the graphs, which hint at four different kinds of semantic behavior of these 14 methods. Dependency Pattern A seems to be the standard case and is, presumably, the pattern desired by the original

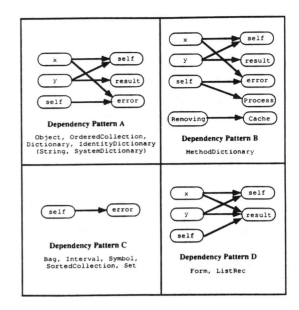

Fig. 3. External dependencies of the Smalltalk/V `at:x put:y` methods.

designers of the system. Each of these methods uses the value of `self` (the receiver) and `x` (the location) to check that the operation can be performed; in other words, there is a valid location `x` within object `self`. (For simplicity we represent the error checking by a graph node called `error`. The actual processing involves calling error handling routines in the Smalltalk/V environment.) The value of `y` is placed at location `x` in `self`, thus changing `self`. Finally, the parameter `y` is returned as the result of the operation. This pattern of dependencies is created by the methods in the classes `Object`, `OrderedCollection`, `Dictionary`, `IdentityDictionary` while very similar patterns, with slightly more error checking, are found in `String` and `SystemDictionary`.

Dependency Pattern B shows more complicated processing since, when the `MethodDictionary` is changed, the Smalltalk/V environment must be updated to make sure that any future message sends will find the new method, not the old. The use of the `at:x put:y` message name is reasonable, but maintainers may need to be aware of this special processing. Dependency Pattern C shows methods which are simple error stubs, since `Bag`, `Interval`, `Symbol`, `SortedCollection` and `Set` do not allow values to be placed at a specified location.

The most interesting case is Dependency Pattern D, for the `Form` and `ListRec` classes. Some external dependencies are similar to those of the standard case but these methods return `self` instead of returning parameter `y`. It would seem likely that these methods were added by a different coder who did not respect the implicit naming conventions of the system. The methods constitute a potential trap for any maintainer who uses them without careful study of their code. We would suggest that projects that use polymorphism heavily should consider comparing the external dependency graphs of methods to detect such problems before they cause trouble.

VIII. DETAILED CODE UNDERSTANDING

Detailed code understanding is at the heart of the maintenance process. Maintainers spend a large fraction of their time doing code reading tasks to understand precisely the module that they are going to modify. The typical question at this point is: "What exactly is this line of code doing?" In conventional programs the answer is normally found by studying the function calls and the data items in the code and then reading the function implementations and searching out the definitions and uses of the data. Cross referencers and browsers aid in this process (e.g., [3], [6], [22]). Such tools have been implemented in many programming environments. Other tools that have been proposed, but more rarely implemented, include ripple effect analyzers [32] and program slicers [27].

The class hierarchy and polymorphism seem to introduce two kinds of complications to detailed code understanding. First, as mentioned in Section IV, the code that must be examined to understand a given method may be quite widely dispersed. Second, as indicated in Section III, hierarchy and polymorphism multiply the number of kinds of relationships that may need to be considered in planning a specific change to an OOP. One approach that may be fruitful would be querying tools and browsers built around the concept of Dependency Analysis given in [29]. Dependency Analysis provides a uniform method of viewing the different kinds of relationship in the system and so can more easily handle the multiple kinds of dependencies of object oriented programs. It also focuses on identifying chains of relationships instead of simple cross-references, and thus may be useful in tracing through widely dispersed code fragments. Browsers may be constructed that display information in multiple windows based on the output of a dependency query [30]. We are currently working on the design of a generalized Dependency Analysis toolset intended to address the problems of OOP.

IX. SOME EXISTING OBJECT-ORIENTED ENVIRONMENTS

This paper does not pretend to be a review of OOP environments, but during its preparation we have seen literature or demonstrations of several of the current commercial products. The products studied include:

- Smalltalk/V with its Application Manager package, from Digitalk, Inc.;
- Objectworks, from ParcPlace Systems;
- Objective-C, from The Stepstone Corp.; and
- Saber C++, from Saber Software, Inc.

Several interesting academic tools have also been described in the literature [13], [23]. It should be remembered that new products are appearing very rapidly and new features are constantly being added to old ones, so our impressions may be out of date.

From the point of view of maintenance, the main kind of static analysis provided by these tools is *cross-reference browsing*. Typically the user can look at the code of one method, select a message or a variable, get a "pick list" of methods implementing the message or of references to the variable, and pop open a window on the corresponding

code. Browsing is typically supported using several different kinds of dependencies, such as the class inheritance structure, methods implementing a message, variable references, file locations of definitions, etc.

The dynamic debugging tools provided by several of the products should also be very useful for detailed code understanding during maintenance. Facilities provided include the insertion of breakpoints, various levels of execution stepping and tracing, insertion of test data, monitoring of test coverage, etc. A most important feature is the ability to examine and manipulate objects and their contents easily so that the user can view the actual state of the complex data structures that are established by an OOP. Graphic displays of object relationships would seem to be very useful.

X. CONCLUSIONS

This paper has attempted to outline some of the main difficulties that can be expected in maintaining OOP's and has proposed directions for possible tool support of the maintenance process. Some of the main proposals may be summarized as follows.

- Environments for object-oriented maintenance need to address the problem of *dynamic binding*. It is unlikely that any single strategy will be appropriate for all cases so tools could be designed to incorporate multiple sources of information about bindings, ranging from dynamic analysis to human input.
- Statistical clustering tools would form a very useful component of an object oriented maintenance environment. Such tools would aid the maintainer in understanding the high level structure of the system. Similarly, tools for analyzing and comparing traces of system behavior might aid the maintainer in identifying the classes and methods associated with a particular functionality.
- The storage and analysis of external dependency information for methods could aid in controlling some of the semantic problems of polymorphism.
- Designers of several different kinds of tools could find an appropriate paradigm in the concept of Dependency Analysis with its emphasis on tracing chains of relationships.

ACKNOWLEDGMENT

The authors would like to thank P. Matthews of Bell Communications Research both for originally directing our attention to the problems of maintaining object oriented systems and for many ideas contributed during discussions of this topic.

Authors' note: The Florida/Purdue Software Engineering Research Center is supported by Andersen Consulting, Inc., Bell Communications Research, Bell Northern Research, Community Sciences Corporation, Digital Equipment Corporation, GTE Data Services, Harris Corporation, IBM, Magnavox Electronics Co., Northrop Electronics Systems, Sun Microsystems, Inc., The United States Army, and Westinghouse Savannah River Co.

REFERENCES

[1] G. Booch, "Object-oriented development," *IEEE Trans. Software Eng.*, vol. SE-12, pp. 211–221, Feb. 1986.

[2] S.C. Choi and W. Scacchi, "Extracting and restructuring the design of large systems," *IEEE Software*, vol. 7, pp. 66–71, Jan. 1990.

[3] L. Clevland, "A program understanding support environment," *IBM Systems J.*, vol. 28, pp. 324–344, 1989.

[4] B.J. Cox, *Object-Oriented Programming: An Evolutionary Approach.* Reading, MA: Addison Wesley, 1986

[5] Digitalk, Inc., Smalltalk/V Mac Tutorial and Programming Handbook, Digitalk Corp., Los Angeles, CA, 1989.

[6] J. Foster and M. Munro, "A documentation method based on cross-referencing," in *Proc. IEEE Conf. Software Maintenance*, pp. 181–185, Sept. 1987.

[7] A. Goldberg D. Robson, *Smalltalk-80: The Language and Its Implementation.* Reading, MA: Addison Wesley, 1985.

[8] J. Graver and R. Johnson, "A type system for Smalltalk," in *Proc. 17th Annual ACM Symp. Principles of Programming Languages*, pp. 136–150, 1990.

[9] R. Helm *et al.*, "Contracts: Specifying behavioral compositions in object-oriented systems," in *Proc. ECOOP/OOPSLA 90-SIGPLAN Notices*, vol. 25, pp. 169–180, Oct. 1990.

[10] D. Hutchens and V. Basili, "System structure analysis: Clusteing with data bindings," *IEEE Trans. Software Eng.*, vol. SE-11, pp. 749–757, Aug. 1985.

[11] R.E. Johnson and B. Foote, "Designing reusable classes," *J. Object-Oriented Programming*, vol. 1, pp. 25–35, June/July 1988.

[12] D.R. Kuhn, "A source code analyzer for maintenance," in *Proc. IEEE Conf. Software Maintenance*, pp. 176–180, Sept. 1987.

[13] M. Lejter *et al.*, "Support for maintaining object-oriented programs," in *Proc. IEEE Conf. Software Maintenance*, pp. 171–178, Oct. 1991.

[14] K.L. Lieberherr and I.M. Holland, "Assuring good style for object-oriented programs," *IEEE Software*, vol. 6, pp. 38–48, Sept. 1989.

[15] K. Lieberherr *et al.*, "Graph-based software engineering: Concise specifications of cooperative behavior," *Tech. Rep. NU-CCS-91-14*, College of Computer Science, Northeastern University, Sept. 1991.

[16] B.P. Lientz and B. Swanson, *Software Maintenance Management.* Reading, MA: Addison-Wesley, 1980.

[17] S.-S. Liu and N. Wilde, "Identifying objects in a conventional procedural language: An example of data design recovery," in *Proc. IEEE Conf. Software Maintenance*, pp. 266–271, Nov. 1990.

[18] D. Mancl and W. Havanas, "A study of the impact of C++ on software maintenance," in *Proc. IEEE Conf. Software Maintenance*, pp. 63–69, Nov. 1990.

[19] B. Meyer, *Object-Oriented Software Construction.* Englewood Cliffs, NJ: Prentice Hall, 1988.

[20] J. Nielsen and J. Richards, "Experience of Learning and Using Smalltalk", IEEE Software, pp. 73–77, May 1989.

[21] D. Perry and G. Kaiser, "Adequate testing and object-oriented programming," *J. Object Oriented Programming*, vol. 2, pp. 13–19, Jan./Feb. 1990.

[22] V. Rajlich *et al.*, "Visual support for programming-in-the-large," in *Proc., IEEE Conf. Software Maintenance*, pp. 92–99, Oct. 1988.

[23] J. Sametinger, "A tool for the maintenance of C++ programs," in *Proc. IEEE Conf. Software Maintenance*, pp. 54–59, Nov. 1990.

[24] R.W. Schwanke and M.A. Platoff, "Cross references are features," in *Proc. 2nd Int. Workshop on Software Con Fig. Management*, pp. 86-95, Oct. 1989.

[25] R.W. Selby and V. Basili, "Error localization during software maintenance: Generating hierarchical system descriptions from the source code alone," in *Proc. IEEE Conf. Software Maintenance*, pp. 192–197, Oct. 1988.

[26] I. Silva-Lepe, "Abstracting graphed-based specifications of object-oriented programs," *Tech. Rep. NU-CCS-92-4*, College of Computer Science, Northeastern University, Mar. 1992.

[27] M. Weisner, "Program slicing," in *Proc. 5th Int. Conf. Software Engineering*, pp. 439–449, Mar. 1981.

[28] N. Wilde and B. Nejmeh, "Dependency analysis: An aid for software maintenance," *SERC-TR-13-F*, Software Engineering Research Center, Univ. Florida, Gainesville, FL, Sept. 1987.

[29] N. Wilde, R. Huitt, and S. Huitt, "Dependency analysis tools: Reusable components for software maintenance," in *Proc. IEEE Conf. Software Maintenance*, pp. 126–131, Oct. 1989.

[30] N. Wilde and R. Huitt, "A reusable toolset for software dependency analysis," *J. Systems and Software*, vol. 14, pp. 97–102, Feb. 1991.

[31] N. Wilde *et al.*, "Describing object oriented software: What maintainers need to know," *SERC-TR-54-F*, Software Engineering Research Center, Univ. Florida, Gainesville, FL, Dec. 1991.

[32] S.S. Yau, "Ripple effect analysis of software maintenance," in *Proc. COMPSAC-78*, IEEE Computer Society, pp. 60–65, 1978.

Chapter 2

Specification and Verification

Software specification describes what needs to be developed and *software verification* checks if the developed result meets the specification. In other words, *verification* is the process that examines the product in detail and reports how true it is to the specification. Hence, specification comes before the product is produced. Typically, during verification one pays little attention to how the product was implemented and more to whether the implementation satisfies the given specification.

It has long been recognized in software engineering that verification and validation (V&V) is an essential activity in ensuring the quality of a software product. Object-oriented (OO) programs are no exception. While validation of OO software may not be different from that of the conventional programs, the major concerns are if the software functionality is complete and consistent with the users' needs. Nevertheless, there is very little research attempting to address the unique issues in the specification and verification of OO software even though it is very important.

Conventionally, software specification and verification issues are addressed in the work related to theorem proving techniques, and hence are considered esoteric. Consequently, the actual use of the tools developed for verification is limited in practice. This situation may not be true anymore for OO software because its specification cannot be avoided and its verification is essential if reuse is the major goal and benefit to a project.

Since the class is the dominant entity in OO programs, the specifications of classes, clusters of classes, and the whole system become the central focus. We are still in our infancy in terms of the ability to produce consistent and complete specifications. In addition, we need to know how to test the program once it is developed.

This chapter on specification and verification will address some specific testing problems, concerns, and solutions in OO programs related to the subject. We focus on how to proceed to verify an OO program with respect to its specification which may be obtained through a design process.

We have selected two papers for this chapter. The first one is by Binder [bind94a] and addresses design for testability in OO systems. It provides an overview and specific guidelines on what to consider in design in order to develop a program with good testability. The second paper is by

Kirani and Tsai [kira94a] and highlights method sequence specification and verification of classes which is a very important issue in testing a class. It is not present in the conventional software testing. The detailed review of the papers is presented below.

The first paper is "Design for Testability in Object-Oriented Systems" by Binder. It presents a comprehensive treatment of testability and how it works in a related discipline such as very-large-scale integration (VLSI). Then it identifies six primary testability factors: representation, implementation, built-in test, test suite, test automation, and process capability. Each of the six primary factors is further refined into its own quality factors and structure. As one can foresee that these factors are broad enough to include both conventional software testing and OO software testing.

To apply the principle to OO software, the author produced four tables to propose some testability metrics for encapsulation, inheritance, polymorphism, and complexity. They are specific to OO software. One can adopt several metrics and apply them to an OO program to check its testability. They can be used for trade-off analysis when appropriate.

A comparison between VLSI testing strategy and possible class testing strategy is described in a table. Based on this, four types of design for testing (DFT) configurations for OO software are recognized. They are no DFT, ad hoc DFT, structured/standardized DFT, and advanced DFT. These are the four levels of testing maturity that a company exhibits in their OO software testing practice. Finally, a detailed advanced DFT architecture is furnished in great length to illustrate an ideal testing process.

The author concludes by emphasizing the importance of a reliability-driven testing process to ensure software reliability and resource economy. Nearly all the capabilities are in place, but it will take serious investment on the part of the OO community to develop an advanced built-in test environment to achieve the capabilities currently enjoyed by VLSI technology.

The second paper by Kirani and Tsai [kira94a] introduces their insight about class method sequence in an OO program, that is, not all method sequences are semantically feasible and meaningful. Kirani and Tsai propose to provide a method sequence specification along with the class specification. This will achieve several purposes: (1) It can set up usage patterns for the allowable method sequences in a class. (2) It can be used to check if the OO program follows the method sequence patterns. (3) We need only to test the valid method sequences when testing a class. (4) Automatic generation of valid method sequences is feasible.

There is a finite set of methods in any given class. It usually needs to string several methods together to accomplish some observable function. However, not all method sequences are possible and desirable. For instance, in a class of bank Account there may be a set of operations (methods) such as {create, open, deposit, withdraw, close, and delete}. To deposit some money into an account the user will have to follow the sequence create, open, deposit. Without these three operations, no deposit can be made. To deposit money into an account not created and opened is purely nonsense. Hence, if the class is specified with the basic method sequences (Sequence Spec) correctly in the first place we need only to test those legal sequences. Any sequence not in the "usage patterns" should not be tested. The Sequence Spec can be used to generate all the allowable sequences (SafeSequences) because it is a regular grammar. Personally, we think some exception cases also need to be tested, such as deposit into an account that has not yet been created.

Construction of Sequence Spec for a class can be derived from its intraclass state transition diagram (STD) given in a class specification. Once the STD is obtained, the generation of the Sequence Spec needs very little effort.

There is an inconsistency problem in the class method sequence specification when the inheritance relationship and multiple interfaces are involved. The authors provide their solution by using their consistency rules. For example, the child class sequence specification is consistent with all the class sequence specifications for its parent classes if any valid method sequence in the parent class is a proper subsequence of some method sequence of a child class. All consistency rules are specified using the equality Boolean operator to verify the consistency between two regular expressions.

In the case of inheritance relationship, one regular expression is the method sequence specification of the parent class, and the other is that of the child class. In the case of multiple interfaces (that is, several objects use only subsets of the methods a server object provides), the two regular expressions will each serve as the specification of separate subinterfaces. All these consistency-checking rules can be implemented using one uniform consistency-checking algorithm proposed by Hopcroft and Ullman [hopc79a] which verifies the equality between two regular expressions.

The technique proposed in this paper can be used in the following ways:

1. Ensuring conformance of the implementation of a class with the corresponding method sequence specification. Using method sequence specification and static control-flow analysis of OO programs, one can identify all invalid method sequences for each object.

2. Constructing a runtime verification system for a class that ensures the correct method invocation sequence for each object of the class. A runtime verification system can be implemented as a part of the object's runtime support system that identifies all inconsistencies not detected by the first method above (due to the presence of dynamic binding, polymorphism and pointer data structures) either at compile time or during execution.

3. Generating sequence-based test cases for testing the low-level design and implementation. Using different coverage criteria, different sequences can be constructed for generating test cases. Sequence-based testing of an object can then be performed either during design as a walk-through or may be implemented by actually executing the program with the test cases.

References

[bind94a] R. Binder, "Design for Testability in Object-Oriented Systems," *Comm. ACM,* Vol. 37, No. 9, Sept. 1994, pp. 87–101.

[kira94a] S. Kirani and W.T. Tsai, "Method Sequence Specification and Verification of Classes," *J. Object-Oriented Programming,* Oct. 1994, pp. 28–38.

[hopc79a] J.E. Hopcroft, and J.D. Ullamn, *Introduction to Automata Theory, Languages, and Computation,* Addison-Wesley, Reading, Mass., 1979.

Robert V. Binder

Design for
Testability
in Object-Oriented Systems

Testability is the relative ease and expense of revealing software faults. This article maps the testability terrain for object-oriented development to assist the reader in finding relatively shorter and cheaper paths to high reliability. Software testing adds value by revealing faults. It is fundamentally an economic problem characterized by a continuum between two goals. A *reliability-driven* process uses testing to produce evidence that a pre-release reliability goal has been met. Time and money are expended on testing until the reliability goal is attained. This view of testing is typically associated with stringent, quantifiable reliability requirements. Other things being equal, a more testable system will reduce the time and cost needed to meet reliability goals.

A *resource-limited* process views testing as a way to remove as many rough edges from a system as time or money permits. Testing continues until available test resources have been expended. Measurement of test adequacy or system reliability are incidental to the decision to release the system. This is the typical view of testing. Other things being equal, a more testable system provides increased reliability for a fixed testing budget.

Regardless of which goal is emphasized, testability is important for both ad hoc developers and organizations with a high level of process maturity. Testability reduces cost in a reliability-driven process and increases reliability in a resource-limited process.

Design for testability (DFT) is a strategy to align the development process so that testing is maximally effective under either a reliability-driven or resource-limited regime. Object-oriented systems present some unique obstacles to testability as well as sharing many with conventional implementations. The cost and difficulty of testing object-oriented systems can be reduced by following some basic design principles and planning for test. Broadly conceived, software testability is a result of six factors:

• Characteristics of the representation
• Characteristics of the implementation
• Built-in test capabilities
• The test suite (test cases and associated information)
• The test support environment
• The software process in which testing is conducted

These six factors are the spine of the testability fishbone (Figure 1). We'll consider each in turn. Before examining the major and minor bones of object-oriented testing, we review related approaches. Although research and practice in software testing has had relatively little to say about testability, it has been given considerable attention in the engineering and manufacturing of VLSI (very large-scale integration) devices.

The Concept of Testability

Testability has two key facets: *controllability* and *observability*. To test a component, you must be able to control its input (and internal state) and observe its output. If you cannot control the input, you cannot be sure what has caused a given output. If you cannot observe the output of a component under test, you cannot be sure how a given input has been processed. With controllable input and observable output, compliance can be decided. These concepts also have an analogous, formal meaning (beyond

the scope of this article) in control system state-space models [20]. There are many obstacles to controllability and observability. In general, they result from the fact that a component under test must be embedded in another system. Removing obstacles to controllable input and observable output is the primary concern of design for testability. As a practical matter, testability cannot be considered apart from the software process. Process *capability* is equally important.

Design for testability in VLSI. The concept of testability has played an increasingly important role in the design and manufacture of integrated circuits (chips or ICs). Chip testing is performed to identify defects resulting from chip manufacturing or physical failures due to a wide range of causes (vibration, heat, cosmic rays). *Design verification* is the engineering development process that assures functional correctness. Chip testing assumes complete functional correctness. In contrast, software testing assumes perfect replication and the presence of functional faults.

Chips are tested by applying input bit strings and observing output bit strings. For example, with a simple AND gate, we expect that a logical 1 is produced only when both input lines are also logical 1. There are three main approaches to integrated circuit design for test.[1] 1) *Ad hoc* solutions are component-specific. These include the ability to disconnect parts, adding more test points, and reducing a network to smaller, more tractable components. 2) The *structured approach* refers to design rules that reduce or make controllable state

[1]Design for test in VLSI is given a comprehensive treatment by Milton Abramovici, Melvin A. Breuer, and Arthur D. Friedman in *Digital Systems Testing and Testable* (New York, IEEE Press, 1990) and by Hideo Fujiwara in *Logic Testing and Design for Testability* (Cambridge, Mass.: MIT Press, 1985). An overview of DFT is presented by Daniel P. Siewiorek and Robert S. Swarz in *Reliable Computer Systems* (2d ed. Digital Press, Bedford, Mass., 1992.) The history, motivation, and key features of IEEE/ANSI Standard 1149.1. are summarized by Maunder and Tulloss in "Testability on TAP," *IEEE Spectrum 29, 2* (Feb. 1992), 34–37. Hagge and Russell offer an excellent summary of DFT approaches and an integrated process model for development and manufacturing of testable multichip modules in "High-yield assembly of multichip modules through known-good ICs and effective test strategies," *Proceedings of the IEEE, 80, 12* (Dec. 1992), 1965–1994.

variables in sequential circuits. Testing a sequential circuit (a state machine) is considerably more difficult than testing a combinational circuit (a decision table). For sequential circuits, these techniques aim to reduce the test problem to one of generating combinational inputs. 3) *Built-in Test* (BIT) adds standard test circuits. The density of logic gates on chips has steadily increased (about an order of magnitude in the last 10 years), while the feasible number of pins (external interfaces) remained about the same.

With present-day VLSI, on-chip testing capabilities are a necessity. Without these capabilities, it is impossible to provide adequate controllability and observability. ANSI/IEEE Standard 1149.1 defines a boundary-scan architecture for BIT functions [14]. Individual chips (embedded in a single package) may be accessed via four to six additional external test lines and a few standardized test circuits on every IC. This provides the ability to place an embedded chip or board into test mode, transmit (or generate) test bit strings to specific embedded components, and capture output bit strings. The basic BIT capabilities can be extended to provide complex, automatically initiated test suites called *Built-in-Self Test* (BIST). Since approval in 1990, ANSI/IEEE Standard 1149.1 has been rapidly adopted by IC manufacturers. Interoperability and reliability of components and systems have improved.

Software testability has received little consideration relative to the large number of books and articles published on other aspects of software testing. Definitions of testability from two U.S. software engineering standards appear in Figure 2.

Some notion of testability is implicit in most testing strategies. Structural and functional test case design methods are typically based on a program or system model and a related fault hypothesis. For example, data flow testing assumes the paths formed by definitions and uses of variables are a good place to look for errors. These models imply a kind of general testability criteria, since certain programs may be easier or harder to test according to these models. For example, it may be prohibitively difficult and expensive to devise path test cases for a program with spaghetti code or self-modifying control. Qualitative discussions of testability appear in [15] and [22]. In general, testable software is small, simple, and explicit.

A pragmatic analysis of unit-level testability is presented in [15]. When a module is embedded in an application system, it may be difficult to fully exercise it (lack of controllability) and the immediate outputs may be obscured (lack of observability). User interface bindings may reduce testability. Accessing and tracing module input and output may require special tools. Several strategies are suggested to increase controllability and observability. Information hiding and separation of concerns improves testability. Test scaffolding (test drivers and stubs) improves controllability and observability. Even with scaffolding, it is often useful to add explicit built-in test functions to report internal state on demand. "With simple modules, this separation of concerns is useful—with complex ones, it is invaluable." Assertions increase and retain observability when the module under test is subsequently integrated with the rest of an application system.[2]

A formal investigation of testability based on abstract data types and their interfaces is given in [14]. Two practices are identified that reduce testability. Global or local state variables reduce observability of procedure or function output, since response is not determined by input explicitly passed to the unit under test. A function or procedure that cannot produce every possible value in the domain of its associated type lacks controllability; part of the output domain cannot be produced under any circumstance. Modules can be made perfectly observable by adding explicit arguments to replace access to global or local state variables. Similarly, they can be made perfectly controllable by defining a data type that exactly corresponds to

[2]An assertion consists of a condition and an associated exception routine. This may be implemented by the assert () macro in C and C++. The assertion statement is simply a Boolean expression that is evaluated when the statement is reached during program execution. If the condition evaluates to true, nothing happens. If the condition is false, the program is terminated or an exception is activated.

the domain of the output variables. The number of changes that must be made to obtain perfect observability and controllability is an index of testability.

An observability metric for every statement in a program is presented in [24]. The metric is based on the

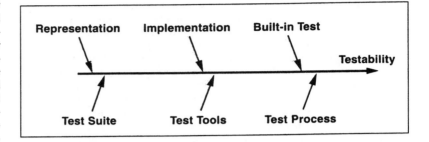

4.3.4 Traceability of requirements to test cases. The contractor shall document the traceability of the requirements in the Software Requirements Specifications (SRS) and Interface Requirements Specifications (IRS) that are satisfied or partially satisfied by each test case identified in the Software Test Description (STD). The contractor shall document this traceability in the STD for each Computer Software Configuration Item (CSCI).

10.3.2 Testability of requirements. A requirement is considered to be testable if an objective and feasible test can be designed to determine whether the requirement is met by the software.

DOD 2167A

Testability. (1) The degree to which a system or component facilitates the establishment of test criteria and the performance of tests to determine whether those criteria have been met. (2) The degree to which a requirement is stated in terms that permit establishment of test criteria and performance of tests to determine whether those criteria have been met.

IEEE 610.12

observable effect of program mutations. "A program's testability is a prediction of its ability to hide faults when the program is black-box tested with inputs selected randomly from a particular input distribution." Testability is defined as *sensitivity* to faults. Sensitivity is determined by systematically mutating a program and its data, running the mutated program, and comparing the output of the mutant to the output of the original program. Given some input set, statement sensitivity is a product of three probabilities: frequency of statement execution, probability that a fault will result in an incorrect data state, and the probability that a fault will result in an incorrect output. A highly sensitive statement is very likely to produce different output when mutated.

Figure 1. The testability fishbone: Main facets

Figure 2. Testability definitions

A less sensitive statement is less likely to produce different output. Lower sensitivity implies that faults are more likely to be hidden, and therefore relatively more testing will be required to reveal them. Sensitivity is computed for each statement. Program sensitivity (testability) is the minimum of all statements sensitivities. Hence, highly sensitive programs are highly testable.

Testability Factors

The preceding definitions of software testability focus on technical aspects. As a practical matter, testability is as much a process issue as it is a technical problem. There are six primary testability factors (see Figure 1). Each may facilitate or hinder testing in many ways. A usable representation is necessary to develop test cases. Implementation characteristics determine controllability and observability. Built-in test capabilities can improve controllability and observability and decouple test capabilities from application features. An adequate and usable test suite (test cases and plan for their use) is necessary. Test tools are necessary for effective testing. High leverage is available with an integrated tool set. Without an effective organizational approach to testing and its antecedents, technical testability is irrelevant.

Representation. The presence of a representation and its usefulness in test development is a critical testability factor. System representations range from natural language statements about desired capabilities to detailed formal specifications. Testing without a representation is simply experimental prototyping—it cannot be decided that a test has passed or failed without an explicit description of the expected result. The best that can be said of "testing" without a representation is that it may force production of a partial representation as part of the test plan. There are many approaches to developing object-

oriented representations, generically known as object-oriented analysis (OOA) and object-oriented design (OOD). For example, [17] outlines a systematic approach to OOA/D which explicitly addresses development of test cases from the representation. Figure 3 shows testability facets of representations.

Requirements include both narrative capability statements and abstract system models. The standards shown in Figure 2 identify essential characteristics for testability. *Objective* requirements are phrased or modeled in such a way that compliance in the system under test (SUT) is not subject to idiosyncratic interpretation. *Feasible* capabilities may be developed and implemented with existing technology. While not all capabilities benefit from a quantitative definition, it certainly eases testing to quantify those that can. For example, "average response time will be 1 second or less," instead of "response time will be quick." IEEE/ANSI standard 830 defines the desirable aspects of software requirements specification: unambiguous, complete, verifiable, consistent, modifiable, traceable, feasible, and useful for maintenance [11]. Each of these attributes contributes to testability.

Specifications describe the detail design for an implementation. IEEE/

ANSI standard 1016 provides a definition of a complete and usable software design description (SDD) [13]. An SDD should define the organization of software components, dependencies, interfaces, and detail of algorithms and data structures. *Completeness* means the specification covers all aspects of the system and that there are no "to be determined" items.

Traceability is a simple, common sense notion that can prevent a wide range of problems. It is simply a bookkeeping operation that records the antecedent of any work product. In testing, we are interested in being able to find which software component implements a given specification, and which specification implements a given requirement. Without this information, it is practically impossible to develop complete and accurate test plans for even a small system. *Currency* means that the specification mirrors the system as programmed. If specifications are not current, they result in incorrect test plans.

Separation of concerns is a first principle of software engineering that is directly related to controllability and observability. A component that can act independently of others is more readily controllable. Separation of concerns is application- and environment-specific, but we suggest a few key issues here. If *user interface* capabilities are entwined with basic functions it will be more difficult to test each function. The *control strategy* (mechanism for allowable sequence of component activation) of object-oriented programming tends to be less explicit (but no less important) than conventional systems. If control is embedded in the structure of the interfaces, it is more difficult to devise explicit tests than if control is an explicit function of a control object. *Collaboration Packaging* refers to the structure of classes participating in a responsibility. *Architectural Packaging* refers to the way classes are allocated to tasks in the target environment and how their runtime interfaces are composed. To the extent that packaging and capabilities are orthogonal, they will be more testable. In a distributed target environment, for example, a single responsibility imple-

Figure 3. Testability: Representation

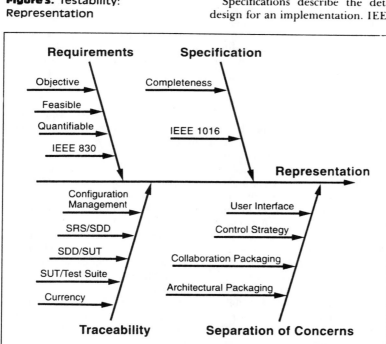

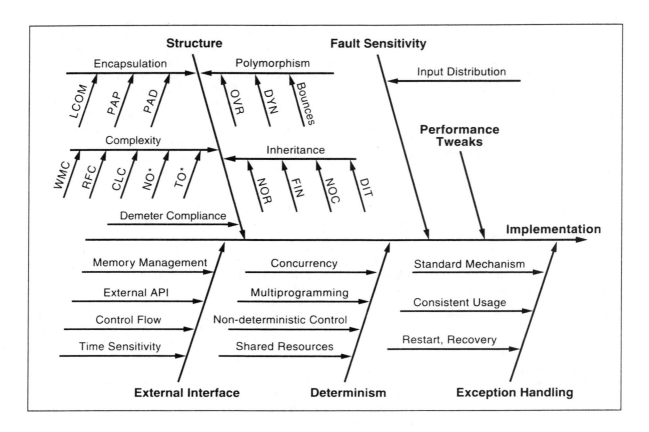

Structure Fault Sensitivity

Encapsulation Polymorphism Input Distribution

LCOM PAP PAD OVR DYN Bounces

Complexity Inheritance   Performance Tweaks

WMC RFC CLC NO* TO* NOR FIN NOC DIT

Demeter Compliance   Implementation

Memory Management Concurrency Standard Mechanism

External API Multiprogramming Consistent Usage

Control Flow Non-deterministic Control

Time Sensitivity Shared Resources Restart, Recovery

External Interface Determinism Exception Handling

Figure 4. Testability: Implementation

mented by objects residing on several hosts will probably be more difficult to test than the same responsibility on a single host.

Implementation. Figure 4 shows the implementation testability fishbone. An object-oriented program that complies with generally accepted principles of object-oriented programming poses the fewest obstacles to testing. *Structural* testability can be assessed by a few simple metrics. These are summarized in Tables 1 through 4. A metric may indicate complexity, scope of testing, or both. The effect of all complexity metrics is the same: a relatively high value of the metric indicates decreased testability; a relatively low value indicates increased testability. Scope metrics indicate the quantity of tests; the number of tests is proportional to the value of the metric. High scope and low complexity suggests many simple tests are indicated; low scope and high complexity suggests a few difficult tests.

For example, with high coupling among classes (CBO) it is typically more difficult to control the class

under test (CUT), thus reducing testability. Good design usually improves testability but even well-designed applications may be inherently difficult to test. These metrics provide information useful for resolving design trade-offs and assessing relative difficulty and cost of testing; they are not some kind of score to be maximized or minimized.

The *Law of Demeter* constrains uses (message sends) to "preferred supplier classes," in effect superclasses, classes of instance variables, and classes of arguments passed to the class under test [18]. Compliance reduces the number of interfaces, the number of stubs and drivers that may be needed, and the number of integration test interfaces. *Fault sensitivity* [24] was discussed previously. Low sensitivity corresponds with low testability. *Performance tweaks* tend to reduce the correspondence of the implementation and a specification and can interfere with both controllability and observability. *External Interfaces* often create difficult testability problems. For example, with an "event-driven" GUI, it may be very difficult

to test application server classes without using the GUI. However, the GUI may decrease both controllability and observability of a CUT. *Determinism* is the extent to which the CUT does not require asynchronous cooperation with other tasks. A high degree of concurrency poses obstacles to repeatable tests. It may be difficult to reproduce and isolate the cause of a failure: the SUT, the environment, or a particular input pattern. Testable *exception handling* requires consistent usage of language-supported features and a related design strategy [20]. Exceptions are typically less controllable than other application functions and may require simulation of failure modes. This may be difficult and time consuming.

Built-in test. Built-in test (BIT) capability provides explicit separation of test and application functionality. The systematic addition of set/reset, reporters, and assertions to a class is a

Table 1. Testability and encapsulation

Encapsulation metric	Complexity effect	Scope effect
LCOM (Lack of Cohesion in Methods). Number of groups of instance variables used by one method only [10]. High LCOM means more states must be tested to prove absence of side effects among methods.	✓	
PAP (Percent Public And Protected). Percentage of data members in a C++ class that are public or protected. Indicates proportion of class data visible to other objects [21]. High PAP means more opportunities for side effects among classes	✓	
PAD (Public Access to Data members). The number of external accesses to a class's public or protected data members. Measures violations of encapsulation [21]. High PAD means more states to test to prove absence of side effects among classes.	✓	

Table 2. Testability and inheritance

Inheritance metric	Complexity effect	Scope effect
NOR (Number of Root Classes, RootCtn.) The number of distinct class hierarchies employed by a program [21]. NOR is one dimension of number of components to test.		✓
FIN (Fan In). The number of classes from which a class is derived. FIN > 1 is only possible with multiple inheritance [21]. High FIN increases the possibility of incorrect bindings. In most cases, all of the inherited methods will need to be retested in the CUT.	✓	✓
NOC (Number of Children). The number of classes derived from a specific parent class. It indicates the number of classes which will be directly impacted by a change to the parent (class fan-out) [10]. In most cases, all of the parent methods will need to be retested in the child CUT.		✓
DIT (Depth of Inheritance Tree). Indicates the level of a class within its hierarchy [10]. In most cases all inherited methods will need to be retested in the CUT.		✓

Table 3. Testability and polymorphism

Polymorphism metric	Complexity effect	Scope effect
OVR (Percent of non-overloaded calls, Pctcall.) Percent of calls throughout the SUT that are not made to overload modules [21]. Overloading may result in unanticipated binding. High OVR indicates more opportunities for faults.	✓	
DYN (Percent of dynamic calls.) Percent of messages throughout the SUT whose target is determined at run time. Dynamic binding may result in unanticipated binding. High DYN means that many test cases will be needed to exercise all the bindings of a method.‡	✓	✓
Bounce-C. Count of the number of yo-yo paths visible to a CUT. A yo-yo path is a path that traverses several supplier class hierarchies due to dynamic binding. A bounce may result in unanticipated binding. High bounce indicates more opportunities for faults.‡	✓	
Bounce-S. Count of the number of yo-yo paths in SUT. A yo-yo path is a path that traverses several supplier class hierarchies due to dynamic binding. A bounce may result in unanticipated binding. High bounce indicates more opportunities for faults.‡	✓	

‡Under investigation by the author.

simple way to provide effective control and observation. Attempts to approximate BIT with application methods is a partial solution at best. If a standard test interface is included in all classes, additional development overhead is minimal and the potential payback is great. The BIT fishbone is shown in Figure 5.

Without set/reset, effective state-based testing is a practical impossibility. A set/reset method allows an object to be set to a predefined internal state, regardless of its current state. Several approaches are possible. The BIT can offer a menu of states with noncontrollable instance variable values, a menu of states with controllable values, or direct manipulation of instance variables.

A reporter returns the concrete (internal, private) state of an object. If the CUT does not offer complete reporting of abstract (external, public) state, the reporter must provide it.[3] A reporter must be trustworthy—we need to be sure its reports are accurate. Reporter code should be subjected to careful scrutiny. For example, the code could be proved correct and then tested with low-level debug probes.

Useful set/reset and reporter methods necessarily violate encapsulation. BIT services should not be used to accomplish application requirements. A *safety* provision is advisable to prevent inadvertent or willful misuse of BIT services. *Source code control* uses compiler-directives to include or exclude BIT features. Either a BIT or a non-BIT version of the SUT can be built. This is problematic because the tested implementation is not necessarily the released implementation. There are many horror stories about systems that inexplicably fail when an apparently innocuous code segment is added or removed. Source code control should be used with due diligence. *Mode control* provides a global parameter to toggle test mode and normal mode. In normal mode, BIT services are disabled. Any BIT invo-

[3]Abstract state is implementation-independent and may be reported via an object's interface. Concrete state is implementation-dependent and is typically not reported. For example, suppose a collection is implemented by a linked list. The abstract state of the collection includes the contents and number of items in the collection; concrete state includes pointers to the first, last, and most recently used nodes [19].

cation is treated as a no-op or an exception. In test mode, BIT services are enabled. *Password control* requires a password of some kind to activate BIT functions. The driver must supply a password value in a parameter defined as part of the BIT interface. A BIT request without the password would be treated as a no-op or an exception. There are many possible safety schemes. Regardless of the BIT approach, some form of encapsulation safety should be provided.

Assertions can be used for many purposes: pre-conditions, post-conditions, class invariants, and sampling

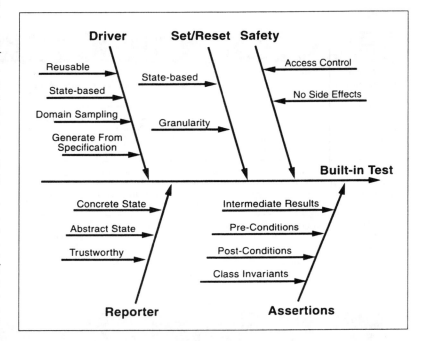

Figure 5. Testability: Built-in test

of intermediate results. For example, they can monitor long-running algorithms to detect failure to converge. After class testing, a class must be embedded in an application system. Once embedded, assertions continue to provide built-in testing and reporting. They contribute to testability by proving built-in observability. A *driver* is a special-purpose class that activates the CUT—drivers are discussed later in this article.

Test suite. A test suite is a collection of test cases and plans to use them. The Test Suite fishbone is shown in Figure 6. There are many possible approaches to the develop-

ment of test cases [8]. A comprehensive list of test suite components is offered in IEEE/ANSI standard 829 [2]. It defines the contents of a test plan, test design specification, test case specification, test procedures, test item transmittal report, test log, test incident report, and test summary. A test suite lacking in these features may pose practical obstacles to testability. A test case schema for object-oriented programs is presented in [7].

Expected results are necessary for test cases. An *oracle* is a mechanism for producing expected results. Typically, expected test results are prepared by manual calculation or simple simulation. Oracle automation and class testing are discussed in [16]. A system for which an oracle is infeasible is fundamentally untestable. For example, the quantity of input or output to consider may be intractably large, or there may be no way to obtain expected output, *a priori*. Such systems require special verification strategies [25].

A test suite represents an asset ac-

Table 4. Testability and complexity

Complexity metric	Complexity effect	Scope effect
WMC (Weighted Methods per Class) is the sum of the cyclomatic complexity of methods implemented within a class [10]. Higher complexity is often associated with a greater number of faults; a proportionally greater number of test cases will be required for decision coverage.	✓	✓
RFC (Response for a Class) is a count of methods implemented within a class, plus the number of methods used by an object not due to inheritance [10]. High RFC indicates a class will either require high number of stubs or must be embedded with many other classes before it can be tested. Each such interface will need to be tested.	✓	✓
CBO (Coupling Between Objects.) The number of non-inheritance couples to classes outside the CUT [10]. High CBO indicates a class will either require high number of stubs or must be embedded with many other classes before it can be tested. Each such interface will need to be tested.	✓	✓
CLC (Class Complexity.) The cyclomatic complexity of the control graph formed by a union of all method control graphs with a state transition graph for the class.	✓	✓
NOM (Nominal Number of Methods per class.) 20 is suggested as an upper limit. NNOM = NNOF + NNOP.‡		✓
NOF (Nominal Number of Functions per class.) Functions report state, but do not change it.‡		✓
NOP (Nominal Number of Procedures per class.) Procedures change state. ‡	✓	✓
TOM (Total Number of Methods per class.) Same as NNOM, but includes all inherited methods. TNOM = TNOF + TNOP. More methods require more testing.‡		✓
TOF (Total Number of Functions per class.)‡		✓
TOP (Total Number of Procedures per class.) If there are n procedures with no sequential activation constraint, at least n^2 tests are necessary to verify state control.‡	✓	✓

‡Under investigation by the author.

Table 5. DFT strategies

DFT approach	VLSI	Class test
None	Manual probes on available test points	Testing embedded class with white/black box tests, use of debugger and ad hoc inline trace
Ad hoc	IC-specific test points	Driver/stub per class
Structured	Addition of set/reset and report circuits to provide combinational test	Driver-stub per class, test interface provides set/reset and report methods
Standardized	Standard Test Access Port and related functions across all components (IEEE 1149.1)	Driver/class pair with standard driver API delivered with class library
Self-Test	Built-in Self-Test (BIST). On-chip ability to generate and execute tests using standard BIT	Generic driver, executable specification packaged with the implementation

quired at considerable cost and should be treated accordingly. The reuse of a test suite (regression testing) provides economic justification for careful test development. Over time, a reusable test suite increases the amount of testing that can be done, and hence increases testability. Effective test suite reuse requires configuration management control and traceability to successive versions of the representation and implementation.

Test case development is a challenging activity that is susceptible to errors similar to those occurring in software development. Faulty test cases can be problematic, in that a correct implementation may be rejected or incorrect implementation may be accepted. Established techniques for work product review and defect prevention will improve test suites and increase their contribution to testability.

Test tools. Testing requires automation. Without automation less testing will be done or greater cost will be incurred to achieve a given reliability goal. The absence of tools inhibits testability. The components of a test environment have been analyzed elsewhere [6]. Basic components include configuration management, test suite manager, static analyzer, instrumentor, run-time trace, comparator, reporting, and integrated debut. Test case development is supported by input capture systems, script editors, spec-based generator, code-based generators, input data generators, and support for other developer-defined tests. The test bed (test environment) needs functions to initialize a system and its environment, execute test scripts, and replay scripts under predefined conditions. There are many commercial offerings for such tools. These components, with the necessary changes, are equally useful for object-oriented implementations. Several test tools for object-oriented systems have recently become commercially available. Interoperability is a key concern, as it is with CASE in general. The Test Tool fishbone is shown in Figure 7.

Process capability. Overall software process capability and maturity can significantly facilitate or hinder testability. The Process Capability

fishbone is shown in Figure 8. The key process abilities of the defined level for software product engineering [23].

Constancy of purpose is necessary for continuous quality improvement [12]. Staff and management need to be empowered to perform adequate testing. This requires sufficient funding, accountability, and an unequivocal, sincere commitment to establishing and improving the process.

The technical approach must be *effective*. The overall development process must be defined and repeatable [23]. A *customer-oriented* test process is driven by customer expectations for cost and reliability. Systems should not be tested unless a *readiness assessment* has been performed. This prevents waste of testing resources on trivial problems more easily prevented by design or programming. *Closed-loop feedback* is necessary to assess testing effectiveness. For example, if the desired level of post-release reliability is not obtained, a process improvement cycle should be initiated to determine and correct the cause of the problem. Testing is a challenging task requiring high *staff capability*. This results from adequate

tool and method training, motivation, and appropriate education and experience.

Testing is most effective when it is viewed as an essential component of a system of production. It is neither a magic filter to remove problems with an upstream source nor a dumping ground for hastily developed code. An *integrated test strategy* views testing in context. Vertical integration means there is a well-defined path among test processes for classes, clusters of classes, and application systems. Hor-

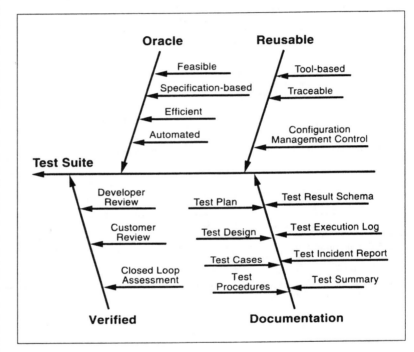

Figure 6. Testability: Test suite

izontal integration means that testability is considered over all stages of development: representation, (requirements and design), implementation (code), test suite (testing), and subsequent iterations of reuse and maintenance. Verification and validation integration means that testing is used in a balanced, optimal manner with other quality assurance practices: prototyping, inspections, and reviews for all stages and work products.

36

Toward High Testability For Object-Oriented Systems

Software testing is an economic problem closely intertwined with nearly all major technical issues in software engineering. The implication of the foregoing analysis is hardly startling: testability results from good software engineering practice and an effective software process. Figure 9 shows the entire testability fishbone. We've seen how these basic facets contribute to testability. However, a manual approach to testing will quickly reach practical limits that are unsatisfactory given the extent of testing needed to assure high reusability and reliability. Just as high testability for VLSI requires an explicit test infrastructure, so will high testability for large object-oriented systems. Advanced test automation is needed.

An extension of the common notion of a driver and BIT functions suggests some intriguing possibilities for advanced test automation. An instructive comparison of levels of abstraction in VLSI and class libraries is provided in [11]. Standardization is needed to achieve a high level of economic efficiency and interoperability. The "gauge" is central to this vision. A gauge is a reusable software component used to test a single class and is routinely produced as part of the implementation. An outline strategy for implementation of the gauge concept follows. Table 5 compares VLSI DFT strategies and class testing. Possible configurations for corresponding object-oriented DFT strategies are depicted in Figure 10 and summarized in Table 5.

Further discussion of elements in Table 5 follows:

• *No DFT.* To the extent that class testing is done, there is no systematic DFT. The implementation is developed and the tester copes. This typically means it is difficult to control and observe the CUT. This approach will result in the highest

Figure 7. Testability: Test automation

Figure 8. Testability: Process capability

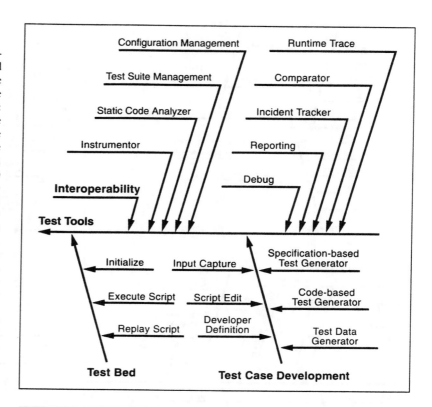

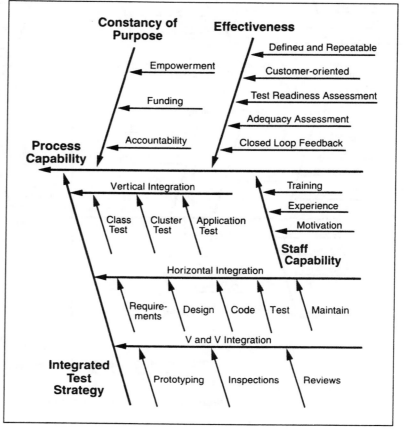

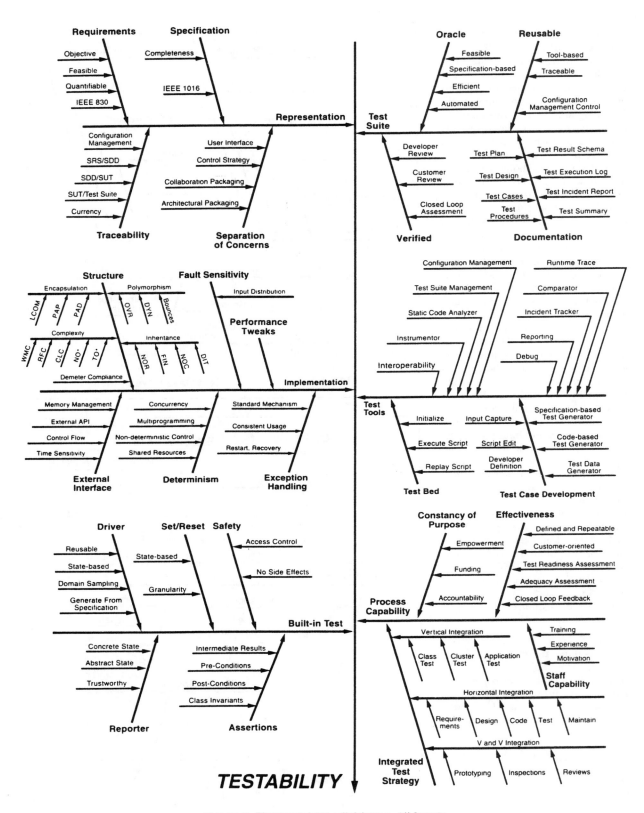

Figure 9. The testability fishbone: All facets

38

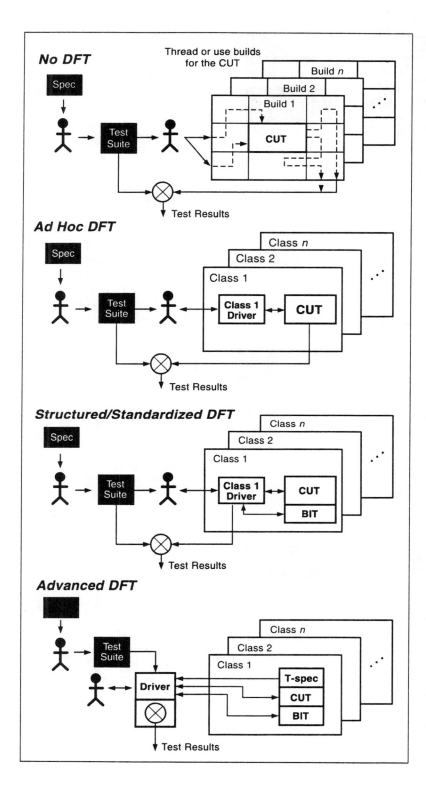

Figure 10. DFT configurations

by developing a driver for each class and stubs (as needed) for the class's servers. Assertions and other forms of inline instrumentation may be added. This improves controllability and observability. However, the absence of explicit set/reset can result in lengthy setup sequences and reliance on debug probes to verify state. This results in a relatively high test cost or less reliability, depending on the basic testing strategy.

• *Structured DFT.* The ad hoc strategy is augmented by including a standard BIT and BIT application programmer interface (API) in all classes. As discussed previously, minimal BIT requires state set/reset, state reporting, and BIT-safe implementation. This can offer complete controllability and observability. However, a single driver must be developed for each class. To develop the driver, the CUT interface is hard-coded in the driver. The requisite interface information is obtained by manual inspection of the CUT. Test cases must be manually prepared for each class.

• *Standardized DFT.* The agreement on and adoption of an industrywide VLSI standard for structured DFT improved IC interoperability and reliability, as well as reducing costs. Individual IC manufacturers with a high degree of vertical market integration practiced structured DFT long before the adoption of IEEE 1149. As the VLSI industry became less vertically integrated, however, interoperability needs provided a win-win economic opportunity, leading to the rapid and widespread adoption of 1149. An analysis of how a similar scenario might develop for commercial class libraries is beyond the scope of this article. However, within a single development organization, there are clear benefits to a standard test API for class drivers and class BIT: one API to learn instead of many, more time for better testing, and consistent test capability over the entire library.

• *Self-Test DFT.* The class testing analog to the structured strategy for calls for a driver to be paired with every class. This has several negatives. With *n* classes to test there are

possible test cost or least reliability, depending on which basic testing strategy is followed.

• *Ad hoc DFT.* Class testing is done

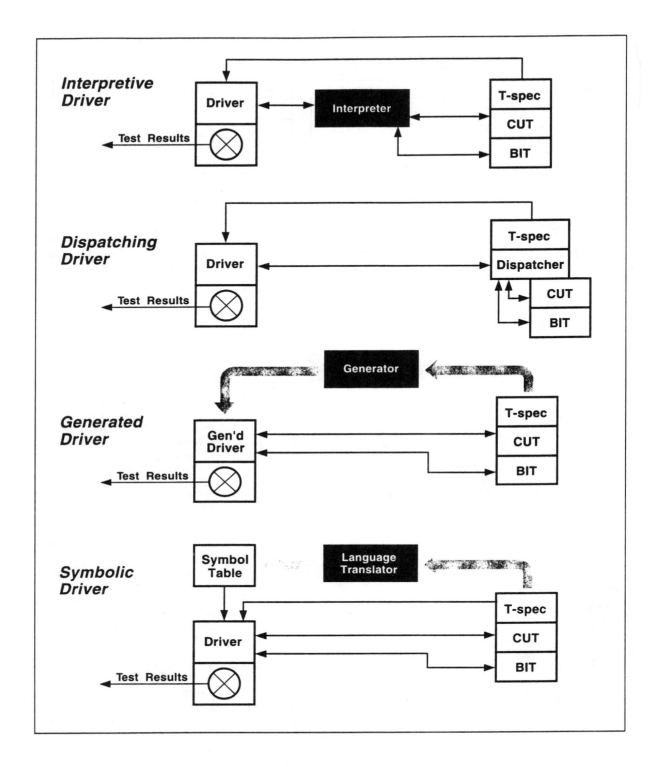

now n additional interfaces to synchronize, the additional development and maintenance effort for every class driver, and limited automation of test case generation, execution, and evaluation.

The use of an implementation as the exclusive basis for automated testing is essentially tautological and therefore insufficient. There must be a specification and a means to generate expected results from the specifi-

Figure 11. Advanced DFT architectures

40

```
t_spec
      = class_name
      + class_invariant         – Boolean expression on all instance variables.
      + {super_class
      + initial_state           – Is a state
      + {state}
      + {transition}

state
      = state_name
      + post_condition          – Boolean expression on all instance variables.

transition
      = accepting state_name    – Is a state
      + method_name
      + pre_condition           – Boolean expression on all instance variables
                                    and arguments.
      + resulting_state_name    – Is a state
      + activation_sequence     – Methods activated in this transition
```

Figure 12. FREE test
specification

_____

cation. Ideally, a single generic driver
would automatically generate a test
suite from an embedded test specification (*t-spec*), activate the CUT with
this test suite, and evaluate the results. The need for a driver paired
with every class is obviated. The self-
test procedure would consist of the
following steps:

1. The driver requests the t-spec
from the CUT.
2. The driver generates a test pattern from the t-spec.
3. The driver generates test case
values by splattering the input parameter domains (random sampling
of from off, on, and in regions in
the domain).
4. The driver uses set/reset to control the state of the CUT.
5. The driver sends the test case
message(s) to the CUT.
6. The driver evaluates the response of the CUT.
7. The driver evaluates the state of
the CUT with the reporter.

The feasibility of this scheme depends on solving two problems. First,
the test pattern method names and
arguments must be bound to messages accepted by the CUT. The manual step of inspecting the CUT to prepare the requisite interface must be
automated. There are several general

solutions to the interface binding
problem, which are depicted in Figure 11. Further discussion of elements of Figure 11 follows:

• Interpreter. The test specification
exported from the CUT contains
the names necessary to create a bin-
dable CUT message. The driver
uses these names to generate a program passed to the interpreter. The
interpreter accomplishes the binding in the normal manner.
• Test dispatcher. Instead of activating features in the CUT directly,
the driver activates test methods in
the CUT which in turn activate
application methods in the CUT.
The same test method interface is
used throughout the application
system. The dispatcher selects the
actual message interface to use and
then sends the message. Control is
returned to the BIT dispatcher,
and then back to the driver.
• Driver generator. Instead of attempting to drive the CUT directly
from a generic driver, the generic
driver reads the CUT source code
and generates an intermediate
driver to activate the CUT under
control of the primary driver. This
scheme has been investigated in the
ASTOOT system [13].
• Language extension. The language translator is modified to accept syntax extensions for test specifications. After translation, portions
of the symbol table and the test
specification are saved as a separate
file that can be directly processed

by the driver. The scheme is essentially an extension of the technique
used to run programs under a symbolic debugger. Thus, automatic test
generation could be developed by
simply using the same input as a
symbolic debugger.

A suitable test specification language with respect to some testing
methodology must be constructed.
Figure 12 provides a sketch of a specification language to automate the
state-based testing approach in the
FREE methodology [9]. Inclusion of
such a specification would not impose
an onerous coding burden. For example, the Eiffel language provides
an elegant executable specification
for pre-conditions, post-conditions,
and class invariants [19]. Only state
control information needs to be
added. Inclusion of an explicit test
specification would also serve other
important software engineering
goals:

• Provide an explicit, specification-
based test plan for every class.
• Prevent fragmentation of specification information and the
implementation.
• Provide an explicit, readable specification embedded with the implementation. This would facilitate
reuse and understandability.

The BIST (built-in self test) approach has limitations—it is not a
replacement for all forms of testing.
Unless a general solution for an automated oracle is found (this is not
likely), manual preparation of test
cases will continue to be necessary.
The test specification language in
Figure 12 can define the bounds of
acceptable input and output, but
does not permit determination of the
exact correctness of a given input and
output. For example, given only the
pre- and post-conditions for a square
root function, we could not decide
whether any given value was indeed
the square root of the argument (e.g.,
is 4.25 the square root of 18.0625?),
but we could decide that was within
the bounds (post-conditions) of a
square root function. The t-spec
should be consistent with all other
representations. A full discussion of
considerations and implementation
of automatic consistence support is
beyond the scope this article.

Conclusion

Testability reduces total test cost in a reliability-driven process and increases reliability in a resource-limited test process. Thus, regardless of the testing strategy employed, it is in the interest of a development organization to improve testability. Testability of an object-oriented system is a result of six primary factors: representation, implementation, built-in test, the test suite, the test support environment, and process capability. Each influences controllability and observability of the implementation, or basic operational effectiveness of the test process. Nearly all the techniques and technology for achieving high testability are well established, but require financial commitment, planning, and conscious effort. The advanced built-in test capabilities sketched here do not yet exist, but are feasible with existing technology. ◪

References

1. *ANSI/IEEE Standard 830-1984: Standard for Software Requirements Specifications.* The Institute of Electrical and Electronic Engineers, New York, 1984.
2. *ANSI/IEEE Standard 829-1983: IEEE Standard for Software Test Documentation.* The Institute of Electrical and Electronic Engineers, New York, 1987.
3. *ANSI/IEEE Standard 1016-1987: IEEE Recommended Practice for Software Design Descriptions.* The Institute of Electrical and Electronic Engineers, New York, 1987.
4. *ANSI/IEEE Standard 1149.1-1990: IEEE Standard Test Access Port and Boundary-Scan Architecture.* The Institute of Electrical and Electronic Engineers, New York, 1990.
5. Beizer, B. *Software System Testing and Quality Assurance.* Van Nostrand Reinhold, New York, 1984.
6. Beizer, B. *Software Testing Techniques,* Second ed. Van Nostrand Reinhold, New York, 1990.
7. Berard, E. *Essays on Object-Oriented Software Engineering.* Prentice-Hall, Englewood Cliffs, N.J., 1993.
8. Binder, R.V. *Testing Object-Oriented Programs: A Survey.* RBSC-94-002. Robert Binder Systems Consulting, Inc., Chicago, 1994.
9. Binder, R.V. *The FREE Approach to Testing Object-Oriented Systems.* RBSC-94-003, Robert Binder Systems Consulting, Inc., Chicago, 1994.
10. Chidamber, S.R. and Kemerer, C.F. A metrics suite for object-oriented design. *IEEE Trans. Softw. Eng. 20,* 6 (Jun. 1994), 476–493.
11. Cox, B.J. Planning the software industrial revolution. *IEEE Softw.* Nov. 1990, 25–33.
12. Deming, W.E. *Out of the Crisis.* MIT Center for Advanced Engineering Study, Cambridge, Mass., 1986.
13. Doong, R.K. and Frankl, P. *The AS-TOOT approach to testing object-oriented programs.* Tech. Rep. PUCS-104-91. Polytechnic University, Brooklyn, N.Y, 1991.
14. Freedman, R.S. Testability of software components. *IEEE Trans. Softw. Eng. 17,* 6, (June 1991), pp 553–64.
15. Hoffman, D. Hardware testing and software ICs. *Proceedings, Northwest Software Quality Conference* (Portland Ore., Sept. 1989), pp 234–22.
16. Hoffman, D. and Strooper, P. A case study in class testing. In *Proceedings of CASCON 93.* IBM Toronto Laboratory, Oct. 1993, pp 472–482.
17. Jacobson, I, Christerson, M., Jonsson, P. and Overgaard, G. *Object-Oriented Software Engineering.* Addison-Wesley, Reading, Mass., 1992.
18. Lieberherr, K.J. and Holland, I.M. Assuring good style for object-oriented programs. *IEEE Softw.* (Sept. 1989), pp. 38–49.
19. Meyer, B. *Object-Oriented Software Construction.* Prentice-Hall, Englewood Cliffs, N.J., 1988.
20. Ogata, K. *Modern Control Engineering.* Second ed. Prentice-Hall, Englewood Cliffs, N.J., 1990.
21. OO tool aids software testing. *The Outlook.* Fall 1993, McCabe & Associates, Columbia, Maryland.
22. Ould, M.A., and Unwin, C. *Testing in Software Development.* Cambridge University Press, Cambridge, UK, 1986.
23. Paulk, M.C., Curtis, B., Chrissis, M.B., and Weber, C.V. *Capability Maturity Model for Software, Version 1.1.* CMU/SEI-93-TR-24. Software Engineering Institute, Pittsburgh, Pa., 1993.
24. Voas, J., Morell, L., and Miller, K. Predicting where faults can hide from testing. *IEEE Softw.* (March 1991), pp 41–8.
25. Weyuker, E.J. On testing non-testable programs. *Comput. J.* 1982 25, 4, pp 465–70.

About the Author:
ROBERT V. BINDER is president of RBSC, Inc. He is researching state-based testing for reliability engineering in object-oriented systems and a systems engineering methodology for client-server development. **Author's Present Address:** RBSC, Inc., 3 First National Plaza, Suite 1400, Chicago, IL 60602; email: rbinder @chinet.com

Shekhar Kirani and *W.T. Tsai*[†]

*U S West Technologies, 4001 Discovery Dr., #270,
Boulder, CO 80303; email: kirani@advtech.uswest.com*
†*Computer Science Department, University of Minnesota,
Minneapolis, MN 55455; email: tsai@cs.umn.edu*

Method sequence specification and verification of classes

THERE IS AN increasing demand for innovative software that satisfies stringent quality and reliability requirements imposed by users. In recent years the object-oriented (O-O) paradigm is gaining acceptance for developing software. O-O software development is based on identifying and modeling real-world entities as objects. The O-O paradigm supports abstraction, decomposition, encapsulation, modularity, and hierarchy. Thus object-based software engineering is seen as a good approach for tackling the intricacies and complexities associated with software construction.[1-3]

The current research so far in O-O software engineering is focused on problem analysis, software design, and implementation techniques, resulting in a potpourri of representations and procedures.[1-6] Even though the importance of verification and validation (V & V) is known, it has commanded little attention in the O-O paradigm. Extensive V & V during software development is essential for building zero-defect software.[7] Most O-O analysis and design techniques proposed to date do not adequately address V & V activities. If successful V & V techniques for this paradigm are not developed, there is a great risk that the object paradigm will fail as a next-generation software development technique.

Meyer proposed the external class specification technique, which specifies different interface methods (operations) and associated preconditions, postconditions, and invariants.[1,8] This technique does not explicitly specify the causal relationship between methods of a class. In this article, we propose a new specification technique called *method sequence specification* that does represent this causal relationship. The method sequence specification documents the correct order in which the methods of a class can be invoked by the methods in other client classes. It can be used and integrated with Meyer's external class specification technique, and can be used for test case generation and runtime verification of the class implementation.

The importance of consistency and completeness (C & C) of specification is well known in software engineering.[9,10] A specification is complete when all the required components are present and completely developed.[9] A specification is consistent if its components do not conflict with each other.[9] C & C of specification is interrelated: often inconsistency leads to incompleteness and vice versa. C & C of class specification is essential for developing an O-O design with less faults. In this article, we provide a set of rules for developing consistent sequence specification in the presence of single and multiple inheritance as well as for multiple interface classes. These rules ensures the consistency of the method sequence specification. We use the regular expression formalism[11] for representing the method sequence specification. We also provide a semi-automatic derivation of class specification from the state-based class design.

In the following section we discuss the basic concepts and definitions of the O-O paradigm. Next, we describe our new regular expression-based technique for representing the method sequence specification. In this section we also describe possible applications of sequence specification. In the fourth section we provide an outline for deriving sequence specification semi-automatically from state-based class design. In the fifth section we provide rules for verifying consistency in the presence of class inheritance and multiple interfaces. We discuss the algorithms for building a tool that automatically verifies the consistency of specification in the sixth section. Finally, we conclude this article and note possible future work.

Related research

In recent years, several techniques have been proposed for analysis, design, and implementation of O-O software. A recent survey article[6] mentions more than 20 O-O analysis and design techniques. The survey article provides a comparative evaluation of these techniques. However, none of these proposed techniques explicitly address the V & V related issues in analysis, design, and implementation. Meyer, in his research on *design by contract*, provides a rigorous usage of preconditions, postconditions, and invariants for specifying and implementing the methods of a class.[1,8] The method sequence specification proposed in this article can be used with the design by contract specification technique. Method

"Method Sequence Specification and Verification of Classes" by S. Kirani and W.T. Tsai from *J. Object-Oriented Programming*, Oct. 1994, pp. 28–38. Reprinted by permission of SIGS.

sequence specification can also be used with multiple interface specifications of classes. An excellent introduction to multiple interfaces for objects is given in Hailpern and Ossher,[12] which provides the various advantages and disadvantages associated with multiple interface specification.

Several issues related to V & V and maintenance of object-oriented programs are discussed in Smith and Robson.[13] Cheatam and Mellinger provide data related to the testing of Smalltalk library software.[14] Issues related to adequate testing of classes is considered in detail in by Perri and Kaiser.[15] A recent article by Turner[16] provides a state-based software testing of O-O programs. In this article, we provide techniques for checking the consistency and completeness of method sequence specification of classes related through inheritance. We also describe a technique that can be used to generate test cases from the method sequence specification.

INTRODUCTION TO O-O CONCEPTS

In an O-O model the fundamental entities are objects, rather than procedures and functions as in imperative programming languages. Objects send messages to other objects, execute a method when a message is received from other objects, and maintain an encapsulated local state. In an object-oriented program, functionality is implemented by sending and receiving messages between objects. In this section we review the concept of objects, interaction between objects, classes, and inheritance.

Object

An object encompasses *state* and *behavior*. The state of an object is determined by a set of *attributes* and their values. The behavior of an object is defined by a set of methods (operations) of the object. These methods are an abstraction of procedures and functions. An object encapsulates its state, and only the methods of the object can refer or modify its state.

Messages are requests sent from one object to another for computing a desired functionality. *Methods* are the functions an object executes in response to a message. There exists a one-to-one relation between the messages an object receives and the method it executes.[17] Before sending a message, an object must uniquely identify the other object to which it is sending the message. In addition, an object accessing the services of other objects must know the proper interface protocol of the objects. All the methods of an object can be classified into define, use, or define-use types. A define type method changes object state by modifying the attribute contents. A use type method (also known as an implementor method) accesses the current value of an attribute. A define-use type method uses as well as changes the contents of attributes.[18] All the objects in a system are created during runtime.

Class

Classes describe the common behavior of a group of unique objects. A class is a static description of a set of objects. It describes all the instance methods and attributes of these objects. During execution, objects are created by instantiating classes. A class provides abstraction by providing an interface and encapsulating its internal structure.

Classes instantiate objects based on receiving a message to create a new object. Each object thus created from a class receives messages from methods in other objects. Thus, each object in its lifetime gets different sets of messages. Even though a class defines several methods, some of its objects may not execute all the methods it supports.

Inheritance

An inheritance model depicts the hierarchical relationship between classes. It is used for expressing specialization. A child class inherits the methods and attributes of its parent class. An inherited property may be redefined by a subclass, nullifying the inherited definition. This feature in inheritance encourages the reuse of code written for parent classes. In single inheritance a child class inherits from a single parent class, and in multiple inheritance a child class inherits from more than one parent class.

O-O software development lifecycle

The O-O paradigm promotes concurrency in software development lifecycle phases. Unlike conventional techniques, in the O-O software lifecycle, several classes can be concurrently analyzed, designed, implemented, and tested. Concurrent development of individual and related classes facilitates better understanding of requirements, alleviates risk, and helps in dividing the complexity of a problem. It also helps developers produce early tangible results.[19] In Figure 1 several threads of software development activities are shown. Each thread corresponds to the development of a class, and usually there is a dependency relation across the threads.

Although it is possible to concurrently perform analysis, design, and implementation of classes in the O-O paradigm, each class is developed sequentially.[19] Early C & C of designed classes helps in the detection of contradictions and gaps and thus promotes reliable implementation. In this article, we address the issue of checking the C & C of the method sequence specification of classes.

CONTRACT SPECIFICATION

Object-oriented analysis and design (OOAD) techniques are used for analyzing and specifying a software system for proper implementation. All the proposed OOAD techniques strive to separate the implementation details from the specification. In the design by

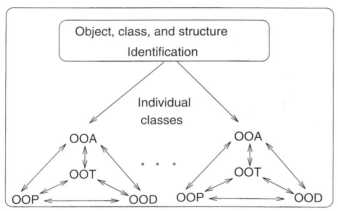

Figure I. Concurrent development of classes in the O-O paradigm.

contract technique, the output of OOAD is a contract between designers and implementors.[8] Another OOAD technique, based on responsibilities, suggests using the responsibilities as a contract of the specification of publicly available services.[20]

Contract specification and separation of the specification from the implementation are useful in many ways. Clear specifications help implementors deliver the software as promised in the contract. The contract specification also helps in documenting a class as a library component, thus facilitating reuse. For multi-person projects, the specification can be used as shared knowledge before implementing different portions of the software. It facilitates test case generation and easy maintenance. The method sequence specification proposed in this article can be used and integrated as a part of the contract specification of classes.

The class interface specification details a contract between the environment and its implementation. The interface specification should specify everything an external user should know for correct use and everything an implementor should know for proper implementation. Although the complete interface specification is of much interest, in this article we concentrate on specifying the inter-method causal relations of a class. Following are some definitions used in the article.

Definition 1. For a class C we define *Methods(C)* as a set of all the methods defined in C that are publicly available. For example, for a Stack class the method set can be Methods(Stack) = {push, pop, isempty?, isfull?, top}

Definition 2: Method sequence. We define a method sequence S of a class C as a finite sequence over a method set M of C, $(m_0 \cdot m_1 \cdot \ldots \cdot m_n)$ where each $m_i \in M$. A method sequence need not contain all the methods in the method set. For example, in the Stack class a method sequence is (push· top· pop· isempty?).

Method sequence specification

Objects instantiated from classes support a set of methods that can be accessed from the methods of other client objects. Each object maintains a state, which is modified when methods change the values of attributes of the object. In addition to specification of individual methods of a class, a complete specification must specify the relations that exist between the methods. When an object receives a message, the result of executing the method corresponding to the received message depends on the state of the object. The state of an object depends on the set of messages the object has already received. The result of any method execution depends on previously executed methods. Thus, correct object behavior is possible only if methods are invoked in a well-defined sequence. Method sequence specification aids in correct object behavior by specifying the causal relationship between methods.

Methods of a class can have different types of inter-method relationships. The causal relationships between methods specify the sequence in which the methods can be executed, such as method m_1 must be invoked before method m_2. We propose the method sequence specification for specifying this causal relationship. The sequence specification for classes is important as it specifies the correct sequences in which objects of the class must receive messages. The methods also can have time-based relationships such as method

m_1 must be invoked within 20 seconds after method m_2. In this article, we model only the causal relationship between methods. We use regular definitions[21] to model the causal relationship between methods. For modeling the timing relationship between methods we need a more powerful formalism than the regular definition.

The strict sequence rules between methods of a class depend on the functionality of the class. For example, the objects of a Stack class should receive a pop() message only after receiving a push() message. Some of the ordering rules can be required due to implementation issues. For example, objects must receive a constructor message before receiving any other messages, and a delete message must be the last message. All other messages must be received between these two types of messages.

To represent the method sequence specification of a class C we use regular definition over the alphabet (usually referred as Σ) consisting of methods from *Methods (C)*. The regular definition is a set of definitions of the form:

$$l_1 \rightarrow r_1$$
$$l_2 \rightarrow r_2$$
$$\ldots$$
$$l_n \rightarrow r_n$$

where each l_i is a distinct label, and each r_i is a regular expression over the methods in *Methods(C)* $\cup \{l_1, l_2, \ldots l_{i-1}\}$. The regular expression can use symbols such as "*" for specifying zero or more instances, and "+" for specifying one or more instances of a method. The regular definition associated with a class defines the set of valid method sequences receivable by all the objects of the class:

Definition 3: *SeqSpec(C)*. A *SeqSpec(C)* is the specification of C that defines a sequence relationship between all the methods of C. We use a regular definition for specifying the *SeqSpec(C)*. We also use RE_c to refer to regular definition.

Example: Let us consider a specification of a simple bank account class as shown in Figure 2. The interface methods defined in the Account class are:

Σ= {Create, Deposit, Open, Withdraw, Close, Delete}

where Create and Delete are constructor and delete methods, the Open method is used for opening an account, the Deposit method is used for depositing positive sums of money into the account, the Withdraw method is used for withdrawing money from the account, and the Close method is for closing the account. In the following we describe a method sequence specification for the Account class. In the sequence specification, the regular definition labels such as *AccountMethods* are shown in italic. The *SeqSpec(Account)* is:

Methods → Create · *AccountMethods* · Delete
AccountMethods → Open · *TransactionMethods* · Close
TransactionMethods → (Deposit · (Deposit | Withdraw)*)

Account Class
Account_No
Name
Balance
Open( )
Close( )
Deposit( )
Withdraw( )
Create( )
Delete( )

Figure 2. Account class attributes and methods.

Definition 4: *SafeSeq(C)*. A *SafeSeq(C)* defines a set of all sequences S_i that can be derived from *SeqSpec(C)* of a class *C*. Any sequence in *SafeSeq(C)* is a valid sequence of messages accepted by any instance of the class *C*. *SafeSeq(C)* is the regular set (or the language) defined by *SeqSpec(C)*.

Example: The sequence specification of Account given in the previous example defines all possible valid sequences of messages that an object of class Account can receive. This set of sequences is *SafeSeq(Account)*. For example, a safe sequence set with sample sequences is:

{(Create · Open · Deposit · Withdraw · Close · Delete),
(Create · Open · Deposit · Deposit · Withdraw · Close · Delete), ...}

Applications of method sequence specification

It is useful to develop a consistent and complete specification of a software as the specification is used throughout the software design, implementation, testing, evaluation, and maintenance phases.[10] The method sequence specification, although only a small portion of the complete O-O specification, can be used throughout the O-O lifecycle. Method sequence specification of a class can be used for numerous purposes. Some uses of method sequence specification related to V & V are:

1. Ensuring conformance of the implementation of a class with the corresponding method sequence specification.

2. Constructing a runtime verification system for a class that ensures the correct method invocation sequence for each object of the class.

3. Generating state-based test cases for testing the low-level design and implementation of the class.

Verification of implementation. The method sequence specification of a class specifies the correct sequence usage for all the objects of the class.* But, in implementation the program may contain method invocation sequences that are inconsistent with the inter-method specification of the objects. It is essential to identify all such inconsistencies and correct the program to make it consistent with the sequence specification. We can use static analysis of the implementation along with the sequence specification to identify such inconsistencies.

A method sequence specification associated with an object specifies all sequences of messages that the object can receive while still providing correct behavior. In practice, an object may receive only a subset of these valid sequences of messages. The goal of static analysis is to determine the actual possible sequences of messages an object can receive. We call such method sequences *use sequences*. Once all the use sequences of an object are identified, they must be verified for compliance with the sequence specification of the object. The control-flow analysis[22] of the O-O program is essential for determining the use sequences. The methods from

which the program execution begins must be identified initially for the control-flow analysis. Conventional control-flow analysis may require modification to make it suitable for identifying all the possible method use sequences for each object. The presence of pointers, polymorphism, and dynamic binding in O-O programs complicates the control-flow analysis.

Thus, method sequence specification of a class can be used for verifying the consistency of the implementation of the class against the specification. However, this verification depends on the result of control-flow analysis in identifying all the use sequences. In this article, we stress the verification aspects of the program rather than the control-flow analysis. In Figure 3, an Account object is shown with three other client objects sending messages. The numbers on the arrows correspond to the sequence in which the methods are expected to execute. Control-flow analysis is used for determining such sequences. From Figure 3 we can see that a sequence of methods the Account can execute is:

(open · deposit · close · withdraw)

This sequence does not belong to the *SafeSeq(Account)* as the withdraw method is invoked after the close method. Using method sequence specification and static control-flow analysis of O-O programs one can identify all such invalid sequences for each object. Each such invalid method sequence may be a potential fault.

Runtime verification system. The static control-flow analysis of an O-O program may not be able to identify all possible use sequences due to the presence of dynamic binding, polymorphism, and pointer data structures. If all the use sequences are not identified and compared for compliance against the method sequence specification, inconsistencies could be left in the program. For safety-critical systems[23] it may be necessary to identify all such inconsistencies either at compile time or during execution. The runtime verification system helps identify the incorrect method invocations.

Although the number of possible use sequences for each object is large, the number of actual runtime sequences is smaller.

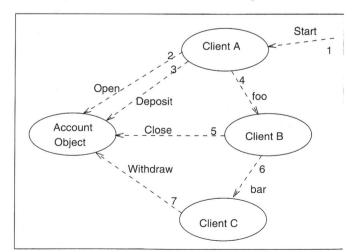

Figure 3. An example for illustrating verification of implementation against the specification. The numbers on the arrows correspond to the temporal sequence in which messages can be sent. Methods invoked are written on the lines.

---

* We are assuming that message-to-method binding is static. For dynamic binding of methods to messages, the static analysis must consider all possible methods that can be bound to a message during analysis.

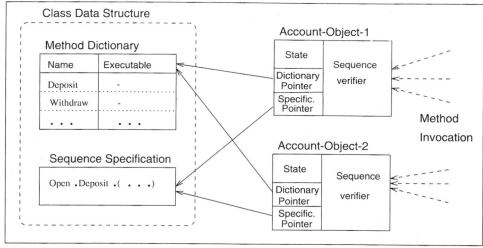

Figure 4. Class and object data structure diagram for implementing a runtime verification system.

In an O-O program, testing a class corresponds to testing the methods supported by the class. Individual methods are similar to conventional procedures. Therefore, methods can be tested similarly to conventional procedures using black-box and white-box testing. In O-O, there is extensive interaction between the methods of a class. These method interactions must be tested for correctness. In this section, we discuss generating test cases for the method sequences of a class using *coverage criteria*.

The runtime verification system is a part of the object's runtime support system. Each object maintains an access pointer to the method sequence specification of the corresponding class. For each invocation of the method, the verification system checks for sequence consistency with respect to the stored sequence specification. If the method invoked is not in correct sequence, an exception is raised and control is transferred to an exception handler. The runtime verification system determines the sequence correctness by checking the sequence with the regular definition specification. This algorithm to check whether a string is part of a regular set is well known[11] and can be implemented easily.

Figure 4 depicts a data structure diagram that can be used to implement a runtime verification system. The method dictionary and sequence specification of a class are shared by all objects of the class. All the method invocations are processed first by the "sequence verifier" that checks each invoked method with the sequence specification for correctness. If the newly invoked method is out of sequence then an exception is raised: otherwise, the method code is accessed from the method dictionary and executed.

Test case generation from sequence specification. Software testing is used for ensuring the correctness of a program against its specification by executing a program on a test case and comparing the result with the expected result.[24] The steps involved in testing are (1) generation of test cases for an identified portion of software, (2) execution of the program using the test inputs, and (3) evaluation of the test results. In this section we focus on test-case generation from method sequence specification of a class.

In Figure 5 a state transition diagram corresponding to the method sequence specification $m1 \cdot m2 \cdot (m3 | m4)^*$ is shown. Using different coverage criteria, different sequences can be constructed for generating test cases. To satisfy the *all-node* coverage criteria, two sequences $m1 \cdot m2 \cdot m3$ and $m1 \cdot m2 \cdot m4$ can be constructed and test cases corresponding to them can be generated. Similarly, all-edge coverage criteria can be satisfied by the sequences

$$m1 \cdot m2 \cdot m3 \cdot m3 \cdot m4 \quad \text{and} \quad m1 \cdot m2 \cdot m4 \cdot m4 \cdot m3$$

For each method in the sequence, data input of each parameter and the expected output must be determined. If a method invokes methods of other objects, then during testing test-stubs may be required to supply the proper return values from those methods. Sequence-based testing of an object can be performed either during design as a walkthrough or implementation by actually executing the program with the test cases. Because sequence-based testing depends on the correctness of individual methods, the testing of individual methods must precede testing the sequences. Method sequence testing helps determine the interactions between methods of a class. A sample program and a sequence test case generated from it are presented in the appendix.

SEQUENCE SPECIFICATION DERIVATION FROM DESIGN

The sequence specification described in the last section is semiformal. It may be difficult for software engineers to become adept at writing such regular-definition-based specifications for the inter-method causal relationships. In this section, we provide an alternative way of deriving the method sequence specification of a class from its state-based design.

Many O-O analysis and design techniques propose state transition diagrams (STDs) for modeling the dynamic behavior of classes.[2,5,25,26] STDs can be used to model both inter-class and intra-class dynamic behavior.[5] For deriving the sequence specification of a class, we use its intra-class STD. The STD model represents all possible states of the class, the events that can cause state transitions, and the actions that result from the state change. The STD model for a class describes how the time sequencing of external events can affect the state of an object of the class.

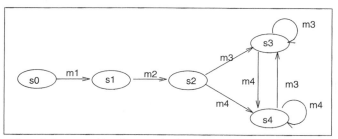

Figure 5. State transition diagram of a class used for generating test cases.

Different states of an object are due to different value combinations of its attributes. The states are linked to one another through state transitions. State transitions are caused by events, which are the stimulus received from the environment. Thus, different values of the instance attributes define states of an object and the messages received from the environment are the events. At each state, all the events are unique and events can be received in any state. The state transition depends on the current state and the message received. In analysis and design, STDs for classes contain states, events, and actions.

The method sequence specification for a class can be derived automatically from the STD specification of the class. For deriving sequence specification, we use only the events. We do not consider the states and actions associated with state transitions. STDs (similar to finite automata) can be modeled as 5-tuple $(S, \Sigma, \delta, s, f)$, where S is a finite set of states, Σ is the set of methods accessible from the outside environment, $s \in S$ is an initial state corresponding to the state after a class receives a constructor message, $f \in S$ is a final state corresponding to a class receiving a delete message, and δ is the transition function mapping $S \times \Sigma$ to S.

The sequences of messages accepted by such an STD of a class C forms the *SafeSeq(C)*. Construction of regular definitions that accept the same language as that of an STD is well studied in literature. Several efficient algorithms exist for deriving the regular expression from the STD (see ref. 11, theorem 2.4, p. 33). As STDs are constructed for each class during analysis and design phases, these STDs can be used for generating the sequence specification of the class. Because efficient algorithms are available, tool support can be provided easily for deriving a method sequence specification of a class. In the following, we provide the STD of class Account and the corresponding regular expression.

Example: Account class. In the example given in the last section, the methods and attributes of class Account were described. The STD corresponding to the dynamic behavior of class Account is given in Figure 6. The STD consists of four states with four types of events, each corresponding to messages.[†] The method Open creates an empty account. The Deposit method creates an actual operational account. Once an operational account is created, Deposit and Withdraw methods can be invoked until the account is closed. The regular expression that can be derived automatically from the STD is:

(Open · Deposit · Deposit|Withdraw)* · Close)

This regular expression is the method sequence specification for class Account.

CONSISTENCY AND COMPLETENESS OF SEQUENCE SPECIFICATION

V & V of software includes all those activities performed on the lifecycle products that increase the quality, reliability, and usability of the software. It is well known that extensive V & V is essential for developing reliable software. The development of software involves various production activities where the opportunity for introducing faults through human error is enormous. It has been

observed that software constructed from an unreliable specification requires major resources and cost during V & V.[27]

Design and construction of a software specification is a highly iterative process. Because the specification for software is written by humans, it is bound to contain gaps and contradictions. The specification is also subjected to continuous changes due to the changing environment and new user requirements. Furthermore, the specifications must represent the complex relationships and associations of the software that is being implemented. Thus, manually developed specifications may contain several inconsistencies.

The inheritance relationship is used extensively in O-O based applications. O-O languages support inheritance to model the hierarchical relationship between classes as well as to promote code reuse.[1,2,28-31] Inheritance allows a class definition that uses the

---

Design and construction of a software specification is a highly iterative process.

---

definition of one or more other classes. If a class C_1 directly inherits from another class C_2, then C_1 is called the *child* class and C_2 is called the *parent* class. The child class thus inherits the specification of the parent class. It is possible that the parent and child class specifications may be inconsistent with one another and therefore consistency verification between the parent and child class specifications is essential. In this article, we propose consistency rules that automatically verify consistency between the method sequence specifications of the parent and child classes depending on the type of inheritance.

Inheritance and sequence specification

In inheritance, a child class inherits both the operations and implementations defined in parent classes. The child class, in addition to inherited methods, can further enhance the class with additional operations or change the implementation of inherited methods.[1,29] Inheritance can be used for *specialization*, *refinement*, or *implementation* (reuse).[1,29] If inheritance is used for specialization, then the child class satisfies the semantics of all the inherited methods from the parent class. The child class may extend the class with

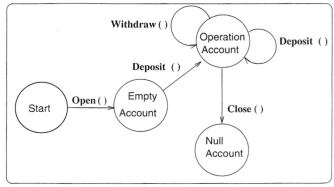

Figure 6. STD corresponding to the Account class.

---

† The methods for creation and deletion are not shown in the figure. The create method can be associated with the start state and similarly the delete method can be associated with the end state of the STD.

48

additional methods. Thus, the child class does not modify the semantics of the inherited methods and obeys the protocol of the inherited methods. In Eiffel, specialization inheritance can be ensured with the help of pre- and postconditions for the parent class methods.[1] If inheritance is used for refinement of the parent class, then the child class may refine or modify the semantics of the inherited methods and the behavior of a child class method may be different from the behavior of the corresponding method in the parent class. If inheritance is used for implementation, then the child class may not inherit all the methods from the parent class, and may modify the semantics of the inherited methods.[29,31]

In this article, we propose a set of C & C rules for consistency checking of method sequence specification of classes for each type of inheritance. Let C_1, C_2, . . . C_k be a set of classes related to one another through an inheritance relationship. In the following we define terms that are used in C & C rules.

Definition 5: ε-*instantiate(RE, S)*. ε-*intantiate(RE, S)* is defined as an operation on the regular definition *RE* where it instantiates all the symbols of *S* in *RE* with ε. For example, if *RE* of a class is $m0 \cdot m1 \cdot (m2|m3)^*$, and $S = \{m1, m3\}$, then ε-*instantiate(RE,S)* $= m0 \cdot (m2)^*$.

Definition 6: *Language(RE_c)*. *Language(RE_c)* defines a set of valid sequences that can be generated from the regular expression RE_c. For example, if *RE* of a class is $m0 \cdot (m2|m3)^*$, then *Language(RE_c)* $= \{(m0 \cdot m2), (m0 \cdot m2 \cdot m3), . . .\}$.

Definition 7: *Subseq(s_1,s_2)*. This is Boolean function returning true if s_1 can be formed by deleting zero or more not necessarily contiguous symbols from s_2. For example, if $s_1 = m0 \cdot m2$, and $s_2 = m0 \cdot m1 \cdot m2 \cdot m3$, then *Subseq($s_1$,$s_2$)* is true because s_1 can be derived from s_2 by deleting $m1$ and $m3$ from s_2.

Specialization inheritance and sequence specification. In specialization inheritance the child class can enhance itself with new methods, in addition to all the inherited methods from the parent classes. However, the child class inherits all the public methods of the parent class and does not modify them. Let class C_k be a proper child class of $C_1 . . . C_{k-1}$.

The sequence specification for the child class C_k must obey the sequence specification semantics of all its parent classes. In class C_k, the *Methods(C_k)* can be split into newly added methods and inherited methods, i.e.,

Definition 8: *NewMethods(C_k)*. A set of methods that are newly added in class C_k and not inherited from parent classes of C_k.

Definition 9: *InhMethods(C_k, C_i)*. A set of methods of class C_k that are inherited from class C_i and $C_k \neq C_i$. Let *IM(C_k)* be the set of methods that are inherited from all the parent classes of C_k.

In specialization inheritance, because the child class inherits all the parent class methods, $IM(C_k) = \cup_{i=1}^{k-1} Methods(C_i)$. The child class sequence specification is consistent with all the parent class sequence specifications if any valid method sequence in the parent class is a proper subsequence of at least one method sequence of the child class. The sequence specification of the child class with respect to all other classes must satisfy the following rule.

Rule: Let C_k be the proper child class of C_1, . . ., C_{k-1}, $S_i = NewMethods(C_k) \cup \{IM(C_k) - InhMethods(C_k, C_i)\}$, and $NRE_i = \varepsilon$-*instantiate(RE_{C_k},S_i)*, where, $i = 1, . . ., k-1$ then, $\forall_{i=1}^{k-1} Language(RE_{C_i}) = Language(NRE_i)$

In the above rule, the set S_i does not include the methods in C_k inherited from the class C_i. It includes the methods inherited from all other classes except C_i, and the new methods introduced in C_k. The symbols in the regular expression NRE_i consist of only those methods inherited from C_i. Because in specialization inheritance the methods are not modified, the derived regular expression must be same as the regular expression corresponding to class C_i.

The above rule uses operations on regular expressions for representing the C & C rule. This rule can be implemented easily using simple operations on regular expressions such as equality, inclusion, and difference between two regular expressions. In the next section we provide a general algorithm for implementing such operations on regular expressions. The rules can be implemented using these described algorithms.

Single inheritance is a specialized case of multiple inheritance. The consistency rule between the sequence specifications of the parent and child class is similar to the one given above. If C_2 is the child class of C_1 then the sequence specification of C_2, given the sequence specification of C_1, must satisfy the following rule.

Rule: If RE_{c_1} and RE_{c_2} are the two regular expressions defining the sequence specification for classes C_1 and C_2, S is the *NewMethods(C_2)*, and $NRE = \varepsilon$-*instantiate(RE_{c_2}, S)* then, *Language(RE_{c_1})* $= Language(NRE)$.

Example: Let us consider a new class Checking_Acc that specializes the parent class Account through specialization inheritance. In this case, the Checking_Acc class inherits all the methods of the parent class Account. Checking_Acc may be enhanced with new methods, e.g., Balance and Report. The sequence specification of Checking_Acc is:

$Methods \rightarrow$ Create $\cdot$ *AccountMethods* $\cdot$ Delete
$AccountMethods \rightarrow$ Open $\cdot$ *TransactionMethods* $\cdot$ Close
$TransactionMethods \rightarrow$ (Deposit $\cdot$ (Deposit|Withdraw|Balance|Report)*

By applying the above consistency rule for single inheritance, we see that the sequence specification of Checking_Acc is consistent with the sequence specification of Account, i.e., the regular expression of Account class can be derived from Checking_Acc class by substituting those methods that are newly added in Checking_Acc with ε.

Refinement inheritance and sequence specification. In refinement inheritance, the child class modifies the semantics of some of the inherited methods from the parent classes. The modification in the inherited methods can be either in the method protocol (also known as method signature) or behavior. The two corresponding methods in the parent and child class that are related through inheritance may produce different results for the same set of inputs. We define another term that is required for the C & C rule.

Definition 10. *RefMethods(C_k,C_i)*: A set of methods in C_k inherited from C_i, whose implementations are modified.

C & C of sequence specification of parent and child classes that are related through refinement inheritance is similar to that described in the previous subsection. The difference is in the computation of the set S_i, which represents all the methods except the ones inherited from the class C_i. For the C & C rule in the case of refinement inheritance, the S_i must include the *RefMethods(C_k, C_i)* where $i = 1, . . . k-1$. Informally, the inherited methods that are

49

refined must be considered as new methods of the child class and must not be considered while applying the rule. The rule is:

Rule: Let C_k be the proper child class of $C_1, \ldots, C_{k-1}$,
$S_i = NewMethods(C_k) \cup RefMethods(C_k, C_i) \cup \{IM(C_k) - InhMethods(C_k, C_i)\}$,
and $NRE_i = \varepsilon\text{-}instantiate(RE_{C_k}, S_i)$, where $i = 1, \ldots, k-1$ then,
$\forall_{i=1}^{k-1} \ Language(RE_{C_i}) = Language(NRE_i)$

Example: In Figure 7, the child class Savings_Acc refines some of the methods inherited from the parent class Account. The methods Deposit and Withdraw of the parent class are modified to compute interest. The specification of the child class can be verified against the parent class by considering these as new methods in Savings_Acc class and not considering them for the rule application.

Inheritance for implementation and sequence specification. If inheritance is used for reuse by excluding some of the methods of a previously defined class, it is generally known as *inheritance for implementation.*[29] In this case, some methods of the parent class are excluded in the child class public interface. The semantics of the inherited methods are not modified. For example, class queue can be implemented using deque by excluding the push2, pop2, and top2 methods of deque and allowing only the push, pop, top, and isEmpty? methods. Some new methods can be added in the child class. Thus, inheritance for implementation promotes reuse of previously developed code. Several languages, such as C++ and CommonObjects, support excluding methods of parent class in child class.[18,29]

The rule that checks the consistency between parent and child class is similar to the one described for specialization inheritance. The only difference is that some of the parent methods are not inherited and therefore these methods must not be considered in parent class regular expressions when applying the consistency rule.

Multiple interfaces and sequence specification

The O-O paradigm promotes strict encapsulation of internal detail of objects from other objects by restricting all interactions to occur only through supported methods. Methods of objects are invoked by methods in other objects. Thus, for each object there exists a set of well-defined client objects. For an object supporting many clients, the requirements of each client can vary. Therefore, it is useful to provide access to only a subset of the methods of an object to each client object. Even though an object defines many external methods, all these methods are not universally available to all client objects. Thus, for each class, multiple interfaces exporting a subset of methods that provide restricted access can be defined.[12,29]

Multiple interfaces are useful as they provide additional encapsulation to object structure. Separate subinterfaces to different users facilitates understanding, maintenance, and proper use. Multiple interfaces thus support the concept of *separation of concern*, which is essential for understanding complex software. Multiple subinterfaces provide well-guarded access control. The access control interfaces are useful for providing a debugging interface to each class so that some specialized users such as debuggers can access the internal details of the object. Multiple interfaces also provide support for implementing trusted users, and for implementing security levels and users in programs such as operating systems.[32]

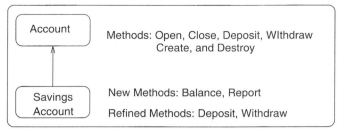

Figure 7. Example illustrating refinement inheritance.

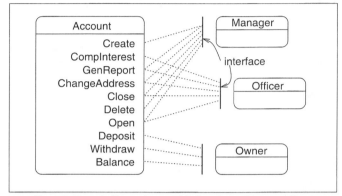

Figure 8. Example illustrating multiple interfaces of Account Class.

An object may support multiple methods and only a subset of these methods may be a part of a subinterface to a client. Some of the methods can also be shared in more than one subinterface. Because each client's view of the server class is through the interface, the method sequence specification for each subinterface defines the proper use of the server class. Therefore, sequence specification of methods for each subinterface is useful. Because methods are shared across interfaces, the method sequence specification of these shared methods must be consistent. In the following we model the multiple subinterfaces and define the consistency rule that the sequence specifications of all the subinterfaces must follow.

C & C of specification in multiple interfaces. For a given class C, let $I_1, \ldots, I_k$ be different subinterfaces the class supports. In the following we define some terms that are useful for defining the rule.

Definition 11: *Methods(I_i, C). Methods(I_i, C)* defines a set of methods of class C that are available to subinterface I_i. This is also denoted by Σ_i.

Definition 12: *SeqSpec(I_i, C). SeqSpec(I_i, C)* defines the method sequence specification for the subinterface I_i of class C.

From the above definitions we can write that $\cup_i \Sigma_i = Methods(C)$. The set of methods, $\Sigma_i \cap \Sigma_j$ ($i \neq j$) need not be a null set, which means that subinterfaces share several methods in common. We model the sequence specification for each subinterface I_i by a regular expression RE_i.

Informally, the consistency rule is that the sequence specification between two subinterfaces that share common methods must represent same method sequences containing the shared methods. In the following we formally describe the consistency rule that each of the subinterface sequence specifications must satisfy:

Rule: Let $I_1, \ldots, I_k$ be the subinterfaces of class C,
$RE_1, \ldots, RE_k$ be the corresponding sequence specification for each interface i,
$NRE_i = \varepsilon\text{-}instantiate(RE_i, \Sigma_i - (\Sigma_i \cap \Sigma_j))$, and
$NRE_j = \varepsilon\text{-}instantiate(RE_j, \Sigma_j - (\Sigma_i \cap \Sigma_j))$, then
$\forall_{i,\,j \wedge i \neq j},\ Language(NRE_i) = Language(NRE_j)$

Example: Figure 8 shows the Account class having three subinterfaces to classes **Manager**, **Officer**, and **Owner**. The **Manager** and **Officer** classes share four common methods, and the sequence specification of these two classes must agree on the inter-method relation of these four methods. This can be verified using the above rule. Further, when new methods are added to one or more interfaces, then the rule can be reapplied to verify the consistency of the sequence specification after adding the method.

ALGORITHM FOR CONSISTENCY CHECKING

All the consistency rules specified in this article can be implemented using one uniform consistency-checking algorithm. The method sequence specification for each class is a regular expression. A regular expression defines a well-defined regular set that contains all possible strings that can be generated from the regular expression. All the consistency-checking rules use the equality Boolean operator to verify the consistency between two regular expressions. The equality between two regular expressions can be expressed as a decision algorithm on the regular sets of each of these regular expressions.

In Hopcraft and Ullman,[11] an efficient algorithm is presented for verifying whether one regular expression is the same as another. Each regular expression defines a *finite automata* (FA). An FA accepts a set of strings and all the acceptable strings form the language defined by the FA. If L_1 and L_2 are the languages represented by two regular expressions, then the two regular expressions are equal if $L_1 = L_2$. One can verify this by constructing a new FA D_1 satisfying $L_1 \oplus L_2$ ($\oplus$ is the exclusive-or operator) and verifying whether D_1 accepts any non-empty string. If D_1 represents an empty regular

set, then $L_1 = L_2$. Efficient methods and proofs for constructing intersection and complement operators are provided in Ref. 11.

FEASIBILITY EVALUATION

The practicality of the method sequence specification technique was evaluated by using it to specify two O-O designs given by Coad and Yourdon.[4] The authors provide a detailed O-O design and program in Smalltalk and C++ for four projects. We chose the Counter and ATM design projects for representing all the classes in each design using the proposed method sequence specification technique.

In Figure 9 the inheritance hierarchy of the Count class is given. In this example, the authors have used refinement inheritance. The IntegerCount class enhances the inherited methods with a new method asBase. All the child classes refine the methods increment and decrement, but do not change their protocol. The sequence specification of the Count class is:

$Methods \rightarrow$ Count $\cdot$ *DataSetup* $\cdot$ Operations $\cdot$ ~ Count
$DataSetup \rightarrow$ set_value $\cdot$ set_reset_value
$Operations \rightarrow$ (increment $\cdot$ decrement $\cdot$ reset)*

In the above sequence specification, *DataSetup* methods can be invoked only once, and once the data is set up all the *Operations* methods can be used. If the designer desires to allow initialization methods to be invoked intermixing with other operation methods, then the specification must be modified. But, the goal of the above specification is to explicitly specify the sequence relation that exists between methods.

The IntegerCount class inherits all the methods from the Count class and a new method asBase is added. The specification of IntegerCount is similar except that of *Operations*:

$Methods \rightarrow$ Count $\cdot$ *DataSetup* $\cdot$ Operations $\cdot$ ~ Count
$DataSetup \rightarrow$ set_value $\cdot$ set_reset_value
$Operations \rightarrow$ (increment $\cdot$ decrement $\cdot$ reset $\cdot$ asBase)*

Even though the specifications of IntegerCount and Count can be verified visually, the consistency rules are useful as a part of a CASE tool used for O-O analysis and design. The algorithm to verify consistency in sequence specification can be implemented as part of a tool that ensures consistency every time an inheritance relation is created. The consistency rules are also beneficial when the inheritance tree grows in depth.

The additional advantage of the above specification is that it helps in understanding the interface of a class. The sequence specification clearly specifies the sequencing information, which is useful during program development so that the class can be used correctly.

CONCLUSION

For successfully implementing O-O programs, a complete and consistent specification and an implementation that is compliant with the specification is essential. In this article, we have proposed a method sequence specification technique for specifying the

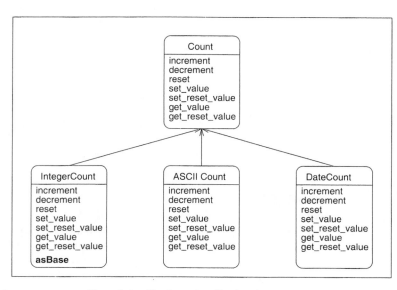

Figure 9. Specification and verification of counter design.

causal relation that exists between methods of a class. Method sequence specification forms only a part of the total O-O specification. The method sequence specification has numerous applications in verification and validation. This sequence specification of a class can be used for ensuring the correctness of inheritance. The sequence specification helps in documenting the proper usage of classes and thus is helpful during implementation. In the presence of multiple interfaces for a class, method sequence specification can be used to ensure consistency among the sequence specification of each of the subinterfaces. The method sequence specification can be used for generating test cases to test the implementation. Further, a runtime verification system can be implemented that uses the method sequence specification to verify the correctness of each method access and thus is useful for identifying runtime faults in method access.

The development of a method sequence specification for each class is not a difficult task. The sequence specification was used to specify the causal relationship between the methods of all the classes in two projects. Further, we have also provided a semi-automated derivation of method sequence specification from a state-based design of the class. We are currently working on integrating sequence specification with an O-O CASE tool. We are also working on generating test cases from the sequence specification and verifying its application and usefulness. ∎

Acknowledgments

The authors thank all the members of the Software Engineering Group at the University of Minnesota for their valuable comments, feedback, and discussion on this research.

References

1. Meyer, B. Object-Oriented Software Construction, Prentice Hall, Englewood Cliffs, NJ, 1988.

2. Booch, G. Object Oriented Design with Applications, Benjamin/Cummings, Menlo Park, CA, 1991.

3. Martin, J. Principles of Object Oriented Analysis and design, Prentice Hall, Englewood Cliffs, NJ, 1993.

4. Coad, P. and E. Yourdon. Object Oriented Analysis, 2nd Ed., Yourdon Press/Prentice Hall, Englewood Cliffs, NJ, 1991.

5. Drake, J.M., W.W. Xie, and W.T. Tsai. Document-driven analysis: Description and formalization, Journal of Object-Oriented Programming 5(7):33–50, 1992.

6. Monarchi, D.E. and G.I. Puhr. A research typology for object-oriented analysis and design, Communications of the ACM, 35(9):35–47, 1992.

7. Dyer, M. The Cleanroom Approach to Quality Software Development, John Wiley, New York, 1992.

8. Meyer, B. Applying design by contract, Computer, October: 40–51, 1992.

9. Boehm, B.W. Verifying and validating software requirement specifications and design specification. IEEE Software, 1:61–72, 1984.

10. Davis, A.M. Software Requirements Analysis and Specification, Prentice Hall, Englewood Cliffs, NJ, 1990.

11. Hopcraft, J.E. and J.D. Ullman. Introduction to Automata Theory, Languages, and Computation, Addison-Wesley, Reading, MA, 1979.

12. Hailpern, B. and H. Ossher. Extending objects to support multiple interfaces and access control. IEEE Transactions on Software Engineering 16(11):1247–1257, 1990.

13. Smith, M.D. and D.J. Robson. Object-oriented programming—The problems of validation. IEEE Conference on Software Maintainance, 1990, pp. 272–281.

14. Cheatam, T.J. and L. Mellinger. Testing object-oriented systems, Proceedings of the 18th ACM Annual Computer Science Conference, ACM, New York, 1990, pp. 161–165.

15. Perri, D.E. and G.E. Kaiser. Adequate testing and object-oriented programming, Journal of Object-Oriented Programming 2(5):13–19, 1990.

16. Turner, C.D. and D.J. Robson. The testing of object-oriented programs, Technical Report TR-13/92, University of Durham, Computer Science Division, SECS, Durham, UK, 1992.

17. Wirfs-Brock, R.J. and R.E. Johnson. Surveying current research in object-oriented design, CACM 33(9):104–124, 1990.

18. Lippman, S.B. C++ Primer, 2nd Ed, Addison-Wesley, Reading, MA, 1991.

19. Coad, P. and J. Nicola. Object-Oriented Programming, Yourdon Press/Prentice Hall, Englewood Cliffs, NJ, 1993.

20. Wirfs-Brock, R.J., B. Wilkerson, and L. Wiener. Designing Object-Oriented Software, Prentice Hall, Englewood Cliffs, NJ, 1990.

21. Aho, A.V., R. Sethi, and J.D. Ullman. Compilers: Principles, Techniques, and Tools, Addison-Wesley, Reading, MA, 1986.

22. Hecht, M.S. Flow Analysis of Computer Programs, North-Holland, New York, 1977.

23. Mojdehbakhsh, R. et al. Life cycle and verification and validation techniques for software hazard analysis, Technical Report TR:93-04, University of Minnesota, Computer Science Department, Minneapolis, MN, 1993.

24. Meyers, G. The Art of Software Testing, Prentice Hall, Englewood Cliffs, NJ, 1979.

25. Rumbaugh, J. et al. Object-Oriented Modeling and Design, Prentice Hall, Englewood Cliffs, NJ, 1991.

26. Zualkernan, I.A. et al. Object-oriented analysis as design: A case study, International Journal on Software Engineering and Knowledge Engineering 2(4):489–521, 1992.

27. Beizer, B. Software Testing Techniques, 2nd Ed., Van Nostrand Reinhold, 1990.

28. Goldberg, A. and D. Robson. Smalltalk-80: The Language and Its Implementation, Addison-Wesley, Reading, MA, 1983.

29. Snyder, A. Encapsulation and inheritance in object-oriented programming languages, Readings in Object-Oriented database systems, Xdonik, D.B. and D. Maier, eds., Morgan Kaufman, New York, 1986, pp. 84–91.

30. Ellis, M. and B. Stroustrup. The Annotated C++ Reference Manual, Addison-Wesley, Reading, MA, 1990.

31. Lee, H.J. and W.T. Tsai. A new partial inheritance mechanism and its applications, Technical Report TR:92-17, University of Minnesota, Computer Science Department, Minneapolis, MN, 1992.

32. Keefe, T.F., W.T. Tsai, and M.B. Thuraisingham. Soda: A secure object-oriented database system, Computers and Security 8(6):517–533, 1989.

33. Dershem, H.L. and M.J. Jipping. Programming Languages: Structures and Models, Wadsworth Publishing Company, 1990.

APPENDIX A:
AN EXAMPLE TEST CASE FOR THE ACCOUNT CLASS

We provided the sequence specification of the Account class in a previous section. In the following we provide the skeleton of the code (adapted from Dershem and Jipping[33]) that implements each method. We use the code and the sequence specification to generate a sample test case.

```
class Account {
public:
    ...
   void open (char * cust_id, char *cust_name, char *date);
   void deposit (char *cust_id, amount amt, char *date);
   void withdraw (char *cust_id, amount amt, char *date);
   amount balance (char *cust_id)
          {return balance;}
    ...
protected:
   amount balance;
   char monthlyreport[1000];
    ...
}

void
Account::open (char *cust_id, char *cust_name)
{
  balance = 0;
  addrep (monthlyreport, date, 0, balance);
   ...
}

void
Account::deposit (char *cust_id, amount amt, char *date)
{
  balance = balance + amt;
  addrep (monthlyreport, date, amt, balance);
   ...
}

void
Account::withdraw (char * cust_id, amount amt, char *date)
{
  if (amt <= balance){
       balance = balance - amt;
       addrep (monthlyreport, date, amt, balance);
        ...
  }else ...
}
```

A possible method sequence from the sequence specification of the Account class is *Open · Deposit · Deposit · Withdraw*. In this sequence we are omitting the creation and deletion methods for convenience. A sequence test case is:

1. **Test Input::** Open ("Foo", "23576")
   Expected State: balance = 0 and number of monthlyreport entries is 1.

2. **Test Input:** Deposit ("23576", 100.00, "03/21/93")
   Expected State: balance = 100.00 and number of monthly-report entries is 2.

3. **Input:** Deposit ("23576", 101.25, "03/25/93")
   Expected State: balance = 201.25 and number of monthly-report entries is 3.

4. **Input:** Withdraw ("23576", 50.25, "04/15/93")
   Expected State: balance = 151.00 and number of monthly-report entries is 4.

The above test case can be used for testing the code for one possible sequence of methods.

53

Chapter 3

Unit Testing and Integration Testing

Software unit testing is one type of software testing. Its major focus is finding various errors in a software component, such as a module. Since unit tests are performed after implementing a software component (or a module), it is very effective to check various errors in a software product's components at an earlier stage of its life cycle. Unlike a traditional program where function modules and functional procedures are considered as its components, an object-oriented (OO) program consists of three levels of components: (1) functions defined in classes, (2) classes, and (3) modules, which are made of a collection of classes.

Although there are many research results addressing unit test problems, most of them focused on function-oriented/procedure-oriented software. These unit test methods can be classified into two types: (1) specification-based test methods, and (2) structure-based (or program-based) test methods. *Black-box* test methods focus on verifying the functions and behaviors of a software component in terms of an external view. *White-box* test methods focus on checking the internal logic structures and behaviors of a software component, for example, basis-path testing based on control-flow graphs.

As mentioned in Chapter 1, OO programs generated some new testing problems for testers. Since classes are the major components in an object-oriented program, testers have to find the answers to the following questions:

- Can existing unit testing techniques be applied on classes and class clusters with a number of related classes?
- What test models, test generation methods, and test criteria can be used in unit tests for object-oriented software?
- How can unit tests for an OO program be performed in a systematic way?

Therefore, new test generation methods, test models, and test coverage criteria for classes are needed in unit tests. Recently, a number of research papers addressing class unit tests have been published. Several of them provide specification-based test methods for abstract data types. The paper in [doon94a], included in Chapter 7, written by Doong and Frankl is one example. This chapter includes two papers that propose new structure-based test methods for class unit testing.

55

The first paper by Parrish, Borie, and Cordes in [parr93a] provides a foundational theory for the application of conventional flow graph-based testing strategies to OO class modules. Based on the conventional flow-graph model, they proposed a general class graph model by extending the basic modeling concept to represent classes. Each class graph consists of: (1) nodes that are the set of class operations; (2) feasible edges which are operation interactions from one to another according to the given specifications; (3) definitions and uses, each consisting of pairs of (operation, type); and (4) subpaths that are infeasible according to the given specifications. Using this conceptual model as the test model, many existing flow graph-based techniques can be applied to classes in both specification-based unit testing and program-based unit testing. The authors provided their insights about how to use this class graph to define a new set of test coverage criteria for class unit testing, including node coverage, branch coverage, definition coverage, use coverage, and du-path coverage. Another important result of this framework is that some systematic test generation techniques are given based on class implementation. This makes the results more applicable to provide a systematic solution in class tests for today's industry practice.

Unlike the first paper, the second paper by Heechem Kim and Chisu Wu in [kimh96a] focuses on data bindings in class testing. In their approach, class testing consists of three steps. The first step is testing each method, in which the existing functional and structural test methods can be used. The second step is testing actual data bindings, in which the major focus of testing is the data bindings between the methods in a class. The authors use an actual data binding to represent a data flow between two methods, so that data bindings between the methods of a class can be used as the basis for measuring intermethod interactions in its class. To reduce the complexity of the state-based testing, they apply state testing only to each simple MM-path (message/message path) which is a sequence of a pair of methods represented by the actual data bindings. The final step is testing of sequences of methods. In this step, the class graph model for a class in [parr93a] is sliced into a set of slices based on data members in the class. Each slice is a subgraph of the class flow-graph. Based on this model, different flow-graph test generation methods given in [parr93a] can be used to achieve various flow-graph-based test criteria. According to the authors, this approach has the advantage of reducing the complexity of state-based testing of class objects, and simplifying test generations.

When software components (or parts) are separately tested, they are integrated together to check if they can work together properly to accomplish the specified functions. The major testing focus here is their interfaces, integrated functions, and integrated behaviors. In the past two decades, a number of software integration testing approaches have been used to perform software integration testing, such as top-down, bottom-up, sandwich, and "big bang." Since all of them were designed for integrating components in a traditional program, they might not be applicable to object-oriented programs due to the differences in their structures and behaviors.

The first is the structural differences between an object-oriented program and a traditional program. For example, a conventional program consists of three levels of components: (1) functions (or procedures), (2) modules, and (3) subsystems. The structures of these components can be represented (or modeled) as call graphs, data-flow and/or control-flow graphs respectively. However, an object-oriented program consists of four levels of components: (1) function members defined in a class, (2) classes, (3) groups of classes, and (4) subsystems. The conventional data-flow graph and control-flow graph can be used to represent the structure of a class function member. A class-flow-based graph [parr93a] can be used to model the interactions between functions defined in a class. A class relation diagram [kung95e] can be used to model various relationships between classes, including inheritance, aggregation, and association relations.

The other major difference between an OO program and a conventional program is the behaviors of each type of program. In a dynamic view, a conventional program is made of a number of active processes. Each of them has its control flow. They interact with one and another through data communications. An OO program consists of a collection of active objects that communicate with one and another to complete the specified functions. In a multiple-thread program, there are a number of object message flows executing at the same time.

These differences bring out some new problems in integrating different components for an OO program. The paper by Paul C. Jorgensen and Carl Erickson [jorg94a] provides their insights about integration testing of OO programs based on their experience with an automatic teller machine (ATM) system. They believe that checking behaviors should be the major focus in the integration of an OO program. In the paper, they suggest five distinct levels of OO testing, including method, message quiescence, event quiescence, thread, and thread interaction. Their basic idea is to model the behaviors of an OO program using an object network, in which nodes (rectangles) are methods and edges (dashed lines) are messages. Each object is a cluster (or a collection) of methods. Based on this model, integration tests are constructed based on different MM-paths (which are sequences of method executions linked by messages) in the object network.

References

[doon94a] R. Doong and P. Frankl, "The ASTOOT Aapproach to Testing Object-Oriented Programs," *ACM Trans. Software Engineering and Methodology*, Vol. 3, No. 2, Apr. 1994, pp. 101–130.

[parr93a] A.S., Parrish, R.B. Borie, and D.W. Cordes, "Automated Flow Graph-Based Testing of Object-Oriented Software Modules," *J. Systems Software*, No. 23, 1993, pp. 95–109.

[kimh96a] H. Kim and C. Wu, "A Class Testing Technique Based on Data Bindings," *Proc. 1996 Asia-Pacific Software Engineering Conf.*, IEEE Computer Society Press, Los Alamitos, Calif., 1996, pp. 104–109.

[kung95e] D. Kung et al., "Developing an Object-Oriented Software Testing and Maintenance Environment," *Comm. ACM*, Vol. 38, No. 10, Oct. 1995, pp. 75–87.

[jorg94a] P. Jorgensen and C. Erickson, "Object-Oriented Integration Testing," *Comm. ACM*, Vol. 37, No. 9, Sept. 1994, pp. 30–38.

A Class Testing Technique Based on Data Bindings

Heechern Kim, Chisu Wu
Department of Computer Science
Seoul National University,
Shinlim-Dong, Kwanak-Gu, Seoul, Korea, 151-742
Email: {khc, wuchisu}@selab.snu.ac.kr

Abstract

We present a testing technique based on data bindings for testing a class. Data bindings can be used to measure the interface between the modules of a system and reflect the possibility of data interactions between modules.

Our approach considers the correctness of a class with regard to data interactions of its member functions and is based on an adaptation of flow graph-based techniques for testing object-oriented classes. A class is fragmented into smaller pieces, called slice-flow graph associated with each data member.

Class testing approaches typically invoke sequences of methods in varying orders. Our approach can generate test cases by applying a flow graph-based class testing technique to each slice-flow graph. It is useful for determining which sequences of methods should be tested. Before applying a flow graph-based testing technique, we apply state-testing only to simple MM-Paths which represents actual data bindings. The result is reflected in the next step to reduce efforts for generating test cases.

1. Introduction

Within object-oriented approaches, testing has received less attention than analysis, design, and coding. This lack of interest is mainly caused by a strong belief that applying an object-oriented development method will eventually lead to quality code. Object-orientedness does not provide correctness by itself. Although an object-oriented design can lead to a better system architecture and an object-oriented programming language enforces a disciplined coding style, they are by no means shields against programmer's mistakes or a lack of understanding of the specification. Therefore testing a software remains an important task even in the presence of object-orientedness. As a matter of fact the testing process is more important for object-oriented software than for traditional software, since the object-oriented paradigm promotes reuse: class will be reused in various context. Object-oriented programmers like to pick up classes from existing, working programs and apply them to new programs being developed. They expect all of the methods of such classes to work, not just the ones required by the originating program [6].

Most work in testing has been done with procedure-oriented software. Without being adapted, traditional methods, despite their efficiency, can not be applied to object-oriented systems. The object-oriented architecture is indeed very different from the procedure-oriented architecture. For object-oriented approaches, the basic unit of organization is the class construct.

Although the operations of a class could be admittedly tested individually, it is impossible to reduce the testing of a class to the independent testing of its operations. They interact with each other by modifying the state of the object by which they are invoked. The context in which an operation is executed is not only defined by its possible parameters, but also by the state of the object by which it is invoked. Furthermore, for methods that effect this state and are accessible outside the class, they can be called in any order. Therefore proper sequences of methods must be executed to be tested for a class in a manageable level and the state must be checked to be consistent when executing the methods of an object.

A class is designed to work as independently as possible from its environment. This is a benefit to testing, as it allows the programmer to write a small test program to exercise the class alone. Testing a class as an independent body ensures that it is loosely coupled to its surrounding program.

The organization of this paper is as follows. In the next section, we briefly overview both data bindings and flow graph-based testing that this paper is based on. In section 3, we present our technique for testing a class and explain the testing process by example. Section 4 briefly discusses the analysis of our testing technique. Finally, section 5 describes the conclusion and outlines further work.

2. Related Work

2.1. Data Bindings

Data organization metrics are measures of data use and visibility. Several types of data organization metrics appear in the literature. Data binding is an example of a module interaction metric. Data bindings will be used in this paper for us to measure the interface between the components of a system and to generate test cases. Several levels of data bindings were defined [4].

A potential data binding is defined as an ordered triple <p, x, q> where p and q are procedures and x is a variable within the static scope of both p and q. Potential data bindings reflect the possibility of a data interaction between two components, based upon the locations of p, q, and x. That is, there is a possibility that p and q can communicate via the variable x without changing or moving the definition of x. Whether or not x is mentioned inside of p or q is irrelevant in the computation of potential data bindings.

A used data binding is a potential data binding where p and q use x for either reference or assignment. It reflects a similarity between p and q (they both use the variable x).

An actual data binding is defined as a used data binding where p assigns a value to x and q references x. The actual data binding only counts those used data bindings where there may be a flow of information from p to q via variable x. The possible orders of execution for p and q are not considered.

A control flow data binding is defined as an actual data binding where there is a possibility of control passing to q after p has had control. The possibility is based on a fairly simple control flow analysis of the program. To be more precise, a possibility is said to exist whenever either 1) there exists a chain of calls from p to q or vice versa, or 2) there exists a procedure r such that there are chains of calls from r to p and from r to q and there exists a path in the directed control flow graph of r connecting the call chain p with the call chain to q.

2.2. Flow Graph-Based Testing

Zweben et al. stated the flow graph model as follows[8].

A node in the graph represents an operation; an edge

between operation A and operation B means that it is permissible for a client module to invoke operation A followed by operation B. Determination of whether or not an edge exists is based on the model-based specification for the class.

Parrish et al. developed a formal framework for modeling classes with flow graphs. They argue that model-based specifications are unnecessary for using flow graph-based sequence-testing techniques. They showed some theoretical results concerning the feasibility of automatically generating operation sequences to satisfy certain flow graph-based criteria[5]. The testing criteria defined for conventional program flow graphs can be viewed as defining sequences of operations based on the class flow graph. The class analog for node coverage requires that a sequence containing every operation in the class flow graph be executed and the class analog for branch coverage requires that a sequence containing every edge be executed. Class analogs for the data flow criteria can be provided similarly, assuming that the underlying data flow concepts are well defined for classes, as follows. First, all definitions and uses are associated with class operations rather than statement blocks. The other general observation that they made about definitions and uses is that data flow concepts must be interpreted in the context of types rather than strictly in terms of variables.

3. Class Testing

This section describes our approach for testing a class as a unit of testing. The following steps are explained by example.

3.1. step 1 : testing each method

An individual method performs a single, cohesive function. This directly corresponds to the unit level of traditional software testing, and both the traditional functional and structural techniques are applicable to testing methods.

When the methods of a class are invoked, these methods act upon the data members (or instance variables) of an object to which the message is sent.

Independent and isolated analysis of methods for detecting anomalies in the usage of instance variables do not give meaningful results. Local variables are also used in the body of methods. If these local variables are not instances of any class then these can be tested using conventional testing techniques.

In testing a public method together with other methods in its class that it calls directly or indirectly, conventional testing techniques are also applicable.

3.2. step 2 : testing actual data bindings

Here we present some informal definition that may be required to describe our approach,

A class can be defined as a tuple, (Data, Methods) where Data and Methods are sets of data members and member functions(or methods) in the class respectively.

The relationship of member functions can be measured. The possibility of a data interaction between two member functions is analyzed using an actual data binding.

Definition : An actual data binding set in a class is defined as an ordered tripple <m1, d, m2> where m1 and m2 ∈ Methods, d ∈ Data, and m1 assigns a value to d and m2 references d.

The actual data binding only counts those used data binding where there may be a flow of information from m1 to m2 via the data member d.

Definition : A sequence is defined as a non-empty, ordered set of methods of a class.

A sequence is defined for a specific data member of the class.

Definition : A simple MM-Path is a sequence of a pair of methods represented by the actual data binding.

An actual data binding reflects the possibility of a data interaction between two methods where there may be a flow of information from one to the other via some data member and the possible orders of execution for one and the other are not considered. So data bindings between the methods of a class provide the basis for measuring inter-method interactions in its class.

In the case of state-based testing, the number of data members that the class possesses has a profound effect on the complexity of the testing and all the transitions can not be tested. Therefore in this step, we apply state-testing only to each simple MM-Path which is a sequence of a pair of methods and belongs to actual data bindings.

As an example, consider the following C++ code. The class Stack will be used as an example to illustrate each step.

```
Class Stack
{ int *s;
  int smax;
  int top;
  int put_elem(int, int);
  int get_elem(int&, int);
public:
    //defines s, top, smax
    // uses
  Stack(int n) { s=new int[n]; smax=n; top=0; };
  int push(int elem);
  int pop(int& elem);
  void print();
};
void Stack::put_elem(int elem, int pos)
    // defines s*
    // uses smax, s, elem
{ if (0<=pos && pos<smax)
    s[pos] = elem;
}
void Stack::get_elem(int& elem, int pos)
    // defines
    // uses smax, s*
{ if (0<=pos && pos<smax)
    elem=s[pos];
}
void Stack::push(int elem)
    // defines top
    // uses smax, top
{ if (top<smax)
    put_elem(elem, top++)
}
void Stack::pop(int& elem)
    // defines top
    // uses top
{ if (top>0)
    get_elem(elem, --top);
}
void Stack::print()
    // defines
    // uses top
  int elem;
  for (int i=top-1; i=0; --i)
  { get_elem(elem, i);
    cout << elem << "\n";}
}
```

In this example, actual data bindings are as follows.

(Stack, s, put_elem)	(put_elem, s*, get_elem)
(Stack, top, push)	(push, top, push)
(Stack, top, pop)	(push, top, pop)
(Stack, top, print)	(push, top, print)
(Stack, smax, put_elem)	(pop, top, push)
(Stack, smax, get_elem) ·	(pop, top, pop)
(Stack, smax, push)	(pop, top, print)

If the public methods incorporate the methods that

they calls directly or indirectly, we have the following results.

(Stack, s, push)	(push, s*, print)
(Stack, top, push)	(push, s*, pop)
(Stack, top, pop)	(push, top, push)
(Stack, top, print)	(push, top, pop)
(Stack, smax, push)	(push, top, print)
(Stack, smax, pop)	(pop, top, push)
(Stack, smax, print)	(pop, top, pop)
	(pop, top, print)

And simple MM paths are as follows.

<Stack, push> <Stack, pop> <Stack, print>
<push, print> <push, pop> <push, push>
<pop, push> <pop, pop> <pop, print>

We assume that it is possible to analyze which values are significant for each data member and which state is inappropriate. Each method would be called with the same object, and the result of the call would be verified against the above analysis.

For example, suppose the conditional in the method pop is omitted as follows.

```
int Stack::pop(int& elem)
{
  get_elem(elem, --top);
}
```

In this case, when the test sequence of methods <Stack, pop> is executed with respect to the data member top , the error can be detected because the value of top is changed to -1.

It is necessary that test cases include the sequence of methods that exposes the fault. Some of the anomalies resulting from the wrong sequence of usage of methods can be detected in this step. This result of testing the wrong sequence is passed to the next step and used to reduce the testing efforts.

If object-oriented application programs are tested instead of a class, control-flow data bindings will be used instead of actual data bindings by a fairly simple control analysis of the program.

If there are situations where all methods in a class is designed defensively, no infeasible path may exist.

This step guides testers in the selection of sequences of methods that should be run, and sequences of methods that need not be run.

3.3. step 3 : testing of sequences of methods

A class encapsulates a set of data members and provides a set of functions that act upon these data members.

We can consider a part of class associated with only a single data member and will call this a slice. We propose that a class be tested one slice at a time. If testing process is repeated for all slices of a class, then it can be concluded that all member functions of the class are correct. The set of member functions of a class associated with a data member d can be classified into three categories; pure-define methods, pure-use methods, and define-use methods exclusively.

Definition : Slice(d) = (D, DU, U)
where
   for all $m1 \in D$, there exists an actual data binding <m1, d, >,
   for all $m2 \in DU$, there exists both actual data bindings, <m2, d, > and < , d, m2>, and
   for all $m3 \in U$, there exists an actual data binding < , d, m3>.

The current state of an object is the combined values from all of its data members at the current point in time. Member functions of a class are the manipulators of the state of its object. To test object-oriented software properly, we must test classes. Class testing approaches typically invoke sequences of methods in varying orders, and verify that the resulting state of the objects manipulated by methods is correct.

Since data members can be considered as the shared variable among member functions, the testing order of the member functions of a class can be defined by the define-use relationships of data members. But the state-based testing has a problem of generating many test cases. So we apply an adaptation of flow graph-based testing technique to our approach.

In our approach a class is fragmented into smaller pieces associated with each data member. Correctness of methods implies that these methods correctly manipulate data members. And correct manipulation of each of the data members by associated member functions gives confidence in the correctness of the class as a whole.

The use of flow graph to model class behavior provides a wide range of class-testing techniques that have been already been analyzed and exploited for conventional programs. Zweben et al.[8] showed that it was possible to associate a flow graph with class modules using formal, model-based specifications. Each node in such a flow graph represents a message; a directed edge between two message A and B represents the possibility that A might be invoked, followed by B. Using this notion of a "class flow graph," a collection of systematic coverage criteria for class modules was defined. Parrish et al. have also developed versions of flow graph-based criteria for which efficient algorithms can be provided to generate satisfactory minimum-length sequences of operations.

In object-oriented software the interactions of methods are performed not by parameters but by shared variables i.e., data members.

It is complicated that a class graph represents all the relations of data and test cases of long sequences of methods may be generated.

In our approach, a class graph consists of smaller segments, called slice-flow graph which also represents the relationship between data and methods additionally.

Testing sequences of methods associated with a corresponding slice-flow-graph are created and tested for the correct manipulation of the data member of that slice-flow graph. Combinations of test cases for each slice-flow-graph comprise a test suit of a class for correctness as a whole.

We have the following graph:
A slice-flow graph, Slice-G , associated a data member is a collection < N, E-I >
Definition : Slice-G(data) = < N, E-I >
where
N is the set of methods with respect to the data member in the class. N can be classified into three categories: pure-define method D, define-use methods DU, and pure-use methods U of the data member.

E consists of all possible edges that are from m1 to m2 in N.

I is a subset of E and consists of those edge that are infeasible. I can be identified from the step 2 by anomaly testing of a pair of methods which represent actual data binding.

E - I states that the possibility of correct interaction between two methods.

A class graph can be considered as a union of all slice-flow-graph.
Definition : Class-G(class) = $\underset{\text{all } i}{U}$ Slice-G(di)

Parrish et al. showed that it was possible to generate minimum-length operation sequences satisfying various graph-based criteria. The details are described in [5]. In our approach it is possible to apply their algorithm to our slice-flow graph.

Our approach considers testing a class one slice at a time. Let us say that we are testing for the given data member top in our example. From the step 2, actual data bindings are as follows: (Stack, top, push), (Stack, top, pop), (Stack, top, print), (push, top, push), (push, top, pop), (push, top, print), (pop, top, push), (pop, top, pop), and (pop, top, print).

We can construct the slice-flow graph associated with the data member top and have Slice-G(top) = < N, E-I > where N = D $\cup$ DU $\cup$ U and D = { Stack }, DU = { push, pop }, U = { print }. In our example all methods are defensively designed and no feasible path exists.

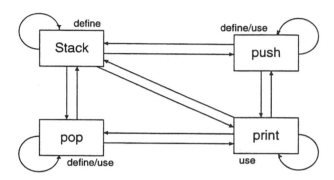

Figure 1. Slice-flow graph associated with a data member top for simple stack

A minimum-length sequence of methods that satisfies weak use coverage can be found. This sequence is <Stack, print, push, print, Stack, pop, pop, push, push, pop, print> which covers all uses: <Stack, push>, <Stack, pop>, <Stack, print>, <push, push>, <push, pop>, <push, print>, <pop, pop>, <pop, push>, and <pop, print>.

A minimum-length sequence of methods that satisfies weak definition coverage is <Stack, push, pop, print>.

If we construct the slice-flow graphs associated with the data member smax, s, or s* in our example, the slice-flow graphs and the test sequences would be simple.

4. Analysis

In object level test, there exists a technique that analyzes methods algebraically with respect to ADT and generates test cases. But ADT defines an object as a relation between operands and operators and this way do not consider the interactions between methods in the object when selecting test cases. Specification based testing only test the external view of the class without any regard for its structure or implementation. There is an alternative way to select test cases with respect to FSM.

In the case of state-based testing, the number of data members that the class possesses has a profound effect on the complexity of the testing. Since there are a lot of state transition paths, this alternative way has a problem of generating many test cases. The number of sequences of all possible permutations of the methods that effect the state of the object can be infinite since the transition path may contain loops. And even if each method appears exactly once in a sequence, the total number of test cases would be n! where the number of those methods is n. Therefore in our approach before applying flow graph-based testing technique with respect to each data member, we apply state-testing only to a simple MM-Path which belongs to actual data bindings. The result of above step is reflected in the next process of the flow graph-based testing to reduce efforts for generating test cases.

Generally the more mutually independent the test cases are, the more effective the testing process can be. But it is often the case that most of the test cases in object-oriented software are mutually dependent. The reason for this is that the result of a test case can easily make an effect on the initial condition for another test case. Our approach proposed in this paper generates test cases associated with each data member, which are independent.

In our approach the test cases are concentrated on individual data members. Although this has the disadvantage of increasing the number of test cases, yet this can generate test cases faster and easier than the other type.

5. Conclusions

When the testing of units is discussed, it is understood that they mean functions or groups of related functions. In object-oriented software a unit can also be a class with its associated methods, classes present some unique testing considerations as well. Programmers tend to think of some classes as general purpose, reusable class while others are held to be application-specific and not reusable.

In this paper we present a technique based on data bindings for testing a class. We consider that data members in a class can be considered as the shared variable among member functions that act upon these data. So we exploit the fact that the data binding is used to measure the interface between the modules of a system and reflects the possibility of data interactions between the modules.

Our approach considers the correctness of a class with regard to data interactions of its member functions and is based on an adaptation of flow graph-based techniques for testing object-oriented classes. A class is fragmented into smaller pieces, called slice-flow graph associated with each data member. The impracticality of wrong sequences is recognized by testing simple MM-Paths to reduce efforts in the next step and then a class is fragmented into smaller pieces, called slice-flow graph associated with each data member. Class testing

approaches typically invoke sequences of methods in varying orders and our approach generates test cases of method sequences for each slice-flow graph.

Our attention has been directed at only a class and its basic features. Now we are extending our approach to the range which covers such features related to the interactions among classes and the concept of inheritance. And an automatic environment for this work will be considered as well.

References

[1] B. Beizer, Software Testing Techniques, Van Nostrand Reinhold, 1990.

[2] E. V. Berard, Essays on Object-Oriented Software Engineering, Prentice Hall, 1993.

[3] V. R. Basili and A. J. Turner, "Iterative enhancement: A practical technique for software development," IEEE Trans. on Software Eng., vol. SE-1, Dec. 1975.

[4] D. H. Hutchens and D. R. Basili, "System Structure Analysis: Clustering with Data bindings," IEEE Trans. on Software Eng., vol. SE-11, Aug. 1985.

[5] A. S. Parrish, R. B. Borie, and D. W. Cordes, "Automated Flow Graph-Based Testing of Object-Oriented Software Modules," Journal of Systems Software, vol. 23, Nov. 1993.

[6] M. Ross, C. A. Brebbia, G. Staples, and J. Stapleton, "The Problematics of Testing Object-Oriented Software," SQM'94, vol. 2, July 1994.

[7] C. D. Turner and D. J. Robson, "The State-based Testing of Object-Oriented Programs," Proc. of Conference on Software Maintenance, 1993.

[8] S. Zweben, W. Heym, and J. Kimich, "Systematic Testing of Data Abstractions Based on Software Specifications," Journal of Software Test, Verification, and Reliability, 1992.

Automated Flow Graph –Based Testing of Object-Oriented Software Modules

Allen S. Parrish, Richard B. Borie, and David W. Cordes
Department of Computer Science, University of Alabama, Tuscaloosa, Alabama

Classes represent the fundamental building blocks in object-oriented software development. Several techniques have been proposed for testing classes. However, most of these techniques are heavily specification based, in the sense that they demand the existence of formal specifications for the module. In addition, most existing techniques generate test cases at random rather than systematically. We present some test case generation techniques that are based entirely on class implementation, involve systematic generation of test cases, and are fully automated. Our techniques are based on an adaptation of existing white-box, flow graph –based techniques for unit testing conventional procedures and functions. We also provide a general conceptual framework to support the modeling of classes using flow graphs. Our framework clarifies the fundamental definitions and concepts associated with this method for modeling classes.

1. INTRODUCTION

Classes represent the fundamental building blocks in object-oriented software development. Several techniques have been proposed for unit testing classes. Most existing work in class testing has involved sending sequences of messages to an object of the class and observing the resulting effect on the object [1–7]. This work normally involves the use of formal specifications (either algebraic [8] or model based [9]) when constructing message sequences.

Test generation techniques for classes fall into one of two categories; random or systematic. A random technique generates message sequences entirely at random; most existing techniques use this approach. A systematic technique uses a repeatable procedure to generate a fixed sequence satisfying particular properties. Although random testing is not without merit, systematic techniques have the advantage of guaranteeing that specific characteristics of a class have been examined in a standard manner, regardless of who applies the technique. For example, a trivial systematic technique would require that every message associated with a particular class be applied at least once to some object. Although different implementations of this technique can produce different sequences, one can guarantee that regardless of how the technique is applied, every message is applied at least once.

Systematic testing can be applied to conventional software using white-box code-coverage techniques (such as branch coverage and path coverage). These techniques associate unique flow graphs with every module and then require test data to execute certain levels of coverage over the flow graph (e.g., branch coverage demands coverage of all edges in the flow graph). Zweben et al. [7] showed that it is possible to associate a flow graph with class modules using formal, model-based specifications. Each node in such a flow graph represents a message; a (directed) edge between two messages A and B represents the possibility that A might be invoked, followed by B. Using this notion of a "class flow graph," a collection of systematic coverage criteria for class modules (similar to the white-box criteria for conventional modules) is defined [7].

The use of flow graphs to model class behavior provides a wide range of class-testing techniques that have been already been analyzed and exploited for conventional programs. The analysis of flow graph –based testing techniques for conventional programs provides a model for the types of analyses that might be useful for class-based analogs. In addition, the experience that many testing practitioners have with flow graph –based techniques for conventional software will likely facilitate effective

Address correspondence to Allen Parrish, Department of Computer Science, University of Alabama, Tuscaloosa, AL 35487-0290.

technology transfer with respect to the analogous class-testing techniques. Consequently, this represents an important area for further investigation.

In this article, we provide a foundation for future work in this area by presenting a general conceptual framework for conducting flow graph modeling of classes. In this framework, we clarify a number of concepts related to how this modeling should be performed, particularly with regard to the feasibility or executability of an edge. The idea of feasibility is universally well understood in the context of flow graph modeling of conventional programs [10], but there are complicating issues in the context of classes. An important result of this framework is the insight that conventional flow graph–based techniques can be applied to classes as either program or specification-based techniques. This means that these techniques may be applied even in the absence of formal specifications, thus making them applicable to current-day development practice.

Based on our expanded conceptual framework, we propose new class-based analogs of conventional white-box techniques that can be automated, in the sense that the techniques may be used to automatically generate sequences of test messages. Previously proposed flow graph–based techniques [7] require manual application. Although our techniques are automated, this automation process does not necessarily ensure a test suite that is as rigorous as those produced by manual techniques. Our automated techniques can thus provide an intermediate plateau, in the sense that the tester can use these techniques to reach a basic level of test coverage satisfaction, and then apply manual techniques to augment the test suite to achieve stronger requirements. We provide guidelines on how to manually augment our testing techniques in this manner.

2. BACKGROUND

2.1 Basic Definitions

We first define a set of standard terms relative to object-oriented development. Our definitions of these terms are similar to those used in the object-oriented testing discussion of Doong and Frankl [2]. We use the term *class* to refer to the implementation of an abstract data type within an object-oriented language. An *object* is an instance of a class. Instances are created by invoking a special constructor operation (such as NEW) on a variable whose type is that of the given class. A class implementation is defined in two parts: an interface consisting of a list of operations that can be performed on instances of the class, and a body consisting of implementations of the operations. Operations are sometimes called methods; invoking a method with respect to a given object is sometimes referred to as "sending a message" to the object. (In the remainder of this article, we use these two forms of the terminology interchangeably.)

We assume that it is plausible for a formal, functional specification to be associated with a class. The specification defines correct behavior for the class. In practice, specifications are frequently informal (or nonexistent). However, classes can also be specified using formal techniques. Much of the research involving formal specification techniques has been related to specifying classes. (See McKim and Mondou, this issue.)

Two formal specification techniques—algebraic specifications [8] and model-based specifications [9]—are commonly discussed in the literature. Weide et al. [11] gives an excellent overview of these specification techniques. An algebraic specification defines the behavior of a module in terms of a set of axioms that characterize the equivalence of combinations of operations, whereas model-based specifications involve the individual modeling (using well-defined concepts) of each operation in the class. Table 1 presents both algebraic and model-based specifications for a stack class (similar to that in Weide et al. [11]).

From Table 1, we first consider the algebraic specification. Algebraic specifications are composed of three separate elements: functions, domain conditions, and axioms. The functions section defines signatures of the class operations. Domain conditions permit restrictions to be placed on the input values for a particular operation. For values not satisfying the domain conditions, the output of the operation is unspecified. Finally, the axioms listed in the specification must be satisfied by the implementation. For example, according to axiom 2, the state resulting from executing the sequence POP(PUSH(s, x)) must be identical to the original state s of the stack.

For model-based specifications, each operation identifies both a *requires* and an *ensures* clause. The requires clause asserts any domain restrictions on the operation, similar to the domain conditions section of the algebraic specification. The absence of a requires clause implies there are no domain restrictions. The *ensures* clause indicates a specific condition that holds true after invoking the operation, provided that the requires clause is met.

With model-based specifications, an independently defined model is chosen to represent the

Table 1. Formal Module Specifications

Algebraic	Model Based

module STACK_TEMPLATE(type T)
   type STACK
   functions
     NEW: $\rightarrow$ STACK
     PUSH: STACK $\times$ T $\rightarrow$ STACK
     POP: STACK $\rightarrow$ STACK
     TOP: STACK $\rightarrow$ T
   domain conditions
     POP(s): not (s = NEW)
     TOP(s): not (s = NEW)
   axioms
     (1) not (PUSH(s, x) = NEW)
     (2) POP(PUSH(s, x)) = s
     (3) TOP(PUSH(s, x)) = x
 end STACK_TEMPLATE
	module STACK_TEMPLATE(type T)
	   type STACK is modeled by STRING
	   interface
	     operation New (s: STACK)
	       ensures $s = e$
	     operation Push (s: STACK, x: T)
	       ensures $(s = \#x \circ \#s) \wedge (x = \#x)$
	     operation POP (s: STACK)
	       requires not ($s = e$)
	       ensures $\exists x \ni \#x = x \circ s$
	     operation Top (s: STACK, x: T)
	       requires not ($s = e$)
	       ensures $(\exists t \ni s = x \circ t) \wedge (s = \#s)$
	 end STACK_TEMPLATE

class. In this case, a string is used to model a stack. Because strings are a well-defined concept from mathematics, the behavior of stack operations can be expressed in terms of string theory operations. For example, e refers to the empty string; the operation *new* returns an empty stack, which is modeled as an empty string. The requires clause for *pop* demands that the stacks provided as input are nonempty; given that this restriction is met, the ensures clause indicates that the new stack s is equal to some element concatenated (denoted by the operator o) with the old value of the stack (denoted using $\#s$). Concatenation is used to model this operation, as it is a well-defined operation within string theory.

2.2 Conventional Flow Graph–Based Testing

To understand flow graph–based testing techniques for classes, we first review flow graph–based testing techniques for conventional program modules. Conventional program modules can be decomposed into blocks of statements. A block is a sequence of statements that can only be entered through the first statement. Once the first statement is executed, all remaining statements are executed in order. No statement can be added to the beginning or end of a block and still retain the property that whenever the first statement is executed, the rest of the statements are executed in order. In our flow graph model, a node represents a block and an edge between two nodes represents the possibility that control is permitted to flow in the direction indicated by the edge. If a transfer between blocks is based on some conditions (e.g., from a predicate in an *if* statement), then the edge corresponding to that transfer is labeled with the condition.

Techniques (sometimes called criteria) used for flow graph–based testing of conventional programs are typically classified as either control flow or data flow criteria. The criteria for which we will discuss class-based analogs are shown in Table 2.

Data flow testing is based on the principle of tracing the definition of the value of a variable through subsequent accesses to that value. Based on this idea, we say that a variable is defined at a node if there is a statement in that node that assigns a value to the variable (e.g., through an input statement or the appearance of the variable on the lefthand side of an assignment statement). A variable is said to be used if a reference is made to its contents. Such a reference can take place in a node (i.e., in an output statement or on the righthand side of an assignment statement) or at a labeled edge (i.e., in a predicate). Uses of the first type are called c-uses (computational uses) and uses of the second type are called p-uses (predicate uses).[1]

Because blocks are executed as a single unit, there is no need to worry abut tracing the variable's definition and access (definition-use pairs) when both definition and use occur within the same block. Instead, attention is focused on global definitions and uses of a variable. Intuitively, a global definition is a definition that is used after exiting the block in which the definition occurs; a global use is a use of a

---

[1] Note that p-uses are really found within nodes rather than edges, because the condition containing the p-use is at the end of the block (node preceding multiple-labeled edges. However, since we require p-uses to be properly covered (meaning that both the **true** and **false** conditions are executed), most authors associate p-uses with the labeled edges rather than the preceding node, to help illustrate that both labeled edges must be executed.

Table 2. Conventional Flow Graph–Based Testing Criteria

Control Flow	Data Flow
Node coverage	Definition coverage
Branch coverage	Use coverage
Path coverage	Du-path coverage

definition from some earlier block. The remaining data flow concepts are summarized in Table 3.

A path is said to cover a def-c-use association (i, j, x) if it contains a definition-clear subpath from i to j with respect to x. Similarly, a path is said to cover a def-p-use association $(i, (j, k), x)$ if it contains a definition-clear subpath from i to (j, k) with respect to x. A path covers a def-use association if it covers a def-p-use association or a def-c-use association.

Formal definitions of the data flow testing criteria definition coverage, use coverage, and du-path coverage are presented in Table 4. Intuitively, definition

Table 3. Basic Data Flow Testing Concepts

- *Simple path.* A simple path is a path where every node, except possibly the first and last nodes, are distinct.
- *Definition-clear path.* Let x be a variable in program p and let $q = (i, n_1, n_2, n_3, \ldots, n_k, j)$ denote a path through the flow graph of p, starting with node i, preceding through nodes $n_1, n_2, n_3, \ldots, n_k$, and terminating at node j. We say that path q is definition clear with respect to x def-clear if the (possibly empty) subpath $(n_1, n_2, \ldots, n_k)$ does not contain a definition of x (i.e., the only definition of x, if there is one, is in the first node i).
- *Global definition of a variable.* Node i has a global definition of x if x is defined at i and there is a definition-clear path from node i to some node, either 1) containing a global c-use of x or 2) having an edge containing a p-use of x emanating from it.
- *Global use of a variable.* A global use of x is either a global c-use or p-use of x. A global c-use of x is a c-use of x in node i, where the value of x is not defined previously in i. (There is no need to define global p-use; since p-uses take place at edges, all such uses are global.)
- *Du-path.* A path $(n_1, \ldots, n_j, n_k)$ is a du-path with respect to a variable x if n_1 has a global definition of x and either 1) n_k has a global c-use of x and $(n_1, \ldots, n_j, n_k)$ is a definition-clear simple path with respect to x, or 2) (n_j, n_k) has a p-use of x and $(n_1, \ldots, n_j, n_k)$ is a definition-clear simple path with respect to x.
- *Def-c-use association.* A def-c-use association is a triple (i, j, x) where i is a node containing a global definition of variable x, j is a node containing a global c-use of x, and there is a definition-clear path from i to j with respect to x.
- *Def-p-use association.* A def-p-use association is a triple $(i, (j, k), x)$, where i is a node containing a global definition of x, (j, k) is an edge containing a p-use of x, and there is a definition-clear path from node i to edge (j, k) with respect to x.
- *Def-use association.* This is either a def-c-use association or def-p-use association of x.

Table 4. Formal Definitions of the Dataflow Criteria

Given a program p and a set of test cases T, we can define definition coverage, use coverage, and du-path coverage as follows:

- T satisfies definition coverage for p iff for every node i in p's flow graph and for every variable x receiving a (global) definition in i, T executes a set of paths covering at least one of either 1) a def-c-use association (i, j, x) or 2) a def-p-use association $(i, (j, k), x)$.
- T satisfies use coverage for p iff for every node i in p's flow graph and for every variable x receiving a (global) definition in i, T executes a set of paths covering 1) all def-c-use associations (i, j, x) and 2) all def-p-use associations $(i, (j, k), x)$.
- T satisfies du-path coverage for p iff for all nodes i and j in p's flow graph and for every variable x receiving a (global) definition in i, T executes all du-paths from i to j such that (i, j, x) represents a def-c-use association and all du-paths from i to (j, k) such that $(i, (j, k), x)$ represents a def-p-use association.

coverage requires covering paths containing at least one use of every definition, use coverage requires covering paths containing every use of every definition, and du-path coverage requires covering every use of every definition along every possible path. Du-path coverage actually requires that every simple path from definition to use be executed by an adequate test set. Without the constraint of simple paths, programs with loops may have an unbounded number of paths from a definition to a use.

Certain flow graph paths may be infeasible in the sense that no test data can cause those paths to be executed. We assume the definitions of Frankl and Weyuker [10], which only require feasible statements (branches, definitions, uses, du-paths) to be executed. Of course, the selection of test data to cover feasible components is undecidable [12], thus making application of these criteria undecidable.

2.3 Flow Graph–Based Class Testing

Our discussion of flow graph–based class testing in this section follows from the work of Zweben et al. [7], whose flow graph model can be stated as follows. A node in the graph represents an operation; an edge between operation A and operation B means that it is permissible for a client module to invoke operation A followed by operation B. Determination of whether or not an edge exists is based on the model-based specification for the class, i.e., on whether the requires clause of B can be satisfied given the ensures clause of A. In the previous example, there would be no edge from NEW to POP because NEW returns an empty stack, thus violating the requires clause of POP.[2] Because the conjunction of arbitrary predicate calculus expressions is undecidable, membership in the set of edges in a class flow graph is undecidable. This is much like the undecidability problem for restricting conventional flow graph coverage criteria to feasible code.

Certain operations are control operations, i.e., they return **true** or **false** and can be used to construct conditions in client modules [7]. For such operations, there are two labeled edges (a **true** edge and a **false** edge) emanating from them to every operation that can follow them in a client program. For example, for the control operation IS_EMPTY found in some stack classes, there is a **true** edge emanating from IS_EMPTY to every operation that a client is permitted (based on the ensures–requires conjunction in the specification) to invoke after IS_EMPTY returns **true**, and a **false** edge emanating from IS_EMPTY to every operation that a client is permitted to invoke after IS_EMPTY returns **false**. Control operations thus have the same role in the class flow graph as conditions have in a conventional program flow graph.

The testing criteria defined for conventional program flow graphs can now be viewed as defining sequences of operations based on the class flow graph. The class analog for node coverage requires that a sequence (or sequences) containing every operation be executed and the class analog for branch coverage requires that a sequence (or sequences) containing every edge in the class flow graph be executed. Class analogs for the data flow criteria can be provided similarly, assuming that the underlying data flow concepts (i.e., definitions, uses, def-use associations, etc.) are well defined for classes, as follows. First, all definitions and uses are associated with class operations rather than statement blocks. A p-use is a use associated with a control operation rather than a condition. Because there are multiple labeled edges emanating from control operations (just as there were from blocks containing conditions), all of the concepts regarding p-uses are the same as before. In particular, each labeled edge emanating from a control operation represents a

p-use to be exercised. A c-use in a use within any other (noncontrol) operation.

The other general observation that we make about definitions and uses in this context is that data flow concepts must be interpreted in the context of types rather than strictly in terms of variables (as is the case for conventional programs). Operations define and use their parameters, e.g., a PUSH operation defines and uses any actual stack instance with which it is parameterized in a client module. Thus, in this example, data flow analysis takes place with respect to type "stack" in general, rather than with respect to a specific variable. Therefore, def-use associations for classes are triples involving the node in which a type is defined, the node or edge where a type is used, and the type itself.

The rules introduced by Zweben et al. [7] for locating definitions and uses can be summarized as follows. An operation is said to contain a definition of a type if a formal parameter to the operation appears of that type and the ensures clause specifies that the parameter is to be changed. Specifically, if the symbol x appears (without #) in the ensures clause and the predicate $x = \#x$ is absent,[3] then Zweben et al. [7] assume that x is defined by the operation (the absence of # means that there is a new value for x). An operation is said to contain a use of a type[4] if a formal parameter to the operation appears of that type and the ensures clause specifies that the parameter is used somehow to produce a result. Specifically, if the symbol $\#x$ appears in the ensures clause in any predicate other than $x = \#x$ (which is considered neither a definition nor a use of x), then x is considered to have been used (since its old value is a part of some predicate that represents the computation of the operation).

A very simple example will clarify these ideas. Consider the model-based specification of a stack module presented earlier. This module has four operations; NEW, PUSH, POP, and TOP. Because of domain restrictions on POP and TOP, there is no edge drawn from NEW to either of these operations. Otherwise, every pair of operations is connected by a single edge (none of the operations are control operations requiring multiple edges) and there is a reflexive edge from every operation to itself (Figure 1).

---

[2] The requires clause and the ensures clause for two different operations are written in terms of variables that are local to those operations. However, Zweben et al. [7] assume that if the parameter lists of the two operations contain common types, then the same actual parameters are used for both operations. Evaluation of the ensures-requires conjunction takes advantage of this observation. For example, in establishing that there is no edge from NEW to POP, the same stack is used in the ensured clause of NEW as in the requires clause of POP.

---

[3] The predicate $x = \#x$ in an ensures clause implies that the formal parameter x is not changed by the operation; the absence of this predicate implies that x could be changed.

[4] Or, in the case of a p-use, the edges emanating from the operation are said to contain p-uses of the type.

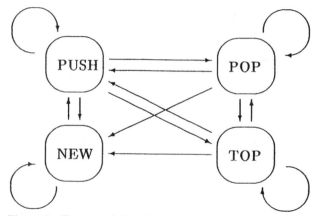

Figure 1. Flow graph for simple stack module.

The left side of Table 5 contains information regarding definitions and uses associated with each operation (node) in the class graph. Because there are no control operations, there are no uses associated with edges. The right side of Table 5 then provides examples of operation sequences satisfying each of the criteria. For a more complex example involving control operations, see Zweben et al. [7].

3. A GENERAL CLASS GRAPH MODEL

In this section, we develop a formal framework for modeling classes with flow graphs. A significant side effect of this framework is that model-based specifications are unnecessary for using flow graph–based sequence-testing techniques, such as those proposed by Zweben et al. [7]. In fact, we argue that formal specifications are not necessary at all to use these techniques. Additionally, the framework provides a basis for deriving results concerning automation of the techniques.

We have the following basic definition: A class graph is a collection $\langle N,E,D,U,I \rangle$ where N refers to the set of all nodes, E refers to the set of all edges, D refers to the set of all definitions, U refers to the set of all uses, and I refers to the set of all infeasible subpaths. A class graph is a formalization of the information that is needed to apply flow graph–based testing techniques to classes. Consider an interpretation of the definitions from Zweben et al. [7] in the context of this framework:

- N (the set of operations) is determined by looking at the set of operations present in the (model-based) specification.

- E consists entirely of those edges that are feasible according to the specifications (i.e., those edges from operation A to operation B, where the ensures clause of A is consistent with the requires clause of B). To provide a better foundation for our later observations, however, we eliminate feasibility from the requirements for E and assume that E contains at least one edge between every pair of operations and two edges (labeled **true** and **false**) from every control operation to every other operation. Thus, the derivation of E is entirely mechanical and does not involve processing semantic information from the specification.

- D and U are determined by following the rules outlined in the previous section to identify definitions and uses from the specification. We assume that definitions and uses each consist of pairs (*operation*, *type*), where *operation* is the operation in which the definition or use occurs and *type* is the type of parameter involved in the definition or use.

- I is composed of subpaths that are infeasible according to the specification.

Table 5. Application of Flow Graph–Based Criteria to Simple Stack Module

Operation			Criterion	Sequence
NEW			node	NEW, PUSH, TOP, POP,
defines		stack	branch	NEW, NEW, PUSH, NEW, PUSH, PUSH, POP, PUSH, TOP,
uses		$\langle \rangle$		TOP, PUSH, POP, POP, NEW, PUSH, PUSH, PUSH, POP,
				TOP, POP, TOP, NEW
PUSH				
defines		stack, T		
uses		stack	definition	NEW, PUSH, PUSH, POP, TOP, PUSH
POP			use	NEW, PUSH, PUSH, POP, POP, PUSH, TOP, PUSH, POP,
defines		stack		TOP
uses		stack		
			du-path	NEW, PUSH, PUSH, POP, POP, PUSH, TOP, PUSH, TOP,
TOP				POP, TOP, POP, PUSH, TOP, PUSH, TOP, NEW, PUSH,
defines		T		PUSH, TOP, POP, PUSH
uses		stack		

With this modification to E, we note that I contains both infeasible edges as well as longer infeasible subpaths. For example, the edge from NEW to POP is in I, given the earlier stack specification. However, the subpath ⟨NEW; PUSH; PUSH; POP; POP; POP⟩ is also infeasible for the same reason that ⟨NEW; POP⟩ is infeasible. Both ⟨NEW; POP⟩ and ⟨NEW: PUSH; PUSH; POP; POP; POP⟩ are in I, given the earlier stack specification.

In defining a general theory for class graphs, it is important to distinguish between four forms of infeasibility that together constitute the set I. We refer to these as type 1, type 2, type 3, and type 4 infeasibility (Table 6).

Types 1 and 2 infeasibility are properties of the specification, while types 3 and 4 infeasibility are properties of the implementation. Because I can contain subpaths associated with all four of these types of infeasibility, we refer to subsets of I corresponding to each type as I_1, I_2, I_3, and I_4, respectively. Note also that membership in each of these subsets is undecidable. Furthermore, when the implementation is correct, there are certain relationships between these subsets, namely

- $I_2 = I_3$: subpaths in both of these sets are related in that the next-to-last operation is a control operation, followed by a labeled edge. The labeled edge that is executed in the implementation (and conversely, the labeled edge that is not executed and therefore infeasible) should be the same edge that the specification implies should be (or should not be) executed.

- $I_4 \subseteq I_1$: any subpath for which the implementation crashes should be a path that the specification implies should not be executed by a client. Otherwise, the implementation is incorrect, in that it crashes on a legitimate sequence of operations. However, the fact that a subpath should not be executed obviously does not imply that a correct implementation must crash on such a subpath.

Of course, when the implementation is incorrect, one cannot guarantee any particular relationship between the specification and implementation forms of infeasibility (without knowing anything about why the implementation is incorrect).

One important design decision in developing classes relates to whether modules are designed to be defensive or nondefensive. In the above framework, a defensive module is a module without type 1 infeasible subpaths. In other words, the specification is written in such a way that no domain restrictions are placed on any operations, i.e., the module is designed to be error catching. An example of a defensive design is to require a particular defined behavior for the POP operation on an empty stack input (i.e., either a no-op or an exception). A nondefensive module is the opposite, i.e., a module where domain restrictions are placed on any or all operations.

Our discussion so far has centered on the possibility that modules might be nondefensive. Much of the literature has suggested that modules should always be defensive, thus eliminating any possibility of type 1 infeasibility [8, 13–15]. This is not the universal view, however; Weide et al. [11] and Meyer [16] both imply that there are at least some cases where nondefensive modules are desirable. The resolution of this issue is outside the scope of this article, but we will maintain the distinction between defensive and nondefensive modules for the remainder of the discussion.

We now reexamine the question raised at the beginning of this section concerning the applicability of flow graph–based criteria to classes without model-based specifications. To apply flow graph–based criteria, a class graph must be constructed. In constructing such a graph, we first observe that although N, E, D, and U are determined from the model-based specification in Zweben et al. [7], this is not strictly necessary in most cases. For most object-oriented languages, N, E, D, and U are ob-

Table 6. Types of Infeasibility for Class Graphs

- *Type 1:* Subpaths are type 1 infeasible if, according to the specification, the subpath should not be executed. This is the form of infeasibility identified at the top of this page. The sequences ⟨NEW; POP⟩ and ⟨NEW; PUSH; PUSH; POP; POP; POP⟩ are type 1 infeasible, according to the specifications in Table 1.
- *Type 2:* Subpaths are type 2 infeasible if, according to the specification, the subpath cannot be executed. This type of infeasibility only arises for subpaths containing control operations with labeled edges. For example, given a standard stack specification, the subpath ⟨NEW; PUSH; PUSH; POP; IS EMPTY⟩, followed by an edge labeled **true** (and leading to any other operation), is type 2 infeasible. This type of infeasibility can be established by sequentially applying the ensures clauses one after the other and noting that the value of the ensures clause of IS_EMPTY is inconsistent with the value of the **true**-labeled edge that follows.
- *Type 3:* Subpaths are type 3 infeasible if, when attempting to execute the subpath, the subpath cannot be executed because the value of a control operation in the subpath is inconsistent with the intended labeled edge that follows. This is the same problem as type 2 infeasibility, except this is a result of the implementation, not the specification.
- *Type 4:* Subpaths where there is a crash in the middle of the subpath are type 4 infeasible. For example, consider the sequence ⟨NEW; PUSH; POP; POP; POP⟩. Suppose that POP crashes on an empty stack. Then this sequence cannot be executed because there will be a crash after the second invocation of POP.

tainable from the class interface (i.e., from the implementation), provided that the class interface has the following properties:

- All operation names are listed.
- For each operation, all parameters must be listed. For each parameter, both type and transmission mode must be listed. (Possible transmission modes and IN, OUT, and IN-OUT; their meanings are obvious).

In most object-oriented languages, the class interface satisfies these properties. Given these properties, the construction of both N and E is trivial, simply by using the names of the operations and interpreting operations that return Booleans as control operations (and therefore constructing labeled edges to emanate from those operations). D and U are constructed as follows. For every IN or IN-OUT parameter to any operation, a definition, i.e., a pair consisting of (*operation*, *type*) is added to set D. Similarly, for every OUT or IN-OUT parameter to any operation, a use, i.e., a pair consisting of (*operation*, *type*) is added to set U.

Using this technique, N, E, D, and U may be constructed from the implementation alone. In addition, even if the specification is used to derive N, E, D, and U, it may not be necessary for the specification to be model based. Most styles of algebraic specifications provide this information as well if the specification has a "syntax" section denoting the signatures of the operations (as in the example from Table 1). Thus, N, E, D, and U can be determined with or without the existence of formal specifications and regardless of whether the specification is model based.

To complete the construction of the class graph, we must be able to construct I as well. Our objective in applying the desired testing techniques is to test the class over sequences that satisfy certain criteria (i.e., coverage of all feasible branches, definitions, uses, etc.). The purpose of constructing I is to allow us to eliminate sequences that are inappropriate or impossible to test. By their nature, I_3 and I_4 are based on properties of the implementation, and so specifications are not used to derive these sets. Moreover, such sequences can never be executed (by definition), so there is no need to consider their explicit elimination.

This leaves I_1 and I_2. We first observe that eliminating the subpaths in I_2 is not desirable. Assuming a correct implementation, subpaths in I_2 are impossible to test anyway (because they are also in I_3). However, if there is a subpath that is in I_2 and not

in I_3, then by our earlier observation that I_2 should equal I_3, the class is incorrect with respect to that subpath. Testing over such a subpath is desirable; we do not want to eliminate such subpaths from our testing process.

Finally, we consider I_1. I_1 is defined by domain restrictions on the class operations, presumably from within the specification. Sequences in I_1 represent unspecified behavior, which we assume is unnecessary to test [7, 17, 18]. Therefore, we would like to identify such sequences and eliminate them from testing. Provided that domain restrictions are present in some discernible form within the specification, it is unnecessary to require the specification to be model based in order to capture such restrictions. For example, the algebraic specification example discussed in section 2.1 contained explicit domain restrictions. Furthermore, we assume that, in the absence of domain restrictions (regardless of specification paradigm), the module design is intended to be defensive by default. Without a way to communicate to prospective clients that certain domain restrictions are in place, a client is unable to knowledgably use a nondefensive module. The bottom line is that, in testing, we must use the specification (if one exists) to find I_1, although there is no reason that the specification has to be model based. However, in the absence of a specification, the question of finding I_1 is eliminated because the module is (by default) defensive and I_1 is empty.

In summary, to find the class graph (and apply the graph-based testing criteria), the specification can be ignored when finding N, E, D, and U, if desired. The specification, if it exists, must be used to find I (specifically, I_1). However, if no specification exists, as may be the case given current development practice, then the specification is no longer needed to find I. Consequently, it is still possible to find the class graph without the specification and apply flow graph–based testing techniques.

4. TOOL SUPPORT

In this section, we consider the issues of providing tool support for flow graph–based class-testing techniques. This discussion is divided into two parts. Section 4.1 contains some theoretical results concerning the feasibility of automatically generating operation sequences to satisfy certain flow graph–based criteria. These results show that efficient generation of operation sequences to satisfy different criteria is possible, but is subject to certain simplifying assumptions regarding both the criteria and the class modules to which the criteria are applied.

Section 4.2 addresses the pragmatics of tool implementation and how the simplifying assumptions used in section 4.1 are handled.

4.1 Theoretical Results

Here we consider the extent to which sequences of operations satisfying various graph-based criteria may be automatically generated. There are two major barriers to automation. One problem involves infeasible paths within the class graph, because finding such paths is undecidable. Consequently, it is impossible to avoid automatically generating sequences that contain such paths. A related problem is that even without infeasible paths, it is impossible to generate a sequence containing subpaths that drive the different conditions returned by control operations.

To deal with these problems, we consider ways of eliminating infeasible paths from the class graph (i.e., from I). This is accomplished in two ways. First, we restrict our attention to class modules that are designed defensively. That is, there are no type 1 infeasible subpaths in the class graph (i.e., I_1 is empty). We are not saying that all class modules should be designed defensively, but we assume that there are situations where modules are designed defensively. Later we will show how to relax this assumption and allow modules to be designed non-defensively, although we are unable to completely automate the sequence generation process under such circumstances (given the undecidability problems).

The second way that we eliminate infeasible paths is to perform a transformation on class graphs as follows: Replace every pair of labeled edges with a single, unlabeled edge. This automatically changes the testing criteria in the obvious way: a criterion that required coverage of either or both of a true/false pair of labeled edges now only requires coverage of the corresponding single unlabeled edge. We call this new version of a class graph a weak class graph and the corresponding versions of the testing criteria weak criteria (i.e., weak node coverage, weak branch coverage, weak definition coverage, weak use coverage, and weak du-path coverage). Weak node coverage is equivalent to (strong) node coverage, because node coverage does not require covering particular edges; however, the other criteria are strictly weaker than their corresponding strong counterparts.

In defining weak class graphs along with the corresponding testing criteria, we have effectively eliminated the infeasibility barriers to automatic generation of sequences to satisfy the criteria. As discussed above, I_1 is empty because of our restriction to defensive modules. For weak class graphs, it should be evident that both I_2 and I_3 are empty, in that these types of infeasibility are associated with labeled edges, which no longer exist. I_4 may be nonempty, but for defensive modules, any subpaths in I_4 are defect revealing (because such subpaths represent crashes); their inclusion is therefore desirable. We have also eliminated the problem that it is impossible to generate subpaths to drive all of the conditions associated with control operations, because it is now necessary only to cover one such condition.

In our results, we are interested in showing not only that it is possible to efficiently generate operation sequences satisfying the criteria, but that it is possible to generate minimum-length operation sequences satisfying the criteria. To this end, it is also necessary to place two additional restrictions:

- We exclude form consideration class modules containing operations involving multiple definitions and multiple uses of the class (e.g., a class containing an operation $Equal(s1, s2)$, where $s1$ and $s2$ contain instances of the type).

- In applying the data flow–based criteria, we restrict our attention to data flow related to the type exported by the class being tested. That is, when constructing D and U in the weak class graph, an operation is assumed to contain a definition (use) only if it defines (uses) an instance of the class being tested. Definitions and uses involving other types are ignored. We do not exclude classes containing operations involving foreign types; rather, we simply ignore such types in the data flow analysis.

The first of these assumptions is indeed restrictive, while the second assumption weakens the amount of testing we do. However, it is possible to relax these assumptions; we consider this issue in section 4.2.

Under these conditions, we are now able to show that it is possible to efficiently generate minimum-length sequences of operations that satisfy most of the weak criteria (except weak du-path coverage) for defensive modules. We also are able to state, in each case, the exact length of such a minimum-length sequence as a function of the number of operations. Before discussing these results, we note that our use of these weak versions of the criteria, as well as the two additional assumptions above, substantially weaken the degree of testing demanded. This would appear to reduce the significance of our results. However, testing to satisfy the weak criteria at least tests certain interesting combinations of operations and has the virtue of being fully automatable. Moreover, in all cases, it is easy to see that a sequence that satisfies a weak criterion is simply a subsequence of the sequence required to satisfy its strong counterpart. Thus, satisfaction of the weak criteria can be viewed as a starting point for achieving satisfaction of the strong criteria, providing the ability at least to automate a subset of the test-generation process. We consider this issue further in section 4.2.

Because of our restrictions involving data flow between operations, we are able to classify operations into three categories: pure OUT operations define a class instance without using it, pure IN operations use a class instance without defining it, and IN-OUT operations both use and define the class instance. In the theorems below, we assume there are n total operations in the class, of which there are a pure OUT operations $A_1, A_2, \ldots, A_a$, b IN-OUT operations $B_1, B_2, \ldots, B_b$, and c pure IN operations $C_1, C_2, \ldots, C_c$. We assume that $a \geq 1$, because there must always be at least one pure OUT operation at the beginning of a sequence to ensure that the class instance is defined before it is used. We also assume that there is at least one operation that uses the class, i.e., $b + c \geq 1$. We would expect any legitimate class to satisfy these restrictions on a, b, and c, so these assumptions are made without loss of generality.

We refer to a pure OUT or an IN-OUT operation as a definition operation; a use operation denotes either an IN-OUT or a pure OUT operation. Also, we assume that there is only one instance of one type of class under consideration. Our results are summarized as follows:

Theorem 4.1. A minimum-length sequence of operations that satisfies weak node coverage can be found in polynomial time.

Proof. The following sequence contains each operation exactly one time, for a total of $n = a + b + c$ operations: $A_1, A_2, \ldots, A_a, B_1, B_2, \ldots, B_b, C_1, C_2, \ldots, C_c$. Obviously, this is a minimum-length sequence that satisfies weak node coverage. It can be constructed in $\mathscr{O}(n)$ time. □

Theorem 4.2. A minimum-length sequence of operations that satisfies weak branch coverage can be found in polynomial time.

Proof. The flow graph has $n = a + b + c$ nodes, each of which has indegree n and outdegree n, so the flow graph is Eulerian. There are a total of n^2 arcs, so the minimum-length sequence must have at least $n^2 + 1$ operations. Denote the n nodes by $V_1, V_2, \ldots, V_n$, where V_1 is a pure OUT operation that is the desired starting and ending vertex for a Eulerian cycle. The following sequence forms an Eulerian cycle with exactly n^2 arcs and $n^2 + 1$ operations:

$V_1, V_1,$
$V_2, V_2, V_1,$
$V_3, V_3, V_2, V_3, V_1,$
$V_4, V_4, V_3, V_4, V_2, V_4, V_1,$
$V_5, V_5, V_4, V_5, V_3, V_5, V_2, V_5, V_1,$
$\ldots$
$V_n, V_n, V_{n-1}, V_n, V_{n-2}, V_n, \ldots, V_n, V_3, V_n, V_2, V_n, V_1$

This sequence satisfies weak branch coverage and can be constructed in $\mathscr{O}(n^2)$ time. □

Theorem 4.3. A minimum-length sequence of operations that satisfies weak definition coverage can be found in polynomial time.

Proof. Each occurrence of a use operation corresponds only to the most recently preceding definition operation, so there are at lest $a + b$ use operations in the sequence. Also, each pure OUT operation appears at least once, which requires a additional operations in the sequence. So the minimum length sequence must have at least $2a + b$ operations. The following sequence satisfies weak definition coverage and has exactly $2a + b$ operations: $A_1, C_1, A_2, C_1, \ldots, A_{a-1}, C_1, A_a, B_1, B_2, \ldots, B_b, C_1$. [As a special case, if $c = 0$, then substitute B_1 for all occurrences of C_1.] This sequence can be constructed in $\mathscr{O}(n)$ time. □

Theorem 4.4. A minimum-length sequence of operations that satisfies weak use coverage can be found in polynomial time.

Proof. There are $a + b$ definition operations, each of which has $b + c$ uses. Each occurrence of a use operation corresponds only to the most recently preceding definition operation, so there are at least $(a + b)(b + c)$ use operations in the sequence. Also, each pure OUT operation appears at least b times (once leading to each IN-OUT operation), which requires ab additional operations in the sequence. So the minimum length sequence must have at least $ab + (a + b)(b + c)$ operations.

To construct such a sequence, first consider the following sequence s with $2ab$ operations:

$$A_1, B_1, A_1, B_2, \ldots, A_1, B_b,$$
$$A_2, B_1, A_2, B_2, \ldots, A_2, B_b,$$
$$\ldots$$
$$A_{a-1}, B_1, A_{a-1}, B_2, \ldots, A_{a-1}, B_b,$$
$$A_a, B_1, A_a, B_2, \ldots, A_a, B_b.$$

Let d denote the sequence $C_1, C_2, \ldots, C_c$ with c operations. Let e denote the sequence with $b^2 + 1$ operations formed by Eulerian cycle through $B_1, B_2, \ldots, B_b$, starting and ending at B_b. [e can be found as described in Theorem 4.2]. Next, insert d into s after the first occurrence of each A_i and each B_j and substitute e for the final B_b in s. This yields the sequence

$$A_1, d, B_1, d, A_1, B_2, d, \ldots, A_1, B_b, d,$$
$$A_2, d, B_1, A_2, B_2, \ldots, A_2, B_b,$$
$$\ldots$$
$$A_{a-1}, d, B_1, A_{a-1}, B_2, \ldots, A_{a-1}, B_b,$$
$$A_a, d, B_1, A_a, B_2, \ldots, A_a, c.$$

This modified sequence satisfies weak use coverage and has exactly $2ab + b^2 + ac + bc$ operations. This sequence can be constructed in $\mathcal{O}(n^2)$ time. ☐

Theorem 4.5. A minimum-length sequence of operations that satisfies weak du-path coverage can neither be found nor tested in polynomial time.

Proof. Consider the special case in which $a = 1$ and $b = 0$, so that the number of distinct operations is given by $n = 1 + c$. But the number of distinct simple paths of length c leading from definition A_1 is $c! = (n-1)!$, and each operation in any given sequence is the final operation of at most one path of length c. Therefore, no polynomial-length sequence that satisfies weak du-path coverage can exist. ☐

We conclude this section by noting some results concerning the relationships among the criteria. The subsumption relation is commonly used to compare testing criteria [10, 19] and can be defined for the sequence testing criteria as follows (as in Zweben et al. [7]): a sequence testing criterion $C1$ subsumes $C2$ if, for every class module and specification, every sequence satisfying $C1$ also satisfies $C2$. The following theorem is then trivial.

Theorem 4.6. The following subsumption relationships hold:

- Node coverage subsumes weak node coverage.
- Branch coverage subsumes weak branch coverage.
- Definition coverage subsumes weak definition coverage.

- Use coverage subsumes weak use coverage.
- Du-path coverage subsumes weak du-path coverage. ☐

Perhaps a more interesting observation concerns the subsumption relationships among the different weak criteria. With strong criteria, use coverage and branch coverage are incomparable, whereas use coverage subsumes both definition and node coverage [7]. It is also shown that du-path coverage is incomparable to all of the other criteria [7].[5] These relationships are depicted in Figure 2.[6]

With weak criteria, there are some additional subsumptions where none held before. In particular, du-path coverage subsumes use coverage because there is always a feasible edge from every definition to every use; therefore, there is always a feasible simple path from every definition to every use. Hence, it is necessary to cover every definition-use association wit du-path coverage. In addition, weak branch coverage subsumes weak use coverage because every definition-use association may be covered on a single branch (i.e., there is a branch between every definition node and every use node and it is not necessary to follow that branch with specific labeled edges in order to cover the definition-use association). The other subsumptions and nonsubsumptions hold correspondingly for the strong and weak analogs. The relationships among the weak criteria are depicted in Figure 3.

Because subsumption is transitive, weak branch coverage and weak du-path coverage both subsume weak node coverage, even though there are no explicit edges associated with these relationships in Figure 3. Also all of the weak criteria (except weak definition coverage) subsume strong node coverage. As pointed out earlier, weak node coverage and strong node coverage are equivalent (i.e., each subsumes the other).

4.2 An Implementation Model

In deriving the theoretical results of the previous section, several simplifying assumptions were needed. Our intention in this section is to show that, despite

---

[5] If the only path between a definition and a use contains a cycle, then du-path coverage does not require coverage of that definition-use association, which may leave certain branches and nodes uncovered as well. However, the other criteria do not subsume du-path coverage either, because in general, du-path coverage is substantially more demanding.

[6] These relationships differ from the corresponding relationships among the analogous conventional testing criteria developed by Frankl and Weyuker [10]. The details involving this discrepancy are discussed in Zweben et al. [7]

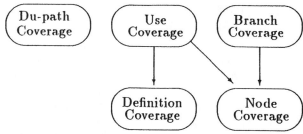

Figure 2. Strong criteria.

those assumptions, the results of the previous section are still useful for implementing practically useful tool support for the class-testing criteria. In particular, we will show that the algorithms identified in the theorems of section 4.1 can be used even when the simplifying assumptions are relaxed.

Our simplifying assumptions of the previous section fall into three categories: 1) restrictions on the set of classes to which the criteria apply; 2) restrictions weakening the criteria; and 3) simplifications to the data flow model. In the remaining discussion, we address these categories separately.

4.2.1 Restrictions on classes. In section 4.1, we restricted applicability of the weak criteria to defensive modules (i.e., modules without domain restrictions on the operations). It is possible to relax this restriction and still use the weak criteria as part of an overall testing paradigm, thus allowing us to automate the sequence generation process. We assume, as in Weide et al. [11], that if domain restrictions are to be placed, then it should be possible using one or more operations on the class (or on other classes) to check whether the domain restriction is violated. For example, if POP is not to be applied to an empty stack, then it should be possible to check with another operation to determine whether the stack is empty. Using this assumption,

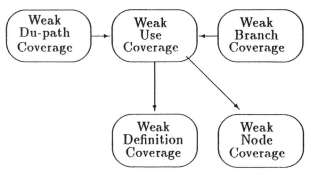

Figure 3. Weak criteria.

we can characterize an implementation model for using the weak criteria to test nondefensive modules. We use branch coverage as an example (Table 7).

This implementation model permits weak branch coverage to be applied to a nondefensive module. Of course, the guarantee of obtaining minimum-length coverage is no longer applicable because of the undecidability of whether edges are type 1 infeasible. However, the basic algorithm identified in Theorem 4.2 can be used to generate the initial sequence. Similar models can be developed for applying the other weak coverage criteria to nondefensive modules.

The above model is only for applying weak branch coverage to nondefensive modules. We consider how a weak coverage criterion can be converted into the corresponding strong coverage criterion in Section 4.2.2.

4.2.2 Restrictions weakening the criteria. The class-testing criteria were substantially weakened from their original definitions in Zweben et al. [7] to derive the results of the previous section. We do not suggest that the weak criteria are, in themselves, completely worthless. In terms of cost, there is sub-

Table 7. Applying Weak Branch Coverage to Nondefensive Modules

1. Automatically generate a sequence to satisfy weak branch coverage.
2. Obtain the domain restrictions. These could be obtained automatically from the formal specifications (assuming the specifications are parsable) or manually from the tester.
3. Modify the sequence generated in step 1 as follows: embed every operation with a domain restriction inside an *if* statement that checks whether the domain restriction is satisfied. For example, if the domain restriction that *pop* could not be applied to an empty stack were present, then every invocation of *pop* would be converted to the following:

    if not IS_EMPTY(*s*) then
        POP(*s*)

4. Test the resulting sequence, recording (automatically) whether any domain restrictions are violated (and the corresponding operation not executed). In particular, the edge consisting of the operation preceding the violation followed by the violated operation (i.e., the operation whose domain restrictions are violated) is recorded as "tentatively (type 1) infeasible."
5. Manually examine the tentatively infeasible operations to determine whether they are really infeasible, or whether there is another sequence preceding the edge that will allow the edge to be executed (i.e., without violating the domain restriction). Then execute any such sequences until all tentatively infeasible edges have been characterized as "definitely infeasible" or have been executed.

stantial benefit in the fact that sequences satisfying weak criteria can be automatically generated. Moreover, all of the criteria except weak definition coverage require executing all of the operations (i.e., they all subsume strong node coverage); some of the weak criteria require executing a substantial number of operation interactions (e.g., weak branch coverage requires executing a sequence of at least $n^2 + 1$ operations).

However, even if a strong form of coverage is desired, the analogous weak-coverage criterion can be used to automatically bootstrap the testing process. For example, an implementation model for strong branch coverage is presented in Table 8.

Similar implementation models can be provided for achieving strong definition and use coverage from their weaker analogs. Of course, as pointed out earlier, weak node coverage is equivalent to strong node coverage (so there is nothing additional to do), and sequences satisfying weak du-path coverage can-

Table 8. Obtaining Strong Branch Coverage from Weak Branch Coverage

1. Automatically generate a sequence to satisfy weak branch coverage.
2. Conduct testing using this sequence. This will involve execution the operations in the sequence and monitoring the results of each operation. (If formal specifications are provided, it may be possible to automatically check the results of each of operation; we do not consider this issue here.) If an error is observed, we assume that the tester will fix the error before proceeding; thus, the weak branch coverage sequence may be partially repeated many times before actually completing the sequence.
3. As the weak branch coverage is completed, monitor (using the automated tool) the condition returned by each control operation on each branch emanating from that operation. The tool should compile a list of the branches that need to be covered in order to cover all branches in the strong class graph. Some of these branches may not be feasible.
4. For each control operation, manually find a sequence of operations (if one exists) that drives the control operation to **true** and manually find a sequence of operations (if one exists) that drives the control operation to **false**. The tool should then be used to prepend these sequences as appropriate to all uncovered branches. For example, if there is a branch (IS_ EMPTY, **true**, PUSH) that is uncovered, the tool should prepend the sequence that drives IS_EMPTY to **true** to this branch. If no sequence can be found that appears to drive a control operation to a particular condition, then we assume that the sequence is type 2 (and/or type 3) infeasible and the branches associated with the desired condition are eliminated in the list returned by step 3.
5. Test the concatenation of all the sequences generated in the previous step. This may require the repeated execution of certain sequences (because it may be necessary to drive a control operation to **true** or **false** more than once each). The tool should allow an option that permits the user to avoid restepping individually through the operations in a sequence that is repeated.

not be generated in polynomial time (so there is no basis from which to start).

4.2.3 Simplifications to the data flow model. We consider simplifications to the data flow model introduced in section 4.1. In particular, we made two simplifying assumptions: 1) data flow with respect to multiple types is ignored (for the purposes of satisfying the data flow criteria, we only consider data flow with respect to the class being tested), and 2) we only permit classes containing a maximum of one definition and one use of the class per operation. In this section, we discuss how these assumptions can be eliminated.

We first consider the assumption that data flow is only measured with respect to the type exported by the module being tested. It is certainly possible to augment the automatically generated sequence to include testing of any additional definition-use associations not already covered involving other types. We can also apply basically the same algorithms used to generate sequences satisfying weak definition and use coverage independently to each individual type found in the parameter lists of the class operations.[7] Using these algorithms, we can generate minimum-length sequences satisfying the desired weak criterion with respect to each type. Of course, the concatenation of all of these sequences may not be of minimum length, but it may be possible to obtain some optimization through an automated tool that prevents definition-use associations appearing in more than one sequence from being covered more than once.

The other issue involves permitting modules containing operations with multiple definitions or multiple uses of the same type in the parameter lists. An example of the problem of blindly using the weak coverage criteria to generate sequences involving such operations is as follows. Consider a sequence where there is an operation with multiple uses of a type, and there has only been one instance of the type previously produced as an OUT parameter in the sequence. In this case, there are not enough defined instances of the type to be used to supply distinct parameter values to the operation in question. An example of this problem is the sequence ⟨CREATE; PUSH; POP; EQUAL⟩ (assuming all of

---

[7] Actually, it may not be possible to apply the exact same algorithms given in the theorems of section 4.1 because some of the properties assumed to hold for the exported type (in terms of number of definition and use operations) may not hold for other parameter types. However, it is possible to generate other configurations of operations to achieve the same results.

these operations were defined for a particular stack module); in such a case, only one stack instance is produced by CREATE and manipulated by PUSH and POP. Yet, to test EQUAL, two stack instances are needed as IN parameters.

One way to address this problem is simply to use the same actual parameter for all instances in an operation invocation. For example, the driver program could invoke EQUAL(S, S) in the above case. This would permit the driver to be well formed and would avoid the type of data flow anomaly where there is a use without a preceding definition. In fact, this would probably be an adequate solution in applying the weak control flow criteria (such as weak branch coverage) because there is no particular semantic requirement (e.g., in the above case, we do not care whether EQUAL returns **true** or **false**). In the case of a control operation, we simply manually augment the sequence to produce the other Boolean value if strong branch coverage is desired.

For data flow criteria, this solution is probably inadequate, because we are not fully taking into account the data flow occurring among the operations. In particular, if there are two operations, A with a definitions and B with b uses, then it may be desirable to attempt to cover $a * b$ definition-use associations between the two operations, thus involving different permutations of actual parameters. For example, with the operation MULTI_DEF containing two definitions and MULTI_USE containing two uses, we would probably like to generate at least the following sequence:

MULTI_DEF(a, b);
MULTI_USE(a, b);
MULTI_USE(b, a);

Of course, we could generate weak coverage sequences using the algorithms discussed previously, and then manually argument the sequence to capture additional data flow. However, the automatic generation of some of these permutations appears to be tractable as well, by a relatively simple extension of the previous algorithms. Fully resolving this issue is an interesting open problem.

5. CONCLUSION

We have provided a foundational theory for the application of conventional flow graph–based testing strategies to object-oriented class modules. In this theory, we have clarified the meaning of basic concepts of flow graph–based class testing, including concepts such as the "feasibility" of a flow graph edge or path. Unlike the analogous concept of feasi-

bility in conventional software flow graphs, several distinct forms of feasibility were identified for class flow graphs. Our theory has shown that analogs of conventional white-box testing strategies based on flow graphs can be applied to object-oriented class modules, with or without formal specifications. This is a generalization of Zweben et al. [7], who restrict the application of the criteria to modules having formal, model-based specifications.

We have also developed versions of flow graph–based criteria for which, under certain restrictions, efficient algorithms can be provided to generate satisfactory minimum-length sequences of operations. Although these restrictions are indeed met by certain realistic testing scenarios, we have shown that, even in their absence, we can still use the same algorithms to assist in automating the testing process. Also, our algorithms may be used to obtain partial satisfaction of stronger versions of the criteria, although manual intervention by the tester may be required.

Future work will fall into two categories. A prototype testing environment to support the ideas presented here would be of significant practical value to the object-oriented community and could provide proof-of-principle with respect to the ideas introduced here. Theoretically speaking, as discussed in section 4.2.3, work is also needed to further develop the data flow criteria. In particular, the criteria should be defined to measure data flow with respect to an arbitrary number of definitions and uses of a variety of types. Ideally, it should be possible to guarantee results regarding the efficient automation of the criteria defined in this manner.

ACKNOWLEDGMENT

This research was supported in part by National Science Foundation grant CDA-9100826 and by Air Force Office of Scientific Research contract F49620-90-C-09076.

REFERENCES

1. L. Bouge, N. Choquet, L. Fribourg, and M. Gaudel, Test Set Generation from Algebraic Specifications Using Logic Programming, *J. Syst. Software* 6, 343–360 (1986).

2. R. Doong and P. Frankl, Case studies on testing object-oriented programs, in *Proceedings of the Fourth Symposium on Software Testing, Analysis and Verification*, IEEE Computer Society Press, Washington D.C., 1991, pp. 165–177.

3. J. Gannon, P. McMullin, and R. Hamlet, Data Ab-

straction, Implementation, Specification and Testing, *ACM Trans. Progr. Lang. Syst.* 3, 211–223 (1981).

4. M. Gaudel and B. Marre, Generation of test data from algebraic specifications, in *Proceedings of the Second Workshop on Software Testing*, IEEE Computer Society Press, Washington, D.C., 1988, pp. 138–139.

5. P. Jalote and M. Caballero, Automated test case generation for data abstraction, in *Proceedings of COMP-SAC '88*, IEEE Computer Society Press, Washington, D.C., 1988, pp. 205–210.

6. P. Jalote, Testing the Completeness of Specifications, *IEEE Trans. Software Eng.* 15, 526–531 (1989).

7. S. Zweben, W. Heym, and J. Kimich, Systematic Testing of Data Abstractions Based on Software Specifications, *J. Software Test. Verificat. Reliabil.* 1, 39–55 (1992).

8. B. Liskov and J. Guttag, *Abstraction and Specification in Program Development*, McGraw-Hill, New York, 1986.

9. J. M. Spivey, *The Z Notation: A Reference Manual*, Prentice-Hall, Englewood Cliffs, New Jersey, 1989.

10. P. Frankl and E. Weyuker, An Applicable Family of Data Flow Testing Criteria, *IEEE Trans Software Eng.* SE-14, 1483–1498 (1988).

11. B. Weide, W. Ogden, and S. Zweben, Reusable software components, in *Advances in Computers*, vol. 33, (M. C. Yovits, ed.), Academic Press, San Diego, California, 1991, pp. 1–65.

12. E. Weyuker, The Applicability of program Schema Results to Programs, *Int. J. Comp. Info. Sci.* 8, 387–403 (1979).

13. E. V. Berard, Creating Reusable Ada Software, EVB Software Engineering Technical Reports, Frederick, Maryland, 1987.

14. P. Hibbard, A. Hisgen, J. Rosenberg, and M. Sherman, Programming in Ada: Examples, in *Studies in Ada Style*, (P. Hibbard, A. Hisgen, J. Rosenberg, M. Shaw, M. Sherman, eds.) Springer-Verlag, New York, 1983, pp. 35–101.

15. G. Booch, *Software Components with Ada*, Benjamin/Cummings, Menlo park, California, 1987.

16. B. Meyer, *Object-Oriented Software Construction*, Prentice-Hall, Englewood Cliffs, New Jersey, 1988.

17. A. Parrish and S. Zweben, Analysis and Refinement of Software Test Data Adequacy Properties, *IEEE Trans. Software Eng.* 565–581 (1991).

18. A. Parrish and S. Zweben, Clarifying Some Fundamental Concepts in Software Testing, *IEEE Trans. Software Eng.*, in press.

19. J. Gourlay, A Mathematical Framework for the Investigation of Testing, *IEEE Trans. Software Eng.* SE-9, 686–709 (1983).

Paul C. Jorgensen and Carl Erickson

Object-Oriented Integration Testing

Object-oriented software development raises important testing issues. Many of these stem from attempts to directly apply theoretical constructs and techniques of traditional software development and testing to object-oriented software. We examine this traditional heritage here, with special emphasis on assumptions and practices that need to be modified or replaced.

We identify five levels of object-oriented testing; four of these map nicely into the commonly accepted unit, integration, and system levels of traditional software testing. (Placement of the remaining level is primarily a management consideration.) We also identify two new testing constructs and a directed graph notation that helps formalize object-oriented integration testing. These are illustrated with an object-oriented formulation of an automated teller machine (ATM) system. The source code (Objective-C) for this system is available from the authors.

We begin with an important distinction: structure vs. behavior. Most of the popular notations used in software development (E/R models, data flow diagrams, structure charts, PDLs, and so on) portray software structure: the components, relationships among these, the interfaces, control and dataflow, and so on. Such information is certainly needed by software developers, but it is only moderately useful to testers. For simple programs, we can understand behavior in terms of structure, but there is a relatively low threshold of program complexity beyond which this derivation becomes untenable. Software testing is fundamentally concerned with behavior (what it does), and not structure (what it is). Customers understand software in terms of its behavior, not its structure. The object-oriented testing constructs we introduce here are deliberately behavioral rather than structural.

To provide a context for object-oriented integration testing, we highlight the traditional software (and system) testing notions that have special implications for object-oriented software testing. Traditional software is

• written in an imperative language
• described by a functional decomposition
• developed in a waterfall life cycle
• separated into three levels of testing

Since these often do not apply directly to object-oriented software, they represent latent assumptions which must be revisited.

Most software developers use an imperative language, in which the order of source statements determines the execution order of compiled object instructions. The familiar languages (Fortran, Cobol, C, Pascal, Ada, and assembly languages) are all imperative, as opposed to declarative languages (e.g., Prolog), in which the source statement order has little to do with execution order. Imperative languages are so widely used (and for so long), they have become "natural" to most programmers. All of structured programming, with the basic control structures of sequence, selection, and repetition, and the single-entry, single-exit precept, is directed at imperative languages.

Imperative languages lend themselves to a rigorous description as a directed graph, or program graph [8], in which nodes are statements (or statement fragments) and edges represent control flow sequence. From this starting point, several graph theory-based testing constructs have been defined: DD-Paths, define/reference nodes, definition clear paths, and program slices, to name a few. These all help the tester give a more accurate description of what is being tested, and all lead to useful test coverage metrics.

In contrast, declarative languages suppress sequentiality, thereby sacrificing the descriptive benefits of directed graphs. (On the other hand, declarative languages are naturally represented by more formal notations, such as the predicate or the lambda calculus, which in turn open possibilities of formal proofs of correctness.)

The event-driven nature of object-oriented systems forces a "declarative spirit" on testing. This is not evident at the unit level (most object-oriented programming languages are imperative), but it is pronounced at the integration and system levels.

Functional decomposition is the natural extension of the systems analysis introduced as a problem-solving technique by the U.S. Army in the 1930s [1]. Known equally often by its synonym, top-down development, functional decomposition can be either prescriptive or descriptive. The prescriptive view (which is enforced in functional languages such as Lisp) demands that software development begins "at the top," and proceeds by subdividing functionality into successively lower levels of detail, resulting in a hierarchy, or functional decomposition tree.

The descriptive view is more tolerant of the way people work, often flitting across levels of abstraction in seemingly random orders [5], and reinforcing analysis with synthesis, a symbiosis found in most other engineering disciplines. The end result is the same: a tree-like decomposition of system functionality into components that exhibit several senses of hierarchy: levels of abstraction, lexical inclusion, information hiding, and corresponding data structures which may have parallel decompositions into various user-defined types.

Functional decomposition has been the mainstay of software development since the 1950s, partly because it fits so well with other hierarchies: organizational structures, program language packaging, hardware packaging (system, frame, rack, card, . . .) and the fan-out of activities in the waterfall model of software development. Despite these reinforcing morphisms, functional decomposition has its vulnerable points. Decomposing a problem so that existing components (to be reused) appear in the tree is tricky, and the decomposition criteria used have an enormous impact on the resulting system. The rival strategy, composition, has been all but lost in the structural revolution.

Functional decomposition has deep implications for testing: first, it emphasizes levels of abstraction (hence, levels of testing), and second, it creates questions of integration order (top-down or bottom-up). Most important (and insidious) is that it stresses structure over behavior.

The well-known waterfall model of software development is sometimes depicted as a "V" in which the development phases (requirements specification, preliminary design, and detailed design) are at levels corresponding to system, integration, and unit testing. The sequential nature of the waterfall model predisposes a bottom-up testing approach in which unit testing produces separately tested components which are eventually integrated to support system testing. The integration portion of this is driven by the functional decomposition tree, where there is another top-down or bottom-up question. Whichever alternative is chosen, it is important to note that the goal is to fit the units together into the functional decomposition tree. Thus the structure of the system is the goal, not the behavior.

Since the mid-1980s, the waterfall model has been critized for several fundamental defects [1]. Most of these pertain to the development side of the model, and to project management considerations, rather than to testing. We believe that the preference of structure over behavior as the goal of integration testing will be recognized as yet another shortcoming of the waterfall model.

The three widely accepted levels of testing—unit, integration, and system need some clarification. There are several definitions of a unit:

- a single, cohesive function
- a function which, when coded, fits on one page
- the smallest separately compilable segment of code
- the amount of code that can be written in 4 to 40 hours
- a task in a work breakdown structure
- code that is assigned to one person
- code that one person designs, codes, and tests in a three-month period

Curiously, many organizations that specifically conduct unit testing have not chosen their definition of a software unit. However defined, a unit is tested "by itself," with adjacent software units being replaced by stubs and drivers to emulate inputs and outputs. The goal of unit testing is to verify that, taken by itself, the unit functions correctly. (Another view is to see how the unit functions, assuming everything else is perfect.)

Once units are separately tested, they are integrated together. Integration testing is the least well understood of the three levels. Part of this can be seen in the symmetries with the waterfall phases: unit testing with detailed design, integration testing with preliminary design, and system testing with requirements specification. These symmetries are comfortable in that the basis for test case identification is clear. Of these, the unit level is best understood (both in terms of detailed design and unit testing), followed by the system level. The "leftovers" are given to preliminary design and integration testing.

Since the mid-1970s, various module interconnect languages have been proposed [3] as descriptions of the information to be produced by preliminary design. In general, this includes the levels of functional decomposition and the major interfaces among components at these levels. This forces the goal of integration testing to address these primarily structural considerations. Here are some frequently used views:

- the gradual replacement of stubs and drivers by separately tested units
- pairwise integration, in which each unit is integrated with its adjacent units
- bottom-up integration guided by the functional decomposition tree
- top-down integration guided by the functional decomposition tree
- "big bang" integration where all units are thrown together at once

The common thread (and deficiency) among these possibilities is that they stress structure and interfaces, rather than behavior. They all presume that correct behavior is guaranteed by correct structure and interfaces.

Where does integration testing end and system testing begin? Distinctions based on waterfall phases beg the question, because it is equally difficult to decide where requirements specification ends and preliminary design begins. We offer an explicit distinction: system testing is

Figure 1. Directed-graph representation of the object network. Three Method-Message Paths (MM-Paths 1, 2, and 3), and two Atomic System Functions (ASFs 4 and 13) are shown.

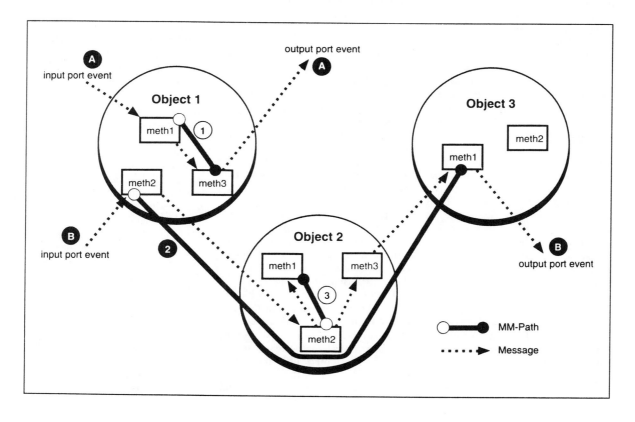

The declarative aspect of object-oriented software lies primarily in its event-driven nature. *Dynamic binding also creates an indefiniteness that resembles that of declarative programs.*

conducted exclusively in terms of inputs and outputs that are visible at the port boundary of a system. A system tester can only have access to those port events that are available to the customer/user. In contrast, integration testing can access memory events and conditions that are invisible at the system level. Another place to see this demarcation is when a system is developed on one platform to be delivered on a different target platform. System testing can only occur on the target platform, while integration testing could occur on the development machine.

To the extent that object-oriented software is declarative, much of the descriptive power of graph theory-based structural testing techniques will not be applicable. Within an object, individual methods remain imperative. All object-oriented languages return control to the calling object when a message is "finished." (We consider a message to be the combination of a receiver object, a method name, and, optionally, method arguments.) The declarative aspect of object-oriented software lies primarily in its event-driven nature. Dynamic binding also creates an indefiniteness that resembles that of declarative programs.

Because the concept of a main program is minimized, there is no clearly defined integration structure. Thus there is no decomposition tree to impose the question of integration testing order of objects. We see this as an advantage for object-oriented integration testing; it is no longer natural to focus on structural testing orders.

The shift to composition (especially when reuse occurs) adds another dimension of difficulty to object-oriented software testing: it is impossible to ever know the full set of "adjacent" objects with which a given object may be composed. Taken by themselves, two objects may be correct; yet when they are composed, errors might result. We are reminded of M.C. Escher's paradoxical drawings which center on deliberate errors of composition. The usual response from the object-oriented community is that if the units (objects) are carefully defined and tested, any composition will work. This was the hope of information hiding as a decomposition criterion in traditional software development. We know from experience that this fails. We know also that unit testing can never reveal integration-level problems.

Object-oriented software development, especially in terms of composition and reuse, usually occurs in a non-waterfall development life cycle; most commonly one based on rapid prototyping, perhaps in conjunction with an incremental approach. The rival models (of waterfall) all have composition as their fundamental underlying strategy, and all make no presumptions about the completeness goal that was so central to waterfall-based practice. We expect to see movement in the direction of operational specification, likely beginning with some form of an executable specification. When requirements specifications are expressed in this way, they create a new problem: the need to make a dynamic-to-static transition. An essentially dynamic, executable specification must somehow lead to static implementation components. This is difficult with traditional languages; the transition is eased by the inherent dynamism of the object-oriented paradigm.

The final implication of traditional software development is that the levels of testing need clarification for object-oriented software. Two levels are clear: object methods are units, and object-oriented unit testing is simply the testing of these methods. Traditional functional and structural testing techniques are fully applicable to this level. At the system level, thread-based testing is completely compatible with object-oriented software. The notion of a thread [4] is a natural construct for system-level testing. Here are several views of a thread:

- a sequence of machine instructions
- a sequence of source instructions
- a scenario of normal usage
- a system-level test case
- a stimulus/response pair (per [2])
- the behavior that results from a sequence of system-level inputs
- an interleaved sequence of system inputs (stimuli) and outputs (responses)
- a sequence of transitions in a state machine description of the system

Threads exist independently of their potential representations. We can interpret a thread to be a sequence of method executions linked by messages in the object network. This will follow from the constructs.

Constructs for Object-Oriented Integration Testing

Taken together, the implications of traditional testing for object-oriented integration testing require an appropriate construct for the integration level. This construct should be compatible with composition, avoid the inappropriate structure-based goals of traditional integration testing, support the declarative aspect of object integration, and be clearly distinct from the unit- and system-level constructs.

We postulate five distinct levels of object-oriented testing:

- a method
- message quiescence
- event quiescence
- thread testing
- thread interaction testing

Taken together, **the implications of traditional testing for object-oriented integration testing** *require an appropriate construct for the integration level.*

An individual method is programmed in an imperative language and performs a single, cohesive function. As such, it corresponds to the unit level of traditional software testing, and both the traditional functional and structural techniques are applicable. As noted earlier, both thread and thread interaction testing are at the system level. To address the two remaining levels, we note that for both cases, method executions are linked by messages, and quiescence provides natural endpoints. This is shown by the object network in Figure 1, in which nodes (rectangles) are methods and edges (dashed lines) are messages. Objects (circles) are not directly represented in the graph; they show related collections of methods.

Definition: A Method/Message Path (MM-Path) is a sequence of method executions linked by messages.

An MM-Path starts with a method and ends when it reaches a method which does not issue any messages of its own. In terms of an executing process, we call this point *message quiescence.* Since MM-Paths are composed of linked method-message pairs in an object network, they interleave and branch off from other MM-Paths. We chose this name to be similar to the DD-Path (decision-to-decision path) construct of traditional structured unit testing; MM-Paths provide analogous descriptive capabilities to object-oriented integration testing. Figure 1 shows three MM-Paths (labeled 1, 2, and 3).

The second construct reflects the event-driven nature of object-oriented software. Execution of object-oriented software begins with an event, which we refer to as a port input event. This system-level input triggers the method-message sequence of an MM-Path. This initial MM-Path may trigger other MM-Paths. Finally, the sequence of MM-Paths should end with some system-level response (a port output event). When such a sequence ends, the system is quiescent, that is, the system is waiting for another port input event that initiates further processing. This fits well with the notion of a reactive system [6] that responds to events in its environment, and with the notion of a stimulus/response pair that is central to the SREM requirements specification technique [2]. Stimulus/response pairs are threads that begin with a stimulus (a port input event), traverse one or more MM-Paths, and culminate with one of several possible port output events. In the case of event-driven, GUI applications, poorly written software may not provide feedback for a user-induced input event, in which case the ending port event is null.

Definition. An Atomic System Function (ASF) is an input port event, followed by a set of MM-Paths, and terminated by an output port event.

An atomic system function is an elemental function visible at the system level. As such, ASFs constitute the point at which integration and system testing meet, which results in a more seamless flow between these two forms of testing. The output port event which defines the end of an ASF may have different values (including null) for multiple executions of the same ASF. Figure 1 shows two ASFs (labeled A and B at the start and stop points). ASF A is composed of a single MM-Path (1). ASF B is composed of MM-Paths 2 and 3.

Example

As a concrete example of the object-oriented testing constructs we have proposed, consider an automated teller machine (ATM) system. All ATM systems must deal with the entry of a customer's personal identification number (PIN), which is known only by the central bank and the customer. The customer's ATM card is encoded with a personal account number (PAN) and is read by the card reader device in the ATM to obtain an expected PIN from the bank. A customer has three chances to enter the correct PIN. Once a correct PIN has been entered, the user sees a screen requesting the transaction type. Otherwise a screen advises the customer that the ATM card will not be returned, and no access to ATM functions is provided.

The following steps occur after the user enters a card:

1. A screen requesting PIN entry is displayed
2. An interleaved sequence of digit key touches with audible and visual feedback
3. The possibility of cancellation by the customer before the full PIN is entered
4. Interdigit time-outs, followed by screens asking if the user needs more time
5. Entry of a yes/no response to the time-out screen
6. A system disposition (valid PIN entered or card retained)

A finite-state machine (FSM) description of PIN entry (to appear in [7]) contains an upper-level FSM with 8 states, 10 transitions, and 4 paths. Three of these states are decomposed to a lower-level FSM that contains 9 states, 18 transitions, and 14 paths, resulting in a cyclomatic complexity of 13.

Classes for ATM PIN Entry. We have implemented an ATM simulator on NEXTSTEP using Objective C. We use this system as a means to ground our work in real code, and as an illustration of our object-oriented testing constructs. The class hierarchy of the ATM simulator is shown in Figure 2, which shows only the classes for the problem domain; we used the standard NeXT AppKit classes for the graphical interface objects.

Identifying MM-Paths. Consider

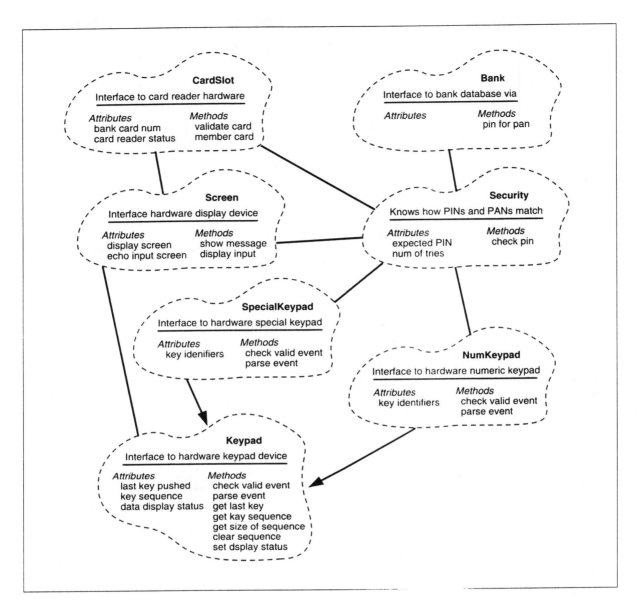

Figure 2. The class hierarchy for the ATM simulator

the following four sequences of behavior visible at the system level of the ATM:

1. Entry of a digit
2. Entry of a PIN
3. A simple transaction: PIN entry, select transaction type, present account details, conduct the operation, report results
4. An ATM session, containing two or more simple transactions

Digit entry (behavior sequence 1) is an example of a minimal MM-Path (see Figure 3). It begins with a port input event (key touch) which acts as a message to the NumKeypad:get

KeyEvents method. It completes (reaches message quiescence) with a message to the parseKeyEvent method to decode the key.

PIN Entry (behavior sequence 2) is an example of an atomic system function. It is composed of six MM-Paths, an input port event, and several possible output port events. Figure 4 shows a mainline portion, in which the correct PIN is entered on the first attempt; several error cases are not shown. The objects in these MM-Paths know about the length of a PIN, the number of bad entry attempts, the PAN/PIN for an account, which bank cards are members of the ATMs

network, and so forth. For clarity, Figure 4 has been simplified by removing the Timer object, and hence the PIN entry time-out. The MM-Path components of this ASF are listed in terms of Object:method sets.

It is instructive to consider where the longest MM-Path in this ASF should end: Screen:showMessage or NumKeypad:parseKeyEvent? The definition of the ASF makes this choice unambiguous, since ASFs are required to end in output port events. If the NumKeypad:parse-KeyEvent were chosen as the end of the PIN Entry ASF, the system would not be in a quiescent state at the end of the ASF. Figure 5 summarizes the PIN Entry ASF.

The simple transaction (behavior sequence 3) is a thread (which can be seen as a sequence of ASFs), and the ATM session (behavior sequence 4) is a sequence of several threads. As an organization for testing, the ASF level focuses on interaction among objects; the thread level entails interactions among ASFs; and the final level stresses thread interaction.

Examples of Errors. Integration testing of the ATM simulator revealed several errors which would not have been found with unit testing. The

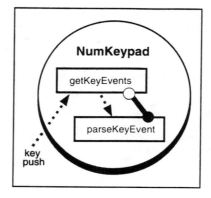

Figure 3. The Digit Entry MM-Path

error described here occurs as an interaction among methods of a single class.

Objective C classes have initialization methods to properly initialize instance variables defined in the class. Since every class inherits from at least one superclass (the Object class), the initialization method of a class should first invoke the initialization code it inherits, then perform the initialization specific to the class, thus ensuring that initialization occurs in the order of inheritance. The error that integration testing discovered was a lack of invocation of the superclass init method in the NumKeypad init method. As a result, the integer variable hideData was not initialized properly. This variable is used by the keypad driver to determine whether or not to send keystroke values to the screen, or just to send a symbol (such as an asterisk) indicating that a key was pressed. The init method in Key-

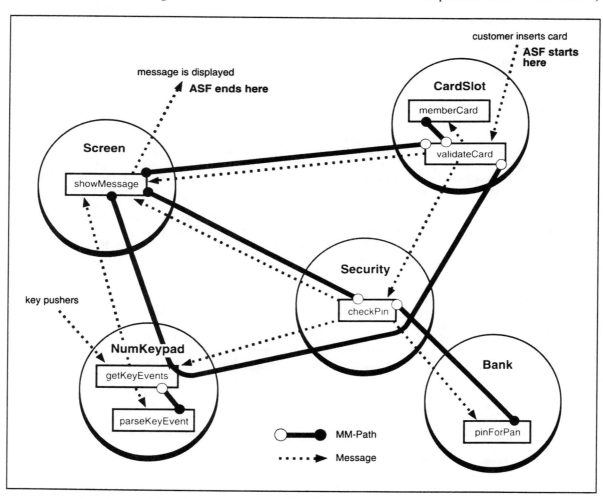

Figure 4. The PIN Entry Atomic System Function

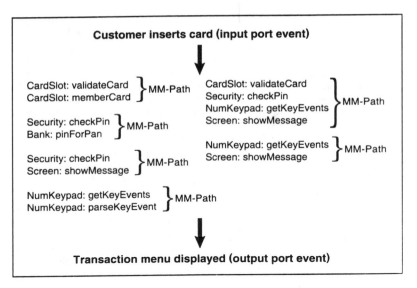

Customer inserts card (input port event)

⬇

CardSlot: validateCard
CardSlot: memberCard } MM-Path

Security: checkPin
Bank: pinForPan } MM-Path

Security: checkPin
Screen: showMessage } MM-Path

NumKeypad: getKeyEvents
NumKeypad: parseKeyEvent } MM-Path

CardSlot: validateCard
Security: checkPin
NumKeypad: getKeyEvents
Screen: showMessage } MM-Path

NumKeypad: getKeyEvents
Screen: showMessage } MM-Path

⬇

Transaction menu displayed (output port event)

pad sets hideData to TRUE. Since this code was not being invoked for NumKeypad, hideData was not properly initialized. The value it had by chance on allocation was 0, the same as FALSE. When we implemented the PIN Entry portion of the ATM, allocating a NumKeypad object to manager PIN entry, the error of not properly initializing the NumKeypad class was discovered, since the digits were echoed to the screen. Unit testing the init method of NumKeypad did not (in fact, could not) reveal the error because the error was the absence of a message call. Integration testing a NumKeypad object with a Screen and a Security object revealed the error.

Observations

The new constructs defined here result in a unified view of object-oriented testing, with fairly seamless transitions across the five levels discussed earlier. We wish to clarify some of our observations about this formulation. In Figure 6, the constructs of interest are entities in an E/R diagram. The first observation is that many-to-many relationships dominate.

An object may be involved in many threads, and threads entail many objects. Similarly, an object may be involved with many atomic system functions, and an ASF may entail many objects. These two mappings guarantee that objects are integrated,

Figure 5. PIN Entry ASF showing all included MM-Paths

and furthermore, the integration is grounded in behavioral rather than structural, considerations. One of the pitfalls of structural testing is the problem of infeasible paths. We might expect similar infeasible connections if objects were integrated with structural criteria. So far, our constructs have avoided the problem

Figure 6. An E/R model for the constructs of object-oriented testing

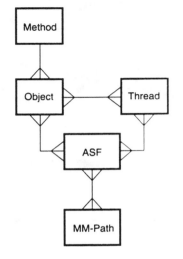

of structurally possible and behaviorally impossible paths.

Degenerate cases are sometimes instructive. In our usage of these constructs, we have noted the following:

• The shortest MM-Path consists of two methods linked by one message.
• The shortest ASF consists of an input port event, a minimal MM-Path, and an output port event.
• An MM-Path is maximal within an ASF, that is, an MM-Path ends either at the point of first message quiescence or with the output port event that ends an ASF.

ASFs sometimes have an initial MM-Path which connects to several MM-Paths that produce different port output events. Such ASFs correspond exactly to stimulus/response pairs. This is a seamless juncture between object-oriented integration testing and system(thread) testing.

The shortest thread consists of one ASF. This degeneracy can be compounded by the possibility of the single ASF consisting of a single MM-Path. In the ATM example, this degeneracy happens with digit entry.

We find that the five levels of object-oriented testing result in distinct, useful testing goals, as well as a bottom-up testing order. The lowest level tests individual methods as standalone functions. Once tested, these become nodes in the object network graph, where separately tested methods are connected by messages. Two levels of object integration are helpful, we test the MM-Paths first, and then test their interaction in an ASF. At the system level, the overlap from ASF testing to thread testing is helpful.

Thread interaction testing is beyond the scope of this article, but we note that such interaction is necessarily with respect to data items. If we took such data to be a mutant form of a message (uncertain destination, no return, but clearly a sender and receiver), the notation only needs a slight extension.

Two final observations: the new constructs are directly usable as the basis for test coverage metrics, and they work well with composition. For spatial reasons we deleted description of our solution to the time-out problems in the ATM example. To add timeouts, the composition affects the existing objects, MM-Paths, ASFs, and threads. What appears complex and intimidating turned out to be straightforward. From this limited experience, we conjecture that these constructs will be even more useful for object reuse, and the composition that must occur when a system is maintained. ▣

References

1. Agresti, W.A. *New Paradigms for Software Development*. IEEE Computer Society Press, Washington, D.C., 1986.
2. Alford, M. SREM at the age of eight: The distributed computing design. *IEEE Comput. 18*, 4 (Apr. 1985), 36–46.
3. DeRemer, F. and Kron, H.H. Programming-in-the-large vs. programming-in-the-small. *IEEE Trans. Softw. Eng. SE-2*, 2 (June 1976).
4. Deutsch, M.S. *Software Verification and Validation: Realistic Project Approaches*. Prentice-Hall, Englewood Cliffs, N.J., 1982.
5. Guindon, R. Knowledge exploited by experts during software systems design. Tech. Rep. STP-032-90, MCC, Austin, Tex., 1989.
6. Harel, D. and Pneuli, A. On the development of reactive systems. In *Logics and Models of Concurrent Systems*, K.R. Apt, Ed. Springer-Verlag, New York, 1985, pp. 477–498.
7. Jorgensen, P.C. *The Craft of Software Testing*. CRC Press, Boca Raton, Fla. To be published.
8. Paige, M.R. Program graphs, an algebra, and their implications for programming. *IEEE Trans. Softw. Eng. SE-1*, 3 (Sept. 1975).

About the Authors:

PAUL C. JORGENSEN is an associate professor of computer science at Grand Valley State University. He also has a consulting practice which combines his research interests with 20 years of industrial software development experience. email: jorgensp@gvsu.edu

CARL ERICKSON is an assistant professor of computer science at Grand Valley State University. His professional interests include object-oriented and distributed information systems, and computer science education. He is a registered NEXTSTEP developer, and an active NEXTSTEP consultant email: erickson @oak.csis.gvsu.edu

Authors' Present Address Computer Science and Information Systems Department, Grand Valley State University, Allendale, MI 49401-9403.

Chapter 4

Regression Testing

Software systems undergo continual changes due to: (1) software deficiencies including inadequacy and incorrectness; (2) hardware changes or hardware deficiencies; (3) new functional requirements; (4) economic savings; and (5) schedule compression or extension.

Regression testing is the process that is performed after changes have been made to a software system. Its purpose is to ensure that the modified software still satisfies its intended functionality. Changes in a part of a software system may affect other parts due to dependencies among the components of the system. Sometimes, the changes may affect only a small number of components but other times they may affect many components. The scope of change impact depends on many factors including the dependency relation among the components, the changes, and the changed components.

The main concern in regression testing is how to effectively and efficiently identify the changes and their impact so that testing can be focused to the changed and affected components. Another consideration in regression testing is reuse of existing test cases and test suites. The papers selected for this chapter address these issues.

The paper by Kung et al. [kung94g] proposed an approach based on a test model called object relation diagram (ORD). It captures the classes and their dependencies, like inheritance, aggregation, and association. A reverse engineering method has been developed to extract the classes' and their dependencies from an OO program and present them in the ORD. Changes to an OO program are automatically identified by comparing two different versions of program source code. The changes then are used to determine which of the classes are changed. Through the dependencies among the classes the impact of the changes are identified. Regression testing then can focus on testing the changed and affected classes.

After identifying the changed and affected classes, a tester will encounter the problem of determining in which order the classes should be tested. This is because in an OO program the classes may be dependent on each other. Therefore when testing a class that invokes methods of other untested classes, test stubs need to be constructed to simulate the untested methods. In some cases the test stub construction may be very costly. The paper also describes a method that computes the minimum cost test order for testing the classes.

The second paper [roth94a], by Rothermel and Harrold, extended their results on selecting retest suites for conventional programs to OO programs. The problem addressed is which of the existing test cases must be rerun to determine whether the modified program still fulfills its functionality. One possible way is to select test cases that will produce different results. To do this, control dependencies and data dependencies among the statements and methods of an OO program and its modified version are identified and represented in two dependency graphs. From these graphs an algorithm identifies the statements in the modified program that will produce different results. Test cases, which traverse through these statements, need to be rerun to test the modified program. Additional test cases are needed to test the new functionalities.

The third paper [hsia97b], by Hsia et al., is a follow-up of the first paper and addresses the same problem as the second paper. However, Hsia et al.'s paper presents a simpler but totally different approach. Unlike Rothermel and Harrold's approach, which analyzes the source codes of the OO program and its modified version, Hsia et al.'s approach involves inserting software probes into the source program. These probes record which test cases touch which of the classes. This information then can be used to establish a relationship between the test cases and the classes. Thus, when the changed and affected classes are identified the test cases that relate to these classes are the ones that must be rerun to test the modified program. Again, additional test cases are needed to test new functionalities.

When reading these papers, the reader should pay attention to the overall approach proposed by the authors. In the first paper, the basic block is a class. It uses only the relationships among the classes to identify the change impact. Therefore the approach is simpler but the retest effort may not be the minimum. The second paper goes down to the statement level and identifies and analyzes all the control dependencies and data dependencies among the statements and methods. This detailed analysis may substantially reduce the regression test effort but the complexity is high. The approach proposed by the third paper is simple but it requires that the changed and affected classes must be known. Again, the retest effort may not be the minimum.

Table 1 summarizes the approaches described by these papers.

References

[kung94g] D. Kung et al., "Change Impact Identification in Object Oriented Software Maintenance," *Proc. IEEE Int'l Conf. Software Maintenance*, IEEE Computer Society Press, Los Alamitos, Calif., 1994, pp. 202–211.

[roth94a] G. Rothermel and M.J. Harrold, "Selecting Regression Tests for Object-oriented Software," *Proc. IEEE Int'l Conf. Software Maintenance*, IEEE Computer Society Press, Los Alamitos, Calif., 1994, pp. 14–25.

[hsia97b] P. Hsia et al., "A Technique for Selective Revalidation of OO Software," *Software Maintenance: Research and Practice*, Vol. 9, 1997, pp. 217–233.

Table 1. High-level summary of the approaches.

	Kung et al.'s approach	Rothermal et al.'s approach	Hsia et al.'s approach
Approach	White-box	White-box	White-box
Key concepts or techniques	Object relation diagram (ORD), firewall, test order	Control dependency, data dependency, dependency graphs, dependency graphs discrepancy, regression tests selection	Class/test case relationship, software probe, class firewall, regression tests selection
Effective	Yes	Yes	Yes
Efficient	May not be optimal	Should be optimal	May not be optimal

Change Impact Identification in Object Oriented Software Maintenance

D. Kung, J. Gao, P. Hsia, F. Wen

The Univ. of Texas at Arlington
P. O. Box 19015
Arlington, TX 76019-0015

Y. Toyoshima, and C. Chen

Fujitsu Network Transmission Systems, Inc.
3099 North First Street
San Jose, CA 95134-2022

Abstract

In the object-oriented (OO) paradigm, new features (such as encapsulation, aggregation, inheritance, polymorphism and dynamic binding) introduce new problems in software testing and maintenance. One of them is the difficulty of identifying the affected components (such as classes) when changes are made in object-oriented class libraries or programs. This paper discusses the types of code changes in an object-oriented class library, and provides an automated solution to identify different kinds of code changes and their impact. In addition, an OO software maintenance environment that implements the research result is described. Our experience with the environment prototype shows promising results.

Key words and phrases: software maintenance, object oriented programming, change analysis, impact identication, regression testing, environment, tool

1 Introduction

One important activity of software maintenance is regression testing, which ensures that the modified software still satisfies its intended requirements. To save effort, regression testing should retest only those parts that are affected by the modifications. In traditional function-oriented programming, only control dependencies exist between the modules; hence, it is relatively easy to identify the affected modules. In the object-oriented (OO) paradigm, a number of new features is supported, such as encapsulation, information hiding, inheritance, aggregation, polymorphism, and dynamic binding. These new features introduce new problems in the maintenance phase, including difficulty of identifying the affected components when changes are made.

Encapsulation and information hiding imply the so-called "delocalized plan" [19], in which several member functions from possibly several object classes are invoked to achieve an intended functionality. This phenomenon means that changes to a member function of a class may affect many classes. Inheritance and aggregation imply structure and state dependent behavior reuse, i.e., the data members, function members, and state dependent behavior of a class are re-used by another class. Thus, there are data dependencies, control dependencies, and state behavior dependencies between the two classes. Moreover, since the inheritance and aggregation relations are transitive relations, the above dependencies also are transitive dependencies. Polymorphism and dynamic binding imply that objects may take more than one form, and the form which an object assumes is unknown until run time. This makes the identification of the affected components much more difficult.

The maintenance complications introduced by the OO features can be summarized as follows: 1) although it is relatively easy to understand most of the data structures and member functions of the object classes, understanding of the combined effect or combined functionality of the member functions is extremely difficult; 2) the complex relationships between the object classes make it difficult to anticipate and identify the ripple effect[1] [6] of changes; 3) the data dependencies, control dependencies, and state behavior dependencies make it difficult to prepare test cases and generate test data to "adequately" retest[2] the affected components; 4) the complex relations also make it difficult to define a cost-effective test strategy to retest the affected components.

This paper discusses types of changes that can be made to an OO library. It also describes a method for identifying the affected classes due to structure changes to an object class library. The method is based on a reverse engineering approach designed to extract the classes and their interrelationships. This information is represented in a multigraph, which is used to automatically identify the changes and the effects of those changes. The method has been implemented in the integrated testing and maintenance environment. The architecture and functionality of the relevant part will be presented.

---

[1] The ripple effect refers to the phenomenon that changes made to one part of a software system ripple throughout the system.

[2] We use this term loosely to mean retesting the software with a certain degree of confidence. We choose not to give a formal definition of adequacy in this paper.

Reprinted from *Proc. IEEE Int'l Conf. Software Maintenance*, 1994, pp. 202–211.

The organization of this paper is as follows: In section 2, a brief review of related work on maintenance of conventional software as well as OO software is given. In section 3, we discuss types of changes and change identification. A formal model is presented to facilitate change identification and impact identification, which is described in section 4. In section 5, we describe a support system for OO testing and maintenance. In section 6, we report our experience on OO software maintenance and in section 7, we present the conclusions and future work.

2 Related Work

Hartmann and Robson examined several regression testing strategies, including methods for capturing the program portion which may be affected by maintenance modifications to a conventional program [8]. A similar study was conducted by Leung and White [14] using a formally defined cost model. Laski and Szermer described an algorithm for identifying the affected parts in conventional program maintenance [11]. The algorithm is based on differentials between the control flow graphs for the original program and the modified program. In [13], impact of data and function changes is addressed using a dynamic approach.

Some conventional program maintenance systems have been reported in the literature. The VIFOR (Visual Interactive FORtran) [17] were developed for FORTRAN programs, the MasterScope [20] for Interlisp, and the CIA (C Information Abstractors) [3] for C. These systems provide editing, browsing, and database supports to a maintainer. In particular, the VIFOR system also provides graphical display and transformations between the textual representation and the graphical representation.

Wilde and Huitt [23] analyzed problems of dynamic binding, object dependencies, dispersed program structure, control of polymorphism, high level understanding and detailed code understanding. The authors then provided a general list of recommendations, including the use of dependency analysis [22] and clustering methods [4] [15], for possible tool support.

Crocker and Mayrhauser addressed problems relating to class hierarchy changes, class signature changes, and polymorphism [5]. The authors then proposed a list of tools to help solve some of the problems. The tools provide information collection, storage, analysis, inference, and display capabilities.

An early system for maintaining C++ programs was reported by Samethinger in [18]. The system utilized the inheritance relation and containment relations (e.g., a class is contained in a file, or a method belongs to a class, etc.) to provide text-based browsing facilities to an OO software maintainer.

The C++ Information Abstractors [7] used program analyzers to extract cross-reference information

Components		Changes
data changes	1	change data definition/declaration
	2	change data access scope/mode/uses
	3	add/delete data
method interface changes	4	add/delete external data usage
	5	add/delete external data updates
	6	add/delete/change a method call
	7	change its signature or messages
method structure changes	8	add/delete a sequential segement
	9	add/delete/change a branch/loop
method component changes	10	change a control sequence
	11	add/delete/change local data
	12	change a sequential segement
class component changes	13	change a defined/redefined method
	14	add/delete a defined/redefined method
	15	add/delete/change a defined datum
	16	add/delete a virtual abstract method
	17	change an attribute access mode/scope
class relationship changes	18	add/delete a superclass
	19	add/delete a subclass
	20	add/delete an object pointer
	21	add/delete an aggregated object
	22	add/delete an object message
class library changes	23	change a class (defined attributes)
	24	add/delete a relation between classes
	25	adde/delete a class and its relations
	26	add/delete an independent class

Figure 1: Different Types Of Code Changes

and stored the information in a database. A maintainer could query the data base to obtain the desired knowledge to maintain a C++ program.

Lejter, Meyers, and Reiss discussed the difficulty of maintaining an OO software system due to the presence of inheritance and dynamic binding [12]. The authors then described the XREF/XREFDB prototype system that provided text editing and relational data base querying support to facilitate OO software maintenance. A similar system was described in [16].

Our system is similar in many aspects to the above systems. It uses program analyzers to collect information and stores the information in a data base. It provides both graphical and textual display and browsing, whereas most of the existing systems provide only textual display and browsing (with VIFOR as an exception). It is capable of automatically identifying the changes to an OO program and deriving the affected parts from the changes. Another difference is that our system is integrated with testing capabilities to facilitate regression test case and test data reuse and generation, result analysis, and report generation.

3   Change Identification

One of the major difficulties in software maintenance is to identify changes and their impact automatically since it is very difficult to keep track of the changes when a software system is modified extensively by several persons. This capability becomes even more crucial when the modifications are performed by one group of persons and regression testing is performed by another group of persons. In this section, we first discuss the different types of code changes. We then describe how to identify the various types of code changes.

3.1   Types Of Code Changes

Figure 1 provides a classification of code changes in an OO class library. These change types are explained as follows:

Data change: Any datum (i.e., a global variable, a local variable, or a class data member) can be changed by updating its definition, declaration, access scope, access mode and initialization. In addition, adding new data and/or deleting existing data are also considered as data changes.

Method change: A member function can be changed in various ways. Here we classify them into three types: *component changes, interface changes,* and *control structure changes.* Component changes include: 1) adding, deleting, or changing a predicate, 2) adding, deleting a local data variable, and 3) changing a sequential segment. Structure changes include: 1) adding, deleting, or modifying a branch or a loop structure, and 2) adding, or deleting a sequential segment. The interface of a member function consists of its signature, access scope and mode, its interactions with other member functions (for example, a function call). Any change on the interface is called an interface change of a member function.

Class change: Direct modifications of a class can be classified into three types: *component changes, interface changes* and *relation changes.* Any change on a defined/redefined member function or a defined data attribute is known as a component change. A change is said to be an interface change if it adds, or deletes a defined/redefined attribute, or changes its access mode or scope. A change is said to be a relation change if it adds, or deletes an inheritance, aggregation or association relationship between the class and another class.

Class library change: These include: 1) changing the defined members of a class, 2) adding, or deleting a class and its relationships with other classes. 3) adding, or deleting a relationship between two existing classes[3], 4) adding, or deleting an independent class.

---

[3]Changing a relationship R1 (between two classes) into a relationship R2 is considered as deleting R1 and adding R2.

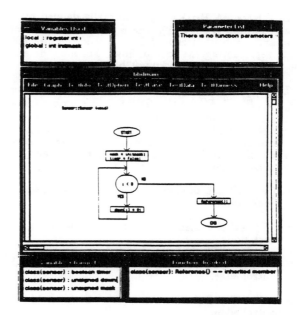

Figure 2: A BBD for a member function in the Inter-Views Library

3.2   Method Change Identification

A directed diagram, called block-branch diagram (BBD) is used to facilitates the understanding of the member functions and their interfaces and relationships to the global data, class data, and other member functions. Figure 2 shows a BBD for a member function of the InterViews library. The various components of a BBD is explained as follows:

- The large window displays the BBD body, denoted B; it encapsulates the program graph for the member function[4].

- The upper left window displays the global and class data that are used by the member function; this is denoted by Du;

- The upper right window displays the input/output parameters, denoted P, of the member function;

- The bottom left window displays the global and class data that are defined (i.e., updated) by this member function; this is denoted by Dd;

- The bottom right window displays functions that are called by this member function; this is denoted by Fe;

Formally, the block branch diagram for a member function f is a quintuple

$$BBD_f = (D_u, D_d, P, F_e, B)$$

where the components are as defined above. When no confusion can arise, we will omit the subscript f

---

[4]The program graph can be used, among others, to generate basis path test cases and test data [2]. However, it is beyond the scope of this paper to explore this issue.

from BBD_f. A BBD body is formally defined by a directed graph $B = (V, E)$, where V denotes the set of program graph vertices and $E \subset V \times V$ the directed edges representing the control flows. For more details the reader is referred to [kung93b].

Let $BBD = (D_u, D_d, P, F_e, B)$, and $BBD' = (D'_u, D'_d, P', F'_e, B')$ be the BBDs for a member function C::f(...) and its modified version C::f'(...) respectively. Recall that $B = (V, E)$ (or $B' = (V', E')$) is a directed graph which represents the control structure of C::f(...)(or C::f'(...)). Method structure and/or component changes are identified as follows:

- if $V - V' \neq \emptyset$ then any $v \in (V - V')$ is a deleted block node.

- if $V' - V \neq \emptyset$ then any $v \in (V' - V)$ is an added block node.

- if $E - E' \neq \emptyset$ then any $e \in (E - E')$ is a deleted control edge.

- if $E' - E \neq \emptyset$ then any $e \in (E' - E)$ is an added control edge.

A member function interface change is identified as follows:

- if $D_u - D'_u \neq \emptyset$, then some data uses are removed.

- if $D'_u - D_u \neq \emptyset$, then some data uses are added.

- if $D_d - D'_d \neq \emptyset$, then some data definitions are removed.

- if $D'_d - D_d \neq \emptyset$, then some data definitions are added.

- if $F_e - F'_e \neq \emptyset$, then some function calls are removed[5].

- if $F_e - F'_e \neq \emptyset$, then some function calls are added.

3.3   Data Change Identification

Data change identification is easy since the needed information is captured by the BBD's (and the internal representation) for the member functions[6]. In particular, information about each data item's access scope, type, access mode, update set (i.e., functions that define the data item), and use set (i.e., functions that use the data item). To identify data change, this information is compared with the information for the original software. If any of the above information is different, the corresponding type of change is identified.

---

[5]Signature change is treated as deleting and then adding a function.

[6]Functions not belong to any class are treated as member functions of a dummy system class in our approach.

3.4   Class Change Identification

A class is a pair $C = (D_{def}, F_{def})$, where D_{def} is a set of defined/redefined data attributes, F_{def} is a set of defined/redefined member functions. Let $C' = (D'_{def}, F'_{def})$ be a modified version of a class C. Then class code change is identified as follows:

- if $D_{def} - D'_{def} \neq \emptyset$, then any $d \in (D_{def} - D'_{def})$ is a deleted data attribute.

- if $D'_{def} - D_{def} \neq \emptyset$, then any $d \in (D'_{def} - D_{def})$ is an added data attribute.

- if any $d \in D'_{def} \cap D_{def}$ is changed, then a residual data attribute is changed.

- if $F_{def} - F'_{def} \neq \emptyset$, then any f in $(F_{def} - F'_{def})$ is a deleted member function.

- if $F'_{def} - F_{def} \neq \emptyset$, then any f in $(F'_{def} - F_{def})$ is an added member function.

- if any $f \in F'_{def} \cap F_{def}$ is changed, then a residual defined/redefined member function is changed.

3.5   Class Library Change Identification

A class library L is a collection of ORDs. An ORD is an edge labeled directed graph $ORD = (V, L, E)$, where V is the set of nodes representing the object classes, $L = \{I, Ag, As\}$ is the set of edge labels (for inheritance, aggregation, and association), and $E = E_I \bigcup E_{AG} \bigcup E_{AS}$ is the set of edges. For a detailed definition and how to reverse code to yield an ORD, the reader is referred to [9]. As mentioned earlier, Figure 3 shows the screen dump of an ORD for part of the InterViews library. In the figure, the inheritance and aggregation relationships are shown using Rumbaugh et al's notation, while association is shown using directed arcs. The figure says that World is associated with OptionDesc, and hence dependent on OptionDesc. MonoScene is a part of Sensor, and hence Sensor is dependent on MonoScene. The figure also shows that World is a derived class of Scene, and hence, it is dependent on Scene.

Modifications to a library can be classified into three basic cases, i.e., adding an ORD, deleting an ORD, and changing an ORD[7]. In the first two cases, there is no impact to the other ORD's, therefore, we will consider only the last case. An ORD can be changed in several ways: changing the defined members of a class, adding/deleting a relation between two existing classes, and adding/deleting a class and its relations. Change identification for a single class has been discussed in the previous subsection. Here, we focus on structure change of a class library.

Let $ORD = (V, L, E)$ and $ORD' = (V', L', E')$ be the ORD's for two versions of the same software. A structure change in an ORD is

---

[7]Note an isolated class is an ORD.

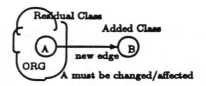

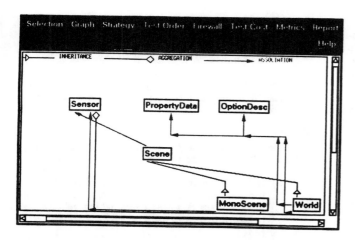

Figure 3: An ORD for a part of the InterViews Library

- if $V' - V \neq \emptyset$ then any $v \in (V' - V)$ is an added class node.

- if $V - V' \neq \emptyset$ then any $v \in (V - V')$ is a deleted node.

- if $E' - E \neq \emptyset$ then any $e \in (E' - E)$ is an added new edge.

- if $E - E' \neq \emptyset$ then any $e \in (E - E')$ is a deleted edge.

- if any v in $V \cap V'$ is changed, then a residual class is changed.

To facilitate understanding, Figure 4 shows the different types of structure changes for an ORD[8]. Figures 4(a) and (b) show the two cases in which a new class node is added into the original ORD by inserting a new relation with an residual class. Two cases of a class deletion are given in Figures 4(c) and (d). Notice that if a class node is removed from an ORD, then all relation edges between the class node and other classes must be deleted. In Figure 4(e), an existing relation edge is removed from two residual classes. In Figure 4(f), a new relation edge between two residual classes is added.

4 Change Impact Identification

After change identification, it is very important to detect the ripple effects of the changes because these changes may affect the software in different aspects, including functions, structures, behavior, and performance. Clearly understanding these effects not only reduces the cost of software maintenance but also saves the regression test effort. For example, if we

---

[8] An independent single class in a class library is considered as an ORD. Thus, adding (or deleting) an independent single class adds (or deletes) an ORD.

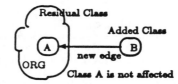

(a) Add a new "superclass"

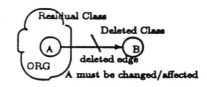

(b) Add a new dependent class

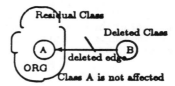

(c) Delete a "superclass"

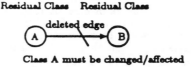

(d) Delete a relation between classes

(e) Delete a dependent class

Residual Class   Residual Class

added edge

Class A must be changed/affected

(f) Add a relation between classes

Figure 4: Different Structural Changes In An ORD

can find all the affected components in the given software, the testers need only to retest these components instead of all of the components in the software. Thus, it is very important to identify and enclose all the affected components after changing a software.

Change impact identification includes data change impact identification, method change impact identification, class change impact identification, and class library change (i.e., class relation change) impact identification. Existing results, e.g., [13], can be used to identify data and method change impacts. A class firewall concept is introduced in [10] to enclose all possible affected classes after some changes are made in a class. In this paper, we focus on changes of classes and their relationships. An automated solution is given to identify the change impact due to changes of classes and their relationships.

4.1 Class Library Change Impact Identification

The major task of class library change impact identification is to find all the affected classes due to changes of interclass relationships. We use a class firewall concept introduced in [10] to enclose all affected classes. The computation of a class firewall is based on the ORDs for the class library.

As shown in Figure 4, there are six types of structure changes in an ORD. Taking into consideration the differences in treating the inheritance, aggregation and association relationships, the impact on a residual class is identified as follows:

1. Adding a new "superclass":

   (a) If the new edge is an inheritance edge, then it expands A's members. According to Weyuko's *antidecomposition* axiom[9], we should retest these new inherited members in the context of class A [24]. In addition, integration testing of class A's new inherited members and its other members is needed to make sure that they work well together.

   (b) If the edge is an inheritance or aggregation edge, then it expands A's state space in terms of state behavior (see Figure 4.1a). That is, its states and transitions are extended by its inherited members from class B. According to Weyukos's *anticomposition* axiom[10], we should retest the state behaviors of class A.

---

[9]There exists a program P and component Q such that T is adequate for P. T' is the set of vectors of values that variables can assume on entrance to Q for some t of T, and T' is not adequate for Q. [21]

[10]There exist program P and Q, and test set T, such that T is adequate for P, and the set of vectors of values that variables can assume on entrance to Q for inputs in T is adequate for Q, but T is not adequate for P;Q.[P;Q is the composition of P and Q. [21]

   (c) If the edge is an association edge, then at least one method of class A must be changed, and hence, A is affected in this sense.

2. Adding a new dependent class.

   Class A is not affected and hence does not need to be retested.

3. Deleting a "superclass".

   This changes class A by removing class B from class A's superclass or component class list:

   (a) If the edge is an inheritance edge, then it reduces the inherited members. This only affects class A's test cases which related to those removed members.

   (b) If the edge is an inheritance or aggregation edge, then it reduces the states and transitions of class A (see Figure 4.1b). According to Weyuko's antidecomposition axiom, we should retest the state behaviors of the modified class A.

   (c) If the edge is an association edge, then at least one method of class A must be changed, and hence, A is affected in this sense.

4. Deleting a dependent class.
   Class A is not affected.

5. Deleting a relationship between existing classes.
   This is similar to (c) above.

6. Adding a relationship between existing classes.
   This is similar to (a) above.

We have discussed the different types of structure changes of an OO library. We have shown how some of the changes affect a residual class A even though its defined attributes were not changed at all. Thus, class A should be retested. A residual class like class A is called an *addition affected class* if it is directly affected by any edge addition (or class addition) in an ORD (cases (a) and (f) above). Similarly, a residual class is called a *deletion affected class* if it is directly affected by any edge deletion (or class deletion) in an ORD (cases (c) and (e) above).

4.2 Class Firewall Generation

The basic idea of computing a class firewall is described in [10]. A class firewall is a set of affected classes when some changes are made in a class library or an object-oriented program. A binary relation R, derived from an ORD $= (V,L,E)$, is introduced to compute the class firewall.

$$R = \{< C_j, C_i > | C_i, C_j \in V \bigwedge < C_i, C_j, l > \in E)\}$$

where R is the dependence relation which defines the dependence between classes, according to the inheritance, aggregation, and association relations.

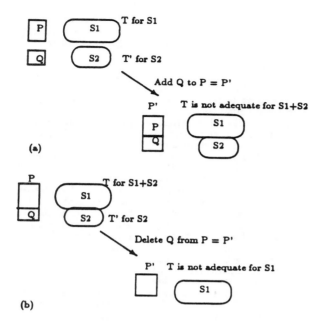

Figure 5: Changes in Object State Space

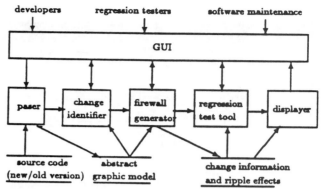

Figure 6: The Architecture Of OOTME

In [10], we have proved that for an ORD, if the modification a class library changes a class C without altering the structure of the ORD, then a class firewall for C, denoted CCFW(C), can be computed as follows:

$$CCFW(C) = \{C_j | < C, C_j > \in R^\bullet\}$$

where $R^\bullet$ is the transitive closure of R. That is, if $< C_i, C_j > \in R$ and $< C_j, C_k > \in R^\bullet$, then $< C_i, C_k > \in R^\bullet$. The transitive closure of R can be computed by the famous Warshall algorithm [1].

Let L be a class library and L' its modified version. Assume that ORD = (V, L, E) is an ORD in L and that ORD' = (V', L', E') its modified version. We define a binary relation R_r as

$$R_r = R \cap (V \times V) \cap (V' \times V')$$

where $\times$ is the Cartesian product operation. In other words, R_r is the relation which defines the dependencies between the residual classes. The class firewalls are generated as follows:

- The class firewall for a changed class C is computed as follows:

$$CCFW(C) = \{Cj | < C, Cj > \in R_r^\bullet\}$$

- The class firewall for addition affected classes is computed as follows:

$$CCFW = \{C_j | (\exists C)(\exists k)((< C_j, C, k > \in E' - E) \land < C, C_j > \in R'^\bullet\}$$

where R' is the dependence relation for the modified ORD.

- The class firewall for deletion affected classes is computed as follows:

$$CCFW = \{Cj | ((\exists C)(\exists k)((< C_j, C, k > \in E - E') \land < C, C_j > \in R'^\bullet\}$$

5   Support System

The objective of a software maintenance system is to help a software maintainer in: understanding a given software, identifying code changes, supporting software updates and enhancement, and detecting change effects. Therefore, any software maintenance system has to fulfill four important requirements: 1) it has to be able to provide the various information about the software, including its structures, and the interfaces and relationships between different components at the different levels; 2) it has to provide an efficient and user-friendly interface to present the various information about software and support maintenance activities; and 3) it has to be able to identify code changes between different software versions and their effects. Figure 5 depicts the architecture of an OO testing and maintenance environment we are currently developing. The components of the environment are described as follows:

- *GUI*: The GUI is constructed based on Motif and X window software; therefore it is user-friendly.

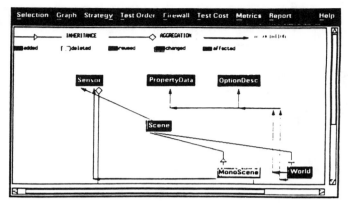

Figure 7: Change impact identification

- *Parser*: There are three different parsers: the ORD parser, the BBD parser, and the OSD parser. The user can use them to extract information from a class library.

- *Displayer*: There are three Displayers: the ORD Displayer, the BBD Displayer, and the OSD Displayer. The user can use them to display the ORDs, BBDs, and OSDs, respectively.

- *Change identifier*: The change identifier can be used to to find the code changes between two different versions of the same class library. It can also be used to automatically identify the impact of a planned code change to help a maintainer to determine whether the change shall be carried out.

- *Firewall generator*: The firewall generator can be used to identify a class firewall to enclose all the possible affected classes in a class library when it is modified.

- *Regression test tool*: The regression test tool consists of a test strategy generator and a test case generator. The test strategy generator produces a cost-effective test order for each class in the library [10]. This test order will be used as a re-test sequence in class unit testing and re-integration testing. The test case generator is used to generate new test cases.

We have applied this tool to many applications, including the Interviews library. Figure 7 shows an example listing of the firewall information for a subset of the InterViews library. We have also compared the two versions (3.0 and 3.1) of the Interviews library using the OOTME. It lists all of the differences between these two versions, including 68 added classes, 76 deleted classes, and 46 residual classes (reused classes). In addition, it also identifies 26 changed residual classes, 16 affected classes, and 4 unaffected classes. The detailed results are given in tables 1 – 3.

6 Experience

Aids to understand an OO software system, anticipate and identify the effects of change, and facilitate regression testing are desirable capabilities of an OO software maintenance environment. Our experience indicates that it is extremely time consuming and tedious to test and maintain an OO software system. This problem becomes even more acute when documentation is either missing or inadequate. Consider, for example, the InterViews library originally developed by Stanford University. An early version of the library consisted of 146 files, more than 140 classes, more than 400 relationships, and more than 1,000 member functions. We felt that it was difficult to obtain a high level of understanding of the classes, member functions, and their relationships. Our initial experiment showed that it took an average of two hours for a C++ programmer to understand a small member function (ranging from a few lines to less than 20 lines) that invokes other member functions. Without tool support, it is almost impossible to anticipate and identify the effect of change because a class can be instantiated by another class which can then use the capabilities of the former. To ensure quality of our products, we often had to retest the entire library when major changes were made.

Software engineers in the industry consider the system useful for testing, maintenance, and reengineering. The application of the system to the InterViews library, an elevator library, and a PBX program shows that it facilitates understanding, test ordering [9][10], test case generation (for which automatic support will be available in the future), and effort estimation (in terms of extended cyclomatic complexity and CO-COMO model).

The application of the automatic change and change effect identification capabilities to the InterViews library has produced promising results. However, our experience is too limited to draw any conclusions. We anticipate that these capabilities will be particularly useful in the maintenance phase. Without tool support, one has to document each change and identify its impact according to one's knowledge of the system. This is both time consuming and inaccurate. The tool will reduce costs significantly and improve productivity in documentation and regression testing by automatically identifying the changes and their impact, thus eliminating many errors. Although the system is still in its prototyping stage, several companies have expressed interests in experimenting with the system and we are porting it to more companies.

7 Conclusion and Future Work

We have described the various types of code changes of an OO system and a formal model for capturing and inferencing on the changes to identify affected components. The model and the inference capabilities have been implemented in a tool prototype. Experience with an earlier version of the tool shows promising results. As reported elsewhere [10][9], the changed and affected classes can be tested in a cost-effective order to avoid extensive construction of test stubs.

Identification of changes and their impact is only one aspect of software maintenance. We are currently extending the capabilities to include various metrics, such as complexity, object-orientedness, and effort, to facilitate the maintenance work. The system is being expanded with these new features and integrated with a test environment to provide retesting support.

8 Acknowledgment

The material presented in this paper is based on work supported by the Texas Advanced Technology Program (Grant No. 003656-097), Fujitsu Network Transmission Systems, Inc., Hewlett-Packard Company, and the Software Engineering Center for Telecommunications at UTA.

9 References

[1] A. V. Aho, J. E. hopcroft and J. D. Ullman, Data Structures and Algorithms, Addison-Wesley Publication Company, 1983.

[2] B. Beizer, "Software Testing Techniques," 2nd ed., Van Hostrand Reinhold, 1990.

[3] Y.-F. Chen, M. Y. Nishimoto, and C. V. Ramamoorthy, "The C information abstract system," IEEE Trans. Software Eng., Vol. 16, pp. 325 – 334, Mar. 1990.

[4] S. C. Choi and W. Scacchi, "Extracting and restructuring the design of large systems," IEEE Software, Vol. 17, No. 1, pp. 66 – 71, Jan. 1990.

[5] R. T. Crocker and A. v. Mayrhauser, "Maintenance Support Needs for Object – Oriented Software," Proc. of COMPSAC'93, pp. 63 – 69, 1993.

[6] T. Gane and C. Sarson, "Structured System Analysis," McDonnell Douglas, 1982.

[7] J. E. Grass and Y.-F. Chen, "The C++ information abstractor," in UNSENIX C++ Conference. Proc., pp. 265 – 277, 1990.

[8] J. Hartmann and D. J. Robson, "Revalidation During the Software Maintenance Phase," Proc. IEEE Conference on Software Maintenance, pp. 70 – 80, 1989.

[9] D. Kung, J. Gao, P. Hsia, J. Lin and Y. Toyoshima, "Design Recovery for Software Testing of Object-Oriented Programs," Proc. of the Working Conference on Reverse Engineering, pp. 202 – 211, IEEE Computer Society Press, 1993.

[10] D. Kung, J. Gao, P. Hsia, Y. Toyoshima, and C. Chen, "Firewall, regression testing, and software maintenance of object oriented systems," to appear in Journal of Object Oriented Programming, 1994.

[11] J. Laski and W. Szermer, "Identification of Program Modifications and its Applications in Software Maintenance," Proc. IEEE Conference on Software Maintenance, pp. 282 – 290, 1992.

[12] M. Lejter, S. Meyers, and S. P. Reiss, "Support for maintaining object-oriented programs, " IEEE Transactions on Software Engineering 18:1045 – 52 Dec 1992.

[13] H. K. N. Leung and L. White, "A study of integration testing and software regression at the integration level," Proc. IEEE Conf. on Software Maintenance, pp. 290 – 301, 1990.

[14] H. K. N. Leung and L. White, "A Cost Model to Compare Regression Test Strategies," Proc. Conf. Software Maintenance, pp. 201 – 208, 1991.

[15] S. Liu and N. Wilde, "Identifying Objects in a Conventional Procedural Language: An Example of Data Design Recovery", Proceedings of IEEE Conference on Software Maintenance, pp. 266 – 271, 1990.

[16] P. D. O'Brien, D. D. Halbart, and M. F. Kilian, "The Trellis programming environment," in Proc. 1987 Conf. Object-Oriented Programming Systems, Languages and Applications (OOPSLA'87), pp. 91 – 102, Oct. 1987.

[17] V. Rajlich, N. Damaskinos, and P. Linos, "VIFOR: a tool for software maintenance," Software: Practice & Experience Vol. 20 pp. 67 – 77, Jan 1990.

[18] J. Sametinger, "A tool for the maintenance of C++ programs," Proc. IEEE Conf. on Software Maintenance, pp. 54 – 59, 1990.

[19] E. Soloway et al, "Designing documentation to compensate for delocalized plans," CACM Vol. 31, No. 11, pp. 1259 – 1267, Nov. 1988.

[20] W. Teitelman and L. Masinter, "The Interlisp programming environment," IEEE Computer, Vol. 14, No. 4, pp. 25 – 34, Apr. 1981.

[21] E. J., Weyuker, "The evaluation of program-based software test data adequacy criteria," CACM, Vol. 31, No. 6, pp. 668 – 675, 1988.

[22] N. Wilde, R. Huitt and S. Huitt, "Dependency Analysis Tools: Reusable Components for Software Maintenance", Proc. IEEE Conference on Software Maintenance, pp. 126 – 131, October 1989.

[23] N. Wilde and R. Huitt, "Maintenance support for object-oriented programs," IEEE Trans. on Software Eng., Vol. 18, No. 12, pp. 1038 – 1044, Dec. 1992.

[24] Dewayne E. Perry and Gail E. Kaiser, "Adequate Testing and Object-Oriented Programming," January/February JOOP, 1990.

class name	class name	class name	class name	class name
ActiveHandler	Adjustable	AllocationInfo	AllocationTable	AllocationTableImpl
BoxImpl	CoordinateSpace	DebugGlyph	Dialog	DialogHandler
DialogKitImpl	Drag	DragZone	DragZoneSink	FieldButton
FieldEditorImpl	FieldStringEditor	FileBrowserImpl	FileChooserImpl	FontBoundingBox
GLContext	InputHandler	InputHandlerImpl	LayoutKit	LayoutKitImpl
LayoutLayer	MFDialogKitImpl	MFKitForeground	MFKitFrame	MFKitImpl
MFKitInfo	MFKitMenuItem	MenuImpl	MonoKitForeground	MonoKitFrame
MonoKitImpl	MonoKitInfo	MonoKitMenuItem	OLKitImpl	OL_AbbrevMenuButton
OL_Anchor	OL_Button	OL_Cable	OL_Channel	OL_CheckBox
OL_CheckMark	OL_Dragbox	OL_Elevator	OL_ElevatorGlyph	OL_FieldEditor
OL_Frame	OL_Gauge	OL_Indicator	OL_MenuMark	OL_Mover
OL_Pushpin	OL_PushpinLook	OL_Scrollbar	OL_Setting	OL_Slider
OL_Specs	OL_Stepper	OL_Tick	OL_ToLimit	Observable
Observer	WidgetKitImpl	WidgetKitOverlay		

Table 1: New added classes in InterViews3.1

class name	class name	class name	class name	class name
ApplicationWindow	BMargin	BoxAllocation	BoxComponent	BreakSet
Center	DeckInfo	FixedSpan	HCenter	HGlue
HMargin	HRule	HitTarget	HitTargetList	IconWindow
LMargin	LRBox	Listener	ManagedWindow	Margin
OptionDesc	Overlay	PSFont	PSFontImpl	Page
PageInfo	Patch	Pattern	PointerHandler	PopupWindow
PossibleHitTarget	Printer	PrinterInfo	PrinterRep	PropertyData
RMargin	Raster	Regexp	ReqErr	Resource
ResourceImpl	Rule	Sensor	Session	SessionIOHandler
SessionRep	Shadow	SimpleCompositor	Stencil	Style
StyleAttribute	StyleRep	StyleWildcard	StyleWildcardInfo	StyleWildcardMatchQuality
Superpose	TBBox	TIFFRaster	TIFFRasterImpl	TMargin
Target	TeXCompositor	Tile	TileReversed	TopLevelWindow
TransformSetter	Transformer	TransientWindow	VCenter	VGlue
VMargin	VRule	ValueString	Window	World
XYMarker				

Table 2: Deleted classes from InterViews3.0

class name	class name	class name	class name	class name
(C)Aggregate	(C)Allocation	(C)Background	(C)Bitmap	(C)Border
(C)Box	(C)Break	(C)Brush	(C)Canvas	(C)Color
(C)Composition	(C)Deck	(C)Display	(C)Event	(C)Extension
(C)Font	(C)FontFamily	(C)Glyph	(C)Handler	(C)Hit
(C)HitImpl	(C)Image	(C)LRComposition	(C)MonoGlyph	(C)Requisition
(C)TBComposition	(A)AggregateInfo	(A)Align	(A)Character	(A)CompositionComponent
(A)Cursor	(A)Discretionary	(A)Glue	(A)Group	(A)HStrut
(A)LRMarker	(A)Label	(A)Layout	(A)ShapeOf	(A)Space
(A)Strut	(A)VStrut	(U)Allotment	(U)ArrayCompositor	(U)Compositor
(U)Requirement				

Table 3: Reused classes in InterView3.1

Selecting Regression Tests for Object-Oriented Software*

Gregg Rothermel and Mary Jean Harrold
Department of Computer Science
Clemson University
Clemson, SC, 29634-1906
{grother, harrold}@cs.clemson.edu

Abstract

Regression testing is an important but expensive software maintenance activity aimed at providing confidence in modified software. Selective retest methods reduce the cost of regression testing by selecting tests for a modified program from a previously existing test suite. Many researchers have addressed the selective retest problem for procedural-language software, but few have addressed the problem for object-oriented software. In this paper, we present a new technique for selective retest, that handles object-oriented software. Our algorithm constructs dependence graphs for classes and applications programs, and uses these graphs to determine which tests in an existing test suite can cause a modified class or program to produce different output than the original. Unlike previous selective retest techniques, our method applies to modified and derived classes, as well as to applications programs that use modified classes. Our technique is strictly code-based, and makes no assumptions about methods used to specify or test the software initially.

1 Introduction

Regression testing is applied to modified software to provide confidence that modified code behaves as intended, and does not adversely affect the behavior of unmodified code. Regression testing plays an integral role in software maintenance; without proper regression testing we are reluctant to release modified software. One characteristic distinguishing regression testing from developmental testing is the availability, at regression test time, of existing test suites. If we reuse such test suites to retest a modified program, we can reduce the effort required to perform that testing. Unfortunately, test suites can be large, and we may not have time to rerun all tests in such suites. Thus, we must often restrict our efforts to a subset of the previously existing tests. We call the problem of choosing an appropriate subset of an existing test suite the *selective retest problem*; we call a method for solving this problem a *selective retest method*.

Although many researchers have addressed the selective retest problem for procedural-language software[2, 3, 5, 9, 11, 15, 16, 18, 20, 24, 26, 29, 30],

*This work was partially supported by NSF under Grants CCR-9109531 and CCR-9357811 to Clemson University.

we are aware of only one technique that addresses the problem with respect to object-oriented software[7], and that approach applies only to test selection for derived classes. The emphasis on code reuse in the object-oriented paradigm both increases the cost of regression testing, and provides greater potential for obtaining savings by using selective retest methods. When a class is modified, the modifications impact every applications program that uses the class and every class derived from the class; ideally, we should retest every such program and derived class[25, 28]. The object-oriented paradigm also alters the focus of test selection algorithms, emphasizing and creating different concerns. For example, since most classes consist of small interacting methods, selective retest approaches for object-oriented programs must work at the interprocedural level. Also, since many methods for testing object-oriented software treat classes as testable entities, and design or employ suites of *class tests* for classes[6, 7, 12, 25, 27], selective retest methods must support the use of class tests.

In this paper, we present a new selective retest method that addresses the selective retest problem for object-oriented software. Our method constructs dependence graphs for classes and programs that use classes; we use these graphs to select all tests in a test suite that may cause a modified class, derived class, or applications program that uses a class to produce different output than the original program or class.

Our approach has several benefits. First, our method is currently the only selective retest method applicable to test selection for applications programs, classes, *and* derived classes. Second, our method selects tests using information gathered by code analysis, and does not require the specifications on which the code is based. Third, our approach is independent of the method used to generate tests initially for programs and classes. Fourth, unlike most selective retest methods, our method selects every test that may produce different output in the modified program. Fifth, unlike many selective retest algorithms, our approach handles both structural and nonstructural program modifications, and processes multiple modifications with a single application of the algorithm. Sixth, where most selective retest methods function at the unit test level, our approach works interprocedurally – a necessity where test selection for classes is concerned. Finally, our method is automatable.

Reprinted from *Proc. IEEE Int'l Conf. Software Maintenance*, 1994, pp. 14–25.

```
E31        int List::search(int& loc, int item)
           {
S32            loc = 0;
P33            while (loc < numentries)
               {
P34                if (list[loc] == item)
S35                    return 0;
                   else
S36                    ++loc;
               }
S37            return -1;
           }
```

TEST HISTORY INFORMATION

test	list	item	region trace
T1	empty	2	E31,R7,P33,R9
T2	1,2,3	2	E31,R7,P33,R8,P34,R11,R10
T3	1,2,3	4	E31,R7,P33,R8,P34,R10,R9
T4	1,2,3	1	E31,R7,P33,R8,P34,R10

Figure 1: Procedure search (upper left), its PDG (right), and test set T (lower left).

In the next section, we provide background information required for the rest of the paper. Section 3 addresses object-oriented program testing issues that are relevant to the paper. Section 4 describes our algorithm for selecting regression tests for modified object-oriented applications programs; our figures and discussion employ C++, but our approach applies, with adaptations, to other object-oriented languages. Section 5 presents our algorithm for selecting regression tests for modified or derived classes. Section 6 discusses some additional issues relevant to this work, and section 7 presents conclusions.

2 Background

In this section, we overview the program dependence graph used by our algorithms. Then, we briefly discuss the regression testing problem. Finally, we discuss the test history that our algorithms require.

Program Dependence Graphs

A *program dependence graph* (PDG) represents both control dependence and data dependence in a single graph. For statements X and Y in a program, if X is *control dependent* on Y then there must be at least two paths out of Y, where one path always causes X to be executed and the other path may result in X not being executed[4]. A *data dependence* exists between statements X and Y in a program if X defines a variable v, Y uses v, and there is a path from X to Y in the program on which v is not defined[1, 14].

Figure 1 shows procedure search and its partial PDG; node labels in the PDG correspond to statement numbers in the procedure. The search procedure is part of the List class shown in full in Figure 6. To facilitate presentation, we present the figure here using the same statement and node numbers used in Figure 6. For our discussion, we assume that a program has a single entry and a single exit. This implies that all procedures return to their callers; thus, we treat

call sites as simple statements. Although we do not discuss it in this paper, with a simple modification in the construction of a PDG, we accommodate the possibility that procedures may exit before returning to their callers.

A PDG contains several types of nodes. Statement nodes, shown as ellipses in Figure 1, represent simple program statements such as assignment, input/output, variable declaration, or call statements. Circles represent region nodes, which summarize the control dependence conditions necessary to reach statements in the region. Predicate nodes, from which two edges may originate, are represented as squares. A hexagon represents the exit from the procedure. Although we do not represent them as such, we may think of statement and predicate nodes as possessing the text of the program statements to which they correspond as labels. We use a single statement node to summarize the variable declarations present in a procedure.

Control dependencies are represented explicitly in the PDG by *control dependence edges*, shown as solid lines in Figure 1. For any control dependence edge (A,B) in a PDG, A is a *control dependence predecessor* (cd-predecessor) of B, and B is a *control dependence successor* (cd-successor) of A. Nodes in a PDG that have no cd-successors are *leaf* nodes; nodes with cd-successors are *interior* nodes. In Figure 1, $S35$ is a cd-successor of $R10$, and $R10$ is a cd-predecessor of $S35$. Furthermore, $S35$ is a leaf node and $R10$ is an interior node. Statements that have the same control dependencies are grouped together into the same region in a PDG.

Data dependencies between program statements are represented in a PDG by *data dependence edges*, shown in Figure 1 as dashed lines. For any data dependence edge (A,B), A is a *data dependence predecessor* (dd-predecessor) of B, and B is a *data dependence successor* (dd-successor) of A. In the PDG in Figure 1, there are data dependence edges from $S32$, where loc is defined, to $P33$, $P34$, and $S36$, where loc is used. Thus, $P33$, $P34$, and $S36$ are dd-successors of $S32$, and $S32$ is a dd-predecessor of $P33$, $P34$, and $S36$.

102

Regression Testing

Given program P, modified version P' of P, and test set T used previously to test P, selective retest techniques attempt to make use of T to gain sufficient confidence in the correctness of P'. These techniques usually consist of the following steps:

1. Identify the modifications that were made to P.
2. Select $T' \subseteq T$, a set of tests to reexecute on P'.
3. Retest P' with T', establishing P''s correctness with respect to T'.
4. If necessary to satisfy some adequacy criteria, create new tests for P'.
5. Create T'', a new test set/history for P'.

In previous work[21], we described a framework for evaluating regression testing techniques. Using this framework, we classify a regression testing technique as *safe* if it selects all tests from T that could possibly exhibit different output when run on P'. However, a safe approach may include many tests in T' that cannot possibly exhibit different output in P'. Thus, we further classify a safe regression testing technique as *precise* if it avoids choosing tests that will *not* cause P' to produce different output than P. Since we cannot find an algorithm to determine, for an arbitrary choice of P', whether a test will exhibit different output in P' than in P, no technique can be both safe and precise[21].

When evaluating the efficiency of selective retest methods, it is important to recognize that regression testing is typically accomplished in two phases. In the *initial phase* of regression testing, while code is being modified, regression testing is not on the critical path; testers may be retesting modified units, developing test plans, and doing limited integration testing, but the bulk of the testing effort awaits inclusion of the final modifications. When modifications are complete, regression testing enters the *critical phase*; where final integration and system tests must be selected and executed. The time allotted to this critical phase is limited by the need to release the product. Efforts to increase regression testing efficiency yield the greatest payoff when they address activities in this critical phase; expensive activities that are confined to the initial phase are less significant.

Test History

To perform regression testing using an existing test suite, we must keep *test history* information about previous testing sessions. For our purposes, test history information lists the execution trace for each test in terms of PDG predicates and regions traversed; we call this a *region trace*. With each predicate and region in the PDG we associate the set of tests in T whose region trace includes that predicate or region. We call this set a *region history*; for a predicate or region R, we use $R.history$ to refer to R's region history. Note that if execution traces of statements instead of regions are provided, we can easily generate region traces from statement traces without rerunning all tests on the original program.

Figure 1 contains a table that describes a set of tests T used initially to test procedure **search**. The table lists the region trace and the initial values for inputs and global variables for each test. In the PDG in the figure, $R9$ only has tests T1 and T3 associated with it while $R7$ has all tests in the test suite associated with it. Thus, $R9.history = \{T1,T3\}$ and $R7.history = \{T1,T2,T3,T4\}$.

3 Regression test selection for object-oriented software

Object-oriented languages raise interesting concerns for regression testing. In this section we discuss concerns relevant to selective retest.

Levels of testing. To test object-oriented software properly, we must test classes[19]. *Class testing* approaches typically invoke sequences of methods in varying orders, and then verify that the resulting state of the objects manipulated by the methods is correct[6, 7, 27].

The object-oriented paradigm provides new applications for selective retest algorithms. When we modify a class, we must retest the class, and classes derived from that class[7, 19]. Moreover, although we expect encapsulation to reduce the likelihood that object-oriented code modules will interact inappropriately, it is still the case that tests run on applications programs may reveal faults in methods that were not revealed by tests of the individual methods[19, 28]. Thus, if we want to be sure that we have rerun *all* existing tests that may expose errors in a modified class (i.e., select a safe test set) we must consider all applications programs that use the modified class[7, 19, 28][1]. Whether retesting applications programs, classes, or derived classes, we can benefit by applying selective retest algorithms to existing test suites.

Drivers, setup routines, and oracles. To perform class testing, we require a driver that invokes a sequence of methods. A typical class test driver first performs "setup" chores, calling constructor routines and/or other methods. Next, the driver invokes the sequence of methods under test. Finally, the driver invokes an "oracle" method that verifies that objects have attained proper states. Code-based selective retest methods must be able to distinguish between drivers, setup routines, oracle routines, and methods actually under test, and select only the tests that are relevant to changes in methods under test.

Polymorphism and dynamic binding. Object-oriented programs employ polymorphism and dynamic binding to a degree beyond that of procedural programs. In an object-oriented program a method invocation can be bound at run-time to a number of methods. For a given call, we cannot always determine statically the method to which it will be bound. Selective retest methods that rely on static analysis must provide mechanisms for coping with this uncertainty.

---

[1] Clearly, in practice it may not be practical to retest all such programs. We discuss this at greater length in section 6.

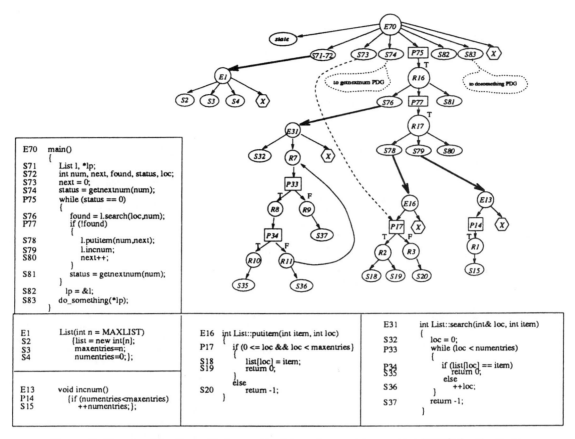

The figure contains the following code listings:

```
E70    main()
       {
S71    List l, *lp;
S72    int num, next, found, status, loc;
S73    next = 0;
S74    status = getnextnum(num);
P75    while (status == 0)
       {
S76        found = l.search(loc,num);
P77        if (!found)
           {
S78            l.putitem(num,next);
S79            l.incnum;
S80            next++;
           }
S81        status = getnextnum(num);
       }
S82    lp = &l;
S83    do_something(*lp);
       }
```

```
E1     List(int n = MAXLIST)
S2     {list = new int[n];
S3         maxentries=n;
S4         numentries=0; };
```

```
E13    void incnum()
P14    {if (numentries<maxentries)
S15        ++numentries;};
```

```
E16    int List::putitem(int item, int loc)
       {
P17        if (0 <= loc && loc < maxentries)
           {
S18            list[loc] = item;
S19            return 0;
           }
       else
S20            return -1;
       }
```

```
E31    int List::search(int& loc, int item)
       {
S32        loc = 0;
P33        while (loc < numentries)
           {
P34            if (list[loc] == item)
S35                return 0;
           else
S36                ++loc;
           }
S37        return -1;
       }
```

Figure 2: Program RemDups that uses the List class, and a partial IPDG for RemDups.

4 Selecting regression tests for modified applications programs

To select regression tests for modified object-oriented application programs, or programs that use modified classes, we use an *interprocedural program dependence graph* (IPDG). Given program P, the IPDG for P consists of individual PDGs for procedures in P, with edges added to represent interprocedural data and control dependencies. Figure 2 depicts a program RemDups and its (partial) IPDG. RemDups uses a List object and methods from a List class. (The figure only shows List class methods used in RemDups; the entire List class is presented in Figure 6.) In the figure, the four bold edges are *call edges*, which summarize the control dependence of code in called procedures on regions enclosing call sites. The figure depicts one interprocedural data dependence edge, from $S73$ to $P17$ (the dashed line). In our IPDG, a *state* node lists all identifier declarations in the program that are not already listed in a declarations node in some PDG. The *state* node is a child of the entry node for the main procedure. In Figure 2 the *state* node contains declarations of variables list, numentries and maxentries, and constant MAXLIST, all of which

appear in the declarations section of the List class (as shown in Figure 6). Note that a call edge connects $S71$-72 to $E1$, because the declaration of variable l invokes the List constructor routine to instantiate a List object. For simplicity, the figure omits the code and PDGs for getnextnum, dosomething, and other List methods not invoked by the application, as well as the remaining data dependence edges.

We use algorithm ConstructIPDG to construct an IPDG. The running time of ConstructIPDG is dominated by the cost of interprocedural dataflow analysis, which is at worst polynomial in the size of the program analyzed[10, 14]. Due to space limitations, we do not present ConstructIPDG here; interested readers are referred to [22].

To select tests for regression testing of applications programs, we use algorithm SelectApplTests, shown in Figure 3. SelectApplTests takes a program P, its modified version P', and a set of tests T used to test P, and selects a safe test set T' for P'. The algorithm finds regions in the IPDGs for P and P' that enclose code which, due to changes or the effects of changes, may cause P' to produce different output than P. For each such pair of regions R and R' in the IPDGs, SelectApplTests selects all tests in $R.history$, because these tests must either reach R', or reach some

```
algorithm      SelectApplTests(P, P', T) : T'
input          P, P' : a program and its changed version
               T : a test set used previously to test P
output         T' : the subset of T selected for reuse
begin SelectApplTests
    G = ConstructIPDG(P); G' = ConstructIPDG(P')
    foreach node n in G and G' do mark n "not visited"
    T' = Compare(E, E'), where E, E' are entry nodes of G, G', respectively
end SelectApplTests
```

Figure 3: Algorithm for selecting tests to rerun on an applications program.

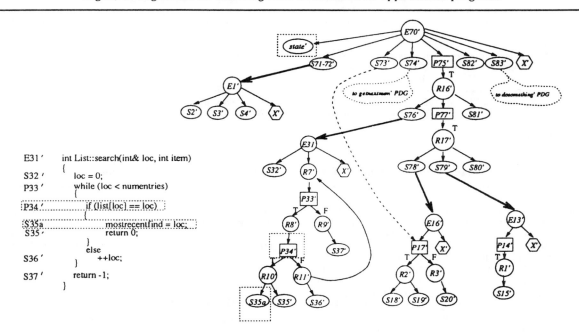

Figure 4: Procedure search2 (left), and the IPDG for RemDups2, with changes enclosed in dotted rectangles.

other pair of regions enclosing code that has been changed. In either case, such tests may produce different output in P' than in P. For more detailed discussion of the algorithm used by SelectApplTests, see [22] and [23]. The following examples demonstrate the use of the algorithm.

Suppose the search method is modified, yielding search2 as shown in Figure 4. In search2, line $P34$ has been (erroneously) modified, and a new line, $S35a$, has been added. Also, a new state variable, mostrecentlyfound, and a new method, getmostrecentlyfound, are added to the List class. Suppose further that the test set T for RemDups contains at least tests $T1$, $T2$, $T3$, and $T4$ that act, with respect to procedure search2, like the four tests given in Figure 1. We wish to determine which tests in T must be reexecuted when RemDups2 is linked with the modified version of the List class. In this case, we call SelectApplTests with RemDups, RemDups2, and T. SelectApplTests first constructs the IPDGs G and G' for the two programs. Figure 4 depicts G' without data dependence edges. G' differs from G

only with respect to the PDG for search, and with respect to the state node; changed parts are enclosed in dotted rectangles. Since getmostrecentlyfound is not invoked by RemDups2, its PDG is not needed or included in the IPDG for RemDups2.

After marking nodes in the graphs "visited", SelectApplTests calls Compare, shown in Figure 5, with entry nodes $E70$ and $E70'$. GetCorresp finds that the children of these nodes differ only in the state nodes: state' contains a declaration of the variable mostrecentlyfound that is not present in state. However, mostrecentlyfound has no uses in G', so Compare marks no nodes "affected" by this change. Compare then invokes itself on nodes $S71-72$ and $S71-72'$, finding no changes beneath these nodes, and then on nodes $S74$ and $S74'$, finding no changes beneath them. Traversal then continues with $P75$ and $P75'$, $R16$ and $R16'$, $S76$ and $S76'$, and down into the PDGs for search and search2; no differences are found until nodes $R8$ and $R8'$ are reached. At this point Compare notes the difference between $P34$ and $P34'$, and selects all tests in $R8.history$ ($T2$, $T3$, and $T4$). The

105

```
procedure Compare( N, N' ): T'
    declare GetCorresp(N, N', Correspondence) : returns f true if traversal is to continue
        in a region; false otherwise, and returns Correspondence, which i ndicates whether cd-successors of
        N and (N') are new, deleted, modified, or equivalent w.r.t. cd-succes sors of N' (N)


    begin Compare
        mark N and N' "visited"
        if GetCorresp( N, N', Correspondence ) then
            T' = φ
            foreach new or modified cd-successor n of N' (or deleted cd-suc cessor n of N) do
                foreach dd-successor U of n in G (G') do
                    if U is "visited" then
                        add to T' all tests in N.history that are also in the .history of U's cd-predecessor
                    else mark U "affected" and attach N.history to U
            if there are "affected" uses in any predicate, output, or control transfer statement control dependent on N or N' then
                T' = N.history
            else
                foreach cd-successor n of N and N' that is a leaf node d o mark n "visited"
                foreach cd-successor C of N' or N marked "affected" do
                    add to T' all tests in N.history that are attached to C
                foreach cd-successor C of N that is an interior node and is not "visited" do
                    T' = T'∪ Compare( C, C' ), where C' is the correspondin g cd-successor of N'
        else T' = N.history            /* processing cannot continu e in N and N' */
        return T'
    end Compare
```

Figure 5: Algorithm for selecting tests to rerun through a PDG node.

algorithm does not continue further beneath $R8$ and $R8'$. Instead, it traverses other portions of the graphs. No further changes are discovered; tests $T2$, $T3$, and $T4$ are selected.

In the example just presented, due to the structure of RemDups and the location of the modifications, it is likely that most tests in T are selected: the only tests not reaching $R8$ are those in which RemDups2 passes an empty or one-element list to search. This test selection is reasonable: all tests reaching $R8$ may exhibit different output and should be rerun. Suppose, however, that the only changes to search were the insertion of line $S35a$ and the declarations of variable mostrecentlyfound and method getmostrecentlyfound. In this case, Compare again finds that the $state$ and $state'$ nodes of the two graphs differ: the $state'$ node listing the new global variable. Again, this variable has no uses in RemDups or RemDups2 so Compare does not mark any nodes "affected" by the global variable insertion. Compare next traverses G and G' until it reaches nodes $R10$ and $R10'$, where it finds a difference in cd-successors. However, this difference involves only an assignment to mostrecentlyfound, and since mostrecentlyfound has no uses in RemDups2, Compare does not select the tests attached to $R10$ or mark any nodes "affected". SelectApplTests recognizes that no tests in T can produce different output in RemDups2 than in RemDups, and returns an empty set of tests.

The running time of SelectApplTests is dominated by the cost of the interprocedural dataflow analysis required to complete construction of the IPDG. The subsequent traversal of the IPDG using Compare is linear in the size of the larger of the IPDGs. Note that construction of the IPDG for P, and collection of test history information, can both be accomplished during the initial phase of regression testing. Thus, only the construction of the IPDG for P' and the traversal of the IPDGs must be performed during the critical phase of testing.

5 Selecting regression tests for modified and derived classes

When a class is modified, we want to find tests in the class's test suite that should be reexecuted. Similarly, when we derive a new class from an existing one, we want to identify the tests from the test set for the base class that should be reexecuted on the derived class. The method of Section 4 does not apply directly to class regression testing, because it requires a program to have a single entry point, whereas a class has multiple entry points. However, by using a *Class Dependence Graph* (ClDG) (a variant of the IPDG) we can depict control and data dependencies within a class in a manner that lets us use an algorithm similar to SelectApplTests to select regression tests for modified or derived classes.

To understand our approach, recall from the discussion in section 3 that to test a class, we create a number of driver programs. These driver programs either assume or instantiate some initial state, and then invoke methods in some required sequence. To retest a modified class, a naive approach is to treat each driver as an application program and use the method of the previous section to retest it. However, this approach has two drawbacks. First, it may require us to construct individual PDGs many times. Second,

106

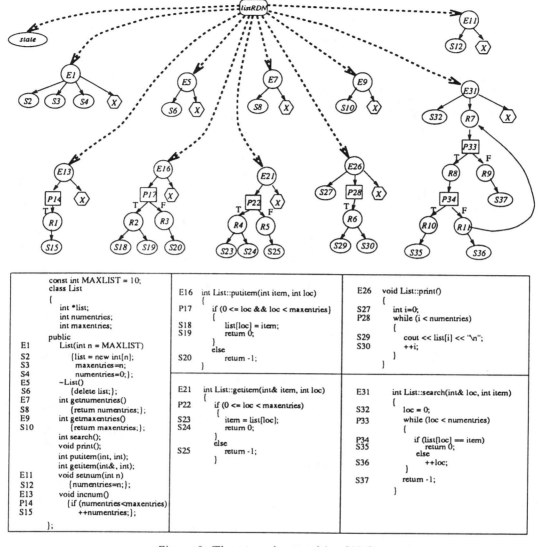

```
         const int MAXLIST = 10;       E16   int List::putitem(int item, int loc)     E26   void List::print()
         class List                          {                                               {
         {                              P17   if (0 <= loc && loc < maxentries)       S27      int i=0;
             int *list;                       {                                       P28      while (i < numentries)
             int numentries;           S18      list[loc] = item;                          {
             int maxentries;           S19      return 0;                            S29         cout << list[i] << "\n";
         public                              }                                        S30         ++i;
E1       List(int n = MAXLIST)               else                                        }
S2           {list = new int[n];       S20      return -1;                               }
S3            maxentries=n;                 }
S4            numentries=0;};                                                         E31   int List::search(int& loc, int item)
E5       ~List()                       E21   int List::getitem(int& item, int loc)         {
S6           {delete list;};                 {                                        S32      loc = 0;
E7       int getnumentries()           P22   if (0 <= loc < maxentries)              P33      while (loc < numentries)
S8           {return numentries;};           {                                          {
E9       int getmaxentries()           S23      item = list[loc];                    P34         if (list[loc] == item)
S10          {return maxentries;};     S24      return 0;                            S35            return 0;
         int search();                     }                                              else
         void print();                     else                                      S36            ++loc;
         int putitem(int, int);        S25      return -1;                              }
         int getitem(int&, int);           }                                        S37      return -1;
E11      void setnum(int n)                                                                }
S12          {numentries=n;};
E13      void incnum()
P14          {if (numentries<maxentries)
S15              ++numentries;};
         };
```

Figure 6: The `List` class, and its ClDG.

in calling `SelectApplTests` for pairs of drivers, this approach may traverse each PDG many times. The ClDG lets us avoid these problems; it provides a single graph in which each PDG is created and traversed at most once by the test selection algorithm.

Figure 6 depicts the ClDG and code for the `List` class used in earlier examples. A "representative driver node" (RDN) labeled "*listRDN*" serves as root of the graph, and summarizes the set of drivers for class tests. Each public method in the class is made a child of the root, by adding *driver edges* (shown as bold dashed lines). A *state* node summarizes variables that make up the state of objects of that class. Since methods in the `List` class make no calls on other methods, the `List` ClDG contains no nesting of methods, and hence has no edges from the PDGs for `List`

methods to other PDGs. ClDGs also contain data dependence edges to depict dataflow dependencies: these are omitted from the figure.

Figure 7 depicts the code and ClDG for a `Stack` class derived from `List`, again omitting data dependence edges. The `Stack` ClDG illustrates how PDGs in a ClDG may be connected both by driver edges to the class's RDN, and by call edges to other call sites within the graph. For example, the `putitem` method in the `List` class is a public method within the `Stack` class, but also is called from both the `pop` and `print` `Stack` methods. Thus, the `Stack` ClDG contains a driver edge from *stackRDN* to *E*21 (the entry node for the `putitem` method), and also contains call edges from *S*48 and *S*60 to *E*21, representing the calls from `pop` and `print`.

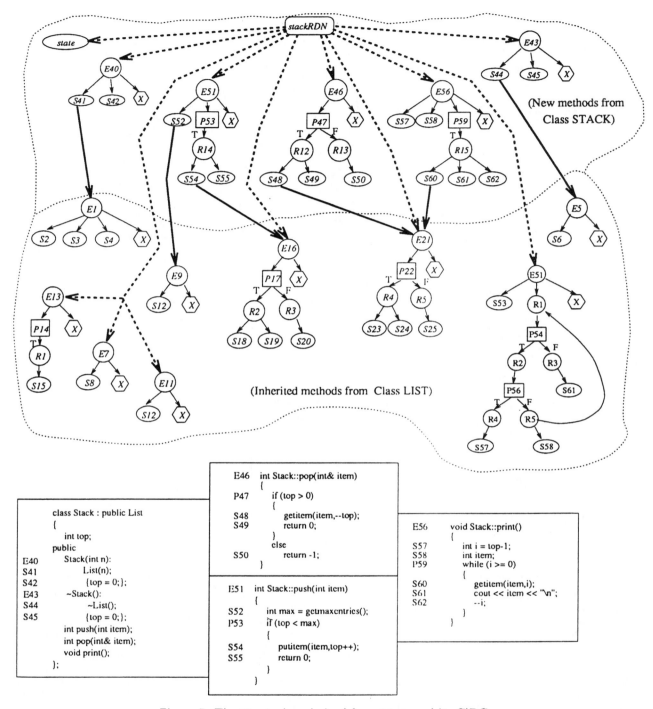

Figure 7: The Stack class derived from List, and its CIDG.

```
algorithm    SelectClassTests(C, C', L, L', T) : T'
input        C, C' : a class and its modified version
             PubM, PubM' : list of public methods in C and C'
             T : a test set used previously to test C
output       T' : the subset of T selected for reuse

begin SelectClassTests
    G = ConstructClDG(C, PubM); G' = ConstructClDG( C', PubM')
    foreach node n in G and G' do mark n "not vi sited"
    foreach new or modified item in state' or deleted item in state do
        mark nodes containing uses reached by that item "affected"
    T' = φ
    let G_RDN and G_RDN' be the root (RDN) nodes of G and G', respectively
    foreach child node N of G_RDN do
        if there is a child node N' of G_RDN' equivalent to N then
            T' = T'∪Compare(N, N')
        else /* N is no longer public in C' */
            T' = T'∪ N.history
end SelectClassTests
```

Figure 8: Algorithm for selecting tests to rerun through modified classes.

We use algorithm ConstructClDG to construct a ClDG. The running time of ConstructClDG, like that of ConstructIPDG, is dominated by the cost of interprocedural dataflow analysis, which is at worst polynomial in the size of the class analyzed. Due to space limitations, we do not present ConstructClDG here; interested readers are referred to [22], where ConstructClDG is presented, and to [8], where we present an algorithm for performing interprocedural dataflow analysis on classes.

To select tests to rerun on a modified class, we use algorithm SelectClassTests, shown in Figure 8, which is similar to algorithm SelectApplTests. SelectClassTests takes as input a class C and its modified version C', the lists of public methods $PubM$ and $PubM'$ in C and C', respectively, and the set of tests T used to test C. We assume that T contains all tests used to test C, by all drivers used for that purpose, but that each test is uniquely distinguished from tests that employ other drivers. SelectClassTests is discussed in more detail in [22]; here we demonstrate the algorithm's use through examples.

To see how SelectClassTests works when a class is modified, suppose the search procedure is modified, yielding the search2 procedure depicted in Figure 4. Assume that a new private variable mostrecentlyfound is declared, and a new method, getmostrecentlyfound, is implemented. When SelectClassTests is invoked, it creates ClDG G shown in Figure 6, and ClDG G' shown in Figure 9. Figure 9 also shows the new method and new declaration, and uses dotted lines to highlight portions of G' that differ from G. Next SelectClassTests marks all nodes "not visited", and then marks the use of mostrecentlyfound in $S39'$ "affected". The only new child of $stackRDN$ is the entry node for getmostrecentlyfound, and T contains no tests for it, so none are selected at that node. All other PDGs in G correspond to PDGs in G', so SelectClassTests runs Compare on them. However, the only changes in

any of these PDGs lie in the PDGs for search and search2. SelectClassTests finds that nodes $P34$ and $P34'$ differ, and selects all tests in $P34.history$. These are the only tests selected for this example.

Now consider the case where a class is inherited. Figure 7 shows the code and ClDG for a Stack class derived from the List class. When SelectClassTests is invoked with the List and Stack classes, it creates ClDGs G and G' shown in Figures 6 and 7. The Stack class contains new constructor, destructor, pop and push methods, and redefines the print method. SelectClassTests does not traverse the PDGs for the new methods, because they have no corresponding PDGs in the List class, and thus no tests of that class executed them. SelectClassTests does call Compare on the entry nodes $E26$ and $E56$ of the print methods, and on discovering that the cd-successors of these nodes differ, selects every test that executed the print method in the List class. Other methods, such as the search method, remain unchanged. SelectClassTests runs Compare on the old and new versions of their PDGs and finds that no tests through these need to be selected. Of course, any tests that called both the search and print functions were selected when SelectClassTests considered the print methods.

As a final example, suppose we have developed and tested our Stack class and created a test set T for it, and suppose we then modify the search procedure in the List class as above, creating search2. To see which tests in T we need to rerun, we use the SelectClassTests algorithm on the Stack class as linked with the first version of List, and the Stack class as linked with the second version of List. The algorithm constructs the ClDGs for the two versions of the Stack class; the ClDG for the new version includes the modified version of search, the new state variable, and the new getmostrecentlyfound method. The algorithm then proceeds precisely as it did when we used it to select tests to retest List.

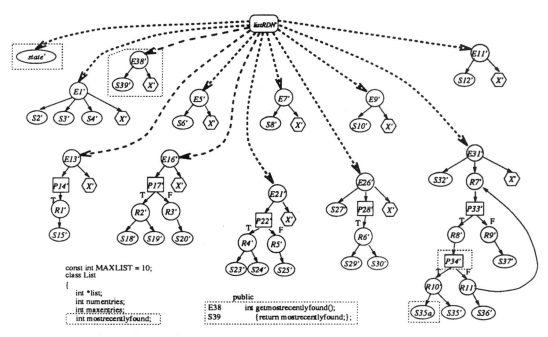

Figure 9: Modified **List** class code, and the CIDG for the modified **List** class.

The running times for `SelectClassTests` and `SelectApplTests` depend on the same factors. Much of the processing required for `SelectClassTests` can be accomplished during the intial phase of testing.

6   Other issues

Several issues raised in the previous sections bear further scrutiny.

Polymorphism and dynamic binding. As detailed in section 3, the polymorphism inherent in object-oriented languages implies that method calls can invoke any of a set of methods. For each call, we can determine a set of methods it can invoke; the size of the set will depend on the precision of our algorithm for determining it, and on how strongly typed our language is. When the set is too large, further graph construction and traversal through that call is impractical. In this case, we summarize a set of callable methods, and summarize the set of variable uses in these methods, as a single node. When our test selection algorithms reach a summary node, if the node contains affected uses or summarizes a method that has been modified, we select all tests through that node.

Drivers, setup, and oracles. With class tests, it is important to distinguish code being tested from code used to drive, setup, or check results of the test. To see why, consider what happens when a constructor is modified. If `SelectClassTests` treats all methods, including setup methods, equivalently, then `SelectClassTests` will select every test that uses the constructor. Clearly, every such test may exhibit dif-

ferent output due to the modifications to the constructor. However, we may not have time to run all such tests. In this case we may choose to test the constructor independently, sign off on it, and select tests for the rest of the class independent of the constructor. An easy way to prohibit `SelectClassTests` from considering the effects of changes in particular methods is to leave those methods uninstrumented when we calculate test histories. Since `SelectClassTests` only selects tests attached to regions enclosing changed code, or attached to both a region enclosing a changed definition of a variable and another enclosing a use of that variable, `SelectClassTests` will select tests only in routines where history information is gathered.

Specification- and code-based testing. When we test programs initially, we must employ some specification-based ("black-box") testing, because only such testing can identify errors of missing functionality[13]. However, if we rely solely on black-box testing we may miss significant faults, since we may fail to test some components of the code. Thus, when we test programs initially we must also employ "white-box" methods that analyze code[19]. The same conclusions may be drawn about regression testing: we must employ both black and white-box methods when selecting regression tests. If the specifications for modified software have changed, and the code modifications necessary to implement the changed specifications have not been made, such a fault can only be detected by black-box test selection, wherein tests related to the changed specification are selected. However, if we rerun *only* the tests identified as related to the changed specifications, we may omit tests that exercise portions of the code that have (inadvertently) been affected by code modifications.

Our selective retest method is strictly code-based, and thus fulfills the need to employ a white-box test selection method. We apply it to a test set T that includes *both* white-box and black-box tests, and thereby select all tests in T that may produce different output in the modified program due to code modifications. However, to achieve adequate confidence in modified software, our method should be used in conjunction with a black-box test selection method that selects tests relevant to changed specifications.

The feasibility of safe selective retest for applications programs. No matter how well we test a class C we cannot be certain, in general, that C behaves correctly for all inputs, because we cannot test C with all inputs. When we test an applications program P that uses C, our tests of P may exercise C with inputs not used during class testing. When we modify C, creating C', if we do *not* retest C' in the context of P, we may fail to detect faults that would be exposed by those inputs. Thus, we cannot confidently state that we have run all existing tests that might expose errors in C' unless we retest C' in the context of each applications program that uses it. Clearly, in practice we may have neither the time to retest all applications programs that use C', nor the ability to identify all such programs. In this case we must settle for less than safe test selection. We may choose instead to retest an identifiable subset of the applications programs that use the class. The algorithm of section 4 may be used to select tests for (and reduce the cost of retesting) this subset of programs.

Encapsulation. Object-oriented programming relies on encapsulation to reduce the likelihood that code modules will interact inappropriately. As the preceding paragraph shows, encapsulation does not eliminate the possibility that a test of an applications program will expose a fault in a class that was not exposed by some test of the class. Nevertheless, we expect that the use of encapsulation will reduce the size of the test sets our algorithm selects for applications programs that use modified classes, by eliminating data dependencies that would, if present, force selection of tests through the modified class. Since our algorithms for test selection use data dependence information to detect both tests that must be rerun, and tests that do not need to be rerun, it selects smaller test sets than algorithms that do not use such information[21].

7 Conclusion

We have presented a new method, based on code analysis techniques, for selecting regression tests for object-oriented software. Our method selects tests from existing test suites that may cause a modified program or class to produce different output than the original program or class. Our approach also selects tests that should be run for classes derived from other classes. The approach is advantageous because it handles selective retest needs in the object-oriented paradigm, is independent of program specifications and methods used to develop test suites initially, and

selects safe test suites.

Selective retest strategies are cost-effective only if the cost of running the tests these strategies let us omit exceeds the cost of applying the strategies[17]. As the size of an applications program increases, the cost of applying a selective retest strategy to that program may become prohibitive. However, we believe that in practice, the analysis our algorithms perform to select tests for *classes* will not be prohibitive. Clearly, experimentation is required to investigate the practicality of our test selection algorithms, and to determine under what conditions these algorithms are cost-effective. We are thus currently implementing our algorithms to select tests for C++ classes and applications programs. When the implementation is complete we will perform empirical studies to measure our methods' efficiency and effectiveness.

Several additional areas are open for future work. First, as Hoffman and Strooper[12] observe, careful test selection does not lower the cost of executing the tests we select; it would be useful to consider combining our approach with an approach like theirs that reduces the cost of test execution. Second, we believe our algorithm, with minor modifications, can be used to help detect obsolete tests and determine not just which tests must be reexecuted, but which tests may be inherited by a derived class. Third, we will consider the problems presented by polymorphism and dynamic binding in greater detail, in order to select more precise test sets. Finally, we will investigate methods for reducing the costs of our algorithm associated with graph construction, by constructing portions of graphs on demand rather than constructing entire graphs up front, and by saving and reusing portions of graphs.

References

[1] A.V. Aho, R. Sethi, and J.D. Ullman. *Compilers, Principles, Techniques, and Tools.* Addison-Wesley, Boston, MA, 1986.

[2] S. Bates and S. Horwitz. Incremental program testing using program dependence graphs. In *Proceedings of the Twentieth Annual ACM Symposium on Principles of Programming Languages*, January 1993.

[3] P. Benedusi, A. Cimitile, and U. De Carlini. Post-maintenance testing based on path change analysis. In *Proceedings of the Conference on Software Maintenance - 1988*, pages 352–61, October 1988.

[4] J. Ferrante, K.J. Ottenstein, and J.D. Warren. The program dependence graph and its use in optimization. *ACM Transactions on Programming Languages and Systems*, 9(3):319–49, July 1987.

[5] K.F. Fischer, F. Raji, and A. Chruscicki. A methodology for retesting modified software. In *Proceedings of the National Telecommunications Conference B-6-3*, pages 1–6, November 1981.

[6] P.G. Frankl and Roong-Ko Doong. Case studies on testing object-oriented programs. In *Proceedings of the Fourth Symposium on Testing, Analysis, and Verification (TAV4)*, October 1991.

[7] M.J. Harrold, J.D. McGregor, and K.J. Fitzpatrick. Incremental testing of object-oriented class structures. In *Proceedings of the 14th International Conference on Software Engineering*, pages 68–80, May 1992.

[8] M.J. Harrold and G. Rothermel. Performing dataflow testing on classes. Technical Report 94-108, Clemson University, Clemson, SC, June 1994.

[9] M.J. Harrold and M.L. Soffa. An incremental approach to unit testing during maintenance. In *Proceedings of the Conference on Software Maintenance - 1988*, pages 362–367, October 1988.

[10] M.J. Harrold and M.L. Soffa. Efficient computation of interprocedural definition-use chains. *ACM Transactions on Programming Languages and Systems (TOPLAS)*, pages 175–204, March 1994.

[11] J. Hartmann and D.J. Robson. Techniques for selective revalidation. *IEEE Software*, 16(1):31–8, January 1990.

[12] D.M. Hoffman and P.A. Strooper. Graph-based class testing. In *Proceedings of the 7th Australian Software Engineering Conference*, September 1993.

[13] W.E. Howden. Reliability of the path analysis testing strategy. *IEEE Transactions on Software Engineering*, SE-2(3):208–215, 1976.

[14] W.A. Landi and B.G. Ryder. A safe approximate algorithm for interprocedural pointer aliasing. In *Proceedings of SIGPLAN '92 Conference on Programming Language Design and Implementation*, pages 235–248, June 1992.

[15] J. Laski and W. Szermer. Identification of program modifications and its applications in software maintentance. In *Proceedings of the Conference on Software Maintenance - 1992*, pages 282–90, November 1992.

[16] H.K.N. Leung and L.J. White. A study of integration testing and software regression at the integration level. In *Proceedings of the Conference on Software Maintenance - 1990*, pages 290–300, November 1990.

[17] H.K.N. Leung and L.J. White. A cost model to compare regression test strategies. In *Proceedings of the Conference on Software Maintenance - 1991*, pages 201–8, October 1991.

[18] T.J. Ostrand and E.J. Weyuker. Using dataflow analysis for regression testing. In *Proceedings of the Sixth Annual Pacific Northwest Software Quality Conference*, pages 233–47, September 1988.

[19] D.E. Perry and G.E. Kaiser. Adequate testing and object-oriented programming. *Journal of Object-Oriented Programming*, 2(5):13–19, January 1990.

[20] G. Rothermel and M.J. Harrold. A safe, efficient algorithm for regression test selection. In *Proceedings of the Conference on Software Maintenance - 1993*, pages 358–67, September 1993.

[21] G. Rothermel and M.J. Harrold. A framework for evaluating regression test selection. In *Proceedings of the 16th International Conference on Software Engineering*, pages 201–10, May 1994.

[22] G. Rothermel and M.J. Harrold. Selecting regression tests for object-oriented software. Technical Report 94-104, Clemson University, Clemson, SC, March 1994.

[23] G. Rothermel and M.J. Harrold. Selecting tests and identifying test coverage requirements for modified software. In *Proceedings of the 1994 International Symposium on Software Testing and Analysis (ISSTA 94)*, August 1994.

[24] B. Sherlund and B. Korel. Modification oriented software testing. In *Conference Proceedings: Quality Week 1991*, pages 1–17, May 1991.

[25] M.D. Smith and D.J. Robson. A framework for testing object-oriented programs. *Journal of Object-Oriented Programming*, 5(3):45–53, June 1992.

[26] A.B. Taha, S.M. Thebaut, and S.S. Liu. An approach to software fault localization and revalidation based on incremental data flow analysis. In *Proceedings of the 13th Annual International Computer Software and Applications Conference*, pages 527–34, September 1989.

[27] C.D. Turner and D.J. Robson. The state-based testing of object-oriented programs. In *Proceedings of the Conference on Software Maintenance, 1993*, pages 302–11, September 1993.

[28] E.J. Weyuker. Axiomatizing software test data adequacy. *IEEE Transactions on Software Engineering*, SE-12(12):1128–38, December 1986.

[29] L.J. White and H.K.N. Leung. A firewall concept for both control-flow and data-flow in regression integration testing. In *Proceedings of the Conference on Software Maintenance, 1992*, pages 262–70, November 1992.

[30] S.S. Yau and Z. Kishimoto. A method for revalidating modified programs in the maintenance phase. In *Proceedings of the COMPSAC '87: The Eleventh Annual International Computer Software and Applications Conference*, pages 272–77, October 1987.

A Technique for the Selective Revalidation of OO Software

PEI HSIA,[1]* XIAOLIN LI,[1] DAVID CHENHO KUNG,[1] CHIH-TUNG HSU,[1] LIANG LI,[1] YASUFUMI TOYOSHIMA[2] AND CRIS CHEN[2]

[1]*Department of Computer Science and Engineering, The University of Texas at Arlington, P.O. Box 19015, Arlington, TX 76019-0015, U.S.A.*
[2]*Fujitsu Network Transmission Systems, Inc., 2540 First Street, #201, San Jose, CA 95131, U.S.A.*

SUMMARY

The object-orientated paradigm provides the power for software development but at the same time introduces some brand new problems. One of these problems is that the relationships among classes are more complex and difficult to identify than those in the traditional paradigm. This problem becomes a major obstacle for regression testing of OO software, in which the relationships among classes as well as those between test cases and classes, must be determined a priori. In this paper we propose a new method to select only a fraction of the test cases from the entire test suite to revalidate an OO software system. This method is based on the concepts of class firewall and of marking all the classes 'touched' by a test case. From the class firewall, we can identify all of the affected classes after a new version of software is released. Together with the markings, we can also identify all the test cases in the test suite that need to be retested after the software change. A step-by-step process is proposed to identify the relationships between classes and test cases, compute the class firewall, and select only the appropriate test cases for retesting. © 1997 by John Wiley & Sons, Ltd.

J. Softw. Maint., **9**, 217–233 (1997)

No. of Figures: 4.   No. of Tables: 6.   No. of References: 17.

KEY WORDS: software validation; object-orientated software testing; regression testing; acceptance testing; class firewall; software maintenance

1. INTRODUCTION

Software revalidation involves retesting the modified software to ensure that the software behaves correctly after the modification. There are essentially four issues in software revalidation:

* Correspondence to: Pei Hsia, Department of Computer Science and Engineering, University of Texas at Arlington, PO Box 19015, Arlington, TX 76019-0015, U.S.A. E-mail: hsia@cse.uta.edu

Contract grant sponsor: Texas Advanced Technology Program; Contract grant number: 003656-097.
Contract grant sponsor: Fujitsu Network Transmission Systems, Inc.
Contract grant sponsor: IBM Center for Advanced Studies.
Contract grant sponsor: Software Engineering Center for Telecommunications.

CCC 1040–550X/97/040217–17$17.50
© 1997 by John Wiley & Sons, Ltd.

Received 21 October 1996
Revised 6 May 1997

1. change impact identification,
2. test suite maintenance,
3. test strategy, and
4. test case selection.

Resolving the first issue involves locating all the modules and other program segments that are affected by the modification. Test suite maintenance attempts to keep the test suite status current and reusable for future revalidation. This involves identifying and eliminating the obsolete test cases and adding new relevant test cases into the test suite. The third issue in regression testing is to find a testing sequence to conduct a cost-effective retesting of the software. The fourth issue, test case selection, involves choosing a subset of the existing test suite to re-test the software after a modification. The objective of test case selection is to achieve maximum coverage with minimal time, cost and effort.

Two major factors contribute to the cost of revalidation. The first factor is maintaining a complete and up-to-date test suite to cover every part of the software. This may require generating new test cases and deleting irrelevant test cases; however, identifying the obsolete test cases so that they can be eliminated from the test suite is rather difficult. The second factor is revalidating the modifications by rerunning an appropriate subset of the test suite. This involves selecting a relevant set of test cases and a test strategy.

Software revalidation is a complex and expensive activity. The introduction of the object-orientated ('OO') paradigm makes this issue even more complicated and difficult to deal with. The problem is due to the use of numerous OO features such as inheritance, messaging, polymorphism and dynamic binding. The current practice of OO revalidation is still in its infancy. The transfer of traditional testing strategies to OO applications is relatively difficult. For example, unlike traditional procedural-language software, a hierarchy of program control structure is not existent in OO software. This prevents the traditional integration testing strategies like top-down, bottom-up and sandwich approaches from being directly applied to OO software. The intricate relationships and interactions between classes make test case design difficult.

This paper is organized as follows. The next section reviews related research on the regression testing of OO software. The proposed test case selection approach is presented in Section 3. Section 4 presents the results of our experiments to illustrate the application and the effectiveness of this approach. The final section gives concluding remarks for future research in this domain.

2. RELATED WORK

A number of studies on the selective revalidation of procedural-language software have been conducted in the past. Harrold and Soffa (1988) proposed an approach for analysing the change effects within a module. They employed a dataflow graph to identify the affected definition-use pairs and/or paths. Testing effort is reduced by retesting only the affected definition-use paths and the new paths. They extended the approach to identify affected modules at the inter-module level (Harrold and Soffa, 1989). Different approaches using a control-flow graph to identify the affected control-flow paths in a module include Prather and Myers (1987) and Laski and Szermer (1992).

Leung and White (1990) introduced the firewall concept to enclose all modules affected by a module modification. They based the identification of the firewall on a call graph. By retesting only the modules that are within the scope of the firewall, test effort can be saved. The firewall concept was later extended to include a data-orientated firewall to enclose the affected modules that are global-data-related to the modified module (White and Leung, 1992). Fischer (1977, 1980) employed the concept of a zero–one integer programming model to find a minimum set of test cases which cover one of the path criteria in unit regression testing. Hartmann and Robson (1989, 1991) extended Fischer's method to investigate other retest criteria and constraints such as retesting at minimum cost, time or effort.

Lee and He (1990) applied the zero–one programming model on a test matrix to minimize testing effort in functional regression testing. Yau and Kishimoto (1987) proposed a selective retesting method based on the concept of input-partitioning. The idea is to partition a program's input domain into several classes and combine the input data to traverse various paths through the code. A minimum set of test cases can be derived by identifying all possible paths that reach the modified code. Leung and White (1988) used the concept of function table to relate the functions and their associated test cases to maintain the test suite. Test cases are classified into reusable, obsolete and retestable so that only the retestable and new test cases are considered as tests in the new regression testing.

Although extensive efforts have been given to the research on traditional software revalidation, the issue of selective revalidation on object-orientated software as yet is not well addressed. Rothermel and Harrold (1994) presented an algorithm to construct dependence graphs for classes and application programs. The dependence graphs are used to determine which tests in an existing test suite can cause a modified class or program to produce a different output from the original.

The approach described in this paper addresses the issue of test case selection and emphasizes the detection of the run-time relationships between object classes and test cases. Our approach can handle not only the class inheritance relationship, but also the aggregation and association relationships. Kung *et al.* (1994, 1995) introduced a concept of class firewall to identify the effect of a class-level modification. A test order generation algorithm was also proposed to help retest the classes within the class firewall. The approach described in this paper applies the concept of class firewall to test case selection in the revalidation process.

3. TEST CASE SELECTION FOR REVALIDATION

3.1. Three steps

To make the OO software revalidation process effective and cost-efficient, we propose an approach in which the revalidation activities are performed in three steps:

1. Determining the relationship between class and test case. Appropriate probes are added to program code to detect the existence of possible relationships between the

use of a class and the execution of a test case. Inserting probes into the program facilitates the detection of the relationships between classes and test cases.

2. Identifying the change impacts of a class. An object relation diagram (ORD) is constructed from the source code to describe the static relationships among the classes. The ORD will be used as the basis for evaluating the cascading class change effects.

3. Selecting test cases for the revalidation. Some test cases in the original test suite have to be retested to ensure the correctness of the desired functionality of the OO software, while certain test cases may be ruled out in the revalidation process because they have no direct or indirect relationship with the changed class.

An OO program may be tested at different levels. In this paper we focus on the selective revalidation at the class level. Our approach can be used to evaluate the change impacts in a class library and to identify the test cases affected by the class changes.

3.2. Determining the relationship between class and test case

The test cases represent the possible inputs to the software from the system environment. In this paper we consider only those test cases that are visible to the end users. Our approach requires that a test log file be created to keep track of the classes that have been traversed by the test cases when the software system undergoes the acceptance testing. To keep track of the classes traversed by a specific test case, a special probe function MARK is inserted into appropriate position within the source code (see Figure 1). This preprocessing step paves the way for identifying the dynamic relationship between the classes and the test cases.

During the preprocessing phase, a script is used to extract the class name for each class in the OO software, and a probe function is then added to each class constructor and each member function in the class. Whenever a class object is declared or accessed by the member functions, the statements in the constructor or member function body will be automatically executed, thus triggering the incorporated probe function.

Definition

For each test case T, a touch set $TS(T)$ is defined as the set of the classes traversed by the execution of T.

Note that a touch set is determined at run-time. From a touch set $TS(T)$, a tester can distinguish those classes that have been used during the execution of T from the classes

```
MARK(classname)
     write the class name to the test log file
     write the test case id to the test log file
```

Figure 1. The probe function

116

that have not been used at all. Although the probe function MARK (see Figure 1) is added to each of the class constructors and member function bodies, MARK may or may not be triggered by a test case. If a class does not declare any constructor, the script will insert a constructor with the probe function MARK inside.

The probe function will not be triggered if no test cases use the class containing the probe function. Therefore, using the strategy of inserting the MARK function enables one to capture the dynamic relationships between classes and test cases. The dynamic features of these relationships are often difficult to detect and describe by the static program analytical techniques (e.g., tracing the program control flows manually).

3.3. Identifying the impacts of changing a class

The identification of class change impacts is a two-step process. The first step is the construction of an object-relation diagram (ORD) that identifies the relationship between the classes in the OO software. The ORD then serves as the basis upon which the task in the second step, called class firewall computation, is carried out (Kung *et al.*, 1995). The firewall for a changed class includes those classes that have been affected by the changes in a class. An object relation diagram represents the relationship of inheritance, aggregation and association among classes. An inheritance relation between two classes means that the properties defined for an object class are automatically defined for all of its subclasses, except where selective or overriding inheritance is specified. By using an aggregation relation, a composite object can be defined on the basis of its component objects, and the composite object is called the aggregated class object. The association relation encompasses a broader range of relationship links such as data dependence control dependence, or message passing between two independent object classes.

Definition

The ORD for an OO program Q is a directed graph $ORD = (V, E)$, where V is a set of nodes representing the object classes in Q, and $E \subseteq V \times V$ is a set of edges which describe the inheritance, aggregation or association relationships between classes. An edge from class A to class B indicates that A is dependent on B.

More specifically, $\langle C_1, C_2 \rangle$, $\in E$ if and only if one of the following conditions holds:

- C_1 is a derived class of C_2,
- C_1 is an aggregate class of C_2 (i.e., C_2 is part of C_1), or
- C_1 is associated with C_2 either by accessing its data members or by passing some messages.

It can be seen that the binary relation E is transitive; that is, if class B depends on class A and class C in turn depends on C, then C also depends on A. Figure 2 shows a portion of the object relation diagram derived from an ATM simulation program. Class TRANSACTION is determined to have an association relationship with class customer because customer is a parameter of member function TRANSACTION(). Since the

117

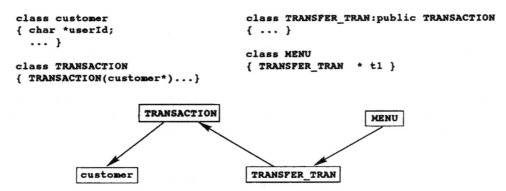

```
class customer                         class TRANSFER_TRAN:public TRANSACTION
{ char *userId;                        { ... }
   ... }
                                       class MENU
class TRANSACTION                      { TRANSFER_TRAN  * t1 }
{ TRANSACTION(customer*)...}
```

Figure 2. Obtaining class dependency relationships from source code

objects of class TRANSFER_TRAN become data members in class MENU, there exists an aggregation relationship between class TRANSFER_TRAN and class MENU. The inheritance relationship between classes TRANSACTION and TRANSFER_TRAN is straightforward.

Any changes made in an OO program will make it necessary for users to redo acceptance testing. The various changes in an OO program can be classified into three categories:

(1) changes that affect the object behaviour represented by the states of the data members;
(2) changes that affect the operations and behaviour of a class's member functions; and
(3) changes that affect the relationships and dependencies between a class and other classes.

In this paper, we consider only the first two types of changes and do not deal with class relation changes.

Definition

The class firewall for a class C, denoted $CFW(C)$, is defined as a set of classes that are dependent on C as described by an *ORD*.

Intuitively, a class firewall for a class C is the set of classes that may be affected by changes to class C. Figure 3 shows a class firewall of the example in Figure 2.

3.4. Test case selection

The changes made to a class in an OO program not only have impacts on other classes but also influence the set of test cases needing to be retested. The problem of identifying the test cases affected by class change is complicated by the fact that the OO paradigm supports a variety of class dependence relationships. Our study indicates that the class change impacts on the test cases can be detected and evaluated on the basis of class

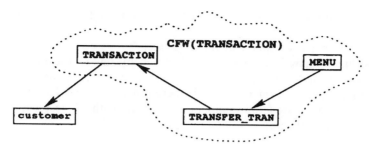

Figure 3. A class firewall

firewall computation. Intuitively, if a programmer makes a change to class C, testers only need to select test case T such that the touch set $TS(T)$ and class firewall $CFW(C)$ have a non-empty intersection.

Our approach uses matrix arithmetic to locate the test cases needed for retesting. Specifically, we define two matrices:

1. a $1 \times n$ class impact matrix M_c to indicate which classes have been included in a class firewall, where n is the total number of classes in the OO program under test; and
2. an $n \times k$ dependence matrix M_d to show the relationships between classes and test cases, where k is the number of test cases in the old test suite.

Once M_c and M_d are defined, the test cases needed for retesting can be determined from a matrix product $M_c \times M_d$. A zero-valued element q_{1i} in $M_c \times M_d$ implies that test case T_i has not been affected by the class changes, whereas each non-zero element q_{1i} indicates that test case T_i may be affected by class changes and therefore should be included in the new test suite for the revalidation.

4. EXPERIMENTS

4.1. ATM simulation software

4.1.1. Objective

This is a Unix-based simulation program written in C++. It consists of six program files and defines 13 object classes. Since the functionalities and behaviours of automated teller machines (ATMs) are well-known, we only give a brief description of each class in the software and assume the software requirements are self-explanatory. The main focus of this ATM experiment is to determine the feasibility of our approach. Specifically, we want to know:

1. whether our OO testing tool can identify the relationships among these 13 classes and perform class firewall computation; and

2. whether the number of test cases can be reduced for the revalidation.

Table 1 lists the classes defined in the software.

The relationships among the classes are identified by our OO testing tool, as illustrated in Figure 4. For example, class MENU turns out to be a subclass of TEXT_DISPLAY, and there exists an aggregation relationship between class TRANSFER_TRAN and class customer. Initially we tested the simulation software with 12 test cases, each testing a special aspect of the software:

T_1: Input invalid user ID, exit.
T_2: Valid user ID, invalid PIN, exit.
T_3: Valid user ID, valid PIN, exit.
T_4: Test transactions of deposition, withdraw, transfer, inquiry, valid input.
T_5: Test the withdraw of money, invalid input.
T_6: Test the deposition of money, invalid input.
T_7: Test the inquiry, invalid input.
T_8: Test the transfer of money, invalid input.
T_9: Input SuperUserID is wrong and exit.
T_{10}: Input SuperUserID is correct, but PIN is wrong and exit.
T_{11}: Test the SuperUser function, valid input.
T_{12}: Test the SuperUser function, invalid input.

4.1.2. Step 1: determining the relationships between class and test cases

A probe function MARK is automatically inserted into the constructor of each class. If there is no explicit constructor, a constructor with a MARK function is inserted. The following is a list of touch sets identified by our testing tool. From these touch sets, a tester can determine which classes are actually used by a certain test case. For example,

Table 1. Classes in ATM simulation software

Class	Class name	Class description
C_1	account	Maintain user account information
C_2	TEXT_DISPLAY	Print out screen messages
C_3	customer	Maintain customer information
C_4	TRANSACTION	Activate a transaction
C_5	WITHDRAW_TRAN	Withdraw money from an account
C_6	DEPOSIT_TRAN	Deposit money into an account
C_7	INQUIRY_TRAN	Retrieve relevant account information
C_8	TRANSFER_TRAN	Transfer money to another account
C_9	MENU	Maintain screen display formats
C_{10}	MSG	Maintain message formats
C_{11}	BAL_MSG	Prepare a message for a balance report
C_{12}	STR	Perform string operations
C_{13}	ATM	Maintain ATM information

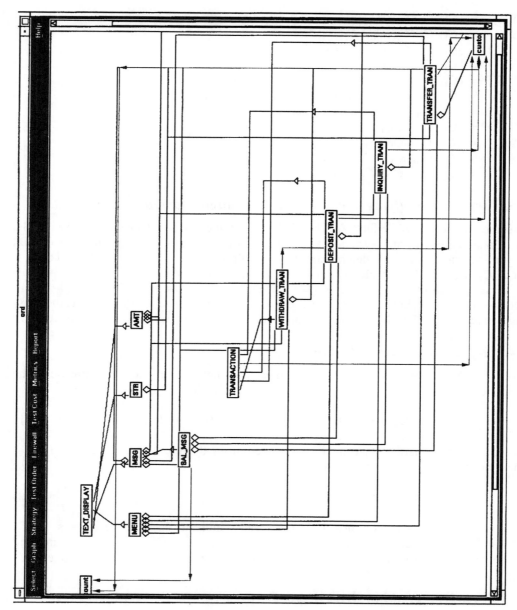

Figure 4. An ORD screen for the ATM experiment

classes TEXT_DISPLAY, MSG, and STR are determined to be used by test case T_1 during its execution.

$$TS(T_1) = \{C_2, C_{10}, C_{12}\}$$
$$TS(T_2) = \{C_1, C_2, C_{10}, C_{12}\}$$
$$TS(T_3) = \{C_1, C_2, C_9, C_{10}, C_{12}\}$$
$$TS(T_4) = \{C_1, C_2, C_3, C_4, C_5, C_6, C_7, C_8, C_9, C_{10}, C_{11}, C_{12}, C_{13}\}$$
$$TS(T_5) = \{C_1, C_2, C_3, C_4, C_5, C_9, C_{10}, C_{12}, C_{13}\}$$
$$TS(T_6) = \{C_1, C_2, C_3, C_4, C_6, C_9, C_{10}, C_{12}, C_{13}\}$$
$$TS(T_7) = \{C_1, C_2, C_3, C_4, C_7, C_9, C_{10}, C_{11}, C_{12}, C_{13}\}$$
$$TS(T_8) = \{C_1, C_2, C_3, C_4, C_8, C_9, C_{10}, C_{11}, C_{12}\}$$
$$TS(T_9) = \{C_2, C_{10}, C_{11}\}$$
$$TS(T_{10}) = \{C_2, C_{10}, C_{11}\}$$
$$TS(T_{11}) = \{C_2, C_{10}, C_{11}, C_{12}, C_{13}\}$$
$$TS(T_{12}) = \{C_2, C_{10}, C_{11}, C_{12}, C_{13}\}$$

4.1.3. Step 2: identifying the impacts of changing a class

Assume that class WITHDRAW_TRAN (i.e., C_5) has to be changed to enhance the ATM functionalities during system maintenance. From the object relation diagram (ORD) in Figure 4, our testing tool determines the class firewall for C_5 as $CFW(C_5) = \{C_3, C_4, C_5, C_6, C_7, C_8\}$. $CFW(C_5)$ clearly indicates that the changes in one class can influence other classes in an OO program. It shows that changes in class WITHDRAW_TRAN will affect six classes, leaving the other seven classes unaffected. The information on the class change impacts can then be used as a guide for the test case selection in the next step.

4.1.4. Step 3: test case selection

From $CFW(C_5)$ we can see that six classes are included in the class firewall. The corresponding class impact matrix P is then determined to be:

$$M_c = [\ 0,\ 0,\ 1,\ 1,\ 1,\ 1,\ 1,\ 1,\ 0,\ 0,\ 0,\ 0,\ 0\ ] \tag{1}$$

The dependence matrix M_d can be constructed from the touch sets $TS(T_1) \sim TS(T_{12})$ as mentioned in Step 1, is shown in Table 2, and hence:

$$M_c \times M_d = [\ 0,\ 0,\ 0,\ 6,\ 3,\ 3,\ 3,\ 3,\ 0,\ 0,\ 0,\ 0,\ 0\ ] \tag{2}$$

The non-zero elements in columns 4, 5, 6, 7 and 8 indicate that only test cases T_4, T_5, T_6, T_7, and T_8 are required to retest the software if class WITHDRAW_TRAN is changed after the initial round of testing. The other seven test cases do not have to be retested.

4.2. Interactive graphic-drawing software

The second software package used in our experiment is a PC-based drawing program (Priestley, 1996). The package consists of 11 program files and 18 header files, which

Table 2. Dependence matrix for ATM simulation software experiment

Class	T_1	T_2	T_3	T_4	T_5	T_6	T_7	T_8	T_9	T_{10}	T_{11}	T_{12}
account	0	1	1	1	1	1	1	1	0	0	0	0
TEXT_DISPLAY	1	1	1	1	1	1	1	1	1	1	1	1
customer	0	0	0	1	1	1	1	1	0	0	0	0
TRANSACTION	0	0	0	1	1	1	1	1	0	0	0	0
WITHDRAWN_TRAN	0	0	0	1	1	0	0	0	0	0	0	0
DEPOSIT_TRAN	0	0	0	1	0	1	0	0	0	0	0	0
INQUIRY_TRAN	0	0	0	1	0	0	1	0	0	0	0	0
TRANSFER_TRAN	0	0	0	1	0	0	0	1	0	0	0	0
MENU	0	0	1	1	1	1	1	1	0	0	0	0
MSG	1	1	1	1	1	1	1	1	1	1	1	1
BAL_MSG	0	0	0	1	0	0	1	1	1	1	1	1
STR	1	1	1	1	1	1	1	1	0	0	1	1
ATM	0	0	0	1	1	1	1	0	0	0	1	1

are compiled and built into executables by using Borland Turbo C++. The software defines 26 object classes to support various figure-drawing functions, such as rectangle selection, ellipse drawing, and graphic element resizing and moving. Since the results from the first experiment indicate that our approach does have the potential to reduce regression testing cost, in this second experiment we are more interested in the overall performance of the approach. Particularly, we want to know (1) the effectiveness of the approach in the average case, and (2) which factors influence the effectiveness.

Table 3 lists all the classes used in the software, where C is a class name, $|CFW(C)|$ is the number of classes in the corresponding class firewall, and α is the ratio of $|CFW(C)|$ to the total number of classes (i.e., $|CFW(C)| \div 26$). Note that $|CFW(C)| = 1$ implies that there is no other class dependent on C, and therefore the changes only affect class C itself. Our initial test suite consists of 14 test cases, as listed in Table 4.

Having identified the class firewalls and developed the initial test suite, we want to examine the impacts of class changes on the test cases. The dependence matrix M_d of this experiment is shown in Table 5. Each column in the matrix represents the touch set of the related test case. A sparse matrix such as this is a clear indication that, in general, a test case uses only a small number of classes defined in the software.

For each of the 26 classes, our testing tool derives the corresponding class impact matrix M_c and computes $M_c \times M_d$. The experiment results are listed in Table 6, where C is the changed class, T' is the set of test cases affected by the changes, $|T'|$ is the size of T', and p is the ratio of $|T'|$ to the total number of test cases in the initial test suite. Recall that owing to the dependence relationships of classes, it may well be the case that more test cases are affected by changes in a class than those directly using the class. For example, all 14 test cases are affected by the changes in class Node, despite the fact that the class is used directly by three test cases only (i.e., T_5, T_6 and T_7).

It can be seen from Table 6 that in the best case the changes made to a class (e.g.,

Table 3. Classes and their firewall sizes

C	$|CFW(C)|$	α
ControlPoint	16	0·62
Collection	10	0·38
Node	11	0·42
Display	21	0·81
Drawing	8	0·31
Rectangle	3	0·12
Ellipse	3	0·12
GraphicsScreen	1	0·04
Mouse	4	0·15
Poller	1	0·04
CreationTool	5	0·19
LineTool	2	0·08
SelectionTool	2	0·08
Application	4	0·15
CollectionEditor	1	0·04
DiagramEditor	1	0·04
DOSKeyboard	1	0·04
Element	15	0·58
Line	3	0·12
EventHandler	2	0·08
Keyboard	3	0·12
MSMouse	1	0·04
Tool	7	0·27
RectangleTool	2	0·08
EllipseTool	2	0·08
ToolManager	8	0·31

Table 4. Test cases in the initial test suite

Test case	Description
T_1	Initiate the program and then exit
T_2	Select the rectangle-drawing operation
T_3	Select the ellipse-drawing operation
T_4	Select the line-drawing operation
T_5	Draw a rectangle
T_6	Draw an ellipse
T_7	Draw a line
T_8	Initiate the select-element operation
T_9	Cancel the select-element operation
T_{10}	Select an element (a rectangle, an ellipse or a line)
T_{11}	Move an element
T_{12}	Unselect an element
T_{13}	Initiate select-element operation and drag (outside of any element)
T_{14}	Resize an element (click on handle and drag)

Table 5. Dependence matrix for graphic-drawing software

Class	Test case													
	T_1	T_2	T_3	T_4	T_5	T_6	T_7	T_8	T_9	T_{10}	T_{11}	T_{12}	T_{13}	T_{14}
Application	1	0	0	0	0	0	0	0	0	0	0	0	0	0
Collection	1	0	0	0	0	0	0	1	0	0	0	0	0	0
CollectionIter.	0	0	0	0	0	0	0	0	1	1	1	1	1	1
Node	0	0	0	0	1	1	1	0	0	0	0	0	0	0
ControlPoint	0	0	0	0	1	1	1	0	0	0	0	0	0	0
DiagramEditor	1	0	0	0	0	0	0	0	0	0	0	0	0	0
Display	1	0	0	0	0	0	0	0	0	0	0	0	0	0
DOSKeyboard	1	0	0	0	0	0	0	0	0	0	0	0	0	0
Drawing	1	0	0	0	0	0	0	0	0	0	0	0	0	0
Element	0	0	0	0	1	1	1	0	0	0	0	0	0	0
Rectangle	0	0	0	0	1	0	0	0	0	0	0	0	0	0
Line	0	0	0	0	0	0	1	0	0	0	0	0	0	0
Ellipse	0	0	0	0	0	1	0	0	0	0	0	0	0	0
EventHandler	1	0	0	0	0	0	0	0	0	0	0	0	0	0
GraphicScreen	1	0	0	0	0	0	0	0	0	0	0	0	0	0
Keyboard	1	0	0	0	0	0	0	0	0	0	0	0	0	0
Mouse	1	0	0	0	0	0	0	0	0	0	0	0	0	0
MSMouse	1	0	0	0	0	0	0	0	0	0	0	0	0	0
Poller	1	0	0	0	0	0	0	0	0	0	0	0	0	0
Tool	0	1	1	1	0	0	0	1	0	0	0	0	0	0
CreationTool	0	1	1	1	0	0	0	0	0	0	0	0	0	0
RectangleTool	0	1	0	0	0	0	0	0	0	0	0	0	0	0
LineTool	0	0	0	1	0	0	0	0	0	0	0	0	0	0
EllipseTool	0	0	1	0	0	0	0	0	0	0	0	0	0	0
SelectionTool	0	0	0	0	0	0	0	1	0	0	0	0	0	0
ToolManager	1	1	0	0	0	0	0	0	0	0	0	0	0	0

class DiagramEditor) influence only one test case, implying that 13 other test cases are not required for the revalidation. However, the table also shows that the changes in four of the classes affect the initial test suite so seriously that all of the 14 test cases must be retested. A better measurement for the overall performance is to look at the average case. If we assume that each class is equally likely to be changed, on average $|T'|$ is equal to 4·54. This indicates that on average only 4·54 out of 14 test cases will be affected by the changes in a class. In other words, we can expect that the approach will provide a savings of 67·6% for the software revalidation.

5. CONCLUDING REMARKS

We have described a selective revalidation technique for OO software. The proposed approach is based on the ideas of object relation diagram, class firewall, class-level probe function and a test-class matrix. The experiments show that our approach can save time and cost. First, the time of applying our approach is minimal because the entire revalidation

Table 6. Test cases affected by class changes

C	T'	$|T'|$	p
ControlPoint	$T_1 \sim T_{14}$	14	1·000
Collection	$T_1 \sim T_4, T_8 \sim T_{14}$	11	0·785
Node	$T_1 \sim T_{14}$	14	1·000
Display	$T_1 \sim T_{14}$	14	1·000
Drawing	$T_1 \sim T_4, T_8$	5	0·357
Rectangle	T_1, T_2, T_5	3	0·214
Ellipse	T_1, T_3, T_6	3	0·214
GraphicsScreen	T_1	1	0·071
Mouse	T_1	1	0·071
Poller	T_1	1	0·071
CreationTool	$T_1 \sim T_4$	4	0·286
LineTool	T_1, T_4	2	0·143
SelectionTool	T_1, T_8	2	0·143
Application	T_1	1	0·071
CollectionEditor	$T_9 \sim T_{14}$	6	0·429
DiagramEditor	T_1	1	0·071
DOSKeyboard	T_1	1	0·071
Element	$T_1 \sim T_{14}$	14	1·000
Line	T_1, T_4, T_7	3	0·214
EventHandler	T_1	1	0·071
Keyboard	T_1	1	0·071
MSMouse	T_1	1	0·071
Tool	$T_1 \sim T_4, T_8$	3	0·357
RectangleTool	T_1, T_2	2	0·143
EllipseTool	T_1, T_3	2	0·143
ToolManager	$T_1 \sim T_4, T_8$	3	0·357

process—change impact identification and test case selection—has been fully automated. Second, the cost of revalidation can be significantly reduced if the number of selected test cases is well below the total number of test cases in the test suite. The cost saving is nearly linearly proportional to the number of unselected test cases.

Future research in this area should be directed at extending the current class-level revalidation technique to the member function and data member levels. Our approach assumes that each data member is private. That is, data member access from outside a class will invoke the class's constructor from which the probe function is executed. The use of the probe function should be expanded to encompass the cases of friend functions, and public data members and member functions.

Acknowledgements

The material printed in this paper is based on the work supported by the Texas Advanced Technology Program (Grant number 003656-097), Fujitsu Network Transmission Systems, Inc., the IBM Fellowship grant from IBM Center for Advanced Studies, Toronto, Canada, and the Software Engineering Center for Telecommunications at UTA.

References

Fischer, K. F. (1977) 'A test case selection method for the validation of software maintenance modifications', in *Proceedings COMPSAC77*, Chicago, IL, IEEE Computer Society Press, Los Alamitos, CA, pp. 421–426.

Fischer, K. F. (1980) 'A graph theoretic approach to the validation of software maintenance modifications', Doctoral dissertation, University of California, Los Angeles, CA, 141 pp.

Harrold, M. J. and Soffa, M. L. (1988) 'An incremental approach to unit testing', in *Proceedings Conference on Software Maintenance—1988*, IEEE Computer Society Press, Los Alamitos, CA, pp. 362–367.

Harrold, M. J. and Soffa, M. L. (1989) 'Interprocedural data flow testing', in *Proceedings of the Third Testing, Analysis and Verification Symposium*, ACM Press, New York, NY, pp. 158–167.

Hartmann, J. and Robson, D. J. (1989) 'Revalidation during the software maintenance phase', in *Proceedings Conference on Software Maintenance—1989*, IEEE Computer Society Press, Los Alamitos, CA, pp. 70–80.

Hartmann, J. and Robson, D. J. (1991) 'Techniques for selective revalidation', *IEEE Software*, 8(1), 31–36.

Kung, D. C., Gao, J., Hsia, P., Wen, F., Toyoshima, Y. and Chen, C. (1994) 'Change impact identification in object-oriented software', in *Proceedings International Conference on Software Maintenance*, IEEE Computer Society Press, Los Alamitos, CA, pp. 202–211.

Kung, D. C., Gao, J., Hsia, P., Wen, F., Toyoshima, Y. and Chen, C. (1995) 'Class firewall, test order, and regression testing of object-oriented programs', *Journal of Object-Oriented Programming*, 8(2), 51–56.

Laski, J. and Szermer, W. (1992) 'Identification of program modification and its applications in software maintenance', in *Proceedings Conference on Software Maintenance*, IEEE Computer Society Press, Los Alamitos, CA, pp. 282–290.

Lee, J. A. N. and He, X. (1990) 'A methodology for test selection', *Journal of Systems and Software*, 13(3), 177–185.

Leung, H. K. N. and White, L. (1988) 'A study of regression testing', Technical Report TR 88-15, Computing Science Department, University of Alberta, Edmondon, Canada, 16 pp.

Leung, H. K. N. and White, L. (1990) 'Insights into testing and regression testing global variables', *Journal of Software Maintenance*, 2(4), 209–222.

Priestley, M. (1996) *Practical Object-Oriented Design*, McGraw-Hill Book Co., New York, NY, 350 pp.

Prather, R. E. and J.P. Myers Jr., J. P. (1987) 'The path prefix software testing strategy', *Transactions on Software Engineering*, SE-13(7), 761–765.

Rothermel, G. and Harrold, M. J. (1994) 'Selecting regression tests for object-oriented software', in *Proceedings International Conference on Software Maintenance*, IEEE Computer Society, Los Alamitos, CA, pp. 14–25.

White, L. and Leung, H. K. N. (1992) 'A firewall concept for both control-flow and data-flow in regression integration testing', in *Proceedings Conference on Software Maintenance*, IEEE Computer Society Press, Los Alamitos, CA, pp. 262–271.

Yau, S. S. and Kishimoto, Z. (1987) 'A method for revalidating modified programs in the maintenance phase', in *Proceedings COMPSAC87*, IEEE Computer Society Press, Los Alamitos, CA, pp. 272–277.

Chapter 5

Object State Testing

Object state testing is an important aspect of object oriented software testing. It is different from the conventional control flow testing and data flow testing methods. In control flow testing, the focus is testing the program according to the control structures (that is, sequencing, branching, and iteration) of the program being tested. That is, test cases are generated according to the control structures and attempt to exercise each part of the program through the control structures. For example, two test cases are generated to test an "if-then-else" statement. One exercises the "then part" while the other exercises the "else part."

In data flow testing, the focus is testing the correctness of individual data define-and-use. A variable x is defined if it is assigned a value and it is used if its value is used in a condition or a calculation. A variable x may be defined at one place and afterward its value will be used in several places. Data flow testing aims at generating test cases to exercise variables' define-and-use pairs in an attempt to detect errors that are caused by improper definitions or uses of variables.

Object state testing focuses on testing the state-dependent behaviors of objects rather than the control structures and individual data. Finite-state machines, also called state transition diagrams, are most often used to model object-state-dependent behaviors. From these models test cases are generated to test the implementation.

This section includes three papers. The first paper "The State-Based Testing of Object-Oriented Programs," by C.D. Turner and D.J. Robson [turn93a], describes a black-box state-based testing method for testing the interactions between the features of an object and the object's state. The features of an object are usually implemented as the object's operations or methods. This approach takes into account the random order in which the features can be invoked. The paper also suggests a suite of tools to support state-based testing of object-oriented programs.

A state of an object is defined as the combination of the attribute values of the object. This view is commonly taken by researchers of the object-oriented paradigm. Since the number of all possible combinations is large, two concepts are introduced to reduce the complexity: (1) specific state values; and (2) general state values.

A specific state value of an attribute of an object has specific significance in the application at hand. For example, the quantities-on-hand of a certain product may drop below a certain level which would trigger a replenishment event. Another example is the NULL value of a linked list head pointer that signifies that the list is empty. Note that an attribute may have more than one specific state value. For example, the attribute used to denote the top of a stack may have "full" and "empty" as its specific values. The general state values of an attribute include all the values that are not specific. Using these concepts, the states of an object are identified according to the specification or design of the object class. States for invalid or exceptional situations are also identified.

The features of a class, when executed, cause state transitions from an "input state" to an "output state." The input states and output states of each feature are identified according to the specification or design. Test cases then are generated to test and validate each state transition. To simplify the process, Turner and Robson's paper also proposes using substates, each of which is a combination of values of a subset of the attributes of a class, instead of states (which considers all the attributes) in the test case generation process. The steps for using this approach are: (1) identifying states which are combinations of attribute values; (2) identifying state transitions from input states to output states resulting in a finite state machine (FSM); and 3) generating test cases from the FSM.

The second paper, "ClassBench: A Framework for Automated Class Testing," by D. Hoffman and P. Strooper [hoff97a], describes a black-box methodology and support tools for testing object-state-dependent behaviors. The methodology consists of three main steps: (1) the tester prepares a testgraph which is essentially a state transition diagram that illustrates the expected state dependent behavior of the class under test (CUT); (2) according to the testgraph the tester implements an oracle class that has exactly the same methods as the CUT; (3) the tester implements test drivers to initialize the oracle class and the CUT; (4) the tester generates test cases according to the state transitions in the testgraph to execute the CUT and the oracle class; and (5) the tester determines whether the CUT implements the desired behavior by comparing the execution results of the CUT and the oracle class.

The third paper, "Object State Testing and Fault Analysis for Reliable Software Systems," by Kung et al. [kung96c] is an extension of an earlier paper on object state testing by the authors [kung94c]. The authors showed that certain object state behavior errors could not be readily detected by conventional testing methods like control flow testing or data flow testing. They then described an object state test method consisting of an object state model, a reverse engineering tool, and an object state test generation tool. The object state test model is an aggregation of hierarchical, concurrent, communicating state machines envisioned mainly for object-state testing. A state machine may be an atomic object state diagram (AOSD) or a composite object state diagram (COSD).

An AOSD is a Mealy-type state transition diagram defined for a single attribute of the class under testing. It represents the state-dependent behavior of the attribute. Since only some of the attributes of a class have state-dependent behaviors, only these attributes require an AOSD. For example, the title of a book in a library never changes, therefore, it does not require an AOSD. A COSD is an aggregate of AOSDs and COSDs. This recursive definition allows the test model to support inheritance and aggregation in OO programming. That is, the state-dependent behavior of a derived class or subclass is a COSD consisting of the AOSDs for its own attributes and the COSD that represents the state-dependent behavior of its parent class. Similarly, the behavior of an aggregate class is a COSD consisting of the AOSDs for its own attributes and the COSDs representing the behaviors of the component classes.

The reverse engineering tool produces an object state model from any C++ program (The tool is being extended to process Java programs.) The object state test generation tool analyzes the object state behaviors and generates object state test cases. Another important feature of the paper is state-based fault analysis which identifies the sequence(s) of method invocations that led to a faulty state. The steps to conduct object state testing can be summarized as follows: (1) selecting the class(es) to be tested; (2) generating the AOSDs for the class(es), noting that the COSDs are simply the aggregates of AOSDs and COSDs; (3) generating object state test cases from the AOSDs and COSDs; (4) generating test data for the test cases (test data generator is another tool not covered by the paper); (5) executing the test cases; (6) analyzing the test results to identify bugs; and perhaps (7) conducting state-based fault analysis to identify possible causes.

The three papers of this chapter all deal with object state testing. As expected, there are similarities and differences. These are summarized in Table 1.

The first two papers [turn93a], [hoff97a] present black-box approaches. That is, the tester constructs an object state test model from the requirements specification or according to her or his knowledge about the application at hand. From the test model the state test cases are generated. The third paper uses a white-box approach. That is, the tester generates the test model from the program code. Test cases are then generated from the test model. The first and the third papers both view an object state as a combination of a subset of attribute values. All three papers view state transitions as the results of method invocations and test cases are generated from the object state test model. Test tools are used by all these approaches. In Hoffman et al.'s approach the tester also implements an oracle class which simulates the behavior of the class under test and uses its results to determine whether the class under test correctly implements the desired behavior. In Kung et al.'s approach, state-based fault analysis is also performed to help the tester identify the possible causes of faults.

Table 1. Similarities and differences.

	Turner et al.'s approach	Hoffman et al.'s approach	Kung et al.'s approach
Approach	Black-box	Black-box	White-box
Test model	Finite state machine (FSM)	Finite state machine (FSM)	Hierarchical, concurrent, communicating FSMs
State view	Combination of attribute values	Depends on the tester's view	Combination of attribute values
Transitions	Method invocations	Method invocations	Method invocations
Test cases generation	From test model	From test model	From test model
Tool support	Yes	Yes	Yes
Other		Uses oracle class to help determine the "correctness" of test results	State-based fault analysis

References

[hoff97a] D. Hoffman and P. Strooper, "ClassBench: A Framework for Automated Class Testing," *Software Practice and Experience,* Vol. 27, No. 5, 1997, pp. 573–597.

[kung94c] D. Kung et al., "On Object State Testing," *Proc. COMPSAC 94*, IEEE Computer Society Press, Los Alamitos, Calif., 1994, pp. 222–227.

[kung96c] D. Kung et al., "Object State Testing and Fault Analysis for Reliable Software Systems," *Proc. 7th Int'l Symp. Software Reliability Engineering*, IEEE Computer Society Press, Los Alamitos, Calif., 1996.

[turn93a] C.D. Turner and D.J. Robson, "The State-Based Testing of Object-Oriented Programs," *Proc. IEEE Conf. Software Maintenance*, IEEE Computer Society Press, Los Alamitos, Calif., 1993, pp. 302–310.

Object State Testing and Fault Analysis for Reliable Software Systems

D. Kung, Y. Lu, N. Venugopalan, P. Hsia

Computer Science Engineering Dept.
The Univ. of Texas at Arlington
416 Yates Street, 300 NH
P. O. Box 19015
Arlington, TX 76019-0015
Tel: (817) 273-3627, Fax: (817) 273-3784
Email: kung@cse.uta.edu

Y. Toyoshima, C. Chen, J. Gao

Fujitsu Network Communication Systems
2540 North First Street, Suite 201
San Jose, Ca. 95131

Abstract

Object state behavior implies that the effect of an operation on an object may depend on the states of the object and other objects. It may cause state changes to more than one object. Thus, the combined or composite effects of the object operations must be analyzed and tested. We show that certain object state behavior errors cannot be detected readily by conventional testing methods. We describe an object state test method consisting of an object state model, a reverse engineering tool, and a composite object state testing tool. The object state test model is an aggregation of hierarchical, concurrent, communicating state machines envisioned mainly for object state testing. The reverse engineering tool produces an object state model from any C++ program. The composite object state testing tool analyzes the object state behaviors and generates test cases for testing object state interactions. We show the detection of several composite object state behavior errors that exist in a well-known thermostat example.

1 Introduction

Object state testing is different from control flow and data flow testings. Object state testing focuses on testing objects' state dependent behavior rather than the control structures and individual data. That is, we need to develop 1) a suitable state test model; 2) a methodology for constructing a state test model, from either a specification or a given OO program; 3) state testing strategies and testing criteria; and 4) methods and techniques for test case generation and result evaluation.

This paper deals with object state testing and its extensions to safety critical software fault analysis. In particular, we describe an object state test model, called *object state diagram (OSD)* to capture state dependent behaviors of objects. We then informally present a methodology for extracting object state behavior from an OO program written in C++ and representing the object state behavior in terms of object

state diagrams. The OSD can also be derived from a specification, as described in [4]. An OSD can be used to generate test cases and fault analysis. These will be described later in the paper.

We wish to point out that the OSD is defined with testing rather than modeling in mind; that is, it is defined to facilitate a tester to understand the state dependent behaviors of the object classes, to generate state test cases, and to evaluate the test results.

The importance of the work can be stated as follows. First, object state testing has not received wide attention and in-depth treatment, although state machines have been used to test conventional software [1] and protocol software [5]. Second, symbolic execution has traditionally been used to prepare test cases for testing a single function, not interactions between the member functions of a class through object state. Third, although integration testing of an OO application program may detect some state behavior errors, the difficulty and cost will be much higher than detecting (and removing) such errors at class level testing. Moreover, the advantage of class library and software reuse will be largely compromised if the classes are not well tested.

The organization of this paper is as follows. In section 2, we discuss the importance of object state testing through a simple example. In section 3, we introduce a state test model for capturing and representing object state dependent behavior. In section 4, we present the methodology for extracting state dependent behaviors from C++ code. In section 5, we discuss the usefulness of the OSD in testing and in section 6 we show fault analysis using an object state approach in opposed to the fault tree analysis approach. Section 7 is related work and new problems introduced by the OO features and some existing solutions. Finally in section 8 we present the conclusions and future work.

2 The Importance of Object State Testing

Conventional functional and structural testings may detect errors that are local to a member function. They are not adequate for detecting errors due to interactions between member functions through object state behaviors. In this section, we show informally the notion of object state and the importance of object state testing through a simple example.

2.1 A Motivating Example

Consider a coin box of a vending machine implemented in C++. For simplicity, we will assume that the coin box has very simple functionality and the code to control the physical device is omitted. It accepts only quarters and allows vending when two quarters are received. It keeps track of the total quarters (denoted totalQtrs) received, the current quarters (denoted curQtrs) received, and whether vending is enabled or not (denoted allowVend). Its functions include adding a quarter, returning the current quarters, resetting the coin box to its initial state, and vending. The C++ source code for this simple coin box is listed below:

```
class CCoinBox {
  unsigned totalQtrs; // total quarters collected
  unsigned curQtrs; // current quarters collected
  unsigned allowVend; // 1 = vending is allowed
public:
  CCoinBox() { Reset(); }
  void AddQtr(); // add a quarter
  void ReturnQtrs() { curQtrs = 0; } // return current
quarters
  unsigned isAllowedVend() { return allowVend; }
  void Reset() { totalQtrs = 0; allowVend = 0; curQtrs =
0; }
  void Vend(); // if allowed, update totalQtrs and curQtrs
};
void CCoinBox::AddQtr() {
  curQtrs = curQtrs + 1; // add a quarter
  if (curQtrs > 1) // if more than one quarter is collected,
    allowVend = 1; // then set allowVend }
void CCoinBox::Vend() {
  if ( isAllowedVend() ) // if allowVend
  {
    totalQtrs = totalQtrs + curQtrs; // update totalQtrs,
    curQtrs = 0;               // curQtrs, and
    allowVend = 0;             // allowVend,
  }                            // else no action }
```

By carefully examining the code above one may discover that there is an error in the implementation. But the error is not obvious. We argue that the error cannot be easily detected by functional testing and/or structural testing of the member functions since: 1) each of the member functions seems to implement the intended functionality; 2) structural testing (such as basis path testing) also would conclude that each basis path is correctly executed; and 3) the most important is that the error was due to interactions involving more than one member function through an object state. Such interaction implies that testing the

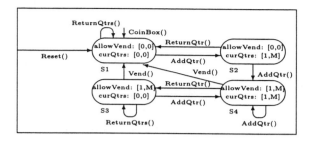

Figure 1: States and state transitions for the coin box example

individual functions is not likely to discover the error.

2.2 Error Detection via State Testing

In our opinion, the states of an object are defined by a subset of the member data of the object class. For the coin box example, the subset of member data that define the states of the coin box are allowVend and curQtrs, because these two member data are checked in a conditional statement to determine whether certain actions need to be performed. For example, the allowVend is checked in Vend() to determine if totalQtrs, curQtrs, and allowVend should be updated. Similarly, curQtrs is checked in AddQtr() to set allowVend. TotalQtrs is not a state defining member datum because the object behaves independently from changes to this datum.

From the two possible outcomes of the test of allowVend we know that there are two possible intervals or states: $[0, 0], [1, M]$, where M denotes the maximum possible value of unsigned for a particular implementation. Similar, there are two states for curQtrs: $[0, 0], [1, M]$. Thus, there are totally four states for the coin box, as illustrated in Figure 1.

As usual, an object changes its state when a member function is executed. The effects of the member functions can be analyzed by identifying the pre-state in which a member function can be applied, and the post-state that results. For example, the AddQtr() function can be applied to any of the four states. Its application in state S1 results in state S2, its application in state S2 results in state S4 in which allowVend is set to greater than zero due to the successful testing of the condition "curQtrs $+ 1 > 1$" (which is equivalent to "curQtrs > 0"). The analysis of all of the functions results in the state transition diagram in Figure 1. State S1 is an initial state since it is the resulting state of a constructor. Note that the pre-state of a constructor is not shown to conceptually indicate that the object is created from scratch. Note also that the transition labeled by Reset() connects the enclosing rectangle and state S1. This is a shorthand notation to mean that the Reset() member function can be executed in any of the states and the execution always results in state S1. The member function isAllowVend() is not shown for simplicity.

From the state transition diagram, we see that the following scenario or member function sequence can occur: AddQtr(); AddQtr(); Vend(). The sequence constitutes a normal and expected behavior of the coin box. However, the diagram also indicates that the scenario AddQtr(); AddQtr(); ReturnQtrs(); Vend() is also possible. This means that a consumer could insert two quarters, instruct the coin box to return the quarters, and Vend() to get a free drink. A state dependent error is detected.

The error is caused by not resetting the member datum allowVend to zero when the ReturnQtrs() member function is executed. It can be removed by changing ReturnQtrs() to

$$void \quad ReturnQtrs()\{curQtrs = 0; allowVend = 0; \}$$

It is important to point out that there are many possible ways to implement the correct semantics. This makes it difficult to detect such errors by conventional functional and structural testings. For example, there could be a disAllowVend() member function, which could be invoked to set allowVend to zero, and Vend() would test both allowVend and curQtrs to determine whether vending is allowed. Thus, ReturnQtrs() would not be changed. Although this latter alternative may not be elegant, but it could exist in practice.

2.3 The Complexity of the Flat State Machine

The state machine in Figure 1 is called a flat state machine since the states and transitions are represented in only one level. Flat state machines are commonly used in modeling and testing function-oriented software. However, our experience showed that flat state machines are not appropriate for modeling and testing in the OO paradigm because these machines tend to introduced excessive complexity. Suppose a class has k state defining member data, each has $n_i, i = 1, \ldots, k$ value intervals (e.g., curQtrs has two intervals: [0,0] and [1,M]). The total number of possible combined states will be $N = n_1 * n_2 * \ldots * n_k$. In the worst case, there could be $N * N = n_1^2 * n_2^2 * \ldots * n_k^2$ directed edges, each of which may be labeled by more than one member function since two member functions may cause the same transition. For the coin box example above, we have four states and in the worst case there can be as many as 16 directed edges representing the state transitions.

3 The Object State Test Model (OSD)

A state of a simple object in C++ is captured by ranges of values of a subset of member data of the object. For instance, a library book is available for check out if its number_of_copies is not equal to zero. In this example, the member data number_of_copies defines the state of book, while the member data book_title does not participate in the definition of the object's state because state changes of the object are independent of the member data.

The complexity of using the conventional flat state machines, as discussed in the last section, suggests

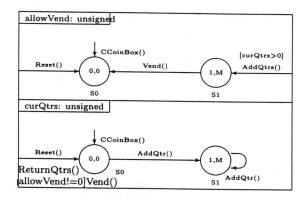

Figure 2: A nonflat state machine for the incorrect coin box class

that a hierarchical, concurrent object state diagram be used to represent the object state behavior. That is, the state behavior of a complex object is viewed as consisting of three parts: 1) the inherited part; 2) the aggregated part; and 3) the defined part. The inherited part consists of state machines of the base classes from which the complex object is derived. Similarly, the aggregated part consists of state machines of the component classes that are part of the complex object. The defined part consists of state machines for the state defining member data (e.g., number_of_copies) of the object. In particular, there is a state machine for each state defining member datum. Our experience showed that the introduction of hierarchy simplifies representation and analysis.

For a more formal and detailed definition, see [6].

A composite OSD, denoted COSD, is defined recursively as follows: 1) an aggregation of AOSD's is a COSD; 2) an aggregation of AOSD's and COSD's is a COSD. A COSD for the erroneous coin box is shown in Figure 2.

4 Reversing Object State Behavior

In this section, we outline a reverse engineering method for constructing a COSD from C++ source code. In particular, we will focus on AOSD construction for a base class because a COSD can be constructed easily and recursively from AOSD's. We will present only a simplified version of the method to avoid going into details. The interested reader is referred to [10] [12]. We will not consider pointers and pointer operations.

The constructed OSD can be used in verification and testing to detect errors in object state behavior. State testing using this method is known as program-based or white-box state testing. The other approach, which uses state machines constructed from a specification [4], is called specification-based or black-box state testing.

The method consists of three main steps: 1) symbolically execute each member function of the class; 2) identify states from the result of symbolic execution; and 3) identify transitions from the result of symbolic execution. Each of these steps will be described in greater detail in the following sections.

4.1 Symbolically Execute Each Member Function

This is the first step of the reverse engineering method. If the member function does not contain a loop, then symbolic execution is easy and the method has been illustrated in [6]. If the member function contains a loop, then the following rules are applied:

- If the loop does not contain any predicates, then symbolically execute the loop along three paths. One that contains zero iterations of the loop, a second that contains one iteration, and a third that contains two iterations. The idea behind this strategy is that zero, one, and two iterations coincide with three classes of loop error and so each should be tested. These three paths would provide reasonable coverage of the loop. This is satisfactory only because the statements in the loop contain no branching and coverage of the loop statements is achieved.

- If the loop contains multiple predicates, then the loop is executed zero times, and as many times as needed to cover each of the basis paths in the loop.

- Repeat the above steps until the entire member function is symbolically executed.

4.2 Identifying States

This is the second step of the method. It identifies states for some of the primitive type data members. To simplify explanation we will only consider integer data types. The method can be extended to other data type without much difficulty.

The aim of creating states is to explain the behavior of the class based on the values the data member takes. The value of the data member effects the class behavior when it takes part in a decision (condition), the evaluation of which at run time controls the execution path. We will exploit this to partition the domain of the data member into intervals where the values of data member lead to different execution paths.

We need to define some terminology. An arithmetic expression is a variable expression involving one or more variables. An atomic condition is an expression involving two variable expressions connected by one of the relational operators: $>, <, ==, >=, <=$ and $! =$. Compound conditions are formed by atomic conditions and logical connectives $\land, \lor$, and $\lnot$ as usual. A conditional literal is either an atomic condition or the negation of an atomic condition. If the only variable of a conditional literal is a data member d, then it is called a conditional literal in d. Finally, We use m to represent the min value and M the max value of the domain of any data member d.

The identification of states for a data member d is achieved by the following steps:

1. Examine all the path conditions of the member functions to look for conditional literals in d.

2. For each conditional literal identified in the last step, form intervals of the domain of d such that the conditional literal is evaluated to either TRUE or FALSE for all values in the interval. The following examples show how this can be done:

conditional literal	intervals formed
$d > 8$, $d <= 8$	$[m,8]$, $[9,M]$
$d < 8$, $d >= 8$	$[m,7]$, $[8,M]$
$d == 8$, $d != 8$	$[m,7]$, $[8,8]$, $[9,M]$

3. The above steps result in a set of intervals over the domain of d. Form states from the intervals as described below.

   (a) Select any two intervals A and B that intersect.

   (b) Form intervals $A - (A \cap B)$, $B - (A \cap B)$ and $A \cap B$.

   (c) Replace A and B by above intervals.

   (d) Repeat the above steps until no intersecting intervals exist.

   (e) The intervals created are the states.

4.3 Identifying State Transitions

In this step we construct the transitions between the states of a data member d. A data member changes its state if its value is changed. It is possible for a transition to start and end at the same state. We will make a simplifying assumption that the data members are defined only by the member functions of its class. That is all the data members are private. Note that any direct assignment to a data member by a non-member can be replaced by a member function that assigns a value to the data member.

A member function has one or more execution paths. A path may update a data member only if the path condition is satisfied. Thus a state transition from a pre-state to a post-state can occur if the member function contains a path whose path condition can be satisfied by the pre-state; and the final value expression of the data member can be satisfied by the post-state; that is, it lies in the interval representing the post-state.

In the following discussion we will first deal with member functions that directly define a member data. The method will be extended later to deal with member functions that call another function or member function to define the data. The reader is reminded that we have restrict ourselves to integer type and are dealing with one member data at a time. That is, the state machine constructed is an AOSD.

We will use the following notations. By definition, a state S_i is an interval $[l,u]$. A data member is said to be in state S_i if its value lies in the interval. We will use $S_i(x)$ to denote the expression that $(x \geq l) \land$

(x ≤ u), where x is either a data member or a variable expression. We will use PC to denote a path condition and E the final value expression of a data member d produced by a path. Both E and PC may have function calls. For treatment of function calls, see [6].

State transitions are constructed by the following steps:

1. Create a set RS of reachable states, initially set to empty.

2. Examine the states identified in the last section, add those that satisfy the final value expression produced by a constructor to RS. These states are the initial states. (If the class does not have a constructor, then add all the states to RS[1].)

3. Select a state $S_i \in$ RS as a pre-state. If S_i is an initial state, then add the constructor transition leading to S_i and label it accordingly.

4. Select a path P_k which defines the data member d. Let PC_k be the path condition of P_k and E the final value expression of d for this path. The path can cause a transition from S_i if $S_i(d) \wedge PC_k$ is consistent (i.e., satisfiable). If this is not so, reject P_k and select the next path.

5. Identify all the post states for the transitions from S_i due to the path P_k as follows:

   (a) Select a state S_j from the set of states, including the initial and potential states, of data member d identified in the last section. S_j is a post-state for a transition from S_i due to P_k if $(S_i(d) \wedge PC_k) \models S_j(E)$. That is, $S_j(E)$ must be true for all cases in which $(S_i(d) \wedge PC_k)$ is true.

   (b) If S_j satisfies the above criteria, then the transition from S_i to S_j is constructed. The guard condition for this transition is $S_i(d) \wedge PC_k \wedge S_j(E)$[2]. If the pre-state implies the guard condition, then the guard condition is omitted.

   (c) Add S_j to RS, i.e., RS = RS $\cup$ { S_j }.

6. Repeat from step 4 till there are no more paths that define the data member d.

7. Remove S_i from RS set.

8. Repeat from step 3 till RS is empty.

---

[1] If the class has not constructor, then objects of that class can be initialized arbitrarily by using the compiler default constructor. Since the states partition the domain of the data member, the arbitrarily initialized value must fall into one of the states. That is, we include all the states in the set of initially reachable states.

[2] This condition is simplified as usual and is omitted in this paper.

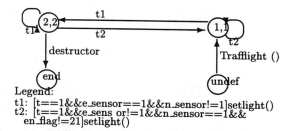

Legend:
t1: [t==1&&e_sensor==1&&n_sensor!=1]setlight()
t2: [t==1&&e_sens or!=1&&n_sensor==1&& en_flag!=21]setlight()

Figure 4: AOSD for north member datum of the traffic light example

4.4 Examples

For the CoinBox example discussed earlier with the error corrected, the symbolic execution step produces the results as shown in Table 1.

From the path conditions we find that the conditional literals for the data member curQtrs are "curQtrs > 0", and "¬(curQtrs > 0)". The two conditional literals yield the following intervals: [m,0], [1,M], since m=0 for unsigned, we have [0,0] and [1,M]. Since the intervals do not overlap, they are the states.

The transitions for the curQtrs member datum are as follows:

$$\delta([0,0], Reset()) = [0,0]$$
$$\delta([0,0], ReturnQtrs()) = [0,0]$$
$$\delta([0,0], [allowVend! = 0]Vend()) = [0,0]$$
$$\delta([0,0], AddQtr()) = [1,M]$$
$$\delta([1,M], AddQtr()) = [1,M]$$
$$\delta([1,M], Reset()) = [0,0]$$
$$\delta([1,M], ReturnQtrs()) = [0,0]$$
$$\delta([1,M], [allowVend! = 0]Vend()) = [0,0]$$

Similarly, the transitions for allowVend can be constructed. In summary, the AOSD's for curQtrs and allowVend, and the COSD for the CCoinBox class are shown in Figure 2.

As an example of loop handling, consider the traffic light example originally used by Leveson in verification of safety critical software [8] (see Figure 3). Three basis paths must be symbolically executed: one that does not go into the while loop; one that executes the *then* part of the *if* statements; and one that does not execute the *then* part of the *if* statements.

The AOSD for the member datum north is shown in Figure 4. Recall from the source code that the coding of the lights is 1 means red, 2 means green and 3 means yellow. We see that the transition from state [1,1] to state [2,2] means that the north-south traffic light changes from red to green without going through the warning yellow light.

5 Detecting Object State Errors

In [6], we showed that using traditional state testing methods cannot detect object state errors due to object interactions or message passing. We also described an algorithm for composite object state testing by constructing a test tree from a composite object state diagram.

The nodes of a test tree for a COSD represent the composite states of the COSD. The edges of the tree

Table 1: Summary of symbolic execution result for the coin box class

Path	Path Condition	Final Expr	Return Value
$CCoinBox().P0$	T	$< totalQtrs, 0 >$ $< allowVend, 0 >$ $< curQtrs, 0 >$	$void$
$Reset().P0$	T	$< totalQtrs, 0 >$ $< allowVend, 0 >$ $< curQtrs, 0 >$	$void$
$AddQtr().P0$	$\neg(curQtrs > 0)$	$< curQtrs, curQtrs + 1 >$	$void$
$AddQtr().P1$	$(curQtrs > 0)$	$< curQtrs, curQtrs + 1 >$ $< allowVend, 1 >$	$void$
$ReturnQtrs().P0$	T	$< curQtrs, 0 >$ $< allowVend, 0 >$	$void$
$IsAllowedVend().P0$	T		$allowVend$
$Vend().P0$	$(IsAllowedVend() == 0)$		$void$
$Vend().P1$	$\neg(IsAllowedVend() == 0)$	$< totalQtrs, totalQtrs + curQtrs >$ $< curQtrs, 0 >$ $< allowVend, 0 >$	$void$

```
class Trafflight                        e_sensor=a[t];
{                                       n_sensor=a[t+1];
private:                                if ((e_sensor==1)||(en_flag==21))
    unsigned east;                          { east=2; north=1;
    unsigned north;                           en_flag=21; direction=1;
    unsigned direction;                       cout<<east<<north<<"\n"; }
    unsigned t;                         if ((n_sensor==1)||(en_flag==12))
    unsigned en_flag;                       { east= 1; north= 2;
public:                                     en_flag=12; direction=2;
    Trafflight();                           cout<<east<<north<<"\n"; }
    void setlight();                    if (direction==1)
};                                          { east=3; north=1; en_flag=31;
                                            cout<<east<<north<<"\n";
Trafflight::Trafflight()                    east=1; north=2; en_flag=12;
{ east= 2; north=1;                         cout<<east<<north<<"\n"; }
  en_flag=21; t=1;                      else { east=1; north=3;
  direction=1;                                en_flag=13;
}                                             cout<<east<<north<<"\n";
                                              east=2; north=1;
void Trafflight::setlight() {                 en_flag=21;
while (t < 4) {                               cout<<east<<north<<"\n"; }
  t=t+2;                            }}
```

Figure 3: The traffic light example C++ code

represent transitions between the states. If the COSD contains k AOSD's, then each state is represented by a k-tuple, where the i-th component denotes the state of the i-th AOSD. Since an AOSD may have more than one initial state and not all of them can be reachable from the other states, there could be several test trees for a COSD. Each of these test trees has a particular initial composite state. Stating more formally, a test tree for a COSD of k AOSD's is constructed as follows:

1. For each of the k AOSD's, construct a set of (inreachable) atomic initial states, denoted $AIS_i, i = 1, 2, \ldots, k$, as follows. If $AOSD_i$ has m initial states whose only incoming edge is labeled by a constructor, then, include these m initial states in AIS_i. If AIS_i is empty, then include any initial state in AIS_i.

2. Compute the set of composite initial states

$$CIS = AIS_1 \times AIS_2 \times \ldots \times AIS_k$$

   In the following discussion, each composite state is denoted $(S_{i1}^1, S_{i2}^2, \ldots, S_{ik}^k)$, where the superscripts denote the AOSD's and the subscripts denote the state of an AOSD.

3. For each composite initial state $(S_{i1}^1, S_{i2}^2, \ldots, S_{ik}^k)$ in CIS, construct a test tree as follows:

   (a) Starting from the initial state $(S_{i1}^1, S_{i2}^2, \ldots, S_{ik}^k)$, the root of the test tree is constructed and labeled by $(S_{i1}^1, S_{i2}^2, \ldots, S_{ik}^k)$.

   (b) We now examine the nodes in the tree one by one. Let the node being examined be labeled by $(S_{j1}^1, S_{j2}^2, \ldots, S_{jk}^k)$.

   (c) If $(S_{j1}^1, S_{j2}^2, \ldots, S_{jk}^k)$ has already occurred at a higher level in the tree, then the node becomes a terminal node and will not be expanded. That is, go to step 3b and examine the next node; otherwise, continue.

   (d) If there is a transition t leading from state S_{jp}^p to state S_{jq}^p in the $AOSD_p$, then we attach a branch and a successor node to $(S_{j1}^1, S_{j2}^2, \ldots, S_{jk}^k)$, the branch is labeled t and the successor node is labeled $(S_{j1}^1, S_{j2}^2, \ldots, S_{jq}^p, \ldots, S_{jk}^k)$.

   (e) If t also triggers other transitions, then the corresponding component(s) of the successor node is updated accordingly. This step is repeated until no transition can be so triggered.

   (f) Repeat from step 3b until no expansion is possible.

The tree, though may be large, must be finite, since k is finite and each AOSD has only a finite number of states.

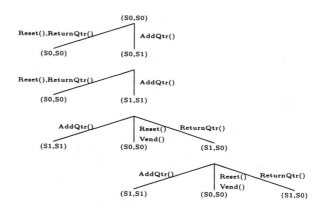

Figure 5: Test tree showing the execution sequences of a COSD

Consider now the COSD in Figure 2 for the incorrect coin box program. A spanning tree for this COSD is shown in Figure 5, from which we can derive the test sequence AddQtr(); AddQtr(); ReturnQtrs(); Vend() (i.e., the second rightmost branch), which should detect the error in the implementation of the Return-Qtrs() member function.

6 State-Based Fault Analysis

Software fault tree analysis is a technique used to verify the safety aspects of software [8]. In the structure of a fault tree, the top event is a hazardous state of the system and Boolean logic is used to describe the combination of events and conditions in the system environment leading to this critical state. These events and conditions constitute the nodes of the fault tree with the hazard as the root. The edges are represented by logical operators indicating the logical relationships between events and conditions which cause the event in the upper level to happen.

Software composite object state testing focuses on testing of interactions of object state behaviors. Composite object state behavior can be represented by a tree with each node representing a reachable composite state and each edge being a transition (event) causing a state change. In particular, the root of the tree represents the initial composite state. A composite state is an n-tuple of component states, each of which is either a composite state or an atomic state. In the latter case, it is a state of an atomic OSD. This recursive, hierarchical structure was designed to best accommodate the inheritance hierarchy and aggregation hierarchy of OO software.

To simulate fault tree analysis technique using composite object state test tree, two modifications are required:

1. Since we want to identify what cause(s) the hazardous state, we adopt a backward approach instead of the forward approach used in object state testing. We begin with the hazardous state as the root of the fault analysis tree.

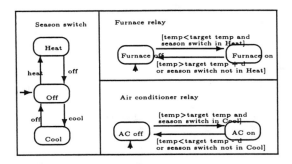

Figure 6: Partial specification of a thermostat system

2. The backward approach implies that all the transitions of the OSD's are reversed. That is, each transition from state S_i to state S_j is replaced by a transition from state S_j to state S_i with the same label.

We have implemented a state-based fault analysis tool and applied it to several case studies. One of them is a thermostat example. The thermostat consists of six objects: season switch, fan switch, furnace relay, air conditioner relay, run indicator, and fan relay. For simplicity, we use only three of the objects in this paper: season switch, furnace relay and air conditioner relay. The dynamic model for these three objects are depicted in Figure 6. An undesirable state (which can be a hazadous state in a safety system) is "Off, FurnaceOn, AcOn", meaning that the season switch is off but the furnace and the air conditioner are both on.

The following rules are used to detect undesirable states:
1) SeasonSwithOff and (FurnaceOn or AcOn)
2) FurnaceOn and AcOn
3) SeasonSwithCool and FurnaceOn
4) SeasonSwithHeat and AcOn

Starting with a hazardous state, say "Off, FurnaceOn, AcOn", and apply our tool to the modified object state diagrams, we obtain the fault analysis tree as shown in Figure 7. The the highlighted paths show how the undesirable state is reach from an initial state. For example, the undesirable state can arise when the system is in the state of "Heat, FurnaceOn, AcOn" or "Cool, FurnaceOn, AcOn" and the switch is turned to Off. Continuing this process, we could see that when the system is in the state of "Heat, FurnaceOff, AcOn" and if the temperature is less than the target temperature the furnace relay will be set to ON, leading to the state "Heat, FurnaceOn, AcOn".

We wish to point out that according to the specification in Figure 6 the furnace will be turned off when the season switch is turned to off. But the "Off, FurnaceOn, AcOn" state still will occur because there is an indefinite delay between the furnace and the season switch. That is, the furnace will not switch to off until after the season switch has been switched to

off. For the thermostat system, this may not be a problem. However, in a safety critical system such as medical treatment equipment like Therac-25, the indefinite delay in shutting down some device (such as a radiator) may result in disaster.

Fault tree analysis and composite object state testing are two techniques applied to different aspects of software testing. However, the above example indicates that modified composite object state testing can be used to simulate fault tree analysis. Though the example provided here is not a typical safty system, composite object state testing shows its applicability in the research of this field.

Fault tree analysis requires expert knowledge which is difficult to find and usually subjective. Composite object state testing has its specific features such as constructing the test tree based on the object state machine which can be derived from the source code, or a requirement specification. The undesirable states can be detected by domain specific rules as above.

7 Related Work

State dependent behaviors of a software system are usually modeled by finite state machines (FSM). State testing is considered complementary to functional and structural testings. A distinguished approach to state testing was due to Chow [1] in which FSM is used to model software components that can be described by *stimuli* and *operations*. Stimuli are inputs from the outside world and operations are executed as responses (to the stimuli). In Chow's approach, a spanning tree derived from an FSM specification of the software is used to generate test sequences, each of which is a sequence of operations. These test sequences can be used to detect errors in operations, state transitions, and extra and/or missing states.

Software testing of OO programs is a relatively new, important, and difficult area. Only a few results are reported [11] [6] [3]. The state test model presented in this paper is superficially similar to existing models [9]. However, the semantics and use are completely different. The existing models are used as analysis and design tools, but OSD is used as a testing tool. As usual, object state testing can be either specification-based or program-based. In specification-based testing, the OSD is derived from the software requirements specification. This has been described in [4] and will not be repeated here. In program-based testing, the notions of state and transition in OSD are associated with specific programming concepts rather than high level application domain concepts. For example, a state of an object is defined by the ranges of values of a subset of member data of the object. State transitions are defined by (possibly conditional) executions of member functions. More importantly, the hierarchy of state machines in our approach resembles the inheritance and aggregation hierarchies of object classes, whereas the existing concept of state hierarchy resembles the decomposition of complex states into a network of simpler states [9].

Object state testing as presented in this paper concerns multiple, hierarchical, concurrent, communicating state machines, constructed from code. It is dif-

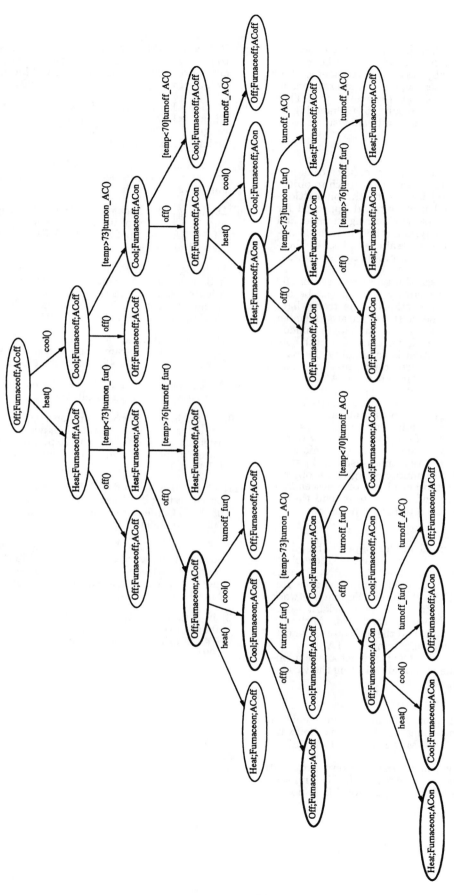

Figure 7: A state based fault analysis tree

141

ferent from Chow's method [1], where test cases are generated from a single state machine; and hence, interactions between the objects are not considered. We shall show in section 5, testing of such interactions is essential in the detection of state behavior errors. This paper extends our previous results [6] to handling of loop statements and software fault analysis using a state based approach.

8 Conclusions

In this paper, we present the importance of object state testing, a reverse engineering approach to object state recovery, a method for testing the interactions among the objects, and a state-based approach for fault analysis. The reverse engineering method and the state based fault analysis method have been implemented and applied to several examples. Application of these tools to industrial production software is being negotiated.

Problems concerning scalability is discussed briefly as follows. The AOSD recovery method can be applied to simple member functions. The traffic light example in Figure 4 is the most complicated member function we have used so far. We anticipate difficulties with member functions having complex path conditions. One partial solution is to simplify the path condition through equivalence transformations. Another problem concerns the layout of an AOSD with a large number of states and a complex graph. This problem can be solved easily by using a matrix representation instead of a graph representation.

We wish to point out the following omissions, which may also be considered as future work: 1) how to extend the composite object state testing technique to testing of object-oriented real time systems; 2) state testing issues relating to mutable aggregate objects which may mute into another object of a descendant type during execution; and 3) how to extend the reverse engineering approach to handle pointers.

Acknowledgment

The material presented in this paper is based on work supported by the Texas Advanced Technology Program (Grant No. 003656-097), BBN Systems and Technologies, Electronic Telecommunications Research Institute (ETRI) of Korea, Fujitsu Network Transmission Systems, Inc., Hewlett-Packard Company, IBM, Office of Naval Research, Sun Microsystems Computer Company, and the Software Engineering Center for Telecommunications at UTA.

Thanks are due to the OOT project team members for developing the tools and collecting the various statistics.

References

[1] T. S. Chow, "Testing software design modeled by finite- state machines," IEEE Trans. Software Eng., Vol. SE-4, No.3, May 1978. pp. 178 - 187.

[2] L. Clarke, "A system to generate test data and symbolically execute programs," IEEE Transactions on Software Engineering, Vol. SE-2, no. 3., 1976.

[3] R. Doong and P. Frankl, "The ASTOOT approach to testing object-oriented programs," ACM Transactions on Software Engineering and Methodology, Vol. 3, No. 2, pp. 101 - 130, April 1994.

[4] J. Gao, D. Kung, P. Hsia, Y. Toyoshima, C. Chen, "Object state testing for object-oriented programs," Proc. of COMPSAC'95, pp. 232 – 238, Dallas, Texas, August 9 – 11, 1995.

[5] Naik, Kshirasagar, Sarikaya, Behcet, and "Testing communication protocols," IEEE Software 9:27-37 Jan 1992.

[6] D. Kung, N. Suchak, P. Hsia, Y. Toyoshima, and C. Chen, "On object state testing," Proc. of COMPSAC'94, pp. 222 – 227, IEEE Computer Society Press, 1994.

[7] D. Kung, J. Gao, P. Hsia, Y. Toyoshima, C. Chen, Y.S. Kim, and Y. Song, "Developing an object-oriented software testing and maintenance environment", Communications of the ACM, Vol. 38, No. 10, pp. 75 – 87, October 1995.

[8] N. Leveson, S. Cha, and T. Shimeall, "Safety verification of Ada programs using software fault trees," IEEE Software, pp. 48 – 59, July 1991.

[9] J. Rumbaugh et al., "Object-Oriented Modeling and Design," Prentice-Hall, 1991.

[10] N. Suchak, "A reverse engineering methodology for extracting object state behavior from object oriented programs," Tech. Rep. no. 9401, Software Engineering Center for Telelcommunicaitons, UTA, 1994.

[11] C. D. Turner and D. J. Robson, "The state-based testing of object-oriented programs," Proc. of IEEE Conference on Software Maintenance, pp. 302 - 310, 1993.

[12] N. Venugopalan, "Loop Handling in Design Recovery of Object State Behaviors," MS Project Report, Department of Computer Science and Engineering, The University of Texas at Arlington, May 1996.

[13] N. Wilde and R. Huitt, "Issues in the maintenance of object-oriented programs," University of West Florida and Bell Communications Research, 1991.

The State-based Testing of Object-Oriented Programs

C.D. Turner and D.J. Robson

Computer Science, SECS,
University of Durham, Durham
DH1 3LE, England

Email: C.D.Turner@durham.ac.uk
            Dave.Robson@durham.ac.uk

Phone: +44 91 374 2635

Abstract

This paper describes a new technique known as state-based testing which is used for the validation of object-oriented programs with emphasis on the interaction between the features and the object's state. Because of the nature of the technique, the random order in which features can be invoked is taken into account. The technique is complementary to other functional and structural approaches to validation. A suite of tools to support the state-based testing of object-oriented programs is also outlined. The adaptation of traditional validation techniques to the object-oriented programming model is also discussed.

1. Introduction

The concepts known today as object-orientation, first appeared in the programming language Simula in the late 1960's (see [1]). Since then a number of object-oriented languages have been developed, for example, Smalltalk, Eiffel and C++. Object-oriented programming presents a different approach to the construction of programs from the more traditional methods. For example, functional decomposition places the main emphasis of the program on the 'functions' or 'operations' that will be performed by the program. In contrast, the object-oriented method places the emphasis not on the operations, but on the types of data that the operations will be performed on. This produces highly modular programs.

Current research into the testing of object-oriented programs has been concerned with the following areas: experience with the application of traditional approaches to object-oriented programs, the application of formal specification to the validation process, the incremental testing of class hierarchies and other more theoretical aspects. These are surveyed in the section on current research.

Testing is an activity that is required both in the development and maintenance phases of the life cycle. Specialist methods, such as regression testing, are required during the maintenance phase. The method described in this paper is equally applicable to both the development and maintenance phases and in the maintenance phase the method is particularly relevant to the direct testing of changes rather than to regression testing.

The remainder of this paper is as follows: a section describing the adaptation of more traditional testing techniques to the object-oriented model, a review of current literature in the area, a detailed description of a new technique for testing object-oriented programs known as state-based testing, a brief introduction to a suite of prototype tools that were developed for the evaluation of the new technique and a summary of the information presented in this paper.

2. Traditional Testing Techniques

There are two basic categories of traditional testing techniques: functional and structural. Functional testing (also known as black-box testing) involves the generation of test cases based purely on the functional specification of the software with no regard for its structure or code. In contrast, structural testing (also known as white-box testing) uses information about the programs structure to generate test cases for exercising specific portions of the code under test. It has been suggested by Herrington et al. in [8] that both types of testing be performed in conjunction with a coverage measure. With functional testing being performed first, followed by structural testing until the required coverage level is achieved.

Functional system testing views the whole system as a single unit with inputs and expected outputs. Functional unit testing views each separate program unit as a single entity with inputs and expected outputs. This implies that although functional unit testing has a degree of knowledge about the systems construction, it still tests units with respect to its specification.

Traditional testing techniques assume the Von-Neumann model of processing (see Figure 1) with a minor adaptation to the model, traditional testing techniques can be relatively easily adapted to the object-oriented paradigm (see figure 2 below).

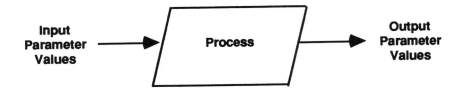

Figure 1. The Von-Neumann model of processing

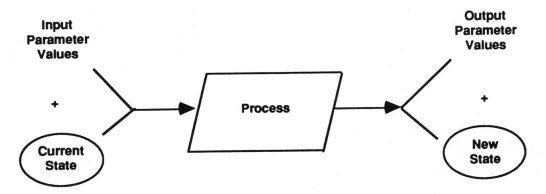

Figure 2. An adaption of the Von-Neumann model of processing

The generation of the starting states and the validation of the finishing states is discussed later.

3. Current Research

As mentioned earlier, there has been an increasing level of research into the testing of object-oriented programs in recent years. Leavens in [9] discusses the application of formal specification to object-oriented programs. He describes the validation of the specification and design of Abstract Data Types (ADTs). However, he does not consider the validation of their implementation. Frankl and Doong in [5] and [3] also describe the application of formally specifying ADTs to the testing of object-oriented programs. Their method and tools rely upon the navigation around a formal specification to generate large numbers of functional test cases.

In contrast, Fiedler in [4] discusses the application of the more traditional McCabe cyclomatic testing method to the testing of C++ class. Both Cheatham and Mellinger in [2], and Harrold et al. in [6] discuss the incremental testing of class hierarchies. Harrold

describes in detail an algorithm for the reduction of the test cases that must be rerun when a feature is inherited from a parent class. Smith in [13] discusses a framework for the testing of object-oriented programs. Various test strategies can be used by the tester to guide the testing.

The vast majority of research conducted into the testing of object-oriented programs fails to address the difference between the object-oriented and more traditional programming techniques. The research which does address this issue is concerned with formally modelling objects as ADTs and therefore the validation is performed purely from a functional testing view of the class. A concept central to object-oriented programming is the interaction that occurs between the features and the state of an object. It is the authors' belief that a new technique is required to address the validation of this fundamental issue.

4. Finite State Automata

As its name suggests, the main emphasis of state-based testing is the values stored in the object's representation (the state). This draws similarities with

Finite State Automata (FSA). FSAs are objects whose next state is determined by the next feature that is called and the current state. The next feature called in conjunction with its parameter values are known as stimuli.

i) It can change the object's state to the appropriate new state.
ii) It can leave the object's state as it is.
iii) It can change the object's state to an undefined state (error).

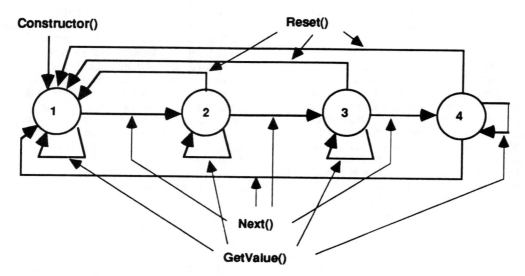

Figure 3. The state diagram of an example Determinisitic Finite State Automata for counting from one to four

As can be seen in the above example (figure 3), the FSA has four states corresponding to the numbers one through to four. There are four different featuresavailable for a client to call (including a constructor) and their effects are shown above. The feature Constructor( ) initialises the FSA to its starting state - one. The feature Next( ) causes the FSA to change to the next state in the sequence. The feature GetValue( ) does not affect the current state, it simply informs the client (caller) what the current value is. The Reset( ) feature allows the state to be returned to the start (one) at any time. The counting FSA would be relatively trivial to test, especially as all features are defined over the whole range of states with no exceptions. Each feature would be called with the object in each of the four states. The result of the calls would be verified against the diagram above.

Any feature has five types of possible responses to a particular state and stimuli combination (see figure 3).

iv) It can change the object's state to a defined, but inappropriate state (error).
v) It can leave the object's state as it is when it is supposed to change it (error).

The aim of state-based testing is to validate all occurrences of i) and ii) and to detect all occurrences of the erroneous iii), iv) and v).

5. State-Based Testing

5.1 Notation

To introduce a degree of formalism, each feature is considered as a mapping from its starting (or input) states, to its resultant (or output) states affected by any stimuli. The notation to be used for expressing this is as follows:

σ = The set of valid states that the object can be in.

ϵI_i = The set of states that the ith feature is expected to accept (by both action, and inaction) as input.

ϵO_i = The set of states that the ith feature is expected to be able to generate as output.

αI_i = The set of states that the ith feature actually accepts as input.

αO_i = The set of states that the ith feature is actually able to generate as output.

If a class is valid (as far as state-based testing is concerned), then $\alpha I_i = \varepsilon I_i$ and $\alpha O_i = \varepsilon O_i$ for all the features of the FSA. This simply means that the states each feature accepts as input are as expected, and the same for the output states.

If the FSA in figure 3 was written as a class, it would only require a single data-member needed to store its state. When applying this type of testing to more complex classes, a number of factors influence the effectiveness of the process. Firstly, the number of data-members of the class has a profound effect on the complexity of the testing. The more data-members, the more time it takes to design and implement the tests. Secondly, data-members are used for two main purposes: data-storage and control-information. Data-storage is simply the storing and recalling of values with minimal processing of the values. Control-information is data-values that are used to trigger events; that is, the features of a class will communicate with each other via values or flags set within the state of the object. The level of control-information and hence the interaction between the features of the class via the representation also affects the time required to design and generate state-based tests. The complexity of the code of individual features of a class also has a bearing on the complexity of the testing.

5.2 Substates

The current state of an object is the combined values from all of its data-members at the current point in time. It is appropriate to therefore define a *substate* to be the value of a particular data-member at a specific point in time; likewise, a *partial state* is the combination of values of a subset of all of the data-members of the class at a particular point in time. The state of an object can now be redefined to be the combination of all of the object's substates at the current point in time.

5.3 Substate-values

Instead of associating every single possible value of a data-member with a substate, it is more appropriate to introduce two types of substate-values:

specific substate values - these are substate values that are tested for directly within the code, or are described in the design (or specification) as being of special significance.

general substate values - these are a group of substate values that are all considered in the same manner; therefore there is no need to distinguish between them for the purposes of state-based testing. Hence an assumption is introduced into the testing, it is assumed that all attribute values that are considered to be part of the same general-substate-value will all behave in the same manner. This assumption is used to significantly reduce the number of test cases that must be generated to a manageable size. This assumption is not used during any structural testing that may take place and so the class will still be fully tested.

A substate's values are therefore a collection of specific-substate-values and general-substate-values. For example,

given an integer data member iValue, and a design that states:
- -1 has special meaning
- that the value is always greater or equal to -1
- and all numbers greater than minus one are treated equally,

then iValue has the following substate values:
- iValue = -1 - a *specific substate value*
- iValue > -1 - a *general substate value*

In a similar way that the substate-values were analysed for specific-values and general-values, parameters can also be analysed. This technique when applied to parameters is known as equivalence partitioning [12].

If the data-member being considered is a pointer (an address of an object, rather than an actual object), then it is most likely that the pointer will only have two substate-values, one specific and one general. The specific-value is likely to be the value NULL, and the general-value will cover all other possibilities, that is, any other than NULL. Nevertheless, it is conceivable that the substate will have more susbtate-values, such as the address of a specific or default object.

Using the example shown below (figure 4), the following substates were chosen:
substate 1 (denoted as S[1]) : The value of pTop
substate 2 (denoted as S[2]) : The value of *pCur
substate 3 (denoted as S[3]) : The value of pCur

From the design of the class (not shown), the following information has been obtained.

pTop points to the first element in the linked list. If there is no linked list then pTop equals NULL.

pCur is a pointer to a pointer to the current element in the list. Therefore to point to the first element in the list, pCur equals the address of pTop, as pTop points to the first element in the list. For pCur to point to the second element, pCur equals the address of pTop->pNext, and so on. pTop will always exist, therefore pCur will always be a valid pointer, even when *pCur is NULL.

```
class list
{
    public:
        // the definition of the interface
        // goes here ....
        // ...

    protected:
        // this structure creates the
        // links of the list
        struct list_element {
            list_element * pNext;
            TYPE tItem;
        };

        // pTop points to the top of the
        // first element of the
        // list (the top)
        list_element * pTop;

        // pCur points to the pointer to
        // the current list_element
        list_element ** pCur;
};
```

Figure 4. The definition of a linked list class written in C++.

The following substate-values become apparent:
For S[1]:
1) pTop equals NULL (a specific-substate-value)
2) pTop is not equal to NULL (a general-substate-value)
For S[2]:
1) *pCur equals NULL (a specific-substate-value)
2) *pCur is not equal to NULL (a general-substate-value)
For S[3]:
1) pCur equals the address of pTop (a specific-substate-value)

2) pCur is not equal to the address of pTop (a general-substate-value)

5.4 Performing the testing
The next part of the testing preparation is to determine the I_i and O_i for all the features of the class. This must be obtained from the design of the class, not from the code, as there may be errors in the code. In the integer linked list example all the features are defined over the whole range of states. This is true for the vast majority of classes written. There are only two exceptions: the constructor, and the destructor of a class. The constructor is called when the object is in an undefined states before it has been initialised. The destructor leaves the object in an undefined state, it must accept all valid states as input.

5.6 Additions to the class
A major part of state-based testing is the determining of the object's current state. To enable this, a new version of the class under test must be produced with at least one new feature per substate. These enable the tester to inspect the value of chosen substates. However, if there is a state change between two values which were both considered to be part of the same general group, then the change is undetectable. This problem is easily rectified by the addition of an extra set of data-members, whose purpose is to mirror the value of the original data members that the user is interested in. For each data-member being mirrored, an extra feature is required to test the difference between the original and the mirroring data-member, and to update the value of the mirror.

As a simple recommendation, it is advisable to insert statements at the beginning and end of each feature to report to the screen (or to a file) the value of the parameters passed and the values returned by the features. It is useful if this is also performed for the substate testing features by tracing the execution of the test case as it provides a useful aid in debugging any errors that might occur. It is usual that some features of a class must perform more than one task or activity to achieve their desired functionality. The greater the number of tasks, the more difficult they will be to test and debug, if errors are present. As a suggestion to aid the tester, it is advisable to insert *assertions* (statements about the current state of the data) into the code between each task, checking that each sub-task as well as the whole task was satisfactorily performed .

5.7 Data Scenarios
State-based testing is useful for more than simply detecting the change in state of an object, it can be used to detect the correct construction of a more complex dynamic data structure; for example, a linked

list. For such dynamic data structures, it is essential to determine which particular changes can occur to the structure, and when they can occur. This analysis produces a list of situations which are significant to the model upon which the data structure is based; these situations will be referred to as *data-scenarios*.

In conjunction with the model upon which the class is based (not shown), two different sets of scenarios are produced: scenarios used by those features of the class that act upon the elements themselves (see figure 5), and the scenarios used by those features which act upon the links between the nodes (see figure 6).

These scenarios are used as additional test cases to the appropriate groups of features. However, unless a change in the composition of the data structure is detectable, the results of using the above scenarios will be difficult to verify. Therefore, additional substates are required for detecting the state of various parts of the dynamic data structure. For the above scenarios, the following additional substates were used:

S[4]   (*pCur)->pNext
i)   invalid (*pCur equals NULL and so cannot be dereferenced)
ii)   (*pCur)->pNext does not equals NULL
iii)   (*pCur)->pNext equals NULL
S[5]   (*pCur)->tItem
i)   (*pCur)->tItem is invalid (*pCur equals NULL and so cannot be dereferenced)
ii)   (*pCur)->tItem is valid

The substate values S[4](ii) and S[4](iii) are relatively self-explanatory; however, S[4](i) has to be included, because there is a possibility that *pCur could be NULL rendering the expression (*pCur)->pNext invalid. This also applies to S[5], which has an added anomaly, it seems to indirectly reflect the value of *pCur (S[2]) only. This is because a list is used to store any range of values; it is pointless to detect every single value, therefore what is required is the ability to detect a change in value stored. This is provided by some of the extra features that have been added to the class under test; but for identification purposes, allocating a substate to the expression eases some problems.

When choosing substates for use with the data scenarios, it is not necessary that they should be able to differentiate between the scenarios; the initial set-up of the test case is driven by the tester, therefore allowing the starting state to be whatever is required. It is for this lack of differentiability between scenarios that the tool MKTC has a separate facility allowing the starting state for test cases to be expressed as a scenario, rather than a state description.

5.8 Generation of Test Cases

In this paper, both substates and data scenarios have been introduced and can now be combined to provide a more general algorithm for state-based testing. The guide is in the form of a list of tasks to be performed.

[1]   Allocate one substate per data-member.
[2]   Determine the data scenarios from the design of the class.
[3]   Allocate any extra substates required for the data scenarios to function properly.
[4]   Determine the specific and the general-values for all these substates. Include the *invalid* values that are required when de-referencing a pointer as mentioned in the previous section.
[5]   Add the features to test for the substate values to the class.
[6]   Determine the substates for which a test for a change of value is required. Add features to the class for their detection. Also add any new data-members required for mirroring.
[7]   From the design of the class, determine which states are the I_i, and the O_i for each feature. In the majority of cases, I_i should be the same as because classes should be written with no implied order for the calling of features [11]. These sets of states form the basis of the test cases.
[8]   Analyse the design for the call graph of inter-feature calls within the class.
[9]   Start with the features at the bottom of the graph, especially those features which are not called by any other feature within the class.
[10]   For each state si_f such that $si_f Œ I_i$, calculate from the design the state so_f such that $so_f Œ O_i$ for feature i (That is, for each state that the feature is expected to handle as input, calculate the state that the feature should leave the object in after the call). This is done for all significant values that can be passed as parameters to the feature. These significant values are the stimuli of the feature.
[11]   Generate the code to create the test case's initial condition, that is, the starting state of the object. Follow this with the test for validating the starting state of the object. After this, add the code for the test case, including the call to the feature under test. Append to all of this, a test for the final state of the object, and any code required to tidy up after the test.
[12]   Go back to item 10 until there are no more features left to test.

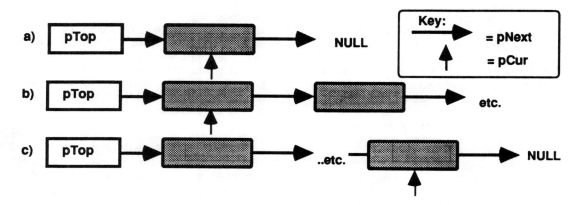

when put into words they are
- a) the only node in the list
- b) the first element of a multiple node list
- c) the last element of a multiple node list

Figure 5. The data scenarios for the features that act upon the nodes of the list

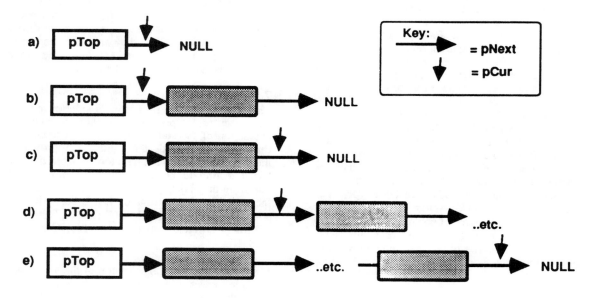

when put into words they are
- a) an empty list
- b) before the only element
- c) after the only element
- d) in between two nodes in a multiple list
- e) at the end of a multiple node list

Figure 6. The data secenarios for the features that act upon the links between the nodes

5.9 Integration Testing

Up to this point the focus has been on unit testing. Integration testing is analogous to unit testing, but with the emphasis on the interaction between features of different classes, rather than within a class [6]. This implies that it involves the creation of states for not only the main object under test, but also the objects that will be passed as parameters.

For Example, given two classes, A and B where an object of class B is passed as a parameter to class A, then:
1. Class B is unit tested alone.
2. Class A could be unit tested using test stubs.
3. Class A and B are then integration tested.

A test case for class B would be similar to:
1. create starting state for object of class B
2. invoke the feature under test
3. validate the resultant state for the object under test

A test case for the integration testing of classes A and B would be similar to:
1. create starting state for object of class A
2. create starting state for object of class B
3. invoke feature under test of class A
4. validate resultant state for object of class B
5. validate resultant state for object of class A

6. Assessment of the Technique

State-based testing, like the majority of other techniques, has particular types of classes on which it is more effective than on others. The types of classes that have been tested by this technique so far have by no means been restrictive. They include file handlers, parsers, lexical analysers, and abstract data types such as lists. The degree of effectiveness of the technique is dependent upon the degree of control-information that exists as part of the data representation of the class. The more the features of a class interact via the representation, the more effective state-based testing is likely to be.

If the class is designed simply as a repository of information, or as a non dynamic data storage structure, then this technique will have limited effect. From the experience of the authors, the number of test cases that can be generated is related to the number of different substate-values for each substate.

The technique is not a substitute for functional testing, nor structural testing. However, it should be considered as a complimentary technique for testing interactions with an object's state. These interactions are central to the object-oriented method, and therefore are particularly prevalent when compared with more traditional languages.

If a class is written with no order imposed upon the execution of features, the less restrictive it is upon any programmer who may to make use of it. This in turn increases one of the aims of object-oriented programming - that of facilitating the increased use of reusable components and therefore reducing the cost of software production [10].

There is one point which has been carefully avoided until now - the emphasis of the test cases. The dilemma is: should the test cases concentrate on individual substates, or should they attempt to concentrate on combinations of substates ?

There does not seem to be a simple answer to this problem. If emphasis is placed on individual substates, the number of test cases increases significantly which although significantly faster and easier to generate (when using automated methods such as those described in the next section), it has the disadvantage of using more testing resources such as machine time and disk space. In contrast, if the emphasis is placed upon the combinations of substate-values then the test cases are more difficult to generate, nevertheless, they are more thorough. It is possible to find a compromise between the two and this must be decided upon by the tester.

7. Tools

This section will briefly outline a suite of tools that have been prototyped by the authors to enable the evaluation of the state-based testing technique. As time has progressed, the tools have grown and increased in complexity. The tools enable the state-based testing to be accomplished with ease, by removing the majority of the tedium associated with the repetitive generation of test cases. The suite comprises of three tools: MKTC (MaKe Test Cases), MKMFTC (MaKe MakeFile for Test Cases), and TESTRUN.

MKTC is used for the generation of the actual state-based test cases. It requires a test script file as input which describes the class under test and the tests that must be created.

MKMFTC generates a Makefile which allows the automatic compilation and linking of all the test cases in the current directory. It not only generates a Makefile for the state-based test cases, but also for the 'ordinary', or traditional test cases.

TESTRUN allows the user to automatically execute all the test cases in the order that they were created. In a similar manner to MKMFTC, it not only deals with the state-based test cases, but also the 'ordinary' ones. TESTRUN allows the resultant output from all of the test cases to be logged to a file for perusal at a later date. In addition, it is possible to generate a file with a description of all the test cases that failed (unless the fail causes an infinite loop, or a system crash). See [14] for a more detailed description of the tools.

The technique has been evaluated by generating test suites for a number of classes. The preliminary results are promising with a high level of code coverage being achieved for the majority of classes. The evaluation was performed in conjunction with an LCSAJ (sub-path) coverage analyser (see [7] for more details). However, 100% sub-path coverage has not been achieved for any class. Hence the technique is not a "stand-alone" one, it must be used in conjunction with both funcitonal and structural testing techniques. The technique is currently undergoing a more thorough evaluation by both the authors and by other parties.

8. Conclusions

This paper has described a new technique for the testing object-oriented programs. The emphasis is on validating the correct interaction between the features of a class. It is this emphasis that is particularly prevalent in object-oriented programming.

An assessment of the technique has been presented, describing the circumstances in which the technique is likely to be particularly effective. At present, the technique is still under going extensive evaluation, and it is hoped that this will provide a much greater insight into the effectiveness of the technique on different types of classes. The classes that are component parts of the suite of tools are also currently undergoing validation by a combination of state-based, functional, and structural testing techniques.

Acknowledgements

C.D. Turner is supported by a Co-operative Award in Science and Engineering (CASE), in conjunction between the Science and Engineering Research Council (SERC) and BT Laboratories, Martlesham Heath, Ipswich (BTL).

References

[1] Birtwistle, G. M., Dahl, O. -J., Myhrhaug, B. and Nygaard, K., *Simula Begin*, Studentlitteratur, Lund, Sweden, 1979

[2] Cheatham T. J. and Mellinger L., Testing Object-Oriented Systems, in *Proceedings of the 18th ACM annual Computer Science Conference*, pp. 161-165, ACM Inc., New York, 1990

[3] Doong. R. K. and Frankl, P., Case Studies in Testing Object-Oriented Programs, in *The 4th Testing, Analysis and Verification Symposium*, pp. 165 - 177, ACM Inc., New York, New York, 1991

[4] Fiedler, S. P., Object-Oriented Unit Testing, *Hewlett-Packard Journal*, pp. 69 - 74, April 1989

[5] Frankl, P. G. and Doong, R., Tools for Testing Object-Oriented Programs, in *proceedings of the 8th Pacific NorthWest Conference on Software Quality*, pp. 309 - 324, 1990

[6] Harrold M. J., McGregor, J. D. and Fitzpatrick K. J., Incremental Testing of Object-Oriented Class Structure, in *14th International Conference on Software Engineering*, ACM, 1992

[7] Hennell. M. A., Testing in the Real World, in *Proceedings of Software Tools*, pp. 59 - 66, 1987

[8] Herington. D., E., Nichols, P., A. and Lipp, R., D., Software Verification Using Branch Analysis, *Hewlett-Packard Journal*, vol. 38, no. 6, pp. 13 - 23, June 1987

[9] Leavens. G. T., Modular Specification and Verification of Object-Oriented Programs, *IEEE Software*, pp. 72 - 80, July 1991

[10] Love. T., The Economics of Reuse, in *IEEE Spring COMPCON Conference*, pp. 238 - 241, IEEE Computer Society Press, Los Alamitos, California, 1988

[11] Meyer. B., *Object Oriented Software Construction*, Prentice Hall, 1988

[12] Myers. G. J., *The Art of Software Testing*, John Wiley, 1979

[13] Smith. M. D. and Robson, D. J., A Framework for Testing Object-Oriented Programs, *Journal of Object-Oriented Programming*, vol. 5, no. 3, pp. 45 - 53, June 1992

[14] Turner. C. D. and Robson, D. J., A Suite of Tools for the State-Based Testing of Object-Oriented Programs, *Tech. Rep. TR 14/92*, University of Durham, Durham, England, 1992

ClassBench: a Framework for Automated Class Testing

DANIEL HOFFMAN

*Department of Computer Science, University of Victoria, P.O. Box 3055 MS7209, Victoria, B.C., V8W 3P6
Canada (email: dhoffman@csr.uvic.ca)*

AND

PAUL STROOPER

*Department of Computer Science, University of Queensland, St. Lucia, QLD 4072, Australia (email:
pstroop@cs.uq.oz.au)*

SUMMARY

In contrast to the explosion of activity in object-oriented design and programming, little attention has been given to object testing. We present a novel approach to automated testing designed especially for collection classes. In the ClassBench methodology, a *testgraph* partially models the states and transitions of the Class-Under-Test (CUT) state/transition graph. To determine the expected behavior for the test cases generated from the testgraph, the tester develops an oracle class, providing essentially the same operations as the CUT but supporting only the testgraph states and transitions. Surprisingly thorough testing is achievable with simple testgraphs and oracles. The ClassBench framework supports the tester by providing a testgraph editor, automated testgraph traversal, and a variety of utility classes. Test suites can be easily configured for regression testing–where many test cases are run–and debugging–where a few test cases are selected to isolate the bug. We present the ClassBench methodology and framework in detail, illustrated on both simple examples and on test suites from commercial collection class libraries. ©1997 John Wiley & Sons, Ltd.

KEY WORDS: object-oriented; automated testing; class library

INTRODUCTION

With object-oriented methods, productivity and reliability can be vastly improved, primarily through reuse. Because reliability depends upon testing, this improvement cannot be realized without effective class testing. The tests for class C must be repeated many times: for the initial version of C, after each modification to C, and when C is used in a new environment, such as the new version of an operating system or compiler. Ideally, a change in environment should not require retesting of a class. With current technology, however, class behavior *is* often affected by environment changes. For example, there is considerable variation across C++ compilers, especially regarding templates, exceptions, and name spaces, key features for class libraries. Classes that run correctly with one compiler may not even compile with another. The requirement for repeatability of test suites suggests that test execution should be automated, to minimize the cost of each test run. Automation of test development is less important because it is performed less often.

Our testing focuses on classes with a call-based interface rather than on graphical user interface classes, whose interface includes the keyboard, mouse, and screen interaction as well as procedure calls. While ClassBench has been used primarily on *collection classes*–those providing sets, lists, trees, etc.–it can be used for any class with a call-based interface. For example, ACE[1] is based on a predecessor of ClassBench and uses a similar, though simpler, testing approach. ACE has been used extensively for testing communications protocols. We also focus on programmatic testing, with little human interaction; both the input generation and output checking are under program control. We do not rely on keyboard and mouse capture and playback, or on file and screen capture and comparison. We have found these techniques unsuitable for automated testing of collection classes, where the interface is through function calls rather than keyboard, mouse, screen, and file.

Methodology

With our methodology, the tester performs three tasks:

1. *Develop the testgraph.* The testgraph nodes and arcs correspond to the states and transitions of the Class-Under-Test (CUT). However, the testgraph is vastly smaller than the CUT state/transition graph.
2. *Develop the* Oracle *class.* The Oracle provides essentially the same operations as the CUT but supports only the testgraph states and transitions. As a result, the Oracle is usually significantly cheaper to implement than the CUT, and is more reliable as well. The Oracle member functions are invoked frequently for output checking and, perhaps surprisingly, for input generation.
3. *Develop the* Driver *class.* The Driver class contains cut and orc, instances of the CUT and Oracle. Driver also provides three public member functions: reset places both cut and orc in the initial state, arc generates the transition in cut and orc associated with the testgraph arc traversed, and node checks that, in each node, the cut behavior is consistent with the orc behavior.

Framework

ClassBench provides a framework in the sense of Gamma *et al.*[2]:

> When you use a toolkit (or a conventional subroutine library for that matter), you write the main body of the application and call the code you want to reuse. When you use a framework, you reuse the main body and write the code *it* calls.

The main parts of the ClassBench framework are a graph editor, a graph traversal algorithm, and support code in the form of skeletons and demonstration test suites.

The testgraph editor provides the facilities commonly available in today's graph editors. Testgraphs can be accessed from disk; nodes and arcs can be added and deleted.

The testgraph traversal classes automatically traverse a stored testgraph, calling the appropriate Driver member functions: reset is called at the start of each path, arc is called each time a testgraph arc is traversed, and node is called each time a testgraph node is visited.

A substantial quantity of code has been developed to ease the task of using the ClassBench framework. Skeleton files are provided for Oracle and Driver, and for test documentation. A modest Collection Class Library (CCL) has been developed, including sophisticated test suites. This library is used heavily by the ClassBench software itself. The test suites have played an important role during development, and are also useful as a starting point for a new test suite. When developing a test suite for a new class, we typically begin with a suite for a CCL class similar to the new class.

```
const int MAXSIZE = 100;

class IntSet0 {
public:     IntSet0();
            void add(int x) throw(DuplicateExc,FullExc);
            void remove(int x) throw(NotFoundExc);
            void removeAll();
            int isMember(int x) const;
            int size() const;
protected:  int s[MAXSIZE];
            int curSize;
};
```

Figure 1. IntSet0 *class declaration*

THE CLASSBENCH METHODOLOGY: BASIC TECHNIQUES

Following IEEE standards,[3] we define a *failure* as the occurrence of incorrect system behavior (an incorrect output), and a *fault* as a defect in the source code.

IntSet0 class and test suite

To illustrate the ClassBench methodology we use IntSet0, a simple bounded integer class whose C++ declaration is shown in Figure 1. The constructor IntSet0 creates an empty set. Assuming that cut is an object of type IntSet0, cut.add(x) adds x to cut, throwing the exception DuplicateExc if x is already in cut and the exception FullExc if cut contains MAXSIZE elements. The call cut.remove(x) removes x from cut, throwing NotFoundExc if x is not in cut; cut.removeAll removes all elements from cut. Finally, cut.isMember(x) returns *true* or *false* according to whether x is in cut, and cut.size returns the number of elements in cut.

A class such as IntSet0 is typically tested by writing a customized test driver. Such a test driver is shown in Figure 2; it uses a simple loop and the C++ macro assert to check the behavior of the CUT. An array of *test suite parameters*, parm, is used to control the set size. In each iteration of the outer loop, IntSet0 is instantiated and assert is used to test size and isMember(i) for all i in [0..*parm*[i] − 1]. The set is then filled with parm[i] elements and size and isMember are again tested.

Although this driver is straightforward to write, it has several problems. The error messages generated by assert contain too little information: only the line number and the assertion that failed are printed. Because the element being checked is not displayed, it is hard to locate the fault in the CUT. In addition, this test suite achieves poor code coverage: the functions remove and removeAll are never called and none of the exception code is tested. To improve the code coverage would require a significantly longer driver even though IntSet0 is a very simple class. This indicates that these customized drivers do not scale up to practical examples if we are interested in systematic, thorough class testing.

```
int parm[] = {2,5,10,MAXSIZE};          // test suite parameter
const int PARMSIZE = 4;

int main()
{
    for (int i = 0; i < PARMSIZE; i++) {
        IntSet0 cut;

        assert(cut.size() == 0);        // check that cut is empty
        for (int j = 0; j < parm[i]; j++)
            assert(!cut.isMember(j));

        for (j = 0; j < parm[i]; j++)  // load cut
            cut.add(j);

        assert(cut.size() == parm[i]); // check that cut is full
        for (j = 0; j < parm[i]; j++)
            assert(cut.isMember(j));
    }
}
```

Figure 2. Assertion-based test driver for IntSet0

Testgraphs

A *testgraph* is a directed graph in which the nodes have unique labels and there is a
designated start node; the arcs of a testgraph are labeled (arc labels need not be unique).
Figure 3 shows a simple testgraph for IntSet0 with two nodes with labels EMPTY and ALL,
and one arc with the label ADDALL. In diagrams of testgraphs, we use an arc with no source
node to indicate the start node, EMPTY in this case.

A testgraph is a partial model of the CUT state/transition graph, where we view the CUT as
a finite state machine. Each testgraph node corresponds to a CUT state and the start node to
the initial state (the empty set in the case of IntSet0); each arc corresponds to a sequence of
CUT state transitions. In Figure 3, beside each node is the CUT state that it represents. While
the CUT typically contains a very large number of states, the testgraph state space is vastly

Figure 3. Simple testgraph for IntSet0 *(test suite parameter is 10)*

155

```
class Driver {
public:   Driver(int parm);
          void reset();
          void arc(int arcLabel);
          void node() const;
private:  IntSet0 cut;
          int curNode,allSize;
};
```

Figure 4. Declaration for class `Driver`

smaller. For example, there are roughly $2^{32} \times MAXSIZE$ different `IntSet0` states, but the testgraph in Figure 3 contains only two states. The CUT state space contains all states that *can* be reached; the testgraph state space contains only those states that *will* be reached by the test suite.

To add flexibility to the testgraph scheme, we associate a *test suite parameter* with each test suite. By supplying a value for this parameter, the tester selects a particular mapping from testgraph nodes to CUT states. Typically, a handful of parameter values are chosen and the suite is run once for each value selected. For the `IntSet0` testgraph, the test suite parameter *N* is the size of the CUT state corresponding to the testgraph node ALL.

We generate test cases by repeatedly traversing the testgraph beginning at the start node; test cases are derived from the resulting paths. We are interested in paths that, in some sense, cover the testgraph. We consider three types of coverage: *node coverage*, *arc coverage*, and *path coverage*–analogous to statement, branch, and path coverage in structural testing.[4] As in structural testing, arc coverage subsumes node coverage; path coverage subsumes arc coverage but is difficult to achieve–impossible if the testgraph is cyclic. For these reasons our testgraph traversal algorithm generates paths that achieve arc coverage. For the trivial testgraph shown in Figure 3, arc coverage is achieved by the single path

$$\langle EMPTY, ALL \rangle$$

The testgraph traversal algorithm generates calls to the member functions of the class `Driver`, which must be implemented by the tester. The declaration for `Driver` is shown in Figure 4. The constructor takes the value of the test suite parameter as its argument. The member function `reset` is called each time a new path is started, `arc(l)` is called when the arc with label *l* is traversed, and `node` is called when a node in the testgraph is visited. The private variables `cut`, `curNode`, and `allSize` store the CUT, the current node in the testgraph, and the current value of the test suite parameter.

The `Driver` implementation is shown in Figure 5. `reset` sets the current node to EMPTY. `arc` adds the elements that are in ALL to `cut` and sets the current node to ALL. Because there is only one arc in this testgraph, `arcLabel` is not used in `arc`. Finally, `node` checks the return value for `cut.size`, and for `cut.isMember(i)` for all *i* in $[0..allSize - 1]$. The functions CHECKVAL and CHECKVALBOOLEAN are provided by the ClassBench framework, and generate the appropriate error messages when the testing reveals a failure.

The code coverage for this testgraph is the same as for the simple customized driver shown

```
1   Driver::Driver(int allSize0)
2   {
3       allSize = allSize0;
4   }
5   void Driver::reset()
6   {
7       curNode = EMPTY;
8   }
9   void Driver::arc(int arcLabel)
10  {
11      for (int i = 0; i < allSize; i++)
12          cut.add(i);
13      curNode = ALL;
14  }
15  void Driver::node() const
16  {
17      if (curNode == EMPTY) {
18          CHECKVAL(0,cut.size());
19          for (int i = 0; i < allSize; i++)
20              CHECKVALBOOLEAN(FALSE,cut.isMember(i));
21      } else {
22          CHECKVAL(allSize,cut.size());
23          for (int i = 0; i < allSize; i++)
24              CHECKVALBOOLEAN(TRUE,cut.isMember(i));
25      }
26  }
```

Figure 5. Implementation for class Driver

```
Test suite parameter:2
reset
Node: EMPTY
*** Value error*** File: DRIVER.CPP. Line: 18. Expected value: 0 Actual value: 100
Arc: ADDALL
Node: ALL
*** Value error*** File: DRIVER.CPP. Line: 22. Expected value: 2 Actual value: 100

Test suite parameter:10
reset
Node: EMPTY
*** Value error*** File: DRIVER.CPP. Line: 18. Expected value: 0 Actual value: 100
Arc: ADDALL
Node: ALL
*** Value error*** File: DRIVER.CPP. Line: 22. Expected value: 10 Actual value: 100

Test suite parameter:100
reset
Node: EMPTY
*** Value error*** File: DRIVER.CPP. Line: 18. Expected value: 0 Actual value: 100
Arc: ADDALL
Node: ALL

Summary statistics
        Number of failures: 5
        Total test cases: 230
```

Figure 6. Test output

in Figure 2. In fact, the calls executed on the CUT will be identical for the two test suites. However, the error messages generated by the testgraph test suite are more informative. For example, suppose that a fault in IntSet0::size causes it to return MAXSIZE regardless of the number of elements in the set. If we run the test suite with the test suite parameter values 2, 5, 10, and 100, the output shown in Figure 6 is generated. For the parameter value 100, only one error message is generated because, for the node ALL, MAXSIZE is the correct return value for size.

To improve the code coverage, we extend the IntSet0 testgraph as shown in Figure 7. The new nodes EVEN and ODD represent the subsets consisting of the even and odd elements of ALL. The arcs DELODD and DELEVEN delete the odd and even elements from ALL using remove, and the arc CLEAR empties the set using removeAll. The required changes to Driver are straightforward: arc and node are both implemented as four-way case statements. With the extended testgraph, we achieve 100% statement coverage of every normal-case statement in IntSet0, as measured by the Unix utility *tcov*.

Oracles

In test suites for realistic classes, the Driver implementation tends to become complex and unmanageable. Driver complexity can be reduced by moving the code for output checking to a separate class, Oracle. Oracle is similar to the CUT, except that it handles only the states and transitions in the testgraph. The Oracle declaration for IntSet0 is shown in Figure 8. It provides the same member functions as IntSet0, but is implemented using an array, s, of

158

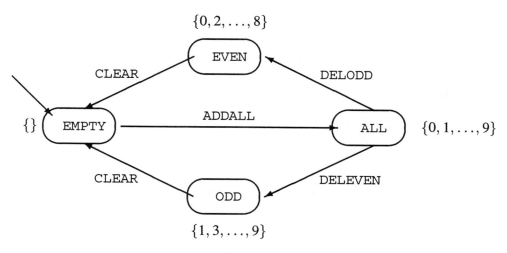

Figure 7. Full testgraph for `IntSet` *(test suite parameter is 10)*

MAXSIZE booleans. To add the element i to the set, `s[i]` is set to *true*; to remove it, `s[i]` is set to *false*. Since the sets in the testgraph contain only elements in the range $[0..MAXSIZE-1]$, this simple implementation is sufficient. `Oracle` also contains a constructor that creates an oracle object from a testgraph node and a value for the test suite parameter. For example, the statement

```
Oracle orc(ODD,10);
```

initializes `orc` to an oracle object representing the set $\{1, 3, 5, 7, 9\}$. Finally, `Oracle` provides `operator=`.

A partial `Oracle` implementation is shown in Figure 9. The constructor creates an empty set by initializing all the entries in `s` to *false*, `add(i)` sets `s[i]` to *true*, and `isMember(i)` returns `s[i]` if $i \in [0..MAXSIZE-1]$ and *false* otherwise. The implementations of the other member functions are also straightforward.

The `Oracle` implementation can be much simpler than the CUT implementation, because:

(i) the `Oracle` needs to only handle the testgraph states and transitions;
(ii) the `Oracle` does not have to be as efficient as the CUT; and
(iii) the `Oracle` does not signal exceptions.

For example, a simple oracle similar to the one discussed here was used to test a set class from the CSet++ Collection Class Library,[5] which was implemented using a B* tree, and a set class from the Standard Template Library,[6] which was implemented using a red-black tree.

As in any nontrivial program, faults in the oracle are inevitable. Since the oracle is the standard for CUT correctness, oracle errors are a serious concern. To minimize these errors, we follow standard software engineering practice by carefully documenting the oracle interface and inspecting the oracle implementation. While the few remaining faults may cause oracle failures, these failures rarely cause a CUT failure to go undetected. That would happen only if the oracle and CUT failed on the same input and produced the same incorrect output for that input.

```
class Oracle {
public:   Oracle();
          Oracle(const Oracle& orc);
          Oracle(int node,int parm);
          void add(int x);
          void remove(int x);
          void removeAll();
          int isMember(int x) const;
          int size() const;
          Oracle& operator=(const Oracle& orc);
private: int s[MAXSIZE];
};
```

Figure 8. Declaration for class Oracle

```
Oracle::Oracle()
{
    for (int i = 0; i < MAXSIZE; i++)
        s[i] = 0;
}
void Oracle::add(int x)
{
    if (x >= 0 && x < MAXSIZE)
        s[x] = 1;
}
int Oracle::isMember(int x) const
{
    return x >= 0 && x < MAXSIZE && s[x];
}
```

Figure 9. Partial implementation for class Oracle

```
void Driver::reset()
{
    cut.removeAll();
    orc.removeAll();
}
void Driver::arc(int arcTag)
{
    switch (arcTag) {
    case ADDALL:
        for (int i = 0; i < allSize; i++) {
            orc.add(i);
            cut.add(i);
        }
        break;
    case REMOVEODD: // ...
    case REMOVEEVEN: // ...
    case CLEAR: // ...
    }
}
void Driver::node()
{
    CHECKVAL(orc.size(),cut.size());
    for (int i = 0; i < allSize; i++) {
        CHECKVALBOOLEAN(orc.isMember(i),cut.isMember(i));
    }
}
```

Figure 10. Partial implementation for class Driver

The version of Driver that uses Oracle is shown in Figure 10. The member variable orc stores an Oracle object. reset removes all the elements from orc and cut. In arc(*l*), for arc ADDALL, the elements in ALL are added to both orc and cut. The other arcs are implemented similarly. The code for node is reduced from four cases to a single case because Oracle supplies the expected values for the calls to size and isMember. Note that the same checks are performed for all nodes in the testgraph. The Oracle class provides a systematic approach for checking the CUT behavior and simplifying the Driver implementation.

Exceptions

The IntSet0 implementation uses C++ exceptions.[7] The implementation detects the occurrence of an exception, and signals the exception using the operator throw. The class user handles exceptions with try and catch.

To test the exception behavior of the CUT, we add checks to Driver::node. Figure 11 shows an implementation of node that includes exception testing. The testing of size and isMember has been moved to the new private member function checkCut. Three other functions test that DuplicateExc, FullExc, and NotFoundExc are signaled correctly. The implementation of node in terms of several 'check functions' standardizes the node

161

```
void Driver::node()
{
    checkCut();
    checkDuplicateExc();
    checkFullExc();
    checkNotFoundExc();
}
void Driver::checkDuplicateExc()
{
    for (int i = 0; i < allSize; i++) {
        if (orc.isMember(i)) {
            int excFlag = 0;
            try {
                cut.add(i);
            }
            catch (IntSet0::DuplicateExc) {
                excFlag = 1;
            }
            CHECKVALBOOLEAN(TRUE,excFlag);
        }
    }
}
```

Figure 11. Exception testing for class IntSet0

implementation, which we rely on below.

In checkDuplicateExc, for every element *i* in orc, a call to cut.add(*i*) is placed inside a try block. Each of these calls should throw DuplicateExc, causing the assignment to excFlag inside the catch block to be executed. If the exception is not thrown, the value of excFlag will remain 0 and the call to CHECKVALBOOLEAN will report a failure. The implementation of checkNotFoundExc is similar. The implementation of checkFullExc generates FullExc by adding an element when the node is ALL and the test suite parameter is MAXSIZE.

In addition to the above changes, there is code to check that no unexpected CUT exceptions occur at any time during the testing. This provides a systematic approach for testing exceptions. The test suite provides 100% statement coverage of all statements in IntSet0, as measured by the Unix utility *tcov*.

Test documentation

With a systematic approach to testing, the testing must be documented so that the test implementation can be understood and maintained. We therefore associate a *test plan* with each test suite. The purpose of the test plan is to determine the feasibility of the test implementation and the adequacy of the test cases. This is especially important *before* the test implementation is written. In addition, the test plan serves as documentation of the test implementation, which facilitates the maintenance of the test implementation.

```
class TestCut : public IntSet0 {
public:
    TestCut() {};
    TestCut(const Oracle& orc);
    void add(const Oracle& orc);
    void remove(const Oracle& orc);
};
int operator==(const TestCut& cut,const Oracle& orc);
int operator==(const Oracle& orc,const TestCut& cut);
```

Figure 12. Declaration for class TestCut

THE CLASSBENCH METHODOLOGY: ADVANCED TECHNIQUES

This section introduces several techniques that have proved useful in applying the ClassBench methodology to commercial class libraries.

The TestCut class

Experience with testing commercial class libraries has shown that the Driver class tends to get complex and lengthy, and that it pays to move as much code as possible to other classes. We therefore introduce the TestCut class, which provides a shell around the CUT. The shell typically provides operations that modify the CUT to match information in the Oracle, and operations that compare the CUT with the Oracle. Although the introduction of TestCut does not reduce the total amount of test code, it provides a decomposition that reduces the complexity of the code by avoiding a long, monolithic Driver.

The TestCut declaration for IntSet0 is shown in Figure 12. The second constructor is like a copy constructor, except that it creates a CUT from an Oracle rather than from another CUT. The add and remove member functions add and remove elements from the CUT that belong to the Oracle passed as an argument. Finally, operator== compares a CUT with an oracle by performing the tests that were previously in Driver::checkCut.

Part of the modified Driver implementation is shown in Figure 13. The code for ADDALL creates a temporary oracle allOrc and initializes it to contain the elements for node ALL. It then adds all the elements belonging to this oracle to cut, which is an instance of TestCut, by calling add. Finally, it changes orc using Oracle::operator=.

By providing a shell around the CUT, the Driver is simplified. Even for a simple example such as IntSet0, it has simplified the driver by removing the loops from arc. In addition, the use of TestCut insulates the test driver from minor changes to the CUT, enhancing the reuse of Driver for variants of the same class. Finally, as we show below, the TestCut simplifies the testing of template classes.

Testing binary operators

Most collection classes provide binary operators, such as operator= and operator==. Because a testgraph models only a single instance of the CUT, we must introduce a second instance of the CUT to test binary operators. In this section, we present a test suite for IntSet1

163

```
void Driver::arc(int arcTag)
{
    switch (arcTag) {
    case ADDALL:
        Oracle allOrc(ALL,allSize);
        cut.add(allOrc);
        orc = allOrc;
        break;
    case REMOVEODD: // ...
    case REMOVEEVEN: // ...
    case CLEAR: // ...
    }
}
```

Figure 13. Partial implementation for class Driver

which extends IntSet0 with operator=, operator==, and operator+= (operator+= calculates the union of two sets).

To test IntSet1, we use the same testgraph and TestCut as for IntSet0. We extend the oracle for IntSet0 by adding the three binary operators that we added to the CUT. Again, because the oracle operates on a restricted state space, these operators are straightforward to implement. We extend Driver by adding three check functions to node: checkOpEqual, checkOpEqualEqual, and checkOpPlusEqual.

Figure 14 shows the implementation of checkOpPlusEqual. The implementation loops over all testgraph states. For each testgraph state, it creates a temporary instance of the oracle and the CUT that corresponds to the testgraph state. It then applies both the oracle and the CUT version of operator+= to the temporary instance and the testgraph instance. For the CUT version of the operator, it tests that the operator returns the correct value, which is a reference to the left-hand-side object. Finally, it tests that the operator has changed the state correctly by comparing the new CUT object to the new oracle object using TestCut::operator==. The implementations of checkOpEqual and checkOpEqualEqual are similar.

Since every node is reached at least once by the testgraph traversal algorithm, and since we loop over all testgraph states, we know that every binary operator is tested for all pairs of objects in the testgraph. This method thus provides thorough coverage of binary operators with relatively little code. With the support provided by Oracle and TestCut, the Driver code is compact and comprehensible.

Iterator testing

Collection classes commonly provide *iterators*, which provide sequential access to the elements in the collection. Frequently performance requirements demand that the iterator implementor be given control over the order in which the elements are returned. For example, an IntSet1 implementation based on a linked list and one based on a hash table would use quite different iterator return orders. Thus, many iterators do not specify the order in which the elements in the collection will be returned.

Figure 15 shows the declaration for IntSetIter, which provides member functions to

```
void Driver::checkOpPlusEqual() const
{
    for (int n = EMPTY; n <= ALL; n++) {
        // create and initialize lhs CUT
        Oracle lhsOrc(n,allSize);
        TestCut lhsCut(lhsOrc);

        // compute and check result
        lhsOrc += orc;
        CHECKVAL(&(lhsCut += cut),&lhsCut); // return value
        CHECKVALBOOLEAN(TRUE,lhsCut == lhsOrc); // object state
    }
}
```

Figure 14. Implementation of `checkOpPlusEqual`

iterate over the elements stored in an object of type `IntSet1`. The class constructor takes as its argument the `IntSet1` object over which it will iterate. The function `reset` reinitializes the iterator, `next` returns the next element in the sequence, throwing `IterEndExc` if all elements have been returned, and `isEnd` returns *true* or *false* according to whether or not all elements have been returned. Testing `IntSetIter` poses a problem for the tester; for a given call to `next`, there may be several correct return values.

To test `IntSetIter`, we use the same testgraph, `TestCut`, and `Oracle` as for `IntSet1`. The only change is to `Driver`, where the functions `checkIter` and `checkIterEndExc` are added. Figure 16 shows the implementation of `checkIter`. It creates an instance of the CUT iterator and `tmpOrc`, a copy of `orc`. It then uses `next` to loop over the elements in the CUT and, for each element returned, tests whether the element belongs to `tmpOrc`. If so, it removes the element from `tmpOrc`; if not, it reports an error. After all elements have been returned, it checks whether the oracle is empty to ensure that all elements were returned by the iterator. The function `checkIterEndExc` also iterates over all the elements in the set, and then calls `next` once more, checking that `IterEndExc` is thrown.

The approach is complete in the sense that if the iterator does not return a correct sequence of elements, a failure will be reported. An alternative approach for testing iterators based on a partial oracle has been described elsewhere.[8]

```
class IntSetIter {
public:      IntSetIter(const IntSet1& intSet);
             void reset();
             int next() throw(IterEndExc);
             int isEnd() const;
};
```

Figure 15. `IntSetIter` *class declaration*

```
void Driver::checkIter() const
{
    IntSetIter iter(cut);
    Oracle tmpOrc(orc);

    while (!iter.isEnd()) {
        int x = iter.next();
        CHECKVALBOOLEAN(TRUE,orc.isMember(x));
        tmpOrc.remove(x);
    }

    CHECKVAL(0,tmpOrc.size());
}
```

Figure 16. Implementation of checkIter

Testing class templates

In most class libraries, the collection classes are actually class templates that can be instantiated to store elements of any given type. For example, rather than providing a class such as IntSet0, these libraries would provide a class template such as Set0 shown in Figure 17. Set0 provides the same member functions as IntSet0, but instead of storing integers, the type of element stored by Set0 is specified by the template parameter Element. The statement

```
Set0<int> s;
```

defines a set of integers s. Set0 can be instantiated to any type that provides a constructor, operator=, and operator==. The problem with testing class templates is that it is not clear which element types to choose and how to develop and maintain a test suite for each type. We certainly cannot afford to simply clone the test suite for each new type that we want to test, because that would produce a maintenance nightmare.

```
template <class Element> class Set0 {
public:    Set0();
           void add(Element x) throw(DuplicateExc,FullExc);
           void remove(Element x) throw(NotFoundExc);
           void removeAll();
           int isMember(Element x) const;
           int size() const;
protected: Element s[MAXSIZE];
           int curSize;
};
```

Figure 17. Set0 *class declaration*

```
class Element : public String {
public: Element() { }

        Element(int x)
        {
            char s[80];
            sprintf(s,"%d",x);
            String& stringRef = (String&) *this;
            stringRef = s;
        }
};
```

Figure 18. Implementation for class `Element`

Fortunately, the C++ type conversion mechanism allows us to easily test template classes for different types. With this method, only a small change to `TestCut` is required; the testgraph, `Oracle`, and `Driver` remain exactly as before. We define a new class `Element` that we create to provide a mapping from `int`, the element type used in `Driver` and `Oracle`, to the type for which we want to test `Set0`. For example, the implementation for `Element` that allows us to test `Set0` for type `String` is shown in Figure 18. Here `String` is the user-defined class presented by Stroustrup.[7] `Element` provides a constructor that maps an `int` to a `char*` using `sprintf`. This `char*` is then copied to a `String` by creating a `String` reference and then using the `String::operator=(char*)`. Every time `Driver` calls a `TestCut` member function and passes an `int`, the C++ type conversion mechanism automatically calls this constructor and converts the `int` to a `String`.

It is important to test template classes for different types, and the C++ type conversion mechanism provides a convenient method to do so. To test a new type `T`, all we need to do is provide a new class `Element` with a constructor that maps `int` to `T`. In practice, we test our classes for one built-in and one user-defined type. For example, we tested `Set0` with types `int` and `String`.

THE CLASSBENCH FRAMEWORK

As described in the previous sections, the tester develops a test suite consisting of a testgraph, a list of test suite parameter values, and `Driver` and `Oracle` implementations. The ClassBench framework supports test suite development and execution. Features are provided so that the same test suite can be used for both debugging and regression testing.

The testgraph editor

The testgraph editor provides the facilities commonly available in today's graph editors. Testgraphs can be loaded from and stored to disk. Nodes and arcs can be added and deleted, and node and arc labels modified. Further, nodes and arcs can be temporarily deactivated to control testgraph traversal for a given test run. During regression testing, all of the nodes and arcs are active; debugging is often done with only a single active arc.

```
for each value X in the parameter file
    for each path P required for arc coverage of the testgraph
        invoke reset
        for each node/arc Y in P
            Y is an arc: invoke arc
            Y is a node: invoke node
```

Figure 19. Framework pseudocode

The test configuration

The ClassBench framework provides three additional features for control of test suite execution:

1. *Test suite parameter file*. This file contains the parameter values used for each traversal of the testgraph. Typically 5–10 values are used to generate CUT states with a variety of sizes.
2. *Mask file*. As shown in Figure 11, node simply calls a list of check functions. For each check function, the mask file contains the function name and a boolean flag. Using the mask file and an enhanced version of node, each check function F can be temporarily disabled; F is invoked only if the flag is *true*. The enhanced version of node is more complex than the one in Figure 11 and is automatically generated from the mask file by the ClassBench framework.
3. *Message level*. ClassBench test suites generate log messages, each with an integer priority, using the macro PRINTLOGMSG(int,char*). The tester supplies a message level with each test run. Invocations of PRINTLOGMSG with priority lower than the message level are ignored. This simple scheme gives the tester control over the message output. For example, when the message level is set to its lowest priority, the IntSet0 test suite described above generates over 12,000 lines of message output.

Using the testgraph editor and the three features just described, a test suite can be reconfigured in many ways, with few key strokes and without recompilation.

Automated testgraph traversal

The testgraph traversal classes automatically traverse a stored testgraph, calling the appropriate Driver member functions. The pseudocode in Figure 19 illustrates how the framework invokes the Driver code. There are three nested loops, all under the tester's control. The outer loop is controlled by the contents of the parameter file. The middle loop is controlled by activating and deactivating the testgraph arcs and nodes. In the inner loop, the check functions invoked by node are determined by the contents of the mask file. In all three loops, the log messages are controlled by the message level.

The ClassBench edit/compile/run cycle

Every programmer is familiar with the 'edit/compile/run' cycle. The steps are (1) edit the source code to remove a fault or provide an enhancement, (2) compile the source code, and (3) run the executable. The programmer repeats these steps until no failures are observed.

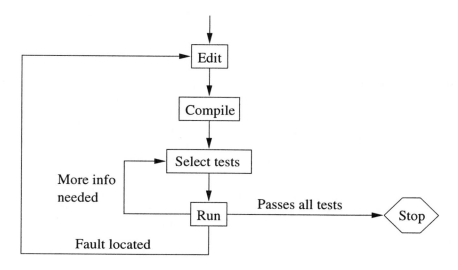

Figure 20. The ClassBench edit/compile/run cycle

The ClassBench framework can make the edit/compile/run cycle more effective. To see how, we must examine the cycle in more detail, as shown in Figure 20. We focus on the inner loop, which iterates over the select and run steps. To run a test, the programmer selects some test cases, typically by modifying an input file or using a debugger. The programmer remains in the inner loop until enough is learned about the CUT behavior to return to the edit and compile steps.

With ClassBench, we use the same flowchart but exploit the configuration features described earlier. In the outer loop, we run all the test cases with all log messages suppressed, so that only failure messages appear. In the inner loop, we isolate the fault with a 'narrow test suite': one with most of the testgraph arcs and nodes deactivated, parameter values removed, and check functions disabled. The goal is to generate the failure with as few test cases as possible. Then the message level is set to print all log messages, to provide as much information about the failure as possible.

With ClassBench, the traditional edit/compile/run cycle is enhanced. In the outer loop, many test cases can be run with a single command. In the inner loop, it is easy to select the most revealing test cases and to adjust the message output, all without recompilation. In our experience, these features make the cycle more effective and enjoyable. The tedious aspects of testing have been automated while still giving the tester the necessary control.

TESTING COMMERCIAL COLLECTION CLASS LIBRARIES

In the previous section, we presented our process for using the ClassBench framework to test and debug a class implementation. This section describes the process we have used to develop test suites for commercial libraries. Because these libraries have a large number of classes, affordable testing depends on exploiting the similarities among the classes. By studying a variety of libraries, we have found that most collection classes fall into one of the following families:

(a) *Unordered collections*, including set, bag, map, and relation.
(b) *Ordered collections*, including list, vector, stack, and queue.
(c) *Trees*, including binary and n-ary trees.
(d) *Graphs*, including directed and undirected graphs.

Our research has shown that it is possible to exploit the commonality between family members and achieve considerable reuse in test suites for classes in the same family. The first time a class family is encountered, substantial effort is required in test suite development. Original work is needed in the testgraph, oracle, and driver design. Trial and error is inevitable and the resulting rework is expensive. A test suite for one class in a family, however, can be converted easily to test another class in the same family. For example, with relatively little effort we have adapted our test suite for a set class to test a bag class. Typically, the adaptation involves little or no change to the `Oracle` and testgraph, and modest changes to the `Driver` and `TestCut`.

Thus, to provide the basis for testing a variety of CCLs, we have developed prototype test suites for a representative class from each of the four families. These representative classes are abstracted from CCLs; the classes are smaller and offer reduced functionality but present the same testing problems as the CCL classes. For example, as explained earlier, testing binary operators poses special testing problems. Therefore, we included a union operation in our representative set class. However, no intersection operation was supplied, because intersection poses no new testing challenges; it can be tested with the same technique used for union. We then wrote and refined test suites for the representative classes. In this way, we were able to inexpensively experiment with many strategies.

We have described the prototype `Set` test suite in the previous sections. We next briefly describe the test suites we have developed for sequence, tree, and graph classes.

Testing sequence classes

Consider the `Sequence` class, providing member functions to insert, delete, retrieve, and modify an element at any position in a sequence. Assignment, equality, and append are also provided for pairs of sequences.

For this CUT, we adapt the approach used for the `Set` class. While no changes are needed to the testgraph, the nodes are interpreted differently: each node represents a sequence of integers rather than a set. For example, in the `Set` testing, the node/parameter pair $\langle EVEN, 3 \rangle$ represents the set $\{0, 2\}$. In the `Sequence` testing, $\langle EVEN, 3 \rangle$ represents the sequence $\langle 0, 2 \rangle$.

The append operation requires further changes. We would like to test append with sequences of various lengths. For example, we could append $\langle 0, 2 \rangle$ and $\langle 4, 6, 8 \rangle$ yielding $\langle 0, 2, 4, 6, 8 \rangle$. However, the second operand cannot be represented with a node/parameter pair. This problem can be overcome with a simple change: represent a sequence with a testgraph node and *two* integers, a low and a high value. Thus, $\langle EVEN, 0, 2 \rangle$ represents $\langle 0, 2 \rangle$ and $\langle EVEN, 4, 8 \rangle$ represents $\langle 4, 6, 8 \rangle$. Their concatenation is $\langle 0, 2, 4, 6, 8 \rangle$, which can be represented as $\langle EVEN, 0, 8 \rangle$.

The `Oracle` implementation uses the node/high/low triple directly, and is simple and fast because it is specialized to the nodes and transitions needed for testing. The `Driver` and `TestCut` implementations are straightforward, following the techniques described in the previous sections.

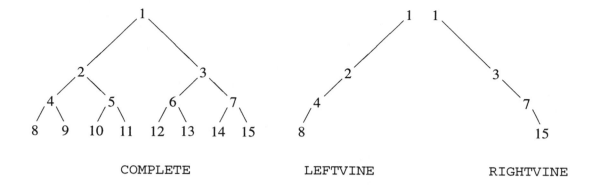

Figure 21. Tree patterns (for height 4)

Testing tree classes

Because trees are more complex than sequences, testing a tree class is more complex than testing a sequence class. Consider the `BinTree` class which can store and traverse a binary tree. Member functions are provided to modify and retrieve the value stored in any node, and to add and delete its left and right child.

In the set and sequence test suites, the oracle represents the testgraph states with a 'pattern': EMPTY, ODD, EVEN, or ALL. The `BinTree` patterns are more complex, as shown in Figure 21. The COMPLETE nodes are numbered breadth-first; in LEFTVINE and RIGHTVINE each node is given the number of the corresponding node in COMPLETE. The oracle represents a tree with a pair $\langle p, n \rangle$ where p is COMPLETE, LEFTVINE, or RIGHTVINE, and $n > 0$ is the tree height. In `Driver::arc`, a `cut` is generated from an `orc` with a simple routine that recursively traverses the tree represented by `orc` and issues add-child calls on `cut`. In `Driver::node`, a similar routine recursively traverses the `orc` tree, checking that `cut` stores the tree represented by `orc`. The entire test suite has been designed so that it is easy to add new tree patterns.[9]

Testing graph classes

The ClassBench framework contains the `TestGraph` class which stores the arcs, nodes, and labels of a testgraph, and traverses a testgraph, returning a sequence of paths that cover every arc reachable from the start node.

The test suite for the `TestGraph` class is similar to the `BinTree` test suite. However, the graph patterns are somewhat more complex, as shown in Figure 22. While the CHAIN, RING, and COMPLETE graphs are straightforward, the STAR graph requires some explanation. In a STAR graph of order k, the label for each node is a permutation of the digits $1, 2, \ldots, k$. A node n is connected to the $k - 1$ other nodes whose labels can be obtained by swapping the first digit of n's label with one of the other digits. For example, Figure 22 shows a STAR graph of order 4. Node 1234 is connected to nodes 2134 (1 swapped with 2), 3214 (1 swapped with 3), and 4231 (1 swapped with 4). We use a STAR graph because it is easy to generate and

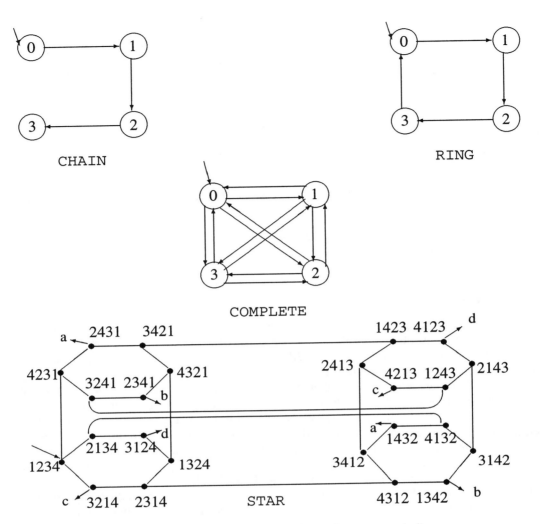

Figure 22. Testgraph patterns (test suite parameter is 4)

produces tests radically different from the CHAIN, RING, and COMPLETE graphs.

The oracle represents a particular graph with an adjacency matrix: a two-dimensional matrix m where m[*src*][*dst*] contains the label for the arc from *src* to *dst*, or 'undefined' if there is no such arc. For each pattern in Figure 22, we write a routine to generate the pattern in the oracle. For the CHAIN, RING, and COMPLETE graphs, these routines are short and simple; for the STAR graph, about 100 lines of C++ is required.

In Driver::arc, a cut is generated from an orc by traversing the adjacency matrix in orc and adding the corresponding nodes and arcs to cut. As for BinTree, the testgraph suite has been designed so that it is easy to add new graph patterns.

172

Set classes
   Set, Key Set, Key Sorted Set, Sorted Set,
   Bag, Key Bag, Key Sorted Bag, Sorted Bag,
   Map, Sorted Map, Relation, Sorted Relation, Heap

Sequence classes
   Deque, Equality Sequence, Priority Queue, Queue, Stack, Sequence

Tree classes
   N-ary Tree

Figure 23. CSet++ class families

Industrial experience

Over the past several years, we have applied ClassBench to classes from libraries developed by several vendors, including IBM,[5] Rational,[10] Rogue Wave,[11] and Borland.[12,13] We have also developed both performance and correctness test suites for the Standard Template Library.[6,14] We repeatedly refined our methodology and framework, resulting in the approach described in this paper.

For concreteness, we briefly review our experience with testing the CSet++ Collection Class Library (CCL) developed by IBM. As with most commercial class libraries, the CCL is large and complex. For clarity, the following discussion presents a slightly simplified view of the CCL classes. The CCL provides 20 classes. For testing purposes, these classes can be divided into the three families shown in Figure 23.

To develop a test suite for a CCL class, we adapted the prototype test suite. The simple metrics in Table I show how this approach worked in practice. We were able to quickly adapt our prototype test suites to the CCL classes. Typically, the testgraphs were used without change and the oracles required only modest enhancement. Because the CCL classes have many more member functions than the classes tested by the prototype suite, most of the adaptation effort was done in `Driver::node`. For each new member function a new check function was written. The check functions were developed quickly from similar check functions in the prototype test suites.

Table I. Metrics for the CSet++ test suites

	Prototype			C Set++		
	Set	Sequence	Tree	Set	Sequence	Tree
TestGraph nodes	4	4	4	4	4	4
TestGraph arcs	5	5	5	5	5	5
Oracle.C (LOC)	93	108	92	123	109	184
Driver.C (LOC)	225	261	328	566	786	997

Overall, we were able to avoid the scaling-up problems so prevalent in software engineering methodologies. For example, our simplified `Set` class has nine member functions, while the CCL `Set` class has 41, or about 4.5 times as many. As Table I shows, the CCL `Driver` is only about 2.5 times as large as the prototype `Driver`. Our test suite achieved 100% statement coverage of all reachable code (less than 1% of the code was unreachable) in the CCL `Set` class, as measured by the Unix utility *tcov*.

Failures found

The most important measure of any testing approach is the failures that are generated. We have used ClassBench extensively to test our own classes, generating many failures. We typically develop a class one member function at a time, implementing both the member function and its check function together. With this approach, most code faults are easy to find because the amount of new code being tested is small, frequently less than 25 lines. Such frequent testing is only feasible if the testing is completely automated.

The test suites that we developed for commercial libraries were run long after many failures were detected by inhouse testing and substantial use. Nonetheless, failures were generated in libraries from Rational, Rogue Wave, and Borland. For example, the testing of the Borland Library revealed a memory management problem, which caused intermittent corruption of one class's data structures. The testing also revealed a number of deficiencies in the documentation of the library, and inconsistencies between the documentation and the observable behavior of the classes. Among these problems are (1) confusion between objects with the same identity–two references to the same object–and objects with the same value–two possibly different objects, (2) references to ordering, for example, 'first element' for classes that store unordered collections of elements, and (3) lack of distinction between single and multiple occurrences of element values in the `Bag` class.

RELATED WORK

Testing classes is similar to testing software modules, and early work by Panzl[15] on the regression testing of Fortran subroutines addresses some of the issues. The DAISTS,[16] PGMGEN,[17,18] and Protest[19] systems all automate the testing of modules using test cases based on sequences of calls.

In object-oriented testing, Frankl[20] has developed a scheme for class testing using algebraic specifications. Fiedler[21] describes a small case study on testing C++ objects. Perry and Kaiser[22] discuss the testing of derived classes and show that, in general, functions inherited from a base class may need retesting in the context of the derived class. Harrold *et al.*[23] extend this work by considering which member functions must be retested, based on how the class is derived from the base class. We have developed a method for testing derived classes by reusing the base class tests and test code.[24]

The September 1994 issue of the *Communications of the ACM* is devoted to object-oriented testing. While all seven of the articles address important issues, only three articles provide techniques for class testing (as opposed to system testing). The ACE tool[1] (an enhancement of PGMGEN[17]) supports the testing of Eiffel and C++ classes and has seen substantial industrial use. Arnold and Fuson[25] discuss class testing issues and techniques. Binder[26] describes how classes can be designed to reduce test cost.

The text by Marick[27] devotes two chapters to class testing, focusing primarily on test plans. With Marick's approach, extensive test documentation is developed for each class. In contrast, our approach minimizes the need to document each test suite by standardizing the structure of all test suites. In other words, the test framework is documented once and reused for each test suite.

CONCLUSIONS

Despite the lack of attention given to object-oriented testing in the literature, it is a crucial area; reuse depends on reliability, which in turn requires thorough, automated class testing.

With the ClassBench methodology, the tester performs three tasks. The first is to define the nodes and arcs of the testgraph; these determine the states and transitions to be tested in the CUT. Second, executable oracles provide the basis for both output checking and input generation. Because full oracles are typically unaffordable, it is important to design the testgraph and the oracle together. Third, the driver class loads the testgraph and provides calls that implement the state transitions and the checking of the CUT behavior for each state.

The ClassBench framework supports the tester by providing a testgraph editor, automated testgraph traversal, and precise control of the test configuration. With this tool support, test suite development is easier and the same test suite can be used for debugging and regression testing.

We have developed test suites for handling a variety of features common in collection classes, including exceptions, binary operators, iterators, and templates. We have also developed strategies and test suites for a representative set of collection classes. Our experience with commercial libraries has shown that many collection classes can be tested by quickly adapting these test suites.

ACKNOWLEDGEMENTS

Many thanks to Kshitij Kumar for his work on testing graph classes, to Jyoti Khera and Greg Kacy for their work on the development of the testgraph editor, and to Jason McDonald for applying ClassBench to the Borland Container Class Library. We also thank David Carrington, Alena Griffiths, and the anonymous referees for their comments on earlier versions of this paper.

REFERENCES

1. G. Murphy, P. Townsend and P. S. Wong, 'Experiences with cluster and class testing', *Communications of the ACM*, **37**(9), 39–47 (1994).
2. E. Gamma, R. Helm, R. Johnson and J. Vlissedes, *Design Patterns*, Addison-Wesley, 1994.
3. Soft. Eng. Tech. Comm. of the IEEE Computer Society, *IEEE Standard Glossary of Software Engineering Terminology*, September 1982.
4. W. E. Howden, 'Reliability of the path analysis testing strategy', *IEEE Transactions on Software Engineering* **SE-2**(3), 208–215 (1976).
5. IBM, *CSet++ for AIX/6000—Collection Class Library Reference*, 1993.
6. D. R. Musser and A. Saini, *STL Tutorial and Reference Guide*, Addison-Wesley, Reading, MA, 1996.
7. B. Stroustrup, *The C++ Programming Language*, Addison-Wesley, Reading, MA, 1991.
8. D. M. Hoffman and X. Fang, 'Testing the CSet++ collection class library', *Proc. CASCON'94*. IBM Toronto Laboratory, October 1994, pp. 314–322.
9. D. M. Hoffman and P. A. Strooper, 'The testgraphs methodology—automated testing of collection classes', *Journal of Object-Oriented Programming*, **8**(7), 35–41 (1995).
10. Rational, *The C++ Booch Components–Class Catalog*, 1991.

11. Rogue Wave Software, Corvallis, OR, *Tools.h++ Class Library*, 1995.
12. Borland International, *The Container Class Libraries*, 1992.
13. J. McDonald and P. A. Strooper, 'Testing inheritance hierarchies in the classbench framework', *TOOLS USA'96*, 1996.
14. D. M Hoffman, 'Testing the standard template library', *Proc. Int. Conf. Software Engineering (submitted)*. IEEE Computer Society, May 1997.
15. D. J. Panzl, 'A language for specifying software tests', *Proc. AFIPS Natl. Comp. Conf.* AFIPS, 1978, pp. 609–619.
16. J. Gannon, P. McMullin and R. Hamlet, 'Data-abstraction implementation, specification and testing', *ACM Transactions on Programming Languages and Systems* **3**(3), 211–223 (1981).
17. D. M. Hoffman, 'A CASE study in module testing', *Proc. Conf. Software Maintenance*. IEEE Computer Society, October 1989, pp. 100–105.
18. D. M. Hoffman and P. A. Strooper, *Software Design, Automated Testing and Maintenance: A Practical Approach*, International Thomson Computer Press, 1995.
19. D. M. Hoffman and P. A. Strooper, 'Automated module testing in Prolog', *IEEE Transactions on Software Engineering* **17**(9), 933–942 (1991).
20. P. G. Frankl and R. K. Doong, 'The ASTOOT approach to testing object-oriented programs', *ACM Trans. on Software Engineering Methodology*, **3**(2), 101–130 (1994).
21. S. P. Fiedler, 'Object-oriented unit testing', *Hewlett-Packard Journal*, 69–74 (1989).
22. D. E. Perry and G. K. Kaiser, 'Adequate testing and object-oriented programming', *Journal of Object-Oriented Programming* 13–19 (1990).
23. M. J. Harrold, J. D. McGregor and K. J. Fitzpatrick, 'Incremental testing of object-oriented class structures', *Proc. 14th Int. Conf. on Software Engineering*, 1992, pp. 68–80.
24. D. M. Hoffman and P. A. Strooper, 'Graph-based class testing', *The Australian Computer Journal*, **26**(4), 158–163 (1994).
25. T. R. Arnold and W. A. Fuson, 'Testing "in a perfect world"', *Communications of the ACM*, **37**(9), 78–86 (1994).
26. R. V. Binder, 'Design for testability in object-oriented systems', *Communications of the ACM*, **37**(9), 87–101 (1994).
27. B. Marick, *The Craft of Software Testing*, Prentice Hall, Englewood Cliffs, NJ, 1994.

Chapter 6

Test Methodology

The word *methodology* originally means the study of methods. However, it has been used to mean a set of methods or techniques for accomplishing a certain goal. In software engineering we have structured analysis and design (SA/SD) methodology, object modeling technique (OMT) methodology, and many others. Each of them prescribes specific steps of activity that are performed in order to arrive at a prespecified state of process. For example, SA/SD starts with a context diagram to identify the system boundary, and a data flow diagram to illustrate the information flows among the processes. It continues by refining the data flow to a detailed level before one can proceed to construct the structure charts of the system. Next, two types of transformations are identified, followed by some adjustment to finalize the structure chart. When this is completed, implementation can commence.

We can also say that a methodology is like a cookbook. It describes in detail a set of sequential and/or concurrent iterative steps that must be carried out to accomplish a specific task. In particular, a methodology should describe for each step the entrance and exit criteria, information representation and manipulation mechanisms, detailed procedures to be carried out in the step, guidelines for carrying out the step, and relationships to other steps.

Similarly, test methodology means a sequence of steps or activities to perform in order to achieve the goal of testing a piece of software. It involves making decisions as to what components to test, when to test them, and how to test them to be cost effective. Testing methodology will use the techniques developed to test individual components, but it has to include much broader considerations such as effectiveness and efficiency on a larger scale. We can use a simple example to illustrate. In OO software, class/object is the fundamental part of a program. It is natural to consider testing classes first, clusters of classes second, subsystems third, and the entire system fourth and last. This is a bottom-up approach similar to conventional bottom-up testing. The only difference is the unit considered in object-oriented (OO) test methodology starts from classes, not procedure or subprograms like in the conventional programs.

This chapter contains two papers. The first paper, "Incremental Testing of OO Class Structure," by Harrold, McGregor, and Fitzpatrick [harr92a], describes a class testing methodology that utilizes the hierarchical nature of classes related by their inheritance relationships to reduce the overhead of testing each subclass. This is accomplished by reusing the test information for a parent class and incrementally updating it to guide the testing of the subclasses. Experiments show that a significant amount of effort can be saved for well-designed hierarchies with a large amount of functionality defined at the top level and modifications and additions are made in the lower levels. Additional savings include the reuse of the parent class' test suites to test the methods of the subclasses.

The second paper, "Integrated OO Testing and Development Process" by J.D. McGregor and T.D. Korson [mcgr94a], proposes a sequence of steps and activities related to software testing that is integrated into the development process. It is inspired by the traditional V-shaped life cycle model and neatly rolls the testing process into the software development phase. If it is done properly, no extra testing time needs to be set aside for a separate testing schedule. However, this integration of testing and development obviously increases the time required for software development. In this day and age when the major focus is on cost cutting and cycle time reduction, it may not be an easy job to sell this process. Nevertheless, we believe that it is a good process that can reduce the duplication of overhead if the testing and development phases are separated as well as enhance software quality.

In their paper, M.J. Harrold et al. [harr92a] address the problem: What is the best way to test a class library? One approach taken by class testing is to validate each class in the library individually. However, this approach requires complete retesting of each subclass although many of its attributes were previously tested since they are identical to those in the parent class. Additionally, completely retesting each class does not exploit opportunities to reuse and share the design, construction, and execution of test suites.

Another approach to class testing is to utilize the hierarchical nature of classes related by inheritance to reduce the overhead of retesting each subclass. However, Perry and Kaiser [perr90a] have shown that many inherited attributes in subclasses of well-designed and thoroughly tested classes must be retested in the context of the subclasses. Thus, any subclass testing technique must ensure that this interaction of new attributes and inherited attributes is thoroughly tested.

Most existing subclass testing techniques do not support automation or reuse of the parent's class test suite. Harrold, McGregor, and Fitzpatrick's paper [harr92a] presents an incremental class testing technique that exploits the hierarchical nature of the inheritance relation to test related groups of classes by reusing the testing information for a parent class and incrementally updating it to guide the testing of the subclass. The technique consists of the following steps:

- Step 1. Initially, base classes having no parents are chosen and a test suite is designed that tests each member function individually and also the interactions among member functions.

- Step 2. A testing history associates each test case with the attributes it tests. In addition to inheriting attributes from its parents, a newly defined subclass "inherits" its parent's testing history. Just as a subclass is derived from its parent class, a subclass's testing history is derived from the testing history of its parent class.

- Step 3. The inherited testing history is incrementally updated to reflect differences from the parent and the result is a testing history for the subclass. A subclass's testing history guides the execution of the test cases since it indicates which test cases must be run to test the subclass.

- Step 4. With this technique, new attributes can be easily identified in the subclass that must be tested along with inherited attributes that must be retested.

- Step 5. The inherited attributes are retested in the context of the subclass by identifying and testing their interactions with newly defined attributes in the subclass.

- Step 6. The test cases in the parent class's test suite that can be reused to validate the subclass and attributes of the subclass that require new test cases can also be identified in the process.

The authors also used a variety of existing C++ class hierarchies as experiments to determine the savings in testing using their technique. The InterView 2.6, a library of graphics interface classes, is used for conducting the experiment. One representative class hierarchies in InterView is base class INTERACTOR, and its subclass SCENE, MONOSCENE, and DIALOG, where SCENE is a subclass of INTERACTOR, MONOSCENE is subclass of SCENE, and DIALOG is a subclass of MONOSCENE.

It is found that the number of member functions to be tested is :

INTERACTOR 100%	SCENE 38%	MONOSCENE 9%	DIALOG 6%

The result shows that for this particular path, in one hierarchy, a significant amount of effort would be saved with this technique. This is a reasonable result for a well designed hierarchy with a large amount of functionality defined at the top level and modifications and additions made in the lower levels.

This analysis did not consider the benefits derived from reuse of the parent test suites. Many of the methods that must be retested will reuse the test cases of their parent, and this results in additional savings.

In the second paper, McGregor and Korson address the problem of coordination of the testing process and development process in the software life cycle. In the traditional waterfall model, the testing and development are two separated phases. The often nonexisting coordination between these two phases leads to a certain amount of overhead in both phases. For instance, most of the system testing effort requires that testers go through the software requirements specification documents and use them as a base to develop test cases. The effort used in this process can actually be saved because it has already been performed in the requirements analysis phase. In reality, testing is one area of software engineering in which the gap between research knowledge and actual practice is very wide.

This paper does not present any novel processes. Instead, the authors present high-level model descriptions for various phases of an iterative development process, and discuss how to integrate testing into each phase. Testing is continuously interwoven into the development process. The paper states that the goals of testing are to give some level of confidence that the software system meets, under specific conditions, at least certain of its objectives and to detect faults in the software.

In addition, McGregor and Korson offer suggestions on how to approach the testing and integration issues. The paper presents various proven methods to aid in completion of these phases. With respect to testing, the paper suggests that test drivers be modeled as classes, so that reuse may be applied. With respect to integration, the paper suggests that stubbing be abandoned and that it be replaced with wave front integration. Wave front integration is a technique in which multiple software development occurs among different teams through the use of software contracts. The required components are first tested when they are developed and inserted to the subsystem for testing as they are used. Wave front integration is a preferred method of integration over stubbing because stubbing usually requires more time and effort than is always anticipated in practice. Furthermore, stubs are usually more complicated than the software being integrated, whereas the wave front technique is more straightforward and requires no wasted effort.

References

[harr92a] M.J. Harrold, J.D. McGregor, and K.J. Fitzpatrick, "Incremental Testing of Object-Oriented Class Structure," *Proc. 14th Int'l Conf. Software Eng.,* IEEE Computer Society, Los Alamitos, Calif., 1992, pp. 68–80.

[mcgr94a] J. McGregor and T. Korson, "Integrating Object-Oriented Testing and Development Processes," *Comm. ACM,* Vol. 37, No. 9, Sept. 1994, pp. 59–77.

Incremental Testing of
Object-Oriented Class Structures[†]

Mary Jean Harrold, John D. McGregor and Kevin J. Fitzpatrick
Department of Computer Science
Clemson University
Clemson, SC 29634-1906

Abstract

Although there is much interest in creating libraries of well-designed, thoroughly-tested classes that can be confidently reused for many applications, few class testing techniques have been developed. In this paper, we present a class testing technique that exploits the hierarchical nature of the inheritance relation to test related groups of classes by reusing the testing information for a parent class to guide the testing of a subclass. We initially test base classes having no parents by designing a test suite that tests each member function individually and also tests the interactions among member functions. To design a test suite for a subclass, our algorithm incrementally updates the history of its parent to reflect both the modified, inherited attributes and the subclass's newly defined attributes. Only those new attributes or affected, inherited attributes are tested and the parent class' test suites are reused, if possible, for the testing. Inherited attributes are retested in their new context in a subclass by testing their interactions with the subclass's newly defined attributes. We have incorporated a data flow tester into Free Software Foundation, Inc's C++ compiler[©] and are using it for our experimentation.

1. Introduction

One of the main benefits of object-oriented programming is that it facilitates the reuse of instantiable, information-hiding modules, or *classes*. A class is a template that defines the *attributes* that an object of that class will possess. A class's attributes consist of (1) *data members* or *instance variables* that implement the object's state and (2) *member functions* or *methods* that implement the operations on the object's state. Classes are used to define new classes, or subclasses, through a relation known as *inheritance*. Inheritance imposes a hierarchical organization on the classes and permits a subclass to inherit attributes from its parent classes and either extend, restrict or redefine them. Subclasses may inherit attributes from a parent class, cancel attributes in the parent, contain new attributes not possessed by the parent, and/or redefine some of the parent's attributes. A goal of object-oriented programming is to create libraries of well designed and thoroughly tested classes that can be confidently reused for many applications.[‡]

Although there is much interest in creating class libraries, few class testing techniques have been developed. One approach is to validate each class in the library individually. However, this approach requires complete retesting of each subclass although many of its attributes were previously tested since they are identical to those in the parent class. Additionally, completely retesting each class does not exploit opportunities to reuse and share the design, construction and execution of test suites. Another approach to class testing is to utilize the hierarchical nature of classes related by inheritance to reduce the overhead of retesting each subclass. However, Perry and Kaiser[16] have shown that many inherited attributes in subclasses of well designed and thoroughly tested classes must be retested in the context of the subclasses. Thus, any subclass testing technique must ensure that this interaction of new attributes and inherited attributes is thoroughly tested. Fielder[3] presented a technique to test subclasses whose parent classes have been thoroughly tested. Part of his test design phase is an analysis of the effects of inheritance on the subclass. He suggests that only minimal testing may be required for inherited member functions whose functionality has not changed. Cheatham and Mellinger[2] also discuss the problem of subclass testing and present a more extensive analysis of the retesting required for a subclass. However, both of these subclass testing techniques require that the

† This work was partially supported by the National Science Foundation under Grant CCR-9109531 to Clemson University.

‡ More detailed discussion of object-oriented programming is given by Korson and McGregor[12].

analysis be performed by hand, which prohibits automating the design phase of the testing. Additionally, neither technique attempts to reuse the parent class's test suite to test the subclass.

In this paper, we present an incremental class testing technique that exploits the hierarchical nature of the inheritance relation to test related groups of classes by reusing the testing information for a parent class and incrementally updating it to guide the testing of the subclass. We initially test *base classes* having no parents by designing a test suite that tests each member function individually and also tests the interactions among member functions. A *testing history* associates each test case with the attributes that it tests. In addition to inheriting attributes from its parent, a newly defined subclass "inherits" its parent's testing history. Just as a subclass is derived from its parent class, a subclass's testing history is derived from the testing history of its parent class. The inherited testing history is incrementally updated to reflect differences from the parent and the result is a testing history for the subclass. A subclass's testing history guides the execution of the test cases since it indicates which test cases must be run to test the subclass. With this technique, we automatically identify new attributes in the subclass that must be tested along with inherited attributes that must be retested. We retest inherited attributes in the context of the subclass by identifying and testing their interactions with newly defined attributes in the subclass. We also identify which of the test cases in the parent class's test suite can be reused to validate the subclass and which attributes of the subclass require new test cases.

The main benefit of this approach is that completely testing a subclass is avoided since the testing history of the parent class is reused to design a test suite for a subclass. Only new or replaced attributes in the subclass or those affected, inherited attributes are tested. Additionally, test cases from the test suite of the parent class are reused, if possible, to test the subclass. Thus, there is a savings in the time to design test cases, the time to construct a new test suite and the actual time to execute the test suite since the entire subclass is not tested. Since our technique is automated, there is limited user intervention in the testing process.

The next section gives background information on procedural language testing. Section 3 discusses inheritance in object-oriented programs as an incremental modification technique. Section 4 presents our incremental testing technique by first giving an overview, and then detailing, both base class testing and subclass testing. At the end of this section, we discuss our implementation. Section 5 discusses experimentation, and concluding remarks are given in Section 6.

2. Testing

The overall goal of testing is to provide confidence in the correctness of a program. With testing, the only way to guarantee a program's correctness is to execute it on all possible inputs, which is usually impractical. Thus, systematic testing techniques generate a representative set of test cases to provide coverage of the program according to some selected criteria. There are two general forms of test case coverage: *specification-based* and *program-based*[9]. In specification-based or 'black-box' testing, test cases are generated to show that a program satisfies its functional and performance specifications. Specification-based test cases are usually developed manually by considering a program's requirements. In program-based or 'white-box' testing, the program's implementation is used to select test cases to exercise certain aspects of the code such as all statements, branches, data dependencies or paths. For program-based testing, analysis techniques are often automated. Since specification-based and program-based testing complement each other, both types are usually used to test a program.

While most systematic testing techniques are used to validate program *units*, such as procedures, additional testing is required when the units are combined or integrated. For *integration* testing, the interface between the units is the focus of the testing. Interface problems include errors in input/output format, incorrect sequencing of subroutine calls, and misunderstood entry or exit parameter values[1]. Although many of the integration testing techniques are specification-based, some interprocedural program-based testing techniques have recently been developed[8, 13].

A test set is *adequate* for a selected criterion if it covers the program according to that criterion [20] and a program is deemed to be *adequately* tested if it has been tested with an adequate test set. Weyuker[20] developed a set of axioms for test data adequacy that expose insufficiencies in program-based adequacy criteria. Several of these axioms are specifically related to unit and integration testing. The *antiextensionality* axiom reminds us that two programs that compute the same function may have entirely different implementations. While the same specification-based test cases may be used to test each of the programs, different program-based test cases may be required. Thus, changing a program's implementation may require additional test cases. The *antidecomposition* axiom tells us that adequately testing a program P does not imply that each component of P is adequately tested. Adequately testing each program component is especially important for those components that may be used in other environments where the input values may differ. Thus, each unit that may be used in another environment must be individually tested. The *anticomposition* axiom tells us that adequately testing each component Q of a program does not imply that the program has been adequately tested. Thus, after each component is individually tested, the interactions among the components must also be tested.

3. Inheritance in Object-Oriented Systems

Inheritance is a mechanism for both class specification and code sharing that supports developing new classes based on the implementation of existing classes. A subclass's definition is a *modifier* that defines attributes that differ from, or alter, the attributes in the parent class. The modifier and parent class along with the inheritance rules for the language are used to define the subclass. The class designer controls the specification of the modifier while the inheritance controls the combination of the modifier and the parent class to get the subclass. Figure 1 illustrates inheritance as an incremental modification technique[18] that transforms a parent class P with modifier M into a resulting class R. The composition operator $\oplus$ symbolically unites M and P to get R, where $R = P \oplus M$.

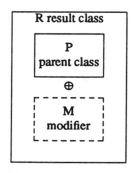

Figure 1. Incremental modification technique

The subclass designer specifies the modifier, which may contain various types of attributes that alter the parent class. These include the redefined, virtual and recursive attributes presented by Wegner[18] along with an additional type of attribute, the *new* attribute. We further classify Wegner's virtual attribute as *virtual-new*, *virtual-recursive* and *virtual-redefined*. In the following discussion, we reference Figure 1 and define these six types of attributes.

New attribute: (1) A is an attribute that is defined in M but not in P or (2) A is a member function attribute in M and P but A's argument list differs

in M and P. In this case, A is bound to the locally defined attribute in the resulting class R but is not in P.

Recursive attribute: A is defined in P but not in M. In this case, A is bound to the locally defined attribute in P and is available in R.

Redefined attribute: A is defined in both P and M where A's argument list is the same in M and P. In this case, A is bound to the attribute definition in M which blocks the definition of the similarly named attribute in P.

Virtual-new attribute: (1) A is specified in M but its implementation may be incomplete in M to allow for later definitions or (2) A is specified in M and P and its implementation may be incomplete in P to allow for later definitions, but A's argument list differs in M and P. In this case, A is bound to the locally defined attribute in the resulting class R but is not in P.

Virtual-recursive attribute: A is specified in P but its implementation may be incomplete in P to allow for later definitions, and A is not defined in M. In this case, A is bound to the locally defined attribute in P and is available in R.

Virtual-redefined attribute: A is specified in P but its implementation may be incomplete in P to allow for later definition, and A is defined in M with the same argument list as A in P. In this case, A is bound to the attribute definition in M which blocks the definition of the similarly named attribute in P.

Although the modifier M transforms a parent class P into a resulting class R, M does not totally constrain R. We must also consider the inheritance relation since it determines the effects of composing the attributes of P and M and mapping them into R. The inheritance relation determines the visibility, availability and format of P's attributes in R. A language may support more than one inheritance mapping by allowing the specification of a parameter value to determine which mapping is used for a particular definition. For example, in C++, the *public* and *private* keywords as part of the specification of the inheritance relationship determine the visibility of the attributes in the subclass. Since inheritance is deterministic, it permits the construction of rules to identify the availability and visibility of each attribute. This feature supports automating the process of analyzing a class definition and determining which attributes require testing. To illustrate some of the different types of attributes, consider Figure 2, where *class* P is given on the left, the modifier that specifies R, a subclass of P, is given in the center, and

class P {	class R : public P {	R's attributes after the mapping	
private:	*private*:	*private*:	
int i;	float i;	float i;	//new
int j;			
public:	*public*:	*public*:	
P(){}	R(){}		
void A(int a,int b)		void A(int a, int b)	//recursive
{i=a; j=a+2*b;}		{i=a; j=a+2*b;}	
	void A(int a)	void A(int a)	//new
	{P::A(a,0);}	{P::A(a,0);}	
virtual int B()	virtual int B()	virtual int B()	//virtual-redefined
{return i;}	{return 3*P::B();}	{return 3*P::B();}	
int C()	int C()	int C()	//redefined
{return j;}	{return 2*P::C();}	{return 2*P::C();}	
};	};		
		hidden	
		int i;	
		int j;	

Figure 2. Class P on the left, subclass R's specification (modifier) in the center, subclass R's attributes on the right.

the attributes for the resulting class R are given on the right. P has two data members, *i* and *j*, both integers, and three member functions, A, B and C; B is a virtual member function. The modifier for class R contains one real data member, *i*, and three member functions, A, B and C. The modifier is combined with P under the inheritance rules to get R. Data member *float i* is a new attribute in R since is does not appear in P. Member function A that is defined in M, is a new attribute in R since its argument list does not agree with A's argument list in P. Member function A in P is recursive in R since it is inherited unchanged from P. Thus, R contains two member functions named A. Member function B is virtual in P and since it is redefined in M, it is virtual-redefined in R. Member function C is redefined in R since its implementation is changed by M and overrides member function C from P. Finally, data members *i* and *j* in P are inherited but hidden in R, which means they cannot be accessed by member function defined in the modifier.

The modifier approach permits a decomposition of the inheritance structure into overlapping sets of class inheritance relations. The left side of Figure 3 shows a simple three-level chain of inheritance relations while the center illustrates an incremental view of the relationship among the classes. Class B can be replaced by A ⊕ M1 since A's attributes and M1's attributes are combined to form B. Once B is defined, there is no distinction in B between A's attributes and M1's attributes. To define a subclass of B, the inheritance relation combines B and M2 in the same way. Thus, the three level inheritance relation can be decomposed into independent structures as illustrated on the right side of Figure 3. Decomposition of

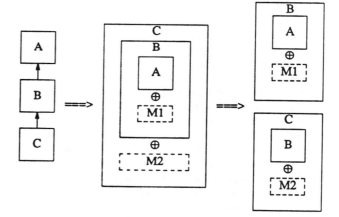

Figure 3. The inheritance hierarchy shown on the left indicates that A is a class with subclasses B and C, B is a class with subclass C. The figure in the center illustrates the incremental format for the class inheritance hierarchy where each new subclass is formed by combining the parent class with some modifier. The figure on the right shows how the class hierarchy can be decomposed into independent structures.

class hierarchies permits us to consider only the immediate parents and the modifier when testing a subclass.

The inheritance relation imposes an ordering on the classes in an inheritance structure. Class C can be determined without considering class A but the relation from A to B must be resolved prior to describing the relation from B to C. The order in which the classes must be defined is a partial ordering and any inheritance structure can be decomposed into a set of partially ordered pairs of classes. This permits us to consider only a class and its immediate parents to fully constrain the definition of that class.[†]

4. Hierarchical Incremental Class Testing

Our class testing technique initially tests a base class by testing each member function individually and then testing the interactions among the member functions. The test case design and execution information is saved in a testing history. Then, when a subclass is defined, the testing history of its parent, the definition of the modifier and the inheritance mapping of the implementation language are used to determine which attributes to (re)test in the subclass and which of the parent's test cases can be reused. The technique is hierarchical because it is guided by the partial ordering of the inheritance relation; it is incremental because it uses the results from testing at one level in the hierarchy to reduce the efforts needed by subsequent levels.

Our testing technique assumes a language model that is a generalization of the C++[17] model but is sufficiently flexible to support other languages such as Trellis[10] with similar features. Our language model is (1) strongly typed and permits polymorphic substitution to provide flexibility, (2) uses static binding whenever possible for efficiency, (3) supports three levels of attribute visibility with the same characteristics as C++'s *private*, *protected* and *public*, although the technique can handle any number of visibility levels, and (4) assumes a parameterized inheritance mapping with the two parametric values used in C++, *private* and *public*. The levels of visibility for attributes are ordered from most visible (*public*) to least visible (*private*) and the inheritance mapping maps an attribute to a level of visibility in the subclass that is at least as restrictive as its level in the parent class.

Our incremental testing technique addresses the test data adequacy concerns expressed by Perry and Kaiser[16]. The antidecomposition axiom cautions that adequate testing of a class does not imply that individual member functions have been adequately tested for use in all contexts. Our technique tests each member function independent of its place in the class. Conversely, the anticomposition axiom states that adequately testing a member function in isolation is not sufficient to assume that it

has been adequately tested as part of a set of interacting member functions. Our technique uses integration testing techniques to test the interactions between member functions without retesting their internal implementations.

4.1. Base Class Testing

We first test base classes using traditional unit testing techniques to test individual member functions in the class. The antidecomposition axiom tells us that adequate testing of the class does not guarantee adequate testing of each member function. Adequately testing each member function is particularly important since member functions may be inherited by the subclasses and expected to operate in a new context. Thus, we individually test each member function in a class using a test suite that contains both specification-based and program-based test cases. The specification-based test cases can be constructed using existing approaches such as the one proposed by Frankl[4]. During this phase of testing, we follow the standard unit testing practice of handling calls to other member functions (procedures) by providing stubs representing called member functions and drivers representing calling member functions. The testing history for a class contains associations between each member function in the class and both a specification-based and a program-based test suite. Thus, the history contains triples, $\{m_i, (TS_i, test?), (TP_i, test?)\}$ where m_i is the member function, TS_i is the specification-based test suite, TP_i is the program-based test suite and 'test?' indicates whether the test suite is to be (re)run.

The anticomposition axiom implies that testing each member function individually does not mean that the class has been adequately tested. Thus, in addition to testing each member function, we must test the interactions among member functions in the same class, *intra-class* testing; we must also test the interactions among member functions that access member functions in other classes, *inter-class* testing. Intra-class testing is guided by a *class graph* where each node represents either a member function in the class or a primitive data member, and each edge represents a message. The class graph may be disconnected where each connected subgraph represents those attributes in the class that interact with each other. For intra-class integration testing, we combine the attributes as indicated by the class graph and develop test cases that test their interfaces. For intra-class testing, we develop both specification-based and program-based test suites. The history for the class contains the root nodes of the class graph subgraphs representing the interacting member functions along with the test suites for each of them. Thus, the second part of the history also consists of triples, $\{m_i, (TIS_i, test?), (TIP_i, test?)\}$ where m_i is the root nodes of the class graph subgraph, TIS_i is the specification-based integration test suite, and TIP_i is the program-based inte-

---

[†] Although a class may have several parents from which it can inherit attributes, for our discussion, we assume that each class has only one parent.

```
class Shape {
private:
         Point reference_point;
public:
         void put_reference_point(Point);
         point get_reference_point();
         void move_to(Point);
         void erase();
virtual  void draw() = 0;
virtual  float area();
         shape(Point);
         shape();
}
```

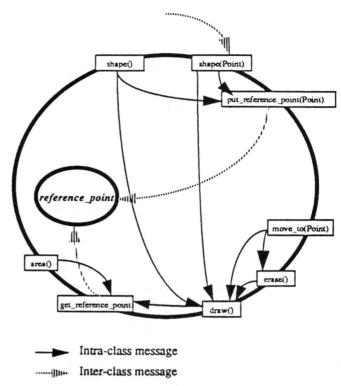

→ Intra-class message

┅┅▸ Inter-class message

Figure 4. Definition for class *Shape* on the left and its class graph on the right.

gration test suite and 'test?' indicates if the test suite is to be totally (re)run (Y), partially (re)run (P), or not (re)run (N).

Inter-class testing is guided by the interactions of the classes that result when member functions in one class interact with member functions in another class. Inter-class interactions occur when (1) a member function in one class is passed an instance of another class as a parameter and then sends that instance a message or (2) when an instance of one class is part of the representation of another class and then sends that instance as a message. The application's design provides a relationship among the class instances that is similar to the class graph produced for intra-class testing. The techniques for handling these interactions are like those described above for intra-class interactions except that interacting attributes are in different classes. We omit the details for inter-class testing since it is analogous to intra-class testing.

To illustrate our technique for testing base classes, consider the simplified example of a hierarchy of graphical shape classes implemented in C++[17]. Class *Shape*, given in Figure 4, is an abstract class that facilitates the creation of classes of various shapes for graphics display. The class definition is abbreviated for the purpose of illustrating the testing algorithm and we omit the bodies of the member functions. Each 'shape' that can be drawn in the

graphics system has a reference_point that is used to locate the position where the shape is drawn in the program's coordinate system.

Class *Shape* defines several member functions that describe the behavior of a shape and includes two virtual member functions, area() and draw(), that contribute to the common interface for all classes in the inheritance structure. Since draw() is a pure virtual member function, it has an initial value of 0 and no implementation. Virtual member function area() is assumed to have an initial implementation that can be changed in subsequent subclass declarations. The put_reference_point() and get_reference_point() member functions provide controlled access to the values of the data members, the shape(Point) and shape() member functions are constructors of instances of the class, and the move_to() member function moves the shape to a new location. Move_to() can be totally defined in terms of member functions in class *Shape* even though some of these member functions are virtual and have no implementation. The erase() member function may be implemented in several ways but if an 'xor' drawing mode is used, erase only calls draw to overwrite, and thus erase, the existing figure. The class graph for *Shape* is also given in Figure 4. Rectangles represent member functions and ovals represent instances of classes. Solid lines indicate intra-class messages while dashed lines indicate inter-class messages. The table in

Testing History for *Shape*		
attribute	specification-based test suite	program-based test suite
individual member functions		
put_reference_point	(TS_1,Y)	(TP_1,Y)
get_reference_point	(TS_2,Y)	(TP_2,Y)
move_to	(TS_3,Y)	(TP_3,Y)
erase	(TS_4,Y)	(TP_4,Y)
draw	(TS_5,Y)	$(\,--\,)$
area	(TS_6,Y)	(TP_6,Y)
shape	(TS_7,Y)	(TP_7,Y)
shape	(TS_8,Y)	(TP_8,Y)
interacting member functions		
move_to	(TIS_9,Y)	(TIP_9,Y)
erase	(TIS_{10},Y)	(TP_{10},Y)

Figure 5. Testing history for Class *Shape* of Figure 4.

Figure 5 shows the testing history for class *Shape*. The analysis of *Shape* is very straight forward. Since *Shape* is a base class, we must test each of its available definitions. The specification-based test suite for draw() can be generated but cannot be run since there is no implementation for draw(). The program-based test suite for draw() cannot be generated since no implementation exists. Since there is an initial implementation for area(), both its specification-based and program-based test suites can be generated and run. The specification-based and program-based test suites for move_to(), erase() and the two shape() constructors are generated. The test suites for the constructors are independently tested since they do not rely on the implementations of either draw() or area(). The advantage of developing the specification-based test suites for draw() and area() in the base class is that these test suites can be 'inherited' in the histories of subclasses.

The class's specification describes how the individual member functions are intended to work together. The input values that test these interactions belong to the integration test suites TIS_i and TIP_i that are part of our intraclass testing member functionality. In addition to the test suites for the individual member functions in Shape, the interface test suites are shown in the history in Figure 5. Member functions move_to(), erase(), shape() and shape(Point) call other class member functions: move_to() calls both erase() and draw(), erase() also calls draw(), shape() and shape(Point) both call put_reference_point() and draw(). The class graph for Shape, shown in Figure 4, illustrates these interactions. The class graph serves as a guide for generating program-based test cases to test each of the interactions.

There are several inter-class messages: messages to construct instances of shape as well as the messages between member functions of class shape and reference_point, which is an instance of class Point. Integration test cases are used to validate these messages but for brevity, we omit them from this example.

4.2. Testing Subclasses

Our testing algorithm, *TestSubclass* given in Figure 6, uses an incremental technique that transforms the testing history for the parent class P to the testing history for the subclass R. *TestSubclass* inputs P's history, HISTORY(P), P's class graph, G(P), and modifier M and outputs an updated HISTORY for the subclass R. The actions taken by *TestSubclass* depend on the attribute type and the type of modification made to that attribute by the inheritance mapping. In section 3, we discussed six types of attributes: new, recursive, redefined, virtual-new, virtual-recursive and virtual-redefined. For each of these types of attributes, different actions may occur. Algorithm *TestSubclass* begins by initializing R's history to that of its parent class P, which has already been tested. The algorithm then inspects each attribute A in the modifier M, and takes appropriate action to update R's history and determine the required testing.

Any NEW or VIRTUAL-NEW member function attribute A must also be completely, individually tested since it was not defined in P. Since the anticomposition axiom tells us that it is necessary to retest each new member function in its new context, A must be integration tested with other member functions in R with which it interacts. We thoroughly test A individually so that when A is inherited by some subclass, only integration testing will need to be repeated. To individually test A, new specification-based and program-based test suites are developed, added to R's HISTORY and marked for testing

186

```
algorithm TestSubclass(HISTORY(P),G(P),M);

input:       HISTORY(P):P's testing history; G(P):P's class graph;
             M:modifier that specifies subclass R;
output:      HISTORY(R):testing history for R indicating what to rerun; G(R):class graph for subclass R;
begin
  HISTORY(R) := HISTORY(P);                              /* initialize R's history to that of P */
  G(R) := G(P);                                         /* initialize R's class graph to that of P */
  foreach attribute A ∈ M do
    case A is NEW or NEW-VIRTUAL:                        /* A is a new/virtual-new attribute */
        Generate TS , TP for A;
        Add {A, (TS, Y), (TP,Y)} to HISTORY(R);
        Integrate A into G(R);
        Generate any new TIS and TIP;
        Add {A, (TIS, Y), (TIP,Y)} to HISTORY(R);
    case A is RECURSIVE or RECURSIVE-VIRTUAL:            /* A is recursive/virtual-recursive */
        if A accesses data in R's scope then
          Identify interface tests to reuse;
          Add (TIS,P) and (TIP,P)} to HISTORY(R);
    case A is REDEFINED or REDEFINED-VIRTUAL:            /* A is redefined /virtual-redefined */
        Generate TP for A;
        Reuse TS from P if it exists or Generate TS for A;
        Add {A, (TS,Y), (TP,Y)} to HISTORY(R);
        Integrate A into G(R);
        Generate TIP for G(R)  with respect to A;
        Reuse TIS from P;
        Add {A, (TIS,P), (TIP,P)} to HISTORY(R);
end TestSubclass.
```

Figure 6. Algorithm *TestSubclass* that determines a testing HISTORY for R by incrementally updating the HISTORY for its parent class. The HISTORY is used to test the subclass.

---

by setting the 'test?' field to 'Y'. A new member function may send messages to existing member functions of the class or may reference existing data members. Thus, A is tested with any other member functions in R with which it interacts by first integrating it into the G(R). Then integration tests are generated, added to HISTORY(R) and marked for testing by setting the 'test?' field to 'Y'. A new data attribute is tested during integration testing when it is integrated into G(R) by testing A with member functions with which it interacts.

A RECURSIVE or VIRTUAL-RECURSIVE member function attribute A requires very limited retesting since it was previously individually tested in P and the specification and implementation remain unchanged. Thus, the specification-based and program-based test suites for A are not rerun. The antidecomposition axiom reminds us that it is necessary to test A in its new context in the subclass. Integration test cases are not reused if they only test the interaction of this recursive attribute with other recursive attributes since this interaction has also been previously tested. However, A may interact with new or redefined attributes or access the same

instances in the class's representation as other member functions. A's interaction with new or redefined attributes is tested when those member functions are integrated into the subclass so there is no need to retest here. This limited testing adequately tests the attributes in the subclass because of the extensive testing that occurred when the attribute was defined.

Consider the case in which a recursive member function accesses the same data as a new attribute. The recursive member function was tested in P and the specification of the recursive member function remains unchanged. Thus, specification-based and program-based test cases need not be rerun. The only test cases that are rerun are those that test the interactions between A and any new member function(s). TestSubclass uses incremental techniques to identify those test cases, marks them for retesting by setting 'test?' to 'P' and updates HISTORY(R) to reflect the changes. 'Y' indicates that the entire test suite is reused while 'P' indicates that only the test cases identified as testing affected parts of the subclass are reused.

```
class Triangle: public Shape {
    private:
        Point vertex2;
        Point vertex3;
    public:
        Point get_vertex1();          //new
        Point get_vertex2();          //new
        Point get_vertex3();          //new
        void set_vertex1(Point);      //new
        void set_vertex2(Point);      //new
        void set_vertex3(Point);      //new
        void draw();      //virtual-redefined
        float area();     //virtual-redefined
        triangle();                   //new
        triangle(Point,Point,Point);  //new
}
```

attribute	Testing History for *Triangle*	
	specification test suite	program-based test suite
individual member functions		
put_reference_point	(TS_1,N)	(TP_1,N)
get_reference_point	(TS_2,N)	(TP_2,N)
move_to	(TS_3,N)	(TP_3,N)
erase	(TS_4,N)	(TP_4,N)
draw	(TS_5,Y)	(TP_5,Y)
area	(TS_6,Y)	(TP_6,Y)
shape	(TS_7,N)	(TP_7,N)
shape	(TS_8,N)	(TP_8,N)
get_vertex1	(TS'_{11},Y)	(TP'_{11},Y)
get_vertex2	(TS'_{12},Y)	(TP'_{12},Y)
get_vertex3	(TS'_{13},Y)	(TP'_{13},Y)
put_vertex1	(TS'_{14},Y)	(TP'_{14},Y)
put_vertex2	(TS'_{15},Y)	(TP'_{15},Y)
put_vertex3	(TS'_{16},Y)	(TP'_{16},Y)
triangle	(TS'_{17},Y)	(TP'_{17},Y)
triangle	(TS'_{18},Y)	(TP'_{18},Y)
interacting member functions		
move_to	(TIS''_9,P)	(TIP''_9,P)
erase	(TIS''_{10},P)	(TIP''_{10},P)
area	(TIS'_{19},Y)	(TIP'_{19},Y)
get_vertex1	(TIS'_{20},Y)	(TIP'_{20},Y)
put_vertex1	(TIS'_{21},Y)	(TIP'_{21},Y)

Figure 7. Definition and History for Class *Triangle*. Test suites marked with 'Y' or 'P' are reused to test the subclass; those marked with 'N' are not rerun. 'Y' indicates that all test cases in the test suite are reused; 'P' means that only part of that test suite is reused. A comment with each of the public attributes indicates its type; all other inherited attributes are recursive.

Both data member and member function attributes are defined in the parent class and inherited by the subclass. The inheritance mapping from P into R may change the visibility of a data member attribute. For example, if the attribute has moved from a visible level to one that is not visible then it cannot interact with any new or redefined attribute. The data attributes that are hidden and the member functions on that data form a tested unit that need not be retested. If the data attribute is visible to any new member functions that are defined in R, then the interfaces between the new member functions and the existing member functions that access the data attributes must be tested. This testing is performed when a new member function that interacts with data attributes accessed by existing member functions is integrated into G(R).

A REDEFINED or VIRTUAL-REDEFINED attribute A in M requires extensive retesting but many existing specification-based test cases may be reused since only the implementation has changed. The antiextensionality axiom tells us that since the the implementation has changed, new program-based test cases may be required. If A is a data member (i.e. an instance of a class) we assume that the class to which the instance belongs has

been tested. No other individual testing is performed on A although it may participate in the integration testing of the member functions defined in M. If A is a member function, the specification of A remains unchanged but the implementation of A will have changed. Thus, A is individually retested by generating new program-based test cases to test the implementation of A. The specification-based test cases stored in HISTORY(R) for the previous definition of A are still valid and are reused. HISTORY(R) is updated to reflect the new test cases and reused existing test cases, and these test cases are marked for reusing by setting 'test?' to 'Y'. Then, A is integrated into G(R). New program-based interface test cases are generated and marked for testing by setting 'test?' to 'Y' or 'P'. HISTORY(R) is again updated to reflect the changes.

To illustrate the way in which algorithm *TestSubclass* works, we consider subclasses of Class *Shape* that was given in Figure 4. The benefits of hierarchical incremental testing can be seen in the testing history for class *Triangle*, given in Figure 7. None of the test suites for the put_() and get_() member functions for reference_point are rerun because they are recursive attributes since no

188

```
class EquiTriangle: public Triangle{
    public:
            float area();                       //redefined
            equi_triangle(Point,Point,Point);   //new
            equi_triangle();                    //new
}
```

Testing History for *EquiTriangle*		
attribute	specification test suite	program-based test suite
individual member functions		
put_reference_point	(TS_1,N)	(TP_1,N)
get_reference_point	(TS_2,N)	(TP_2,N)
move_to	(TS_3,N)	(TP_3,N)
erase	(TS_4,N)	(TP_4,N)
draw	(TS_5,N)	(TP_5,N)
area	(TS_6,Y)	(TP_6',Y)
shape	(TS_7,N)	(TP_7,N)
shape	(TS_8,N)	(TP_8,N)
get_vertex1	(TS_{11},N)	(TP_{11},N)
get_vertex2	(TS_{12},N)	(TP_{12},N)
get_vertex3	(TS_{13},N)	(TP_{13},N)
put_vertex1	(TS_{14},N)	(TP_{14},N)
put_vertex2	(TS_{15},N)	(TP_{15},N)
put_vertex3	(TS_{16},N)	(TP_{16},N)
triangle	(TS_{17},N)	(TP_{17},N)
triangle	(TS_{18},N)	(TP_{18},N)
equi_triangle	(TS_{22},Y)	(TP_{22},Y)
equi_triangle	(TS_{23},Y)	(TP_{23},Y)
interacting member functions		
move_to	(TIS_9'',P)	(TIP_9'',P)
erase	(TIS_{10}'',P)	(TIP_{10}'',P)
area	(TIS_{19}'',P)	(TIP_{19}'',P)

Figure 8. Definition and History for Class *EquiTriangle*. Test suites marked with 'Y' or 'P' are reused to test the subclass; those marked with 'N' are not rerun. 'Y' indicates that all test cases in the test suite are reused; 'P' means that only part of that test suite is reused. A comment with each of the public attributes indicates its type; all other inherited attributes are recursive.

changes are made in their definitions. Virtual-redefined member functions draw() and area() are retested since they have new implementations. However, only new program-based test cases are developed since existing specification-based test cases can be reused. Test suites are developed and run for the new member functions defined in *Triangle*. Three member functions have been added to the list of interacting member functions: area() calls the get_vertex() member functions and both get_vertex1() and put_vertex1() call the get_() and put_() member functions for reference_point respectively. The interfaces between these pairs of member functions must be tested, but get_reference_point() and put_reference_point() need no further individual testing. No member function-interaction test suites for move_to() and get_reference_point() are executed since no member function defined in *Triangle* can directly access reference_point. In Figure 7, test suites marked with ' are newly developed, test suites marked with " may have newly developed test cases, while all others are reused from the parent.

The last class in the hierarchy is *EquiTriangle* which adds no new member functions other than the constructors for the class. However, *EquiTriangle* redefines the implementation of area() to provide more efficiency. Only the program-based test cases for area() are regenerated, although all test cases for area() are rerun. Integration test cases to test the interactions of the new and redefined member functions with the inherited attributes are also run. The definition of class *EquiTriangle* and its testing history are given in Figure 8.

4.3. Implementation

The implementation of our testing system consists of two main parts. The first part uses our algorithm *TestSubClass* to automatically identify the required retesting in a subclass. The second part assists in performing the subclass testing. Although, our hierarchical incremental algorithm is independent of the testing methodology, we are using a type of program-based testing known as data

Table 1: Interactor Class Hierarchy							
class	lines of code	number of attributes of each type					
		new	recursive	redefined	virtual new	virtual recursive	virtual redefined
Interactor	908	79	0	0	14	0	0
Scene	195	21	59	0	8	14	1
MonoScene	98	1	73	0	4	16	4
Dialog	84	3	74	0	1	24	0

flow testing[6, 11, 15] to demonstrate the feasibility of our technique. The underlying premise of all of the data flow testing criteria is that confidence in the correctness of a variable assignment at a point in a program depends on whether some test data has caused execution of a path from the assignment (i.e., *definition*) to points where the variable's value is used (i.e., *use*). Definition-use pairs are determined by considering the reachable uses of each definition. Test data adequacy criteria are used to select particular definition-use pairs or subpaths that are identified as the *testing requirements* for a program. Test cases are generated that satisfy the testing requirements when used in a program's execution. One criterion, 'all-uses'[6], requires that each definition of a variable be tested on some path to each of its uses. The 'all-uses' criterion has been shown to be effective in uncovering errors [5] and feasible since relatively few test cases typically are required for its satisfaction[19].

Data flow testing is also used to validate the interfaces between procedures[7, 8]. When validating the interface, the focus of the testing is the definitions and uses of variables that extend across procedure boundaries and includes global variables and reference parameters. We use data flow testing to validate the class member functions individually and to test the interface among the member functions. Stubs and drivers are used to represent any incomplete implementations. We are incorporating our testing technique into the Free Software Foundation, Inc's C++ compiler© (g++) and are using it for our experimentation. We have modified the data flow analysis performed by the g++ compiler to gather the definition-use pairs for the testing and we can currently test individual member functions. Each member function is compiled with the modified g++ compiler and stubs are used to return appropriate values at runtime.

5. Experimentation

We are using a variety of existing C++ class hierarchies for our experiments to determine the savings in testing gained using our technique. We are considering the class hierarchies in InterViews 2.6 [14], which is a library of graphics interface classes. One representative class hierarchy in InterViews is base class *Interactor*, and its subclasses, *Scene*, *MonoScene* and *Dialog*, where *Scene* is a subclass of *Interactor*, *MonoScene* is a subclass of *Scene*, and *Dialog* is a subclass of *MonoScene*. Table 1 gives statistics about these classes.

We used our algorithm to determine which of the methods in each class required retesting. The results of that analysis are shown in Tables 2 and 3. The only comparison possible was with a technique that retests all methods. The results show that for this particular path, in one hierarchy, a significant amount of effort would be saved with our technique. This is a reasonable result for a well-designed hierarchy with a large amount of functionality defined at the top level and modifications and additions made in the lower levels.

This analysis did not consider another potential benefit of the technique; the benefits derived from reuse of the parent tests suites. Many of the methods that must be retested will reuse the specification-based test cases that were developed for their parent class. Reusing test suites from the parent class results in substantial additional savings of time for the testing process.

6. Conclusion

We have presented an incremental technique to validate classes that exploits the hierarchical structure of groups of classes related by inheritance. Our language model is a generalization of the C++ [17] language. Base classes are initially tested using both specification-based and program-based test cases, and a history of the testing information is saved. A subclass is then tested by incrementally updating the history of the parent class to reflect the differences from the parent. Only new attributes or those inherited, affected attributes and their interactions

Table 2: Number of member functions to be tested (specification/program-based)

class	retest all	our technique	our method/retest all
Interactor	93	93	100%
Scene	96	30	31%
MonoScene	99	9	9%
Dialog	103	4	4%

Table 3: Number of member functions to be tested (interaction/interface)

class	retest all	our technique	our method/retest all
Interactor	93	93	100%
Scene	96	36	38%
MonoScene	99	9	9%
Dialog	103	6	6%

are tested. The benefit of this technique is that it provides a savings both in the time to analyze the class to determine what must be tested and in the time to execute test cases. We are initially incorporating data flow testing into our hierarchical testing system for both individual member functions and interacting member functions to provide base class testing and subclass testing. Later, we will include a specification-based testing technique in the testing system.

References

1. B. Beizer, in *Software Testing Techniques*, Van Nostrand Reinhold Company, Inc., New York, 1990.

2. T. J. Cheatham and L. Mellinger, "Testing object-oriented software systems," *Proceedings of the 1990 Computer Science Conference*, pp. 161-165, 1990.

3. S. P. Fielder, "Object-oriented unit testing," *Hewlett-Packard Journal*, pp. 69-74, April 1989.

4. P. Frankl, "A framework for testing object-oriented programs," *Technical Report, Department of Electrical Engineering and Computer Science*, Polytechnic University, New York, 1989.

5. P. Frankl and S. Weiss, "Is data flow testing more effective than branch testing? An emperical study," *Proceedings of Quality Week 1991*, May 1991.

6. P. G. Frankl and E. J. Weyuker, "An applicable family of data flow testing criteria," *IEEE Transactions on Software Engineering*, vol. SE-14, no. 10, pp. 1483-1498, October 1988.

7. M. J. Harrold and M. L. Soffa, "Interprocedural data flow testing," *Proceedings of the Third Testing,*

Analysis, and Verification Symposium (TAV3 - SIGSOFT89), pp. 158-167, Key West, FL, December 1989.

8. M. J. Harrold and M. L. Soffa, "Selecting Data for Integration Testing," *IEEE Software, special issue on testing and debugging*, March 1991.

9. W. E. Howden, in *Software Engineering and Technology: Functional Program Testing and Analysis*, McGraw-Hill, New York, 1987.

10. M. Killian, "Trellis: Turning designs into programs," *CACM*, vol. 33, no. 9, pp. 65-67, September 1990.

11. B. Korel and J. Laski, "A tool for data flow oriented program testing," *ACM Softfair Proceedings*, pp. 35-37, December 1985.

12. T. Korson and J. D. McGregor, "Understanding object-oriented: A unifying paradigm," *Communications of the ACM*, vol. 33, no. 9, pp. 40-60, September 1990.

13. U. Linnenkugel and M. Mullerburg, "Test data selection criteria for integration testing," *Proceedings of the 1990 Conference on Systems Integration*, pp. 45-58, April 1990.

14. M. A. Linton and P. R. Calder, "The design and implementation of InterViews," *Proceedings of USNIX C++ Workshop*, pp. 256-267, 1987.

15. S. C. Ntafos, "An evaluation of required element testing strategies," *Proceedings of 7th International Conference on Software Engineering*, pp. 250-256, March 1984.

16. D. E. Perry and G. E. Kaiser, "Adequate testing and object-oriented programming," *Journal of Object-*

Oriented Programming, vol. 2, pp. 13-19, January/February 1990.

17. B. Stroustrup, in *The C++ Programming Language*, Addison-Wesley Publishing Company, Massachusetts, 1986.

18. P. Wegner and S. B. Zdonik, "Inheritance as an incremental modification mechanism or what like is and isn't like," *Proceedings of ECOOP'88*, pp. 55-77, Springer-Verlag, 1988.

19. E. J. Weyuker, "The cost of data flow testing: An empirical study," *IEEE Transactions on Software Engineering*, vol. SE-16, no. 2, pp. 121-128, February 1990 .

20. E. J. Weyuker, "Axiomatizing software test data adequacy," *IEEE Transactions on Software Engineering*, vol. SE-12, no. 12, pp. 1128-1138, December 1986.

John D. McGregor and Timothy D. Korson

Integrated Object-Oriented Testing
and Development Processes

Testing is one area of software engineering in which the gap between research knowledge and actual practice is very large. One of the reasons often cited is the amount of "extra" effort required in practice to develop the infrastructure necessary for a comprehensive testing process. A primary reason the effort is considered extra is that the testing process is often not integrated with the development process.

The integration of the testing and development processes provides an opportunity for better coordination between the deliverables of the two processes. This coordination can lead to less redundancy between the processes and thus to a reduction in the overhead of both processes. In this article, we present an integrated development/testing process model utilizing an iterative approach to apply object-oriented methods to software system development. We consider several problems encountered in the testing portion of this process and discuss possible solutions to those problems, taking the point of view that "testing" includes the verification and validation of any development product, not just the code. While we briefly outline a development method, our focus will be on the testing portion of the integrated process.

In writing this article, we have presumed the reader is familiar with the basics of object-oriented analysis, design and programming. For those who are not, an overview of the basic concepts and issues can be found in [8]. We also make assumptions about the process model adopted by a project and the development method used during the project.

Basic shape of the process model. An iterative approach to development is often used in projects that adopt an object-oriented perspective. The information-hiding and loose-coupling attributes of object technology facilitate the rework that results from the iterations. Most of the widely used object-oriented methods, described in the literature, advocate the iterative approach. Thus a realistic testing process for object-oriented projects should accommodate this style of development.

The Software Architects' SYnthesis model (SASY) [9] is a process model that is a synthesis of the most effective

aspects of a number of object-oriented methods. These include 1) domain analysis as a source of classes and models, 2) an iterative structure supporting successive refinement of workproducts, and 3) an incremental approach that solves large problems a piece at a time. Figure 1 shows a listing of the key activities as well as the flow of the iterative cycle of development phases. We will use this model as we describe the interaction between the testing and development processes.

The development process produces many work products. Those of interest to testers include models, designs, and implementations. Each of these products should be tested as a product independent of any other, but there are also many interrelationships in which one product contributes to the development of test cases for a related product. The sections of this article on testing models and implementations will detail techniques that can be used with each of the development products.

The relationship of the development process to the various development products is often a source of confusion to those new to the object-oriented paradigm because they may

be used to having unique activities and notations for each phase of the development process. For example, one might be accustomed to using data flow diagrams to represent analysis information and structure charts to represent design information. In the object-oriented process, work products flow across process phase boundaries. For example, object models that are started during Domain Analysis are focused and refined during Application Analysis, and clustered and enhanced with design mechanisms during Application Design. From a testing point of view this implies that many of the work products will have to be iteratively and incrementally tested. Figure 1 illustrates the flow of SASY activities.

In the sidebar on SASY products we have listed the work products that we will reference in the remainder of the article. We recognize that there are many variants on the development process and work products produced, but it should be relatively easy to adapt our recommendations to any process for object-oriented software development.

Inheritance model. A central issue to the development effort for any object-oriented project is the philosophy concerning the use of inheritance. Many of the algorithms and techniques described in the testing

Figure 1. The flow of SASY activities

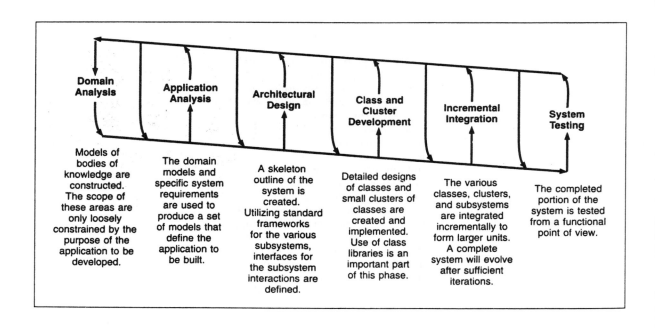

process assume the use of a "strict" inheritance approach. This approach is similar to several other design guidelines including Liskov's [11]. In this philosophy of use of inheritance:

• the preconditions of each method in a child class must be no stronger than the preconditions of that method in the parent class;
• the postconditions of each method in a child class must be no weaker than the postconditions of that method in the parent class; and
• the invariant of a child class is a superset of the invariant of its parent class(es).

This approach to the use of inheritance supports the development of hierarchies that represent classifications of the concepts contained in the structure. Each class represents a special case of its parent. This produces a logical structure in which once a method is part of the specification of a superclass, it is never removed and its intention is never changed in any subsequent subclass. This results in a semantically equivalent set of classes that may be safely polymorphically substituted for one another.

An Integrated Development/ Testing Process
The integration of the development and testing processes can best be described by paraphrasing a description of iteration, often attributed to Grady Booch: "analyze a little, design a little, code a little, test a little" to read "analyze a little, test a little, design a little, test a little, code a little, test a little." In other words, testing is continuously interwoven into the development process. This not only locates faults early, it makes subsequent phases less likely to create new faults based on existing ones. This assumes an iterative incremental approach in which the steps of the development process are repeated and the product is developed through successive refinements. The goals of a testing process are twofold:

• A testing process can give some level of confidence that a software system meets, under specific conditions, at least certain of its objectives.
• A testing process can detect faults in the software.

Selected SASY Work Products

SASY Work product	Work product description
Modified CRC card	English text description of a single class, its responsibilities and its client relationships with other classes.
Class specification	Complete specification of a class including method names, number and type of parameters, return values, pre- and post-conditions and class invariants along with standard information such as revision history.
Class stub	"Header file" completely coded with the implementation stubbed in.
Class Implementation	Completely coded and tested class.
Rumbaugh Object Model	Shows the static structural relationships (association, aggregation, classification) between classes in the model.
Harel Statecharts	Standard state transition diagrams for classes, clusters, and subsystems.
Interaction diagrams	A model of the important algorithms that span objects, clusters, or subsystems.
Clusters, subsystems, and architectures	Sets of related classes and the relationships between these sets
Modified use cases	A transformation of the specification model into a structured hierarchy of system usages.
Text and diagrams	The specification is a model of the real system requirements as they exist in the business world.

Classifying SASY Work Products

Type of work product	Type of model		
	Static	Dynamic	Functional
Class	• Modified CRC card • Class specification • Class Implementation	• Class Implementation • Harel Statecharts	• Class Implementation • Modified use cases
Cluster	• Rumbaugh Object Model • Cluster patterns and frameworks	• Harel Statecharts	• Interaction diagrams- • Modified use cases
Subsystem	• Rumbaugh Object Model • Subsystem architecture	• Harel Statecharts	• Interaction diagrams • Modified use cases
System	• Rumbaugh Object Model • System architecture	• Harel Statecharts • Text and diagrams	• Interaction diagrams • Modified use cases

The Relationships between SASY Work Products and the SASY Development Process

Specific SASY Work product	Relationships to other products and to the process
Modified CRC card	A core product in Domain Analysis, but can be created any time the need for a new class arises; CRC cards are a precursor to class specifications and input to the process of building object models.
Class specification	A transformation and elaboration of CRC cards, responsibilities map to methods. Classes are specified at this level during Application Design.
Class stub	A first pass implementation of the class specification. This evolves into the class implementation during the class development phase.
Class implementation	Elaboration of class stubs done during class development.
Rumbaugh Object Model	A core product across all the phases. The object model starts during domain analysis as unannotated relationships between informally specified classes. The object model evolves to rigorously annotated relationships among formally specified classes. Application Analysis adds software objects and relationships. Later phases add design mechanisms and implementation detail to the analysis models.
Harel Statecharts	Classes that participate in the object models along with clusters and subsystems that participate in the architecture may have their dynamic behavior modeled with state charts. Consistency among the models is an important issue. State information is modeled as needed. Domain standards specify the dynamic behavior of certain classes.
Interaction diagrams	Like statecharts, interaction diagrams are developed as needed. These functional models integrate individual class, clusters and subsystems.
Clusters, subsystems, and architectures	While primarily a design activity, clusters and standard architectures may be identified during Domain or Application Analysis.
Modified use cases	As transformation of the specification model, use cases can be used both to test the specification for accuracy and to test object models for completeness. Use cases are initially developed during early iterations of Domain and Application Analysis, but should be incrementally expanded as each successive system increment is built.
Specification text and diagrams	Contrary to most traditional processes, a detailed system specification is not the first product developed. Domain models are developed first, detailed specifications are developed during Application Analysis.

From the earliest iterations through the software development activities, we are interested in both goals. Before proceeding to a subsequent iteration we would like to have some level of confidence that the work performed to date is correct, but at the same time we know that in large complex projects errors do occur and we want to remove them at the earliest possible time in order to minimize the costs of rework and maintain high quality. Finding faults early not only keeps costs down but increases quality because systems reworked and debugged at the last minute often contain workarounds and other compromises to the integrity of the design. Furthermore these last-minute changes are often not reflected in the analysis and design documents.

To allow for early fault identification, the viewpoint presented here is that "testing" goes beyond the execution of code. It is used here to indicate activities such as formal reviews, comparisons, or any activity in which criteria are used to detect misconceptions, omissions, and mistakes and to provide feedback for improvement. In fact our definition of testing will include all activities in which our intent is to detect faults. This view of testing supports the increased emphasis on "front-end" activities prevalent in object-oriented methods.

A basic objective of testing is to uncover the maximum number of *weighted* errors for a given amount of effort. We use the term *weighted* errors since some errors have a larger impact, both on customers and on the amount of rework required to fix them. We use risk analysis to identify those classes that are more "critical" to the system. The definition of critical will vary from one project to another and from one company to another. Critical classes will be more closely examined and consume a disproportionate share of the testing resources.

The three major categories of testing activities are discussed in the following list. The goal of the first category is to locate faults in the software development process itself. The goal of the second category is to locate faults in nonexecutable products such as models, CRC cards, designs and frameworks. The goal of the last category is to locate faults in the executable code. The 3 categories are:

1. *Testing of the development process and the supporting documents.* There is a need to evaluate and improve the processes as much as the products. The process is embodied as a set of activities and supported by a set of documents that describe the activities. The iterative approach supports continuous improvement through feedback. Specifically, the testing of the process examines the goals for each iteration and evaluates the level of achievement at the end of the iteration. It also examines a cross section of successive iterations to identify problems and improvements in a particular activity across the iterations. Other factors to test include the continuity between successive phases in the life cycle.

2. *Testing analysis and design models.* The object-oriented approach places increased importance on the analysis and design models and the identification of abstractions. Since these directly shape the code, testing analysis models and designs is especially important. As with the testing of the process, comparison among versions of products across iterations is one approach for testing, as is the examination of the mapping of the products from one stage for the next.

3. *Static and dynamic testing of implementations.* Our goal is to locate as many errors as possible early in the process, but errors in the code of large complex systems are inevitable. Many procedural projects are relying more heavily on code inspections (static testing) to find simple logic errors [15]. The smaller methods used in object-oriented systems are even more amenable to this type of detection. Dynamic testing concentrates on executing test data to find faults in the code.

We will focus on the last two categories of testing activities. We believe that reviews of the development process are an important and very high leverage part of testing, but the topic is beyond the scope of this article.

Testing Models

The object-oriented approach emphasizes the creation of models of analysis and design information. When an iterative process model is adopted, these models begin as informal representations and evolve into more formal, and more precise, models. The testing of the informal models must be fast and cheap, since the models change rapidly. The feedback from this testing provides direction to the evolution of the models by pointing out missing entities or inconsistencies in the treatment of entities. The formal models are tested more carefully and completely, since they will have a longer life and play a central role in the shape of the final system.

Criteria for testing models. We will consider three interrelated attributes that are common to all models: correctness, completeness, and consistency. These attributes are similar to those presented in Lindland et al. [10], who provide a framework for achieving quality in conceptual models. In particular, Lindland et al. consider three aspects of the model: syntax, semantics and pragmatics, identifying four criteria for quality models: correctness, completeness, validity, and comprehension.

We will utilize a portion of their framework to address our more narrowly focused concerns with fault detection. We consider both syntactic and semantic correctness and completeness as outlined in their framework. We use consistency, which is included within their definition of validity, but the other facets of their definition of validity pertain more to a quality perspective than fault detection.

These attributes must be interpreted in the context of the iterative incremental approach. That is, early versions will not be expected to attain the same level of detail as later versions. The emphasis in the testing process is the feedback into the development process. Correctness and completeness are judged against the aspects of reality which the model is intended to represent. The set of analysis entities are semantically correct if they are an accurate model of reality. Early models will not contain the level of detail that later versions

will, but the information that is present should be judged to be accurate at that level of abstraction. Correctness criteria can be applied to the syntax of the model as well.

The model is complete if it is judged that the entities describe the aspects of the knowledge being modeled in sufficient detail for the goals of the current iteration. In particular, the model should be understandable to domain experts as a comprehensive representation of standard knowledge within its field. For software engineers who are not domain experts, the model should contain sufficient information to support their development efforts during the current iteration.

Consistency is judged by considering the relationships among the entities in the model. An inconsistent model has representations in one part of the model that are not correctly reflected in other portions of the model. These may be contradictions or differences in level of detail. Incremental models will be segmented across the increments, but the interfaces between the pieces of models should contain sufficient "interface" entities to support a consistent treatment of entities across model boundaries.

The process of mapping one model into another model can introduce errors whenever one model is used to build another model. Testing of the new model is partially accomplished by comparing it to the original model. The transformations from one representation to another are usually made to support a more precise notation. For example, the CRC card model is the basis for the more formal object model.

One of the ways in which object-oriented methods result in higher-quality code is by having fewer mappings and transformations that are less radical than in other development methods. Analysis models, design models, and implementation models all use classes and instances of classes as the primary vehicles of representation. Even though a model shows some particular view that is different from another model, all of the models are illustrating aspects of classes or objects.

The correctness of a mapping is

In a typical development process,

the object, dynamic, and functional models are used to represent both the analysis and design models.

judged by comparing the original model to the derived model to determine that the information has been accurately represented. The mapping should be complete in that every entity in the original model should be accounted for in the transformation. The mapping may result in an existing entity being eliminated from future models or that entity may be split into two or more smaller, more specific entities. The mapping should maintain the same relationships among entities in the new model as existed between the entities in the previous model. Our testing process uses a number of techniques to apply these criteria to the various work products. Reviews of the products are carried out by the model developers assisted by experts in the domains in which the system works, experts in the object-oriented development process, and potential users of the system. Products may also be compared to previous versions of the same product or to earlier products. Some of the models will be executable and their execution will help answer many questions about the content of the model.

The testing carried out during reviews can be integrated with the development reviews that are typically conducted at the end of each iteration. The primary difference between the two reviews is the level of specificity. The development review usually includes a presentation of the models developed during the iteration. The testing portion of the review includes the use of test cases to exercise the model at a detailed level.

The development of model-level test cases provides a vehicle for making these tests repeatable, a necessity in an iterative environment. Each test case is a detailed scenario that requires some action on the model such as instantiating a portion of the model or building extensions at specific locations in the model. These cases should be reviewed by the do-

main experts and applied during the end of iteration review. The nature of these test cases usually requires explicit verification by experts, since correct results are difficult to formally specify.

The test cases should address the goals of those models. The goals of object-oriented system design usually include being reusable, extensible, and reconfigurable. Every model's test suite should include test cases that ascertain whether the model fully represents what is currently intended. Specific scenarios are created, driven through the model using instance diagrams that show the resulting network of objects, and this network is examined to determine that the representation meets the criteria stated previously. For those models that are explicitly intended for reuse, such as that for a framework, some cases addressing hypothetical extensions should be included in the test suite. These test cases require the specification of proposed new classes that extend the existing design. Instance diagrams can then be created to examine the viability of the extension. The key element in both cases is that explicit test cases be constructed so specific objects can be created from the representation.

Specification models. A major problem in software development is errors in the specification. In spite of the high frequency of errors in specifications and the costly consequences of these errors, there exist few techniques for testing specifications. Although object-oriented techniques do not eliminate this problem, we have found that user participation in the testing of domain models coupled with delaying application analysis until after domain analysis results in much higher-quality specifications.

Errors, ambiguities, and omissions not apparent in the specification often become more obvious when use cases [6], descriptions of specific interactions between the system and a

specific user, or scenarios [18], informal descriptions of how the system will be used are developed as part of the work products. This is especially true when the use cases, or scenarios, explicitly include a "rationale" section. When customers review the developers' *understanding* of their requirements they are better able to pinpoint omissions, errors and misleading information in the specification.

The testing of the use-case model's content is conducted by a review group that should include representatives from the testing team, members of the development organization, and potential users of the system. A testing-by-comparison approach is carried out by comparing the interaction model to some version of the system requirements. This activity is completely integrated into the customer review cycle.

The interaction model is correct if the user interactions portrayed in the model accurately describe valid user interactions. In part this can be determined from the requirements. This review also has the effect of testing the mapping of the use cases from the requirements. The model is complete if all legal user interactions with the system are represented. This includes identifying all users of the system as well as all of their possible uses of the system. This results in a set of use cases that can be used to guide system development without repeated reference to the much more detailed requirements.

The model is tested for consistency by examining the hierarchical structure of the use cases. Similar interactions from the specifications should all map into a single hierarchy. A similar exercise can be carried out for scenarios by grouping them based on common entities required in the model. Again, similar interactions should map into a single grouping.

The more formal specification model is often tested by building an executable model. The development of these prototypes provides two tests of the models. First, during the development of the prototype, many inconsistencies will be identified and that feedback should directly affect the models. The second test, the execution of the model, allows developers to conduct "what-if" tests to determine the completeness and correctness of the representation. In these tests the developer uses the executable model in the same ways that users will use the completed system, as described in the use-case model. This examination will identify missing relations among classes as well as finding some relations in the model that should not be present.

Individual class models. The initial models for individual classes are often Class-Responsibility-Collaborator (CRC) cards [1]. This very simple notation links each class to its set of collaborators, classes that provide service to the originating class. The usefulness of the CRC model is in its informality and ease of modification. The major errors that can be made in the CRC model include naming as a collaborator a class that does not exist; not including concepts that should be part of the analysis model; a collaborator not providing a needed service as one of its responsibilities; and grouping together unrelated responsibilities.

A testing-by-inspection process can be built into the CRC construction exercise by providing a checklist for developers to use during the exercise. The checklist considers the interconnections illustrated in Figure 2. The individual creating a CRC card is responsible for using the checklist to test the class they are describing. The steps and checks are as follows:

• Locate the CRC card for each of the listed collaborators. *The creator of Controller will find the creator of Detector.*
• Inspect each collaborator's CRC card to determine if the delegated responsibility is included on the collaborator's card. *The creator of Controller asks if a Detector will acknowledge the presence of Vehicles when queried.*
• Record the classes that come to you seeking service. Note the ser-

vices that are being requested by these classes. *The creator of Controller maintains a list of all cards listing Controller as a collaborator, such as an Intersection (not shown).*
• Use this tracking information to determine whether there are clear groupings of responsibilities/classes that are disjoint or largely so from other groupings. This points to the need for a realignment, creating classes for each of the groups of responsibilities from the one existing class. *The creator of Controller might find that responsibilities for controlling the lights at a single intersection was a different set of responsibilities than coordinating the settings of signals between two adjacent intersections. Two classes such as LocalController and NetworkController might be created.*
• The tracking information can also lead to cleaner definitions of the responsibilities. For example, if every class that uses the fifth responsibility of a class also uses the

second and fourth, perhaps these three responsibilities should be combined. *The creator of Detector might find that many of the requests to read status are immediately followed by a request to reset itself. Were this true, a single responsibility, ReadandClear, would be added as a responsibility.*
• The resulting set of cards is reviewed by domain experts to judge the model.

By applying these simple checks, problems can be quickly found and the feedback can lead to an improved set of CRC cards. Since the CRC cards will be used to produce the object model, finding mistakes at this point makes the creation of that model more efficient and increases its quality.

The formal models of classes are

Figure 2. Testing CRC cards

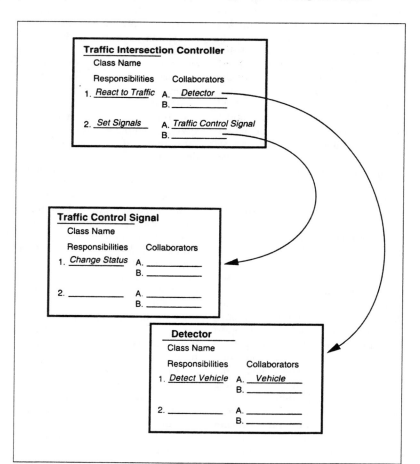

developed as component specifications. Each method has an associated set of pre- and post-conditions and the class as a whole supports a class invariant. The class specification is evaluated by a comparison against its CRC description and against its role in the total system. The class model is complete if the specification includes methods that implement all of the required responsibilities. It will be judged correct at a specification level if a prototype implementation illustrates that the specification provides the appropriate behaviors. The implementation will be judged correct only after an actual implementation is tested as described in a later section.

System models. The analysis models that are developed in a project are either domain-related or application-related. Each domain-related model is intended to represent some area of knowledge whose scope is roughly determined by the depth and breadth of our interest. A typical application will involve multiple domains and therefore multiple models. Testing these models will require the collaboration of persons knowledgeable about each domain. The models are compared to standard knowledge in the field as found in official standards and the literature of the field.

The application-related models provide early views of the actual system being built. The models of a set of relevant domains are used to develop the model for an application. The application model adds the system-specific details needed for domain entities to be related and productive in a computer system. The collaboration of potential users of the system are needed for this testing, since the model is tested from the perspective of the system use cases.

The application model is developed by combining several domain models, the user interaction model, and additional classes that support the application. The mapping from these various models must be complete and correct. The model is not complete in the sense of including everything from the initial models. It should provide the entities necessary to model the portion of the domains required by the application. The application model should be compared to the set of use cases to ensure com-

pleteness. The review team should be able to trace every user interaction into the set of classes that define the interface of the application. The CRC cards should provide a basis for verifying that each class is correctly mapped. The application model should contain correct descriptions of the classes that are mapped into it and it should account for the relationships among those classes. With models being combined, consistency is a concern. Domains often overlap and the new model needs to be reviewed to determine whether similar entities from different domains have been recognized, integrated or differentiated, and handled consistently across the model. The resulting application model should combine the various views of the system into a cohesive whole. The entities from the various models should interact and these interactions should have been captured in the original models as interface issues.

The early modeling techniques, such as the CRC model, have the flexibility that supports quick and easy modifications. As those models become more stable there is a need to support a more precise and integrated view of the classes. These models describe a set of classes that may represent a domain of knowledge, a complete application, or a subsystem of some larger product. A description of this set of classes should include a representation of the relationships among the classes, models of the state representation of each class, and models of the important algorithms provided by the set of classes. SASY utilizes the object and dynamic models of the Object Modeling Technique (OMT) [16] and object interaction diagrams [6] to represent the analysis and design information about this set of classes. Any development method will have similar representations and similar documents to represent the static and dynamic behavior of the entities.

Much of the testing of these descriptions will consist of comparisons with the initial representations described previously to ensure the accuracy of the translation. However, as the models mature from analysis into the more detailed design models, more information will be available to

examine. In particular, with three different views of the system, consistency across the views is an important consideration. The detailed models can be examined for completeness by tracing classes in the initial models into the formal models, and for consistency by examining the treatment of individual classes and relationships among classes across the three models.

In a typical development process, the object, dynamic, and functional models are used to represent both the analysis and design models. As the process moves from identifying objects into describing and specifying the objects, these same models can be used and simply elaborated. Different design methods may also add instance diagrams or other supporting detail to provide additional views of the system. There is less likelihood of an error in developing the design model, since object-oriented development techniques derive the design models directly from the analysis models.

An *object model* is created for each set of classes in order to show the classes, their attributes, and the relationships among classes. The object model contains at least all of the classes defined by the CRC cards for that grouping. One test of the object model is to be certain that all of those informally defined classes are present in the formal model. The collaborations from the refined CRC cards should also be accurately represented as various types of associations. To make certain relationships explicit, object models may have circular dependencies among the entities. These paths should be identified and checked for consistency.

Figure 3 illustrates an object model that has been developed from a set of CRC cards. (For those not familiar with the OMT notation, the relationship between Traffic Control Signal and Intersection is aggregation; that between Traffic Control Signal and Crosswalk Signal is specialization; and that between Intersection and Controller is a many-to-one association.) The testing of this mapping can be part of the object model review. Each component of the previous model should be accounted for in the new model. Elements may be eliminated, split, or combined but the materials supporting the new model should describe what has happened to each element. The mapping should consistently handle elements. That is, similar situations should be handled the same way by the mapping. Testing at this level is a review of the two models side-by-side to determine that all elements from the first model are appropriately represented in the second.

The *dynamic model* is developed at a variety of levels, whenever there is a need to represent the dynamic behavior of a class or set of classes. A dynamic model includes a set of states and the transitions between those states. The states should be observable, and therefore confirmable. The methods through which these states are observed and by which the state is changed are behaviors of the class. The appropriate object model should be checked to determine that those behaviors are present. The dynamic model should be verified against the functional model to ascertain that the sequence of messages required for an algorithm leads to valid sets of state transitions for the participating classes.

The *functional models* will include representations of the algorithms that are significant to the set of classes. Each model will include the sequences of messages corresponding to some algorithm. In cases where the algorithm corresponds to system functionality, the appropriate use cases will be used to verify the completeness and correctness of the formal model. The functional model should be compared to the object model to determine that every class used in an algorithm is represented in the object model and that all of the messages necessary to implement an algorithm are present as associations in the object model.

Figure 4 illustrates the mapping of the use cases into the functional and object models. Every use case should be traceable through the relationships illustrated on the object model. Some of these interactions should be represented as functional models if they involve a significant number of objects within the system. The testing of the mapping is a part of the review for the system-level object model.

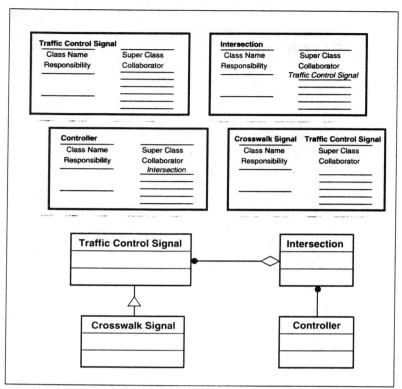

Figure 3. Testing mappings

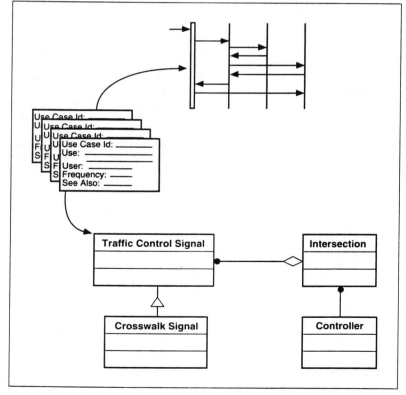

Figure 4. Test for traceability and consistency

201

Integrating testing and development *provides opportunities to improve both processes.*

The classes that are in the analysis model are the nucleus of the set of classes in the design model. Therefore the design model will typically already possess the standard qualities of completeness, correctness, and consistency. There are additional qualities that are important in the design model including efficiency, extensibility, testability, and conformance to accepted design practices such as minimal coupling. Each of these qualities is measured by reviewing the designs, comparing to standard practice, and, in some cases, building scenarios to consider "what-if" extensions to the system.

The recent work on patterns [3, 7] provides a preliminary basis for testing the correctness of the structures in the design model. By defining "standard" patterns of object specification and interaction, researchers are defining pieces of a system's architecture and establishing artifacts against which the design can be repeatedly tested across iterations. As designers begin to use the patterns, and to identify them in their design documents, it will be possible to compare the designer's use of a pattern to accepted practice. For example, Figure 5 shows the well-known Model-View-Controller pattern and a system cluster designed around that pattern. The identification of the missing relationship from Window to Document is equivalent to having no communication from the View to the Model. Departures from standard use should not automatically be taken as an error; however, they do indicate areas needing further review. There may be a specific reason for not having the relationship between Window and Document, but it is sufficiently different from the typical pattern to be identified as a potential fault in the design.

Testing Implementations

We previously stated that a basic ob-jective of testing is to uncover the maximum number of weighted errors for a given amount of effort. With this assumption in mind, we can break this down into the following subobjectives and heuristics for our implementation testing process.

Create the minimal number of test cases necessary to achieve a given level of test coverage. The number of test cases that must be created can be reduced if there is a systematic approach to reusing existing test cases. For example, Harrold and McGregor [4] provide a technique, Hierarchical Incremental Testing (HIT) for constructing the minimal number of subclass test cases that are needed to supplement the test cases that are inherited from a parent class.

At any point in the development process, execute the minimal number of test cases necessary to achieve a given adequacy criteria. In the iterative approach, pieces of a tested design or implementation may change. Should everything be retested when a piece changes? Harrold and McGregor [4] address a related question at the class level. Suppose that a superclass is completely tested. How extensively must a subclass be retested? Some methods will not need to be completely retested after they are inherited, but the test cases are still inherited. Harrold and McGregor also show how to identify those test cases that do not need to be rerun, thus reducing the number of test results that must be validated.

Use an adequacy criteria that allows one to incrementally increase the level of testing coverage. A testing method describes a technique that constructs test cases based on some criteria. The method results in a certain amount of coverage of the work product being tested. For example, the test cases might be selected to exercise every statement in the code. The testing techniques described here allow for increasing the amount of coverage in a systematic way. Risk analysis is used to identify those classes that should have more testing resources allocated than the norm. McGregor and Dyer [13] describe one such technique for state-based testing. McDaniel and McGregor [12] present an interaction-testing technique based on orthogonal arrays that allows the tester to incrementally increase the number of interactions simultaneously being tested.

Use existing work products as the basis for deriving test cases. A critical factor in reducing the amount of perceived effort in the testing process is to use as many products as possible that are created for analysis and design purposes. This reuse of effort supports a more extensive testing process.

Levels of testing. The testing of code is organized around the recognized units of object-oriented design. Three levels of units are discussed in the following list:

- *Class testing.* This level of testing is somewhat comparable to the unit test of the procedural approach. The name change is not superfluous, however. It is intended to denote a real difference. A class is a different scope from that of a single procedure. With its local attributes and private methods, a class is more complex than a procedure. Class testing is a first level of integration testing. Because of this, "unit testing" in the object-oriented world has a higher payoff than "unit testing" in the procedural world.

It is not productive to attempt to treat anything smaller than a class as an independent test unit. A properly designed class is cohesive, and the test driver that would be required to test an individual method would essentially be a reinvention of the class. A class test suite can test those methods that are simple accessor methods before testing the modifier methods. This will reduce the complexity of trying to test a complete set of methods at one time.

- *Cluster testing.* A cluster of classes is a grouping of cooperating classes. A cluster represents a second level of integration. The focus of cluster testing is the interaction among the instances of the classes in the cluster. It is assumed that each class has been tested individually. To aid in recognizing a cluster, a specification should be developed for each cluster that is similar to the specification for a class. This will include those methods from each class that will be accessed from outside the cluster and pre- and post-conditions for each.

Depending on the range of classes in the cluster and the size of the project, one or more teams will be charged with providing the test suite for a cluster. Special attention must be given to clusters that include classes from more than one team. We will discuss the coordination needed for these products later.

- *System testing.* The system is tested functionally using test cases derived from the use cases and other system requirements. System testing of object-oriented systems has the same objectives as those for systems developed using other techniques; however, the process used to develop the test cases is somewhat different. There may also be additional objectives related to testing the extensibility of the system. In spite of these differences, there is very little difference in system-level functional testing of object-oriented software unless the project has also adopted changes in development objectives (e.g., to emphasize reuse) or adopted a different process model (e.g., an iterative model).

Test case perspectives. The complete test suite for a class can be conceptually divided into three sections. Each section is constructed based on a different perspective of the component under test. This allows the tester to make statements about the degree to which that perspective has been covered. The three views correspond to the levels of concern of the development team.

- *Functional.* The functional perspective is an external view that considers the behavior promised by

the class to those that interact with it. Functional test cases are constructed based on the specification of the component. The specification of a class includes a specification for each method plus a class invariant. Coverage is stated as a percentage of the total class specification that is covered. Typically, every method is executed at least once to verify conformance to the stated pre- and post-conditions. Additional test cases may be constructed based on the invariants.

- *Structural.* The structural view is an internal view that is guided by the relationships among individual lines of code. Structural test cases are constructed by identifying individual paths through the code. The coverage will usually be stated in terms of the percentage of the lines of code that have been executed based on the test cases. Every line of code is typically executed at least once; however, it is seldom possible to execute all the paths through the code. A larger percentage of the paths through an individual method can be executed than paths through the complete program.

Functional testing receives more emphasis than structural in object-

oriented development. There are several reasons for this: First, the methods in classes are sufficiently small that an aggressive inspection program can catch many statement-level errors early. Second, the information-hiding property of objects makes the internals of individual objects less likely to cause problems for other objects. Third, the focus on abstraction, prevalent in object-oriented systems, makes the functional view the natural approach for testing.

- *Interaction.* There are two levels of interactions that are of interest to us. Interactions among methods within a class, and interactions among methods in different classes. At the lowest level, interaction test cases investigate two methods that may directly or indirectly cause each other to produce incorrect results. The test cases are constructed by identifying values that are set or

---

Figure 5. Using patterns to test designs

Figure 6. Testing polymorphic messages

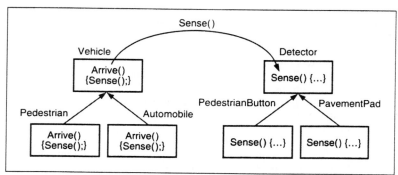

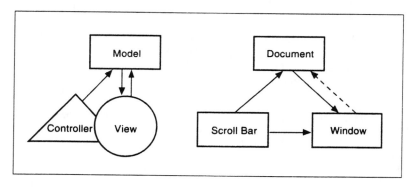

used by two or more methods including cases of parameters being passed between two methods. The two methods may both be in the same class (intraclass) or in different classes (interclass). Typically each such pair of methods would be executed.

Object technology complicates interaction testing by using dynamic binding. Certain interclass relationships cannot be uniquely defined at compile time and thus a definite interaction cannot be identified. Strongly typed object-oriented languages do restrict the associations that can be formed at run time and make the identification of a set of potential associations possible. McDaniel and McGregor [12] analyze the possible interactions and utilize orthogonal array algorithms to provide a technique for constructing appropriate test cases. In this approach, the set of legitimate interactions among inheritance hierarchies of classes are identified. For example, in Figure 6, instances of classes in the first hierarchy send a message to an instance of one of the classes in the second hierarchy. The set of interactions can be very large, so a sample to be tested is drawn from that set. The sample is drawn using an orthogonal array to select all possible pairs of interacting factors. Pairwise interactions are first tested, but higher-order interactions are not. Higher levels of quality can be systematically attained by increasing the complexity of the interactions that are tested.

Testing Activities—Production of Test Cases
Test cases are produced in at least two ways: reusing the test cases from other classes and creating new test cases by examination of the development products.

Functional test cases. These test cases are created by examining the specification of the class. State-based testing [13, 14, 17] considers the state representation for a class. The state representation is validated by an expert and is compared for consistency with the post-conditions of the class's modifier methods. The technique selects test cases that exercise each of the transitions in the representation. A breadth-first traversal of the state

representation provides the ability to generate test cases that cover single transitions or that group sets of transitions into longer sequences termed "*n*-way switches" by Chow [2]. The breadth-first sequence ensures that when a new transition is tested only previously tested transitions are used.

Alternatively, the test cases may be constructed by examining the post-conditions for each method that modifies the state of the object. These conditions provide the boundary conditions for each method. Test cases are constructed to ensure that each method is supporting its post-condition. This is an example of the use of standard development information (e.g., state diagrams, pre- and post-conditions) to drive the testing process.

Structural test cases. The test cases are created by examining the implementation of each method. The significant consideration here is the presence of polymorphic messages that are not bound until execution time.

Interaction test cases. One product of the development process that can be useful during cluster testing is the contract defining the interactions of the classes involved in a cluster. Software contracts [5] define the interfaces that are provided to other classes in the cluster. The message patterns within a cluster can be exercised by selecting test cases that traverse these interactions.

Testing Activities—Management of Test Cases
The inheritance relation that is used to define the classes can also be used to coordinate and manage the other products of the testing process. Two examples will be considered here.

Interaction test cases. Most of the test cases for a class are developed from information contained within the class. Interclass test cases, however, require information from two classes and these may well not be owned by the same developer. The project must provide a management strategy that ensures an adequate number of test cases are generated that examine the interactions between a class and its clients.

Certainly many of the interactions among classes are tested incidentally

because they are integrated into a single higher-level aggregate class. Each time a class defines instances of the two classes within the same environment, the interaction between them is used to provide part of the behavior of the encapsulating class. As test cases for the encapsulating class are defined and executed, their success is some evidence for the correct interaction between the two encapsulated classes. How much of the full range of interaction is really exercised is impossible to answer using this approach. Additionally, the developers of the interacting classes are not aware of the amount of testing being done nor will they necessarily hear about problems that are discovered. A systematic way to develop these test cases is to require a developer to exercise their class with every class related to their class by a software contract. It is not possible, nor is it even necessary, to test a class in combination with every other class defined in a system. By using the software contract as the guide, the class's developer is in control of the test cases that are generated and can guarantee that the appropriate coverage is achieved.

Test drivers. Testing each class requires a test driver that can send the appropriate messages to the object under test and can validate the results received back from the messages. These drivers are classes. This approach further integrates the testing and development processes, since all of the techniques and tools used to develop production classes may now be applied to tests as well. The inheritance relation provides an appropriate structure for defining those classes and achieving reuse in the definition process. Individual test drivers are derived from the abstract test driver class or from the test driver of its parent class. The test driver is a management tool that includes methods for:

- logging and displaying test results in a consistent manner across the project,
- methods that represent actual test cases including validation of results, and
- methods that execute a sequence of test case methods.

The test driver class will provide

behaviors for logging, displaying and analyzing the test results following the procedures used by a specific company. An abstract class, developed for project use, provides the detailed implementations of these output behaviors. Depending on the project, the output may be a simple stream that creates a file or prints directly to a printer. Alternatively, the fault information may be directed to a database that manages the test reporting process. The test driver creates an instance of the class under test and creates the test environment required, such as associated objects that will be sent messages.

Each test case method must set the object under test to the appropriate initial condition, send a sequence of messages, and verify the result of the message sequence. Each test case method should be as independent of other test cases as possible. This can be partially realized by having each method create a "clean" instance of the class under test. This may not always be feasible if creation of the instance requires large amounts of data or other compute-intensive activities. Each test case method should be able to determine whether the object under test has returned the appropriate value and has placed itself in the appropriate state.

The third component in the test driver class is a set of test scripts. These scripts provide a means of sequencing and executing a series of test cases. For most objects, there are particular sequences of methods that are used more often than other sequences. These are not encapsulated in a single convenience method because the object sending the messages must accomplish some computation in between those messages. These scripts allow a class developer to investigate these sequences and to provide appropriate parameters to each of the messages in the sequence.

Figures 7 and 8 illustrate a strategy that coordinates the construction and management of the incomplete production classes and the test driver classes. Figure 7 illustrates the classes and objects that are produced for a specific test case. Vehicle needs an instance of VehicleTiming as part of its definition. The creation of the VehicleTiming instance is always the responsibility of the encapsulating class, Vehicle. Vehicle needs to be able to message an instance of Detector in order to provide some cluster-level behavior. Some external entity will be required to set up a test environment that creates and contains both instances. Automobile is a class derived from Vehicle. It will inherit all of the relationships with VehicleTiming and Detector.

The strategy requires that an inheritance hierarchy of test driver classes be defined in parallel to each inheritance hierarchy of production classes. The specification of the test driver classes is determined by the abstract test driver class. This strategy handles a number of updating issues automatically. In Figure 8, Automobile inherits an association with one class and an aggregation relationship with another from Vehicle. The associated test driver for Automobile inherits how to set up the inherited, associated class. The management of external relationships in which one class is the peer of another class, such as that between Automobile and Detector, is handled by the test driver classes. Classes are responsible for managing their own components, such as the relationship between Automobile and VehicleTiming.

Test execution and validation. Execution of the cases can be controlled by script methods defined in the test driver class. This approach allows for the repetition of tests and for the modification of the testing sequence by providing multiple script methods.

The results of test case execution must be validated via some independent source. This comes in two forms: the creator of the test case and a formal review of the test case database. In many cases the test case is of the form: <initial state, message, resulting state>. Both the initial and resulting states are observable states in that there are methods in the class specification that can determine whether the class is in each of the states. The test method can be written to test the validity of the result by comparing the actual state of the object under test with the expected resulting state. The developer is responsible for ensuring that the test case includes the information needed to determine

whether the test has been passed or failed. The side effect of returning a value as the result of a method must sometimes also be considered.

The test cases are "tested" during the class development review process. Appropriate individuals, including members of the testing team, are assigned to inspect selected test cases and to validate their correctness. The testing team member assigned to the review will also judge the completeness of the test suite for the class. This will be done by considering the test plan for the class, the coverage criteria mandated by the project's test plan and the methods used to select the test cases. One difficulty with validating results is the information-hiding property of objects. If there are few accessor methods in the class, it can be very difficult to determine the value of particular attributes. A detailed discussion of this problem is beyond the scope of this article, but there are several potential solutions to this problem.

• Test methods can be built directly into the class to overcome this problem but then they must either be shipped as part of the system or they are removed and the product being shipped is different from the product that was tested.
• For C++ programs, an alternative is to declare the test harness to be a *friend* of the class under test. This allows the harness to have access to the private areas of the class without being a part of the class.
• The third possibility is the one advocated in this article. Emphasize functional testing and check for externally observable states for which observer methods are provided. This respects the privacy of the object's internal representation.

Issues in Integration

Integrating testing and development provides opportunities to improve both processes. These opportunities fall into the following four categories.

Feedback. The results of the testing process provide feedback concerning the development products. The feedback is intended to direct the corrective actions of the developer. Providing feedback is complicated in the context of an iterative life cycle. By

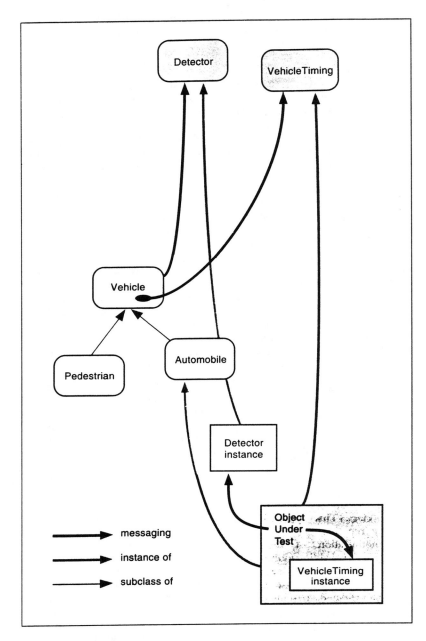

messaging

instance of

subclass of

Figure 7. Objects needed for a specific test case

the time a product is tested, it may have been modified but not necessarily corrected. Even locating the site of the error may be difficult if an extensive modification has taken place. At the class level this is additional evidence that the class developer should be the one to test the class. In this way, the feedback can be more timely. This also supports the idea of a project test team that is responsible for system-level testing as opposed to testing by some group that is independent of the project structure. The

feedback from a group that is separate from the project will most often be too late to be of value.

Coordination. The approaches used for class, cluster, and system testing will determine how much coordination is required. If the class testing is carried out by the class developer, there will be a decreased need for coordination. If an independent group is responsible for class testing, the group must be informed of the portion of the class that is considered completed and ready for testing and they must, in return, feed information forward into the next iteration as quickly as possible.

These problems occur to differing degrees in the class (i.e., unit) and system testing areas. The classes that comprise an object-oriented system are very volatile in the early iterations and some will be eliminated altogether as the design is refined. However, representations of these classes will also be some of the earliest products available for testing. The "system" exists in the early iterations as threads through the object model. Even when classes in the model disappear, these threads are often simply rerouted. This system view, while changing fairly rapidly early in the project, will nevertheless change more slowly than the individual class view. By testing these products, a progression of validated products, each relying on the products from the previous phase, is established.

The incremental approach to development also increases the need for coordination in the testing process. A class is defined in terms of instances of other classes. In order to test a given class, the supporting classes must have been developed at least to the level required by the class in question. This can be accomplished in a number of ways.

Stubbing. In this approach, each class is delivered with an accompanying stub class. Appropriate methods in the stub class have been written to return specific dummy values rather than doing an actual computation. This allows the class to be used before the actual implementation has been completed.

A disadvantage of this approach is that stubbing often requires more effort than anticipated. The stub must be capable of responding to multiple messages and it must return the appropriate value each time. This also requires that a separate stub instance be created for each test case so that the stub will produce the appropriate return values for that test case. These multiple instances can be created by overloading constructor methods, but the individual methods must still return the appropriate values. The result of all this is that a stub can evolve into a more complex implementation than the actual method code.

An additional disadvantage is that the work done to create the stub classes does not contribute to the overall completion of the system. With each iteration, the stubs must be reworked to reflect the incremental implementation improvements to the class. This effort can be somewhat reduced using a scheme such as that shown in Figure 7. By deriving the stub class from the base class, the complete and correct implementation for a method can be inherited. Those that are not completed can be overridden to provide the stub behavior.

Wave front integration. In our preferred approach, development proceeds across all of the classes at the same time. Developers reach agreement on the functionality to be achieved for each component during each iteration. That functionality should be sufficient for all dependent classes to achieve their negotiated level of behavior. This approach requires much communication, but has the advantage that the work done is actual development work—not "extra" work, as is the case with the stubbing approach.

The communication required by this approach can be provided by a simple extension to the software contracts described previously for coordinating design. A contract defines the interface between two specific components, classes (illustrated in Figure 9), clusters, or subsystems. By adding a section to the contract that specifies dates by which various portions of a component will be completed, developers can establish an integration and testing schedule for the level of component represented by the contract. This scheduling be-

comes particularly important when the two parties in the contract are in separate teams or even in separate development organizations. The advantage of the use of contracts is that they are a standard technique for assuring that appropriate interfaces are built among components independent of the testing issues.

Automation. The automation of test case generation, execution, and validation is critical in an iterative environment. Repeatability is also an

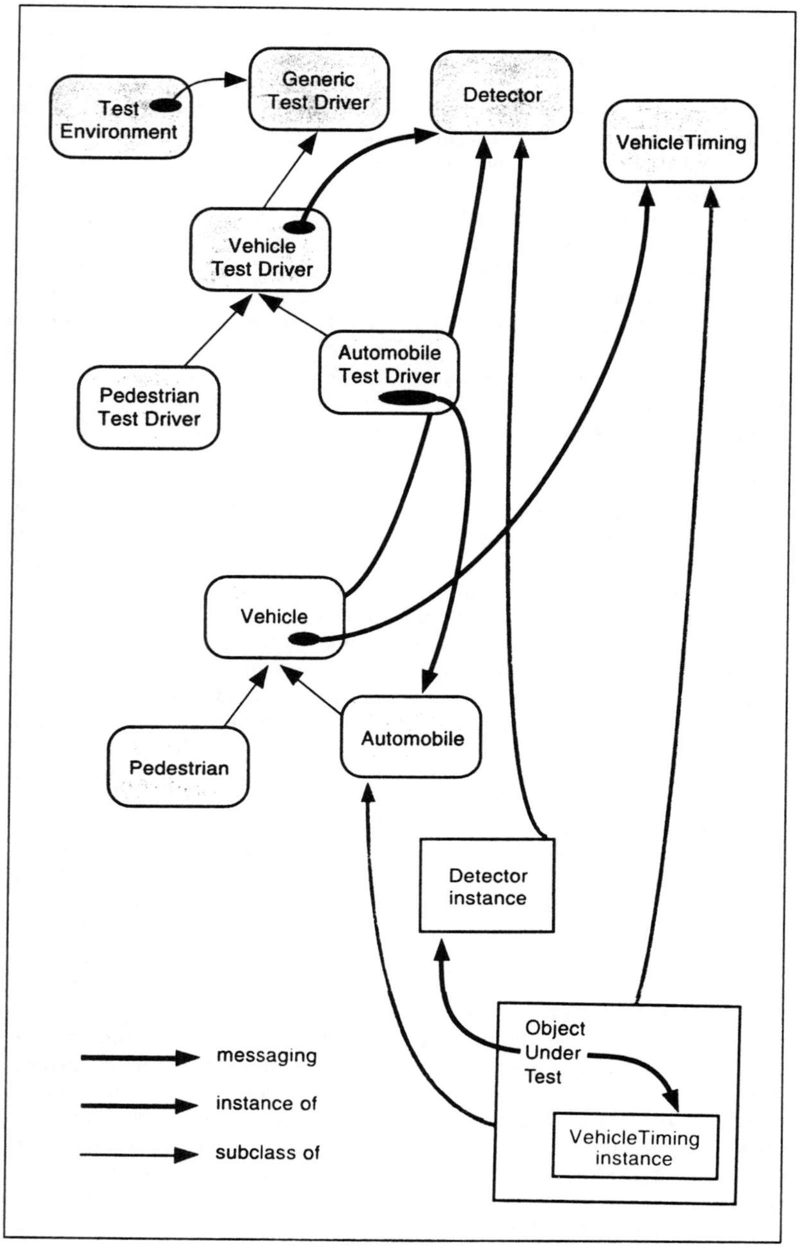

Figure 8. A parallel hierarchy for test driver classes

207

important feature, since each class will evolve across the iterations.

Automation is facilitated by having ready access to the developed products. A number of the techniques described and referenced in this article derive test cases from specific forms of program representation. For example, a number of functional test cases can be developed from the dynamic model for a class. The algorithm for deriving these test cases, given a simple representation of the state machine, is easy to program. The previously referenced reports on HIT and OATS have sets of algorithms that provide the basis for tool development.

The previously discussed technique of coding the test cases as methods of the test driver also supports automation of the regression testing effort. This approach provides for the inheritance of test cases just as other methods are inherited. This is a natural implementation of the HIT algorithm for reuse of test cases, as described in [4]. Changes to classes that are made in later iterations, are reflected in the test drivers and propagated down inheritance structures. The same maintenance advantages touted for object-oriented systems apply to these test driver classes.

Use of development products. A natural byproduct from the interaction of the testing and development processes is the improvement of products from both processes. Table 1 summarizes the set of products from a typical object-oriented development project. It also illustrates the contribution of each product to the generation of test cases. By deriving test cases from these various products, the developers see immediate use for the documents, rather than the distant beckoning of the actual implementation phase. Using an almost algorithmic approach to the derivation supports iteration by making it easier to understand how test cases must be refined as the individual products are refined over several iterations.

Organizational Considerations

The previous discussion about levels of testing activities (e.g., class, cluster, and system) described a set of organizational responsibilities that are not very different from what might be

assigned in a procedural approach. The difference is in the amount and the type of coordination that is required. To take advantage of the increased reuse provided by inheritance and the flexibility of the iterative life cycle, an increased amount of coordination is required.

Groups involved in testing. There are typically four groups involved in the testing process regardless of the organizational strategy: the individual class developers, the development teams, a project testing team, and a corporate-level testing group.

The *class developer* has the most direct knowledge of the class's specification and is the best source of information on details within the class. The involvement of the developer in testing the individual classes ranges from complete responsibility for class testing to a minimal advisory role in the process.

A *development team* is a grouping of developers that are working on a related set of classes. Within the team, communication is informal and quick. Working under one manager, the team usually has a unified set of priorities and a coordinated schedule for delivery.

A *project testing team* is designated to coordinate the testing process. This team, working with project managers, determines a project testing philosophy. The group disseminates the philosophy to the project staff, prescribes procedures to ensure the philosophy is implemented and provides specific testing tools such as generic test driver classes to the developers. The philosophy includes a set of standard practices such as levels of adequacy for test case coverage.

The *system testing group* offers specialized expertise in testing systems and products and may have special facilities for testing embedded software systems for example. This group can apply corporate standards of quality independent of the pressures of project schedules.

Patterns of communication. There are several communications patterns that should be established and supported to facilitate the use of testing information in the development process. The coordination of both the testing and development processes should follow the lines of the architec-

ture of the system. This architecture is provided by the inheritance relations among classes, the containment relations between classes and the messaging patterns between objects.

Developer to developer. Within a development team there will be informal communication between the developer of a class and a developer who uses that class as part of the definition of another class. This communication will provide feedback about problems encountered when integrating objects from the class into a larger context through containment and when deriving a new class from an existing class. Within a team there should be no need for formal coordination of this communication, but the communication should refer back to the specification of the component. The communication indicates whether there is an incorrect specification or a failure to correctly implement the given specification.

Developer to team. A developer will need to provide teammates the test cases developed for a class. This will be necessary if the approach supported by the HIT algorithm is chosen in which test cases are reused down an inheritance hierarchy. This avenue of communication is facilitated by having a standard technique of using a test driver class as the encapsulator of test cases. Then developers subclassing from the original developer's class will also subclass from that developer's test driver class.

Team to team. As classes are "released" for use by other teams, there must be an avenue for reporting integration problems. This type of communication can be facilitated by the use of software contracts. The contract lists a set of requirements that one team has for the components it will receive from the other team. The contract provides contact people on each team who monitor the contract and respond to requests for modification of the contract or to reports of problems with delivered classes.

A model organization for responsibilities. There are several possible models for assigning the responsibility for coordination of the various products of the testing process. These basic approaches can be mixed and adapted to fit a particular project's needs. We present here one possible model and discuss some criteria for tailoring the model.

In this model the individual developer performs the class-level testing. The developer will want to run numerous small test cases during development anyway, so there is not as much extra effort required as would be the case if an independent tester were responsible. The developer constructs components, selects the functional, structural and intraclass interaction test cases, derives a test driver, and executes the test scripts. Each of the developers owns their work and is responsible to the other members of the project staff for meeting the project's quality standards.

The deliverables associated with a class include the class's specification and implementation, the class's test suite, and a test driver class. The class will evolve over the iterations, and this implies updating of test suites as well as repetition of tests. The developer is in the best position to efficiently manage the evolution of all of these products. Each development team has responsibility for facilitating the sharing of test cases among developers down a complete inheritance hierarchy. The team also provides an organization within which the first level of integration occurs and the first inter-class interaction test cases are constructed.

The project test team provides a variety of services to the development teams and plays a central role in the testing process. The team establishes and enforces a set of criteria that determines when a developer has performed an adequate number of tests. The team evaluates, and perhaps constructs, testing tools and provides those to the developers. Members of the testing team play an active role in the inspection process and periodically audit the test suites for particularly critical classes.

The project test team also coordinates the interaction of the development teams through the administration of software contracts. The test team assists development teams in writing, negotiating, and modifying the contracts that coordinate the development process. The system test group provides the traditional system testing responsibilities such as func-

Table 1. Development products as sources of test cases

Test suites	Development Products					
	CRC cards	Object model	Dynamic model	Functional model	Class contracts	Use cases
Class-level functional			X			X
Class-level structural				X		
Class-level interaction	X		X		X	
System		X				X

```
Contract DetectorController
Class Detector will provide:
    StatusCode ShowStatus() by: May 15
    voidReset() by: June 1

Class Controller will provide:
    voidNotifyOfArrival(Detector) by: May 20

...

endContract;
```

Figure 9. Software contract

tional testing and stress and performance testing. The group performs additional duties in an object-oriented project. The system group can be assigned the responsibility of validating the use cases against the system requirements. This provides an early validation that the software being built, and based on the use cases, is at least synchronized with the current requirements even though they are expected to change during the life of the project.

The size and complexity of the project will be major factors in determining the appropriate organization. The model described here is appropriate for a moderate- to large-sized project, where a separate test organization is too formal or requires too much overhead, but the project is too complex to rely on individual developers to handle the coordination. A major benefit of this strategy is that by being an integral part of the project the project test team can more easily coordinate the testing of the various products in the iterative pro-

cess model. Since members of the team are dedicated to the one project, their knowledge of project details can be deeper and they do not require extra time to remain current.

Smaller projects may not be able to justify all of the levels outlined in this strategy. The informality of a small project and the ease of communication can eliminate the need for software contracts. The developers may still wish to designate a small group of developers that will take the lead in establishing the testing philosophy for all the developers.

Larger projects or projects with critical, or regulated, quality goals may utilize an independent test group (ITG), a separate organization responsible for certifying the quality of the products of the company. The ITG provides sets of requirements for submission of materials for testing to the development teams. The ITG may test only the end product of development or every product throughout the life cycle, including individual classes. This organizational structure and level of detail is often difficult to accommodate in the iterative approach because this separate organization must be synchronized with the development team's need for timely feedback.

The major concern that often results in the use of an ITG is the question of how thoroughly individual developers will test their own code. Some believe the objectivity of an independent group is needed to ensure adequate testing. The organization that we have proposed avoids this pitfall by prescribing project wide adequacy criteria, standard test case construction procedures, and a review and audit process.

Strategy for iterative incremental testing. Testing products being developed using an iterative incremental approach requires careful coordination and planning. Several issues have been identified and discussed in previous sections. In this section we will summarize these discussions and present a coordinated strategy.

• *Organize the project to provide clear lines of communication for testing information.* This can be accomplished by having public ownership of classes so that it is clear to whom to report problems. Software contracts can also be used to establish clear communication between the provider of a class and the consumers of its services. The incremental nature of our process often separates these two groups into teams that are not even in the same development phase at a point in time. Rapid communication of faults allows for optimum integration of the information into the development process.

• *Assign, and incrementally adjust, development responsibilities to minimize the need for communication.* Class developers should be responsible for the testing and quality of the components they create. Initial object models can be used to determine closely related classes and these can be assigned as clusters to a single team. This sets the stage for early

integration and cluster-level testing. It is a truism that the architecture of a software system reflects the organization of the development staff. Consequently, a successful iterative object-oriented project will need to adjust the team structure as the project progresses and class clusters are reformulated to reflect emerging relationships.

• *Provide developers with the infrastructure needed to support the testing aspect of their task.* Abstract classes for standard exceptions and generic test drivers are examples of the supporting classes that can be defined and provided to the developers. An error-reporting database, standard reporting formats, and templates for test plans for individual classes can also be provided.

• *Take advantage of the characteristics of the object-oriented products to facilitate the automation of testing.* Classes, with their encapsulation and information-hiding properties, provide a continuity from the earliest analysis phases through implementation. We have already discussed the need to test the mappings of a product from one form to another. The object-oriented approach facilitates these mappings, since even from the initial models, it is classes that are being mapped, modeled, and implemented. The reuse between classes provided by inheritance can be exploited in the defining of test cases as methods in the test drivers. The project's development tools that are intended to manipulate classes can be used to manipulate the testing structure as well. Use cases provide a close link between the system test cases and the classes representing the entities referenced in the use cases. These use cases improve the traceability of requirements through the application and into the system test cases. This traceability speeds the communication, making it more timely.

• *Establish project-wide guidelines to ensure consistency of products.* These guidelines should include specific goals for adequate testing of the various products. The use of a standard set of algorithms such as those we have presented means that test cases can be understood by other

developers. This will facilitate the audit process of selected classes during end of iteration reviews.

• *Schedule periodic integrations across parallel development teams.* In an incremental approach several pieces are being developed separately, often concurrently. These integrations give more exacting tests of the compatibility of interfaces than can be achieved at the design model level.

• *Use the information gained from testing to guide project management as well as development.* Testing can provide assurance of progress toward the finished product over a series of iterations. As the project progresses, obviously, the number of errors are expected to approach zero. Deviations from the downward trend should be able to be explained by a major restructuring of some piece of the system and this explanation should be part of the testing documentation. Larger projects will usually keep these statistics at the cluster level rather than attempting to manage data on every class. A second interesting metric is the change across iterations in the number of errors being detected. The rate of change in error rates across iterations should also approach zero. As the rate of fault detection goes down, confidence in the product should rise. Table 2 illustrates the matrix approach that can be used to analyze faults and the detection rate.

Summary

A comprehensive testing strategy has been presented that is closely related to the iterative incremental development process model. The approach takes advantage of the products of the development process to construct test cases and conduct tests efficiently. The strategy begins the testing process early in the development cycle, so that errors and misconceptions are identified as quickly as possible and corrected for the least cost.

One advantage of this approach is that it improves the probability that project staff will spend the time necessary to achieve quality. The increased overlap between development effort and testing effort provides the time and the motivation to more thoroughly test the components.

One disadvantage of the approach is that it makes the complete testing effort more visible. In some cases this makes it appear that more effort is being directed toward testing than in a typical project. The technique simply makes explicit some processes that have been followed informally but not included in process descriptions.

By integrating the development and testing processes, developers have more reasons to keep documents synchronized with the developed products, and the project realizes a greater return on both its development and testing efforts.

Future directions. This research is part of a comprehensive effort, under the auspices of the COnsortium for the Management of emerging SOFtware Technologies (COMSOFT) and its corporate sponsors, to provide the necessary infrastructure for supporting object-oriented software development. Plans include the continued development of tools that automate and assist the implementation of the techniques described in this article, as well as new versions of handbooks that elaborate on these testing strategies. Our research group is also actively involved in integrating a metrics program into the testing and development process.

Acknowledgments
We would like to thank David A. Sykes for constructive comments. We would also like to thank the corporate sponsors and the members of their development staffs who have provided valuable feedback as the process has matured. **C**

Table 2. Error rates per class and per iteration

	Iteration 1	Iteration 2	Iteration 3	Iteration 4	Iteration 5
Class 1	32	26	19	13	3
Class 2					0
Class 3					
Class 4					
Total errors					0

References
1. Beck, K. and Cunningham, W. A laboratory for teaching object-oriented thinking. In *Proceedings of OOPSLA '89*, ACM, New York, 1989, pp. 1–6.
2. Chow, T.S. Testing software design modeled by finite-state machines. *IEEE Trans. Softw. Eng. SE-4*, May, 1978.
3. Gamma, E., Johnson, R.E., and Vlissides, J. Design Patterns: Abstraction and Reuse of object-oriented design. In *Proceedings of ECCOOP'93— Object-Oriented Programming*. Springer-Verlag, Lecture Notes in Computer Science No. 707, pp. 406–431.
4. Harrold, M.J. and McGregor, J.D. Incremental testing of object-oriented class structures. In *Proceedings of the Fourteenth International Conference on Software Engineering*, 1992.
5. Helm, R., Holland, I.M. and Gangopadhyay, D. Contracts: Specifying behavioral compositions in object-oriented systems. In *Proceedings OOPSLA'90*, ACM, New York, 1990.
6. Jacobson, I., Christerson, M., Jonsson, P., and Overgaard, G. *Object-Oriented Software Engineering: A Use-Case Driven Approach*. Addison Wesley, Reading, Mass., 1992.
7. Johnson, R. Documenting frameworks with patterns. In *OOPSLA'92 Proceedings, SIG-PLAN Notices 27*, 10, pp. 63–76.
8. Korson, T.D. and McGregor, J.D. Understanding object-oriented: A unifying paradigm. *Commun. ACM 33*, 9 (Sept. 1990), 40–60.
9. Korson, T.D. and McGregor, J.D. *Managing Object-Oriented Software Development*. ACM Press, New York. To be published.
10. Lindland, O.I., Sindre, G., and Solvberg, A. Understanding quality in conceptual modeling. *IEEE Softw. 11* 4, pp. 42–49.
11. Liskov, B. and Wing, J.M. Specifications and their use in defining subtypes. In *Proceedings of the Eighth Annual Conference on Object-Oriented Programming Systems, Languages, and Applications (OOPSLA)*. ACM, New York, 1993, pp. 16–28.
12. McDaniel, R. and McGregor, J.D. Testing the polymorphic interactions of classes. Tech. Rep. TR-94-103, Clemson University, 1994.
13. McGregor, J.D. and Dyer, D.M. A note on inheritance and state machines. *Software Eng. Not. 18*, 4 (Oct. 1993) 61–69.
14. McGregor, J.D. and Dyer, D. The selection of state-based test cases. In *Proceedings of the 1993 Pacific Northwest Software Quality Conference*, 1993.
15. Mills, H.D. Stepwise refinement and verification in box-structured systems. *IEEE Comput.* (June 1988), 23–35.
16. Rumbaugh, J., Blaha, M., Premerlani, W., Eddy, F., and Lorensen, W. *Object-Oriented Modeling and Design*. Prentice-Hall, Englewood Cliffs, N.J., 1991.
17. Turner, C.D. and Robson, D.J. A Suite of tools for the state-based testing of object-oriented programs. Tech. Rep. TR-14/92.
18. Wirfs-Brock, R., Wilkerson, B., and Weiner, L. *Designing Object-Oriented Software*. Prentice-Hall, Englewood Cliffs, N.J., 1990.

About the Authors:
JOHN D. McGREGOR is an associate professor of computer science at Clemson University and a principal partner in Software Architects, a consulting firm that specializes in object technology. He conducts research on testing object-oriented software systems and conducts classes on design and testing of object-oriented software. **Author's Present Address:** Department of Computer Science, Clemson University, Clemson, SC, 29634-1906; email: johnmc@cs.clemson.edu

TIMOTHY D. KORSON is the director of COMSOFT, a research associate at Clemson University, and a principal partner in Software Architects. He conducts research on metrics and management strategies for object-oriented software projects. **Author's Present Address:** COMSOFT, P.O. Box 263, Clemson, SC 29633; email: korson@cs.clemson.edu

This research was partially supported by a grant from COMSOFT, IBM, and BNR.

Chapter 7

Test Tools

Software test automation has been recognized by today's software industry as the most effective means of reducing software test cost and of shrinking the testing cycle for a software product. Effective software test methods and efficient test tools play a very important role in a process of software test automation for a software workshop. Although there are now a number of software tool vendors that provide effective software test tools, most of them were developed for traditional programs. In other words, they focus on how to test and validate traditional procedure-oriented and/or function-oriented programs in various aspects of their features, structures, interfaces, and behaviors. Because of new problems (addressed in the first chapter) in the testing of OO programs, there is a very strong demand for new test tools for OO software systems, even though a number of test tools are available in today's market. The new test tool kit (SunStar, SunTestSuite, JavaPureCheck, JavaScope, and JavaSpec) for Java programs, from Sun Microsystems is a typical example (see http://www.suntest.com).

The major theme of this chapter is the exploration of software test automation for OO software in terms of systematic approaches, adapted test models, and test generation methods, as well as applications of test tools in the software testing phase. This chapter is composed of three papers. Each of them provides different insights on how to achieve systematic test automation of OO programs using effective test tools or systems.

Kung et al. in the first paper [kung95e] reported their developmental work on an OO testing and maintenance environment (OOTME.) In this system, a reverse engineering approach is used as a systematic way to recover the design of an OO program (or a class library) into a collection of test models (called OO test models) based on its source code (such as C++ code). These test models are classified into three types:

- object relation diagrams (ORD), which represent the relationships between different classes,
- object state diagrams (OSD), which depict the object state behavior for a class object, and
- block branch diagrams (BBD), which provide the control flow as well as the interface of a function member in a class.

Based on these test models, different tools are developed to assist testers in their testing and regression testing of OO programs. For example, a tool called Test Order Generator can be used to compute an optimal test order (or a test sequence) based on the extracted ORDs in class unit tests and class integration. Following the generated test order, testers can reduce a lot of test cost on test stubs and test drivers during tests. Another tool in the OOTME, called Class Firewall Generator, is also based on different class dependency relationships in ORDs. This tool can be used to identify the class firewall (which encloses the changed and affected classes) after various class changes. In addition, the OOTME consists of two types of test generations using OOSDs and BBDs, respectively. Based on an object state diagram, test cases can be generated for checking object behaviors of a class object. A BBD for a class function is used to generate test cases to exercise the basis paths of the function.

The second paper [doon94a], by Roong-Ko Doong and Phyllis G. Frankl, reported their systematic approach to unit testing of OO programs and a set of test tools, called ASTOOT. The major focus of this approach is how to automate the unit testing of Abstract Data Types (ADTs) in object-oriented programs in test data generation, test execution, and test checking. ASTOOT system consists of a set of tools, including the driver generator and two test generation tools, called the compiler and the simplifier. The driver generator takes as input the interface specifications of the Class Under Test (CUT) and of some related classes, and outputs a test driver. This test driver, when executed, reads test cases, checks their syntax, executes them, and verifies the results. The compiler and simplifier together form an interactive tool for semiautomatically generating test cases from an algebraic specification, called LOBAS. The compiler reads in a specification and does some syntactic and semantic checking on the specification, then translates each axiom into a pair of ADT trees (in which nodes represent operations of an ADT along with their arguments). Each path from the root of a leaf of an ADT tree represents a possible state of the ADT. The simplifier inputs an operation sequence, supplied by the user, translates it into an ADT tree, and applies the transformations to obtain equivalent operation sequences.

The third paper [post94a], by Robert M. Poston, describes how to reuse common object models (stored in repositories) for automated testing with a minimum of work and expense. Step by step through an example system, this article shows how to use an integrated set of software tools to perform the specification-based testing based on automated models during the development of object-oriented programs. This tool set includes three different tools, including a model-drawing tool, called StP/OMT, a test case generator called T, and a test execution tool, called XRunner. StP/OMT (Software Through Pictures/Object Modeling Technique) uses James Rumbaugh's object modeling technique (OMT) as its model to record the design information of OO programs. To make the model test-ready, testers need to prepare the instances of data items, events, and states that cause logical conditions to be true and false and actions to be performed. Test case generator T provides the capability of generating test cases automatically. Xrunner, an execution or capture-replay tool, can be used to exercise or run a given OO program on the integration level as well as on the system level. Robert Poston pointed out a very important fact, that is, when the OMT life cycle is supported by automated testing tools, the work of defining, designing, and writing test cases can be performed in parallel with the work of defining, designing, and implementing objects. Thus, the life cycle of an OO software product is shortened significantly.

When reading these papers, readers should pay more attention to the following aspects:

- the proposed systematic approaches and their advantages and disadvantages;
- the testing problems, testing areas, and related test tools focused on;
- adapted test models and their limitations;
- test generation methods and techniques;
- different application experience with these test tools.

In the first paper, a reverse engineering approach is used to recover the designs of an OO program (or a library) from its source code (C++ code) into a set of OO test models. Thus, the test models are program-based and contain enough information for automatic test generation. However, the major problem in this approach is the complexity and difficulty in recovering object state behavior. Unlike the first paper, the paper by Poston describes a forward engineering approach based on James Rumbaugh's OMT model. Since the OMT model is a high-level specification model for OO programs, it does not provide enough information as a test model. Therefore, testers need to do extra manual work to provide enough information in the models for specification-based test designs. Doong and Frankl in their paper also use a forward engineering approach. Unlike Poston's work where the OMT model is used to define an OO program, they use a format specification language to define abstract data types and their operations. An ADT tree is used as a model for generating tests to check the correctness of different operation sequences in an ADT.

The major focus of ASTOOT, in [doon94a], is on how to automate unit tests for ADTs by systematically generating and checking various operation sequences of an ADT. Unlike ASTOOT, the primary focus of the OOTME, in [kung95e], is on how to reduce the regression testing cost for a class library (or an OO program) by providing systematic methods for identifying class firewalls and optimal class test order. The focus of Poston's paper is on automating the specification-based testing of OO programs based on the OMT model.

All three papers reported their application experience with their test tools, and provided detailed results on their case studies. For example, the experiment results given in the paper by Kung et al. showed significant cost reduction on test harnessing during class unit tests/retests and class integration/reintegration tests. In the second paper, Doong and Frankl provided case studies on the effectiveness of their ASTOOT in ADT unit tests. In the third paper, Poston reported his data indicating the significant reduction of testing cost for specification-based testing in the development life cycle of an OO program due to the usage of different test tools.

References

[kung95e] D. Kung, et al., "Developing an Object-Oriented Software Testing and Maintenance Environment," *Comm. ACM*, Vol. 38, No. 10, Oct. 1995, pp. 75–87.

[doon94a] R. Doong and P. Frankl, "The ASTOOT Approach to Testing Object-Oriented Programs," *ACM* Trans. *Software Engineering and Methodology*, Vol. 3, No. 2, Apr. 1994, pp. 101–130.

[post94a] R. Poston, "Automated Testing From Object Models," *Comm. ACM*, Vol. 37, No. 9, Sept. 1994, pp. 48–58.

[rumb91a] J. Rumbaugh et al., *Object-Oriented Modeling and Design*, Prentice-Hall, Englewood Cliffs, N.J., 1991.

David Kung, Jerry Gao, Pei Hsia, Yasufumi Toyoshima, Chris Chen, Young-Si Kim, and Young-Kee Song

Developing an Object-Oriented Software Testing and Maintenance Environment

The object-oriented (OO) paradigm is rapidly gaining acceptance in the software industry. However, the powerful features of this new paradigm also introduce a new set of OO software testing and maintenance problems. The pioneering work in identifying these new problems includes [7, 10–12, 14, 16, 18]. The problems can be summarized as: 1) the understanding problem; 2) the complex interdependency problem; 3) the object state behavior testing problem; and 4) the tool support problem. Detailed discussions of these problems will be provided later. Our industrial experience confirms these discoveries.

In an attempt to solve these problems, the Software Engineering Center for Telecommunications at the University of Texas at Arlington (UTA) and Fujitsu Network Transmission Systems, Inc., have undertaken a major effort in the past three years to develop

a methodology for OO software testing and maintenance. The results we have obtained so far include: 1) an OO test model and a reverse engineering approach to recovering the designs of C++ programs, 2) a three level schema and algorithms for data flow testing of OO programs, 3) definition and identification of class firewalls and a test strategy for regression testing of C++ programs, 4) a program-based method for object state behavior testing, and 5) a scenario-based method for integration and acceptance testing. Parts of these results have been implemented in an integrated object-oriented testing and maintenance (OOTM) environment.

Currently, most software development organizations are still in the process of observing and/or making the transition to the OO paradigm; only a few have experienced the difficulties of testing and maintaining an OO program. Most OO methods do not address testing. One notable exception is Fayad's Object-Engineering Technique (OET) [4], in which test cases and test procedures are defined for object classes. A recent issue of *Communications* raised the issue of the importance and reported several interesting results of OO testing [2]. Strictly speaking, OO testing and maintenance tools have not been seen in the commercial market; most CASE tool vendors are advocating the use of conventional testing tools to cope with OO testing problems. The objective of this article is to share our experience in the development and application of the OOTM environment. We use the well-known Inter-Views library as a case study throughout the article, except for experiment and object state behavior testing, where we use a vending machine example.

Basic Object-Oriented Concepts

Objects are the basic building blocks of an OO system. In the OO paradigm, the real world is viewed as consisting of objects; hence, many real-world applications can be considered OO systems. The notion of an object includes the following:

- An object models an entity or thing in the application domain. For example, a book or an employee in the real world can be modeled by an object.
- An object has a set of attribute values that define a state of the object. For example, the status attribute of a library book may have as its values 'available', 'checkout', 'on reserve', 'missing', and 'removed'. These values may be used to determine the state of a book object at any time. Attributes are called member data in C++.
- An object has a set of operations it is capable of performing to change its attribute values, which may cause changes to attribute values of other objects. For example, filling an order in a retail company may cause the following changes: 1) the order changes its state from 'new order' to 'filled order'; 2) the customer's balance is changed to reflect the additional amount charged to the customer; and 3) the inventory level or quantities-on-hand of the merchandise is updated to reflect the amount sold to the customer. Object operations are called member functions in C++.
- An object has an identity that can be used to uniquely identify the object, or distinguish the object from similar objects. Each object has its own identity, so that even if two objects have the same attribute values, they can still be identified by using their identities. Object identity is not relevant to our discussion in this article; we include it for the sake of completeness.

An object-oriented system may be typeless, like Smalltalk, or strongly typed, like Eiffel and C++. An object class defines the type or structure of a set of objects—that is, the attributes and their types, and the operations of the objects.

Encapsulation means modeling and storing with an object the attributes and the operations the object is capable of performing. In a conventional paradigm, the modeling of these two aspects is done separately. For example, in structured analysis, the operations that can be performed on book objects are modeled using data flow diagrams and implemented by functions/procedures, while the attributes of book objects are specified in a data dictionary and implemented by data structures.

Encapsulation is closely related to the notion of information hiding, which suggests that a software module designer should try to hide or localize the internal linkage of data structures and implementation details of the procedures. Encapsulation provides an effective way to enforce information hiding, because the data aspect of an object may be made private and access to these private data can be achieved only through operations of the object. Thus, the ripple effect of change may be minimized.

An object class is a subclass of another object class if every object of the former is also an object of the latter. The latter is called a superclass of the former. Superclass corresponds to base class and subclass corresponds to derived class in C++.

Inheritance means that properties (i.e., attributes and operations) defined for an object class are automatically defined for all of its subclasses. The most promising benefit of inheritance is software reuse, which has been utilized widely by software engineers. Since properties of a superclass are automatically defined for all of its subclasses, software that implements the operations of the superclass can be reused by the subclasses. For example, a *print* operation for a *document* object class may be reused to print a technical report if the printing of a technical report requires the same actions to be performed. OO programming also allows different printing methods for different types of documents. The appropriate method will be invoked at run time, according to the type of the document object. This ability is called polymorphism and/or dynamic binding, to be explained shortly.

An object class may have more than one superclass. For example, graduate teaching assistants are a subclass of both students and employees. This is usually referred to as multiple inheritance.

Methods inherited from a superclass must be retested in the context of the subclass, because the testing using the context of the superclass may not include all the cases that may occur in the context of the subclass [15].

Polymorphism means the ability to take more than one form: An attribute may have more than one set of values, and an operation may be implemented by more than one method. A commonly used example is from computer graphics, in which different drawing methods may be implemented for a draw operation. The drawing method (e.g., draw_arc, draw_rectangle) appropriate to the object to be drawn will be executed at run time.

Table 1. InterViews Invocation Chains.

Invocation chain length	0	1	2	3	4	5	6	7	8	9	10	11	12	13	14
No. of chains	246	305	568	783	742	492	514	482	330	172	82	59	31	10	2

Dynamic binding means the method that implements an operation is unknown until run time. It is an effective mechanism to implement polymorphism. As discussed previously, an operation may have more than one implementation. The choice of which implementation to use when an operation is invoked is determined at run time according to the types, the number of arguments, and/or the function pointed to by a function pointer.

Some Object-Oriented Testing and Maintenance Problems

As discussed in the introductory section, the major OOTM problems are 1) the understanding problem, 2) the complex interdependency problem, 3) the object state behavior testing problem, and 4) the tool support problem.

The Understanding Problem

The understanding problem is introduced by the encapsulation and information-hiding features. These features result in the "delocalized plan," in which several member functions from possibly several object classes are invoked to achieve an intended functionality. Often, a member function of a class in turn invokes other member functions, resulting in the so-called invocation chain of member functions [18]. To illustrate, we show in Figure 1 a hypothetical example. The rectangles represent member functions belonging to various classes, which are denoted by capital letters. The edges represent function invocations from left to right. For example, the LOAN.check_out() function invokes LOAN.check_patron(), which in turn invokes PATRON.get_category() and then PATRON.copies_chkout(). Thus, a preorder traversal through the tree in Figure 1 gives the following sequence of member function invocations, where comments are given after '//':

LOAN.check_out () // check out a book by a patron.
LOAN.check_patron () // does he borrow too many books?
PATRON.get_category () // faculty, staff, and student have different check-out limits.
PATRON.copies_chkout () // how many books has the patron checked out?

BOOK.get_type () // reference book is not allowed to be checked out.
BOOK.available () // is the book available?
COPYLIST.empty () // if the book's copylist is empty, then it is not available.

Table 1 summarizes the number of invocation chains of different lengths for the InterViews library. The result does not take into consideration overloading, polymorphism, and dynamic binding[1] because these features require actual execution of the member functions. We see that there are 4,818 member function invocation chains. The longest chain involves 14 member function calls in sequence, and the majority of cases involve

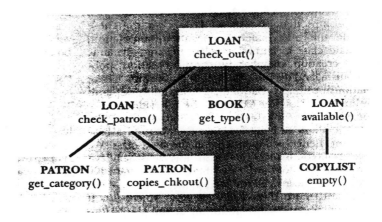

chains of two to nine member functions. By "a chain of member functions calling in sequence," we mean that the first function calls the second, which calls the third, and so forth. Thus, the longest such chain in Figure 1 is 3, not 7.

The implication of the invocation chains is that a tester/maintainer has to understand sequences of member functions and the semantics of the classes prior to preparing any test cases and/or modifying the intended functionality. Since it is necessary to understand all the parts in sufficient detail before testing/modification,

Figure 1.
An example of a function invocation chain in OO programming

---

[1] When these features are considered, the invocation chains will be longer and more difficult to comprehend, because one does not know which code segment will actually be executed at run time.

this adds tremendous complexity to testing and maintenance of OO systems.

We have also conducted an experiment to find out how much time a tester would spend to test three simple, small member functions from an elevator program written in C++. The testers are students who have learned and programmed in C++. They are required to manually prepare basis path test cases and test data for testing the member functions. Although each of the member functions is very small (a total of 15 lines of code, or an average of 5 lines per member function), it took, on average, 0.95, 0.93, and 0.79 person-hours to prepare the test data, test driver, and test stub, respectively. We know that automatic test data and test driver generation is possible and that this would save about 1.88 (i.e., 0.95 + 0.93) person-hours per member function. Automatic test stub generation is not possible, because it requires understanding of the semantics of the called functions. Therefore, reducing the effort needed to construct test stubs will result in additional savings.

The Complex Dependency Problem

The dependency problem was caused by the complex relationships that exist in an OO program. These include the inheritance, aggregation, association, template class instantiation, class nesting, dynamic object creation, member function invocation, polymorphism, and dynamic binding relationships. These relationships imply that one class inevitably depends on another class. For example, the inheritance relationship implies that a derived class reuses both the data members and the function members of a base class and hence is dependent on the base class. We have applied our tools to a version of the InterViews library, which contains 122 classes, more than 400 inheritance, aggregation, and association relationships, and more than 1,000 member functions. It does not contain template class or nested class. However, the 122 classes are related to each other, forming a strongly connected cyclic graph. Another industrial library we have examined contains many template classes, some of which are derived classes of other template classes. The InterViews library is considered a small library compared to some of the class libraries that currently exist in the industry.

The complex relationships that exist in an OO program make testing and maintenance extremely difficult:

- It is very difficult to understand a given class in a large OO program if that class depends on many other classes.
- Without sufficient insight, a tester may not know where to start testing an OO library.
- It is extremely costly to construct test stubs, since the tester has to understand the called functions, possibly create and properly initialize certain objects, and write code to simulate the behaviors and effects of the called functions.
- It is impossible to predict, and equally impossible

to test, all possible uses of a template class.
- It is difficult to identify and test the effect of polymorphism and dynamic binding.
- It is difficult to identify change impact in OO maintenance, since the impact may ripple throughout the OO program through the complex dependencies [12].

The State Behavior Testing Problem

Objects have states and state-dependent behaviors. That is, the effect of an operation on an object depends on the state of the object and may change the state of the object. Thus, the combined effect of the operations must be tested [3, 5, 8, 9, 11, 17]. Consider a coin box class of a vending machine implemented in C++. For simplicity, we will assume that the coin box has very simple functionality and the code to control the physical device is omitted. It accepts only quarters and allows vending when two quarters are received. It keeps track of the total quarters (denoted totalQtrs) received, the current quarters (denoted curQtrs) received, and whether vending is enabled or not (denoted allowVend). Its functions include adding a quarter, returning the current quarters, resetting the coin box to its initial state, and vending. The C++ source code for this simple coin box is shown in Figure 2.

By carefully examining the code shown in Figure 1, one may discover that there is an error in the implementation, since the operation sequence *AddQtr(); AddQtr(); ReturnQtrs(); Vend()* can be successfully performed. This means that a customer can get a free drink by inserting two quarters, requesting that the two quarters be returned, and pressing the vend button to obtain a drink. We wish to point out that this error was not discovered until the programmer applied the object state behavior testing method. We argue that the error cannot be easily detected by unit functional testing and/or unit structural testing of the member functions, nor can it be easily detected by integration testing of the member functions. This is because 1) each of the member functions seems to implement the intended functionality; 2) correctly exercising each of the basis paths would not detect the error unless the object is properly put into a certain state; 3) integration testing detects errors only in the interfaces of the member functions.

Object state behavior testing can be specification-based or program-based. Since we assume that documentation is either missing or poor, we adopt a program-based approach. That is, we derive from the source code the state-dependent behaviors of the objects and represent this information in an object state diagram (OSD); we then generate test cases and test data from the OSD to test the program and observe the output.

The Tool Support Problem

CASE tools to support OO testing and maintenance are still in their infancy. Many commercial tools still implement conventional testing and maintenance methods and techniques. However, we have found these methods and techniques, though applicable, are not

```
class CoinBox
{
        unsigned totalQtrs; // total quarters collected
        unsigned curQtrs; // current quarters collected
        unsigned allowVend; // 1 = vending is allowed
public:
        CoinBox() { Reset(); }
        void AddQtr(); // add a quarter
        void ReturnQtrs() { curQtrs = 0; } // return current quarters
        unsigned isAllowedVend() { return allowVend; }
        void Reset() { totalQtrs = 0; allowVend = 0; curQtrs = 0; }
        void Vend(); // if vending allowed, update totalQtrs and curQtrs
};
void CoinBox::AddQtr()
{
    curQtrs = curQtrs + 1; // add a quarter
    if (curQtrs > 1) // if more than one quarter is collected,
        allowVend = 1; // then set allowVend
}
void CoinBox::Vend()
{
    if ( isallowedVend() ) // if allowVend
    {
        totalQtrs = totalQtrs + curQtrs; // update totalQtrs,
        curQtrs = 0;                      // curQtrs, and
        allowVend = 0;                    // allowVend,
                                          // else no action
    }
}
```

adequate for OO programs because they do not address the OO testing problems.

Software testing is a tedious process. It requires the preparation, execution, and analysis of tens of thousands of test cases and test data sets. Using a specification-based approach, the test cases can be derived from a software specification. This requires that the specification be written in a formal specification language so that a tool can be used to derive the test cases. The tester may or may not be required to provide test data for each of the test cases, depending on the level of detail of the formal specification. According to our observation, formal methods are rarely used in practice for various reasons. A tester has to manually prepare the test cases and test data sets. Therefore, extensive tool support is important in software testing, and OO testing is no exception.

As indicated previously, changes to an OO program may ripple throughout the entire program. Manually identifying the change impact is both difficult and time-consuming. This approach is also associated with the risk of omitting certain affected parts. An alternative is to retest the entire program, but this is very costly. Therefore, tool support is also crucial in the maintenance phase. Tools may help in the identification of the changes and change impact, generation and/or reuse of test cases and test data sets, and retesting only the parts that are changed and/or affected.

An Object-Oriented Testing and Maintenance Environment

In this section, we describe the test model and the capabilities of the OOTM environment. This information may be useful for understanding our experience (described in the next section).

The Test Model and Its Capabilities

Central to the environment is a mathematically defined test model, consisting of three types of diagrams: 1) the object relation diagram (ORD), 2) the block branch diagram (BBD), and 3) the object state diagram (OSD). These diagrams are extracted from code using a reverse engineering approach [10]. The ORD, BBD, and OSD are summarized as follows:

- An ORD represents the inheritance, aggregation, association, (template class) instantiation, uses (in template class instantiation), and nested_in relationships among the object classes and template classes. The usefulness of ORD will be explained with an example later.

- A BBD represents the control structure of a member function and its interface to other member functions so that a tester will know which data is used and/or updated and which other functions are invoked by the member function. Information contained in the BBD diagrams can be used to prepare functional test cases, structural test cases, and test harnesses in member function unit testing; to derive data dependence relations across multiple functions and objects; and to display statement, branch, and path coverage information. These capabilities are similar to conventional unit testing of the member functions [1] and hence will not be discussed further in this article.

- An OSD is similar to Statechart [6] and Rumbaugh et al.'s object state diagram. It represents the state behavior of an object class. To reduce complexity, we construct a state machine for each state-dependent data member of a class. The state behavior of a class is represented as an aggregation of the data members' state machines. If a data

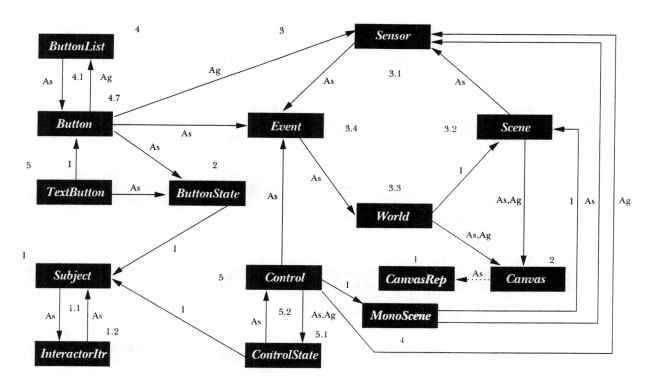

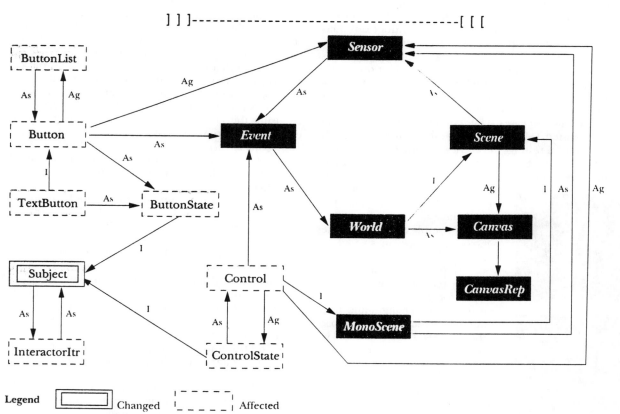

Legend ⬜ Changed ⬚ Affected

member is a simple datum (e.g., integer, float, or string, etc.) then the member's state machine is called an atomic OSD (AOSD). A composite OSD (COSD) is an aggregation of AOSDs and/or COSDs. This recursive definition allows us to model the inheritance and aggregation of object state behaviors in a hierarchy of state machines.

Examples

We show in this section some examples of the application of the OOTM tools. Figure 3 shows an ORD diagram, along with the class test order for a subset of the InterViews library.

The diagram in Figure 3 indicates that *Scene* is a part of *Canvas* and *World* is a subclass of *Scene*. The test order is computed according to the degree of dependencies between the classes, so that if class A is dependent on class B, then class B should be tested before class A. A more detailed description can be found in [13]. In this way, the testing of A can reuse the data structure and functionality of B, instead of having to construct test stubs to simulate the behavior of B. We will show later that this can result in tremendous savings in OO unit testing and integration testing. The test order consists of two components, the major test order and the minor test order. The classes are tested according to their major test order, followed by their minor test order. In Figure 3 the test order is indicated by x.y, where x denotes the major test order whereas y denotes the minor test order.

The test order may be used to conduct unit class testing and integration testing. In unit testing, the individual classes are tested according to the test order. That is, each of the member functions of the class is tested using structural testing and functional testing as in conventional testing. The BBD can be used to generate the basis path test cases as well as functional test cases. The state behavior of the class is then tested using the OSD and the test utilities. In integration testing, the classes are integrated and tested according to the test order, and we focus on testing the member functions' interfaces with other classes and interactions between the state behaviors of the integrated classes.

The complex dependencies between the classes in an OO system imply that changes to one part would ripple throughout the system. The real problem is that it is difficult for a tester to remember and record the changes and for a maintainer to identify the impact of the changes. The firewall tool we have developed automatically identifies the changes and computes the affected classes. Figure 4 shows the changes and their impact on two versions of the InterViews library subset. The figure also displays the test order for retesting the affected classes. Currently the firewall constructed by the tool is based on a static approach, which does not take into consideration the polymorphism and dynamic binding features. A dynamic approach is being studied and will be used to improve the accuracy of the firewall. For a description of the firewall computation method, see [12].

The firewall tool can be used in two different ways:

• Before making actual changes, a developer can use the tool to identify the impact of the planned changes and estimate the effort in terms of number of test stubs and test cases needed to retest the affected classes.
• After making the changes, a regression tester can use the tool to identify the actual changes and their impact. The tool can also compute the optimal test order to retest the affected classes.

Object state behavior testing is an important aspect of OO testing. Our experience indicates that even though each member function of a class has been structurally and functionally tested correct according to the member function's specification, the combined effect of invoking the member functions of the class in a certain sequence may produce an incorrect result. This is due to the failure to check the side effects of the member functions in the specifications and/or code. An example is the CoinBox program we discussed earlier. We wish to point out that the CoinBox program is a simplified version of a real application program and that the error was discovered by the programmer attempting to reconstruct the state diagram for the object class. By using the OSD tool, we generated the state diagram for the CoinBox class as shown in Figure 5. The OSD construction method can be found in [11].

The COSD for the CoinBox in Figure 5 consists of two AOSD's for its two state dependent data members. Note that totalQtrs is also a data member of the CoinBox. But since it does not affect the state behavior of CoinBox, it does not have an AOSD. The notation and semantics of our OSD are similar to those in the literature (see [6]). That is, predicates or guard conditions are enclosed in brackets, and transitions are labeled by member functions. In our model, the states are labeled by disjoint intervals of the data member, such as [0,0] and [1,M], where M denotes the maximum value of the data member. A directed edge from the boundary of the enclosing rectangle to a state is used to represent transitions that can initiate from any state and result in the state pointed to by the directed edge. For example, the Reset() member function can be applied in any state and will result in state [0,0].

Our OSD can be characterized as hierarchical, concurrent, communicating state machines. Hierarchical because we want to support the inheritance

Figure 3.
ORD and class test order for a subset of InterViews

Figure 4.
Class firewall for the subset of InterViews library

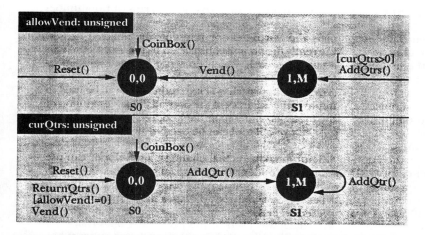

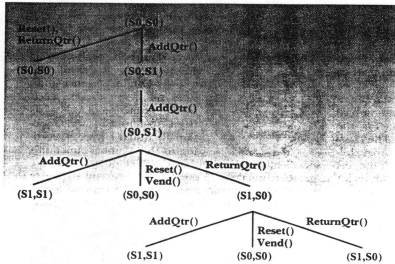

component denotes the state of the i-th AOSD. The root of the test tree is denoted by the initial states of the component AOSDs. For example, in Figure 6, the root is denoted by (S0, S0). A transition from a composite state to another composite state can occur if and only if a corresponding transition can occur in an AOSD. For example, for the curQtrs AOSD, there is a transition from S0 to S1; therefore, we add the edge AddQtr() and the successor node (S0, S1) to the root node in Figure 6. A directed arc from the contour of the AOSD-enclosing rectangle to a state means that there is a transition from every state to the state pointed to by the directed arc. For example, the directed arc labeled by '[curQtrs > 0] AddQtrs()' in the allowVend AOSD represents the fact that there is a transition from S0 to S1 and a transition from S1 to S1. This explains why there is a transition from (S0, S1) to (S1, S1) in the tree in Figure 6.

From the test tree, we can derive the test sequence AddQtr(); AddQtr(); ReturnQtrs(); Vend() (i.e., the second rightmost branch), which will detect the error in the implementation of the member functions. We have also applied the OSD tool to a traffic light example, which was used in the literature to illustrate error detection for safety critical software. The tool easily detected an error in the original code that caused a traffic light in one direction to change from green to red without the yellow warning light.

Experience and Limitations

We have presented OO testing problems and some of the tools we have developed to solve these problems. In particular, the test model (ORD, BBD, and OSD) makes different levels of abstraction of an OO software system to facilitate understanding (problem 1). The OSD facilitates testing of object state behavior (problem 3). The tool set generates, among other things, the test model, test order and firewall (using dependencies), and object state behavior test cases and test data (problems 2 and 4). In this section, we present our experience in the development and application of the OOTM environment.

An OO Test Model Is Extremely Useful

The first lesson we learned is that an OO test model is extremely useful, especially a formally defined test model. Several years ago, some of us were involved in the development of a commercial product using C++.

Figure 5.
A nonflat state machine for the incorrect Coin-Box class

Figure 6.
Test tree showing the execution sequences of a COSD

and aggregation features of OO programming. That is, a derived/aggregate class inherits the state machines of its base classes/component classes. Concurrent because objects are viewed as concurrent processes. And communicating because objects can send and receive messages from each other.

In the following discussion, we show how test cases can be generated from the COSD in Figure 5 to detect the error we mentioned earlier. The basic idea is to construct a test tree, as in Figure 6, from which test cases are derived.

The nodes of a test tree for a COSD represent the composite states of the COSD. The edges of the tree represent transitions between the composite states. If the COSD contains n AOSDs, then each state is represented by an n-tuple, where the i-th

We were astonished by the lack of systematic OO testing methods and supporting tools to help a tester to carry out the testing process. We discovered that the traditional testing techniques and methods were inadequate, since they did not address the complexity of an OO program. When we started to test one class, we soon found out that one had to trace and understand many other classes in order to construct the test cases and test stubs. We realized that an OO test model that would provide a high level abstraction of the OO program was needed. This model should help a tester in understanding the complex relations and coping with the complex dependencies among the various components of the OO program. The development of the ORD and the test order tool was motivated by this experience. The usefulness of the OO test model is summarized as follows:

- It helps the tester and maintainer understand the structures of and relations between the components of an OO program.
- It provides the tester and maintainer a systematic method to perform OOTM. In particular, it assists the tester and maintainer to find better test strategies to reduce testing and maintenance effort.
- It facilitates the definitions and analysis of OO testing criteria.
- It facilitates the development of the various algorithms and capabilities for OOTM.

Optimal Test Order Significantly Saves Test Costs

The significance of the optimal test order is re-affirmed by the number of test stubs needed for unit testing of the InterViews library using a randomly generated test order, as shown in Figure 7. The total number of stubs required is 400 (i.e., 3.27 per class X 122 classes). If we use the result obtained in our experiment mentioned earlier, each stub requires 0.79 person-hours to prepare; then 400 stubs would require 316 person-hours, or almost 8 person-weeks. In comparison, if the optimal test order is used, then it requires only 8 test

stubs. That is, a 93% saving, in terms of the number of stubs needed, is achieved. Using the test order still require 8 test stubs because there are cyclic dependencies among the classes. The weakest dependency in a cycle must be simulated by a test stub(s) so that the remaining dependencies become acyclic and a (topological) test order can then be defined for the classes. The effort or savings may be estimated more accurately by counting the number of lines of executable source code of the functions that need to be simulated by the test stubs. This approach assumes that the effort required to understand a function and construct a stub for it depends on the size of the function. A simpler approach is to assume that on average, each stub requires a certain degree of effort. The latter approach was used in the preceding material.

It should be noted that the test order assumes bottom-up testing, which is also advocated by other researchers [7, 8]. Effort is saved by significantly reducing the number of test stubs. The effectiveness of the test case, which also affects the test effort, is not considered. We believe that the test order and the test case effectiveness are two orthogonal issues and should be addressed separately. The latter depends on the test case generation technique.

Class Firewall is a Useful Concept in OO Regression Testing

Programs undergo continual changes, and OO programs are no exception. In structured programming, a programmer can strive to reduce the ripple effect and achieve a better design by enforcing the scope of effect within the scope of control. However, this design principle is sometimes difficult to enforce due to the nature of OO programming, because a decision of an object may affect the action of another object. Therefore,

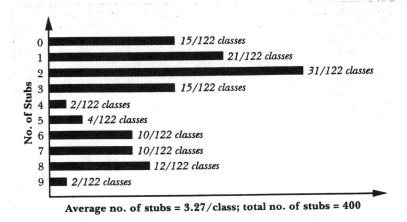

Figure 7. Stubs for unit testing of InterViews using a random test order

No. of Stubs	
0	15/122 classes
1	21/122 classes
2	31/122 classes
3	15/122 classes
4	2/122 classes
5	4/122 classes
6	10/122 classes
7	10/122 classes
8	12/122 classes
9	2/122 classes

Average no. of stubs = 3.27/class; total no. of stubs = 400

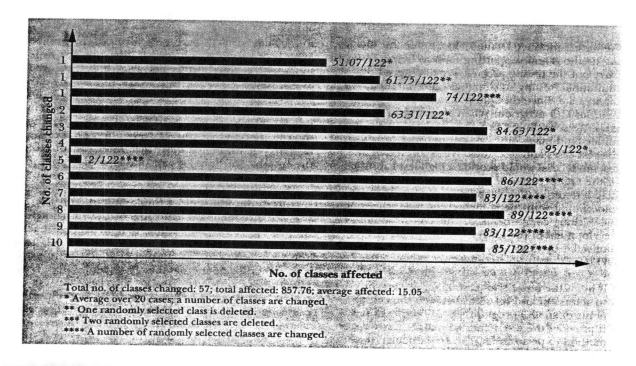

Figure 8. Statistics for change impact identification

The first case in Figure 8 is an average over 20 cases, in each of which a single class is changed. We see that less than 50% of the classes need to be retested. The next two cases concern the deletion of one or two randomly selected classes. Most of the cases show that fewer than 75% of the classes need to be retested. The average is 15.05 affected classes per class changed. In other words, only 12.33% of the 122 classes need retesting, achieving a 87.67% savings in terms of the number of classes need to be retested. It should be noted that retesting effort may be affected by the effectiveness of the test cases. Generally speaking, the more effective the test cases, the less retest effort is required with respect to a given quality requirement. This issue is orthogonal to the firewall concept. In other words, for any given regression test case generation/reuse technique, effort can be saved by retesting only a subset of classes. Similarly, for any given set of classes, effort can be saved by using more effective test cases.

We anticipate that the tool will be particularly useful in the maintenance phase. Without using this tool, one has to document the changes and identify the impact according to one's knowledge of the system. This is both time-consuming and inaccurate. With this tool, the problem is solved in seconds.

without tool support, it is almost impossible to anticipate and identify the effect of change. The application of the firewall tool to the InterViews library has produced promising results. Figure 8 shows the number of affected classes due to changes to one through 10 classes.

Using ORD and Test Order in Integration Testing

Integration testing is not an easy task. Traditionally, there are several integration strategies, including top-down, bottom-up, and sandwich approaches [1]. It has been recognized that a bottom-up strategy is preferred for OO programs. However, how to conduct bottom-up OO testing is still an open problem. One notable contribution is [7], in which a bottom-up methodology was proposed for testing the inheritance hierarchy of OO programs. Jorgensen and Erickson [8] proposed and outlined a five-level testing approach that also advocates bottom-up integration. Our experience indicates that the ORD and the test order not only are useful for conducting class unit testing but also provide a detailed road map for conducting integration testing. That is, after class unit testing is conducted, the classes are to be integrated according to the test order. In this way, the effort required to construct test stubs and test drivers can be reduced to a minimum.

Consider, for example, the integration testing of the InterViews library. Figure 9 shows the statistics of test stubs required for 100 random integration sequences. We see that the average number of stubs required is 191.88 per sequence. If each stub requires 0.79 person-hours to prepare, then testing would require about 152 person-hours or almost 4 person-weeks.[2] When the test order is used, only 8 test stubs are needed.

Limitations and Enhancements

One obvious limitation is that we focus only on white-box testing; hence the limitations of white-box

---

[2] Fewer test stubs are required than the random unit test sequence because the result in Figure 9 is an average over 100 sequences and the result in Figure 7 is for one random sequence, which may happen to be a costly one.

testing are the limitations of our OOTM environment. Although the BBD interface can be used to generate functional testing cases and test data, the testing of member functions is only a small portion of OO testing.

Applying the ORD tool to realistic programs has revealed some design and implementation limitations of our OOTM environment. The ORD display tool works fine for a small set of classes. The display would spread over several screens/paper sheets when the number of classes is large. For example, the display of the complete InterViews library takes up five screens, and a user has to use the scroll bar to view the entire ORD diagram. This "scaling-up" problem is common to many CASE tools. Three promising solutions have been proposed:

- Supporting multiple class libraries. A large OO system involves several libraries. A library dependency graph, in which nodes represent libraries and directed edges represent interlibrary dependencies, can be created to provide an additional level of abstraction. A user can click on a node to view a library's ORD or on an edge to view the relationships among the classes of two libraries. Interlibrary dependencies are identified from "#include" statements.
- Supporting multiple subsystems. Another level of abstraction can be provided by a subsystem graph, in which nodes represent subsystems and directed edges represent interactions among the subsystems. A user can click on a node to view a subsystem's ORD or on an edge to view the class relationships among the classes of two subsystems. A subsystem may contain a *main()* function, and it and its related files may be assumed to reside in a header file directory and a source file directory, respectively.
- Supporting large ORD display. Several techniques can be used to effectively display a large ORD in a library or subsystem. For example: 1) A

matrix representation, in which rows and columns denote classes and entries denote relationships among the classes, is a straightforward alternative. 2) A diagonal matrix is a matrix in which the nonblank entries are clustered around the diagonal. A user can navigate along the diagonal and view the clusters one at a time. 3) The ORDs associated with clusters can be displayed one at a time. 4) An ORD that contains one or more types of relationships can be displayed. 5) A user may specify a class and a distance so that only classes that are within this distance, measured in terms of the length of the path from the specified class, will be displayed. 6) A user may request display of only the classes that contain a particular character string.

Our OSD construction is based on symbolic execution to identify the effects of the member functions of a class. Loop statement handling is a known weakness of symbolic execution. Our solution is to symbolically execute loops using boundary values and include the boundary values in the guard conditions of the transitions. For example, if the values of a loop variable x can range from a to b, then as boundary values, we use $x = a - 1$, $x = a$, $x = a + 1$, $x > a + 1$ and $x < b - 1$, $x = b - 1$, $x = b$, $x = b + 1$, respectively, to execute the loop and derive the effect. We are satisfied with the results for testing purposes. However, since only boundary values are used, the OSD constructed may not be complete.

An important lesson we have learned is that the complexity of object state behavior testing is very high, despite our use of an efficient object state model. When we applied the tool to a class of a vending machine simulator, the AOSD of a data member (i.e., CurrentCash) consists

Figure 9.
Test stubs required for random integration testing sequences

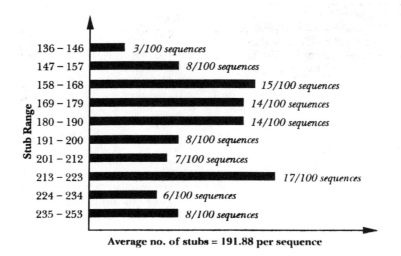

Average no. of stubs = 191.88 per sequence

of 7 states and 94 transitions. The number of state transition sequences is 881. This implies that 881 test cases and test data suites should be generated and exercised. Without tool support, a tester would have to spend a lot of time to prepare the test cases, and test data suites, and execute the tests.

However, even with tool support, the tester still had to specify the expected result for each of the 881 test cases. OO systems usually involve many classes. Class libraries containing thousands or even tens of thousands of classes are not uncommon. Therefore, tools to further reduce the tester's effort are needed.

Objects interact through message passing, resulting in concurrent state transitions in several state machines. The combined state space of these state machines can be unmanageably large. This makes test case generation and test execution extremely difficult, time-consuming, and costly. Our experience in testing interacting object state behavior is still very limited. We had not tried large examples due to the complexity and lack of tool support. (The tool is under development.) The good news is that it seems reasonable to test only those events that cause concurrent state transitions, because the nonconcurrent state transitions have been tested in AOSD testing prior to COSD testing of object interactions.

We wish to point out that not all classes of an OO system require state behavior testing. Our experience indicates that, depending on the nature of the application, only a certain percentage of classes have state-dependent behaviors. We also felt that not all of the 881 transition sequences generated by the tool must be tested to ensure quality. For example, some of the sequences are subsequences of other sequences. There are other application-dependent reasons to exclude some of the sequences. We need better methods to handle the complexity of state behavior testing of real application programs.

One effective way to reduce state behavior testing effort is constraint-directed testing. A constraint specifies that under certain conditions (i.e., combination of object states) something good must eventually happen, or something bad must never happen. Thus, state behavior testing can focus on ensuring that such constraints are not violated. Effort is reduced by not testing the other transition sequences.

Conclusions and Future Directions

We have described some major OO testing problems and the OOTM environment. We also reported our experience in the development and application of the OOTM environment. Although the system is still in its prototyping stage, the tools have been ported to some companies and several other companies have expressed interest in experimenting with the system.

We are currently working on testing and regression testing of dynamic binding features. We found that the OO test model is useful for solving these problems. Another effort is the design and implementation of an OO database to support the environment.

Future research and development will focus on improving the robustness of the existing tools; enhancing the OOTM environment, including black-box testing, distributed real-time embedded software system testing, and interoperability; conducting controlled experiments on large OO programs to quantitatively assess the effectiveness of the results; and incrementally commercializing the environment for technology transfer.

Acknowledgments
The authors wish to thank Lan Chou, Premal Desai, Wen Feng, Kyung Ook Lee, and Hwan Wook Sohn for collecting the statistics of the InterViews library. The material presented in this article is based on work supported by the Texas Advanced Technology Program (Grant No. 003656-097), the Electronic Telecommunications Research Institute (ETRI) of Korea, Fujitsu Network Transmission Systems, Inc., Hewlett-Packard Company, IBM, and SECT. ▣

References
1. Beizer, B. *Software Testing Techniques*, 2d ed., Van Nostrand Reinhold, NY 1990.
2. Binder, R. Object-oriented software testing. *Commun. ACM 37*, 9 (Sept. 1994), 28–29.
3. Doong, R. and Frankl, P. The ASTOOT approach to testing object-oriented programs. *ACM Trans. Softw. Eng. and Methodology 3*, 2 (Apr. 1994), 101–130.
4. Fayad, M.E. Object-oriented software engineering: Problems and perspectives. Ph.D dissertation, University of Minnesota, June 1994.
5. Haffman, D. and Fang, X. Testing the C set++ collection class library. In *Proceedings of CASCON'94*, (Toronto, Canada, Oct. 31–Nov. 3, 1994), 314–322.
6. Harel, D. On visual formalisms. *Commun. ACM 31*, 5 (May 1988), 514–531.
7. Harrold, M.J., McGregor, J.D., and Fitzpatrick, K.J. Incremental testing of object-oriented class structure. In *Proceedings of the Fourteenth International Conference on Software Engineering* (1992), pp. 68–80.
8. Jorgensen, P. and Erickson, C. Object-oriented integration testing. *Commun. ACM 37*, 9 (Sept. 1994), 30–38.
9. Kirani, S. and Tsai, W.T. Method sequence specification and verification of classes. *J. Object-Oriented Programming* (Oct. 1994), 28–38.
10. Kung, D., Gao, J., Hsia, P., Lin0, J., and Toyoshima, Y. Design recovery for software testing of object-oriented programs. In *Proceedings of the Working Conference on Reverse Engineering* (Baltimore, MD, May 21–23, 1993), pp. 202–211.
11. Kung, D., Suchak, N., Hsia, P., Toyoshima, Y., and Chen, C. On object state testing. In *Proceedings of COMPSAC'94*, IEEE Computer Society Press, 1994.
12. Kung, D., Gao, J., Hsia, P., Wen, F., Toyoshima, Y., and Chen, C. Change impact identification in object-oriented software maintenance. In *Proceedings of the International Conference on Software Maintenance* (1994), pp. 202–211.
13. Kung, D., Gao, J., Hsia, P., Toyoshima, Y., and Chen, C. A test strategy for object-oriented systems. *In Proceedings of Computer Software and Applications Conference* (Dallas, Texas, August 9–11, 1995).
14. Lejter, M., Meyers, S., and Reiss, S.P. Support for maintaining object-oriented programs. *IEEE Trans. Softw. Eng. 18*, 12 (Dec. 1992), 1045–1052.
15. Perry, D.E.. and Kaiser, G.E. Adequate testing and object-oriented programming. *J. Object-Oriented Programming 2* (Jan.–Feb. 1990), 13–19.

16. Smith, M.D. and Robson, D.J. Object-oriented programming: The problems of validation. In *Proceedings of the IEEE Conference on Software Maintenance* (1990), 272–281.
17. Turner, C.D. and Robson, D.J. The state-based testing of object-oriented programs. In *Proceedings of the IEEE Conference on Software Maintenance* (1993), pp. 302–310.
18. Wilde, N. and Huitt, R. Maintenance support for object-oriented programs. *IEEE Trans. Softw. Eng. 18*, 12 (Dec. 1992), 1038–1044.

About the Authors:

DAVID KUNG is an associate professor in the Department of Computer Science and Engineering at the University of Texas at Arlington. Current research interests include object-oriented software testing and conceptual modeling. **Author's Present Address:** Department of Computer Science and Engineering, The University of Texas at Arlington, P.O. Box 19015, Arlington, TX 76019. email: kung@homer.uta.edu

PEI HSIA is the director of the Software Engineering Center for Telecommunicatons at the University of Texas at Arlington, and is currently is serving as a visiting professor at the U.S. Military Academy at West Point. Current research interests include functional testing of object-oriented programs. **Author's Present Address:** Department of EE and CS, USMA, West Point, NY 10996. email: hsia@eecs1.eecs.usma.edu

JERRY ZEYU GAO is a member of the technical staff at Fujitsu Network Transmission Systems, Inc. Current research interests include methodologies and supporting tools for object-oriented software testing and maintenance, software testing techniques, and requirements engineering.

YASUFUMI TOYOSHIMA is a vice president of Fujitsu Network Transmission Systems. Current research interests include software engineering for object-oriented technology and software process management.

CHRIS CHEN is a senior manager of Fujitsu Network Transmission Systems. Current research interests include software engineering methods and object-oriented technology and test techniques.

Authors' Present Address: Fujitsu Network Transmission Systems, Inc., 2540 N. First St. Suite 201, San Jose, CA 95131.

YOUNG-SI KIM is a principal member of engineering staff working in the Switching Technology Division of the Electronics and Telecommunications Research Institute. Current research interests are switching system software, distributed real-time system software, software testing, and object-oriented software development. email: yskim@tdx.etri.re.kr

YOUNG-KEE SONG is a principal member of the engineering staff working in the Switching Technology Division of the Electronics and Telecommunications Research Institute. Current research interests include software development environments, CASE tools, software testing, and object-oriented software development.

Authors' Present Address: Switching Technology Division, ETRI, P.O. Box 106, Yousong, Taejon, Korea. email: yksong@tdx.etri.re.kr

The ASTOOT Approach to Testing
Object-Oriented Programs

ROONG-KO DOONG
Sun Microsystems Laboratories
and
PHYLLIS G. FRANKL
Polytechnic University

This article describes a new approach to the unit testing of object-oriented programs, a set of tools based on this approach, and two case studies. In this approach, each test case consists of a tuple of sequences of messages, along with tags indicating whether these sequences should put objects of the class under test into equivalent states and/or return objects that are in equivalent states. Tests are executed by sending the sequences to objects of the class under test, then invoking a user-supplied equivalence-checking mechanism. This approach allows for substantial automation of many aspects of testing, including test case generation, test driver generation, test execution, and test checking. Experimental prototypes of tools for test generation and test execution are described. The test generation tool requires the availability of an algebraic specification of the abstract data type being tested, but the test execution tool can be used when no formal specification is available. Using the test execution tools, case studies involving execution of tens of thousands of test cases, with various sequence lengths, parameters, and combinations of operations were performed. The relationships among likelihood of detecting an error and sequence length, range of parameters, and relative frequency of various operations were investigated for priority queue and sorted-list implementations having subtle errors. In each case, long sequences tended to be more likely to detect the error, provided that the range of parameters was sufficiently large and likelihood of detecting an error tended to increase up to a threshold value as the parameter range increased.

Categories and Subject Descriptors: D.2.1 [**Software Engineering**]: Requirements/Specifications—*languages*; D.2.5 [**Software Engineering**]: Testing and Debugging—*symbolic execution; test data generators*; D.3.2 [**Programming Languages**]: Language Classifications—*object-oriented languages*; D.3.3 [**Programming Languages**]: Language Constructs and Features—*abstract data types*

General Terms: Algorithms, Experimentation, Languages, Reliability

Additional Key Words and Phrases: Abstract data types, algebraic specification, object-oriented programming, software testing

This research was supported in part by NSF grants CCR-8810287 and CCR-9003006 and by the New York State Science and Technology Foundation, and was performed while the first author was at Polytechnic University.
Authors' addresses: R. K. Doong, Sun Microsystems Laboratories, 2550 Garcia Avenue, Mountainview, CA 94043; email: roongko@arkesden.eng.sun.com; P. G. Frankl, Department of Computer Science, Polytechnic University, 6 Metrotech Center, Brooklyn, NY 11201; email: phyllis@morph.poly.edu.

Permission to copy without fee all or part of this material is granted provided that the copies are not made or distributed for direct commercial advantage, the ACM copyright notice and the title of the publication and its date appear, and notice is given that copying is by permission of the Association for Computing Machinery. To copy otherwise, or to republish, requires a fee and/or specific permission.
© 1994 ACM 1049–331X/94/0400–0101 $03.50

"The ASTOOT Approach to Testing Object-Oriented Programs" by R.-K. Doong and P.G. Frankl from *ACM Trans. Software Eng. and Methodology,* Vol. 3, No. 2, Apr. 1994, pp. 101–130.
Copyright © Association for Computing Machinery, Inc. 1994. Reprinted by permission.

1. INTRODUCTION

Object-oriented programming, based on the concepts of data abstraction, inheritance, and dynamic binding, is becoming an increasingly popular software development methodology. Much research has been done on developing object-oriented analysis and design techniques, developing object-oriented programming languages, and exploring how the methodology changes the software development process. Yet relatively little research has addressed the question of how object-oriented programs should be tested.

We have developed a new approach to unit testing object-oriented programs, which is based on the ideas that the natural units to test are classes, and that in testing classes, one should focus on the question of whether a sequence of messages puts an object of the class under test into the "correct" state. In this approach, roughly speaking, each test case consists of a pair of sequences of messages, along with a tag indicating whether these sequences should result in objects that are in the same "abstract state." A test case is executed by sending each sequence of messages to an object of the class under test, invoking a user-supplied equivalence-checking routine to check whether the objects are in the same abstract state, then comparing the result of this check to the tag. This testing scheme has several nice properties:

- Expected results of tests are included in test cases in a concise format (one Boolean) which is independent of the class being tested. This facilitates automatic checking of test results.
- Test drivers for different classes are very similar to one another, hence can be automatically generated from class interfaces.
- If an algebraic specification for the class under test is available, term rewriting can be used to generate test cases automatically. If no algebraic specification is available, a person can develop test cases by reasoning about an informal specification.

This approach is embodied in the prototype testing system ASTOOT, **A Set of Tools for Object-Oriented Testing**, which includes an interactive specification-based test case generation tool and a tool that automatically generates test drivers. For any class C, ASTOOT can automatically generate a test driver, which in turn automatically executes test cases and checks their results. Additionally, when an algebraic specification for C is available, ASTOOT can partially automate test generation. Thus the system allows for substantial automation of the entire testing process.

The current version of ASTOOT is targeted to testing programs written in Eiffel.[TM] Throughout this article we assume that the classes being tested are written in Eiffel. However, the underlying ideas and tools can be adapted relatively easily to other object-oriented languages.

In Section 2, we review relevant background material on software testing, object-oriented programming, and algebraic specification of abstract data types. Section 3 describes the ideas underlying ASTOOT—correctness of a

---

[TM] Eiffel is a trademark of the Nonprofit International Consortium for Eiffel (Nice).

class that implements an abstract data type, test case format, and test result checking. The tools are described in Section 4. Section 5 describes two case studies performed in order to gain more insight into how to generate good test cases. We compare our approach to related work in Section 6 and note directions for future work in Section 7.

2. BACKGROUND

2.1 Background on Software Testing

Testing is one of the most time-consuming parts of the software development process. Increased automation of the testing process could lead to significant saving of time, thus allowing for more thorough testing. Three aspects of the testing process which could potentially be at least partially automated are test data generation, test execution, and test checking. Our approach to testing object-oriented programs involves all three of these areas.

Perhaps the most obvious opportunity for partially automating testing is the generation of test cases. In order to automate test generation it is necessary to analyze some formal object, such as source code or a formal specification. Most research on automated test generation has involved *program-based* or *white-box* techniques, i.e., techniques based on analysis of the source code of the program being tested. However, white-box testing suffers from certain limitations, such as its inability to generate test cases intended to exercise aspects of the specification that have inadvertently been omitted from the program. *Black-box* or *specification-based* techniques, based on analysis of the program's specification, overcome some of these limitations, but cannot be automated unless some kind of formal specification is available. Manual black-box test generation techniques, based on informal specifications, are widely used in practice. The testing scheme described in this article is a black-box approach which is automatable when a formal algebraic specification is available and which can be applied manually, otherwise.

Another area for potential automation is in the construction of test drivers. Many testing methods can be applied to individual subprograms. When the program unit being tested is a whole program, the inputs and outputs are usually a set of files. When the unit being tested is a procedure or function the inputs and outputs may include values of parameters and of global variables, as well as values read from and written to files. In order to test a procedure, it is necessary to build a *driver* program which initializes global variables and actual parameters to the appropriate values, calls the procedure, then outputs final values of relevant globals and parameters. It can be quite cumbersome to initialize the inputs and check the values of the outputs. It is particularly unwieldy if, as is often the case in object-oriented programming, the parameters have complicated types. The model described below for testing object-oriented programs circumvents this problem.

Another problem which arises in testing software is the *oracle problem*—after running a program P on a test case, it is necessary to check whether the result agrees with the specification of P. This is often a nontrivial problem, for example, if there is a great deal of output, or if it is difficult to calculate the correct value [Weyuker 1982]. Our testing method uses a novel approach which allows the correctness of test cases to be checked automatically by the test execution system.

2.2 Overview of Object-Oriented Programming

Object-oriented languages support *abstract data type*, *inheritance*, and *dynamic binding*. An abstract data type is an entity that encapsulates data and the operations for manipulating that data. In object-oriented programming, the programmer writes *class* definitions, which are implementations of abstract data types. An *object* is an instance of a class; it can be created dynamically by the instantiation operation, often called "new" or "create." A language supports *inheritance* if classes are organized into a directed acyclic graph in which definitions are shared, reflecting common behavior of objects of related classes.

A class consists of an *interface* which lists the operations that can be performed on objects of that class and a *body* which implements those operations. The state of an object is stored in *instance variables* (sometimes called *attributes*), which are static variables, local to the object. A class's operations are sometimes called *methods*.

In object-oriented programs, computation is performed by "sending *messages*" to objects. A message invokes one of the object's methods, perhaps with some arguments. The invoked method may then modify the state of its object and/or send messages to other objects. When a method completes execution, it returns control (and in some cases returns a result) to the sender of the message.

The inheritance mechanism of object-oriented languages facilitates the development of new classes which share some aspects of the behavior of old ones. A descendent (subclass) C_d of a class C inherits the instance variables and methods of C. C_d may extend the behavior of C by adding additional instance variables and methods, and/or specialize C by redefining some of C's methods to provide alternative implementations.

A dynamic binding mechanism is used to associate methods with objects. In strongly typed object-oriented languages, it is legal to assign an object of class C_d to a variable of class C, but not vice versa. After doing so, a message sent to this object will invoke the method associated with class C_d. For example, consider a class POLYGON with subclasses TRIANGLE and SQUARE, each of which redefines POLYGON's perimeter method. Assigning an object of class SQUARE to a variable of class POLYGON, then sending the perimeter message will invoke SQUARE's perimeter method. This allows construction of *polymorphic* data types.

Some examples of object-oriented languages include Smalltalk, C++, and Eiffel [Goldberg and Robson 1983; Meyer 1988; Stroustrup 1991]. While Ada and Modula-2 are not, strictly speaking, object-oriented languages, they do provide support for data abstraction; thus, some of the ideas discussed here are relevant to them. See Meyer [1988] for an overview of the object-oriented approach.

2.3 Algebraic Specification of Abstract Data Types

Before we can talk about how to test a class C, we must have some concept of what it means for C to be correct. Thus, we must have some means, formal or informal, of specifying the entity that C is intended to implement and of stating the conditions under which the implementation conforms to the specification. In the case where C is intended to implement an abstract data type, algebraic specifications provide a formal means of doing this.

An algebraic specification has a syntactic part and a semantic part. The syntactic part consists of function names and their signatures (the types they take as input and produce as output). In an algebraic specification of type T, functions which return values of types other than T are called *observers*, because they provide the only ways for us to query the contents of T. Functions which return values of type T are called *constructors* or *transformers*.[1] The distinction between constructors and transformers is clarified below.

The semantic part of the specification consists of a list of axioms describing the relation among the functions. Some specification techniques allow for a list of preconditions describing the domains of the functions, while others allow functions to return error values indicating that a function has been applied to an element outside of its domain.

Term rewriting [Knuth and Bendix 1970] has been used to define a formal semantics for algebraic specifications [Goguen and Winkler 1988; Musser 1980]. Two sequences S_1 and S_2 of operations of ADT T are *equivalent* if we can use the axioms as rewrite rules to transform S_1 to S_2.[2] A specification can then be modeled by a *heterogeneous word algebra*, in which the elements are equivalence classes of sequences of operations.

For a specification $\mathscr{S}$ to be useful, it must be *consistent* and *sufficiently complete* [Guttag and Horning 1978]. A consistent specification must not contain contradictory axioms, i.e., no contradiction should be derivable from any operation sequences of the specification. Let W be the set containing all the operation sequences consisting of constructors or transformers of $\mathscr{S}$. $\mathscr{S}$ is sufficiently complete, if for every sequence w in W, the result of applying each observer of $\mathscr{S}$ to w is defined. Discussion of how to construct useful algebraic specifications can be found in Antoy [1989] and Guttag [1977; 1980].

Most algebraic specification languages use a functional notation. For convenience, we have designed a specification language, LOBAS, whose syntax is similar to OO programming language syntax [Doong 1993]. The syntactic part of a LOBAS specification includes an *export* section which lists operations available to the users of the ADT. In LOBAS, the designer of a

---

[1] Transformers are called *extensions* in Guttag and Horning [1978].
[2] This definition follows the assumption of Goguen et al. [1978]; Guttag et al. [1978] makes the opposite assumption, i.e., that two sequences *may* be assumed to be the equivalent unless provably inequivalent.

specification has to classify the operations into three categories—constructors, transformers, and observers. This classification process helps the designer produce a sufficiently complete specification and facilitates the test generation scheme described in Section 4.2. An additional advantage of this notation is pointed out in Section 3.1.

Algebraic specifications of a priority queue in LOBAS and in functional notation are shown in Figure 1(a) and Figure 1(b). Sequences of operations (separated by dots) are to be read left to right, so that, for example, create.add(5).add(3) represents the result of creating a priority queue, then adding items 5 and 3 to it, in that order. According to the specification, create.add(5).add(3).delete is equivalent to create.add(3) because we can apply axiom 6 twice to give

$$\text{create.add}(5).\underline{\text{add}(3).\text{delete}}$$

$$\Rightarrow \quad \text{create.}\underline{\text{add}(5).\text{delete}}.\text{add}(3)$$

$$\Rightarrow \quad \text{create.add}(3).$$

The difference between constructors and transformers becomes clear at this point. After the simplification is complete, only constructors are left in the operation sequence. The role of transformers is to transform a sequence of constructors into another sequence of constructors.

Note that the appearance of operation sequences in LOBAS bears a strong resemblance to *trace specifications* which describe data abstractions by specifying the legality, equivalence, and values of traces (operation sequences) [Bartussek and Parnas 1986; Hoffman and Snodgrass 1988; Hoffman and Strooper 1991]. Two advantages of trace specifications over LOBAS are their ability to specify functions (observers) with side effects and their ability to handle operation sequences with intermingled procedures and functions. However, the axioms of LOBAS (and other algebraic languages) facilitate automatic test case generation, as discussed in Section 4.2.

3. SELF-CHECKING TEST CASES

In this section we describe the main concepts that underlie ASTOOT. These include a notion of correctness for classes, a model of test cases and their execution, and a test-checking mechanism.

In one of the early articles on specification of data abstractions, Liskov and Zilles [1975] pointed out that it is possible to specify a data abstraction by specifying the intended input-output behavior for each of its operations individually, but doing so is usually cumbersome and may lead to overspecification of the underlying representation of the data. Instead, they and other [Goguen et al. 1978; Guttag 1977; Guttag et al. 1977] proposed algebraic specifications of abstract data types (ADTs), which define the intended behavior of an ADT by giving axioms describing the interaction of operations.

Similarly, it is possible to test a class by testing each of its methods individually, treating each as a function mapping some input space to some output space, selecting elements of that input space, and examining the outputs to see if they are correct. However, doing so shifts the focus of testing away from the essence of the data abstraction—the interaction among opera-

234

```
class Priority_Queue export                    type Priority_Queue
   create, largest, add, delete, empty, eqn     syntax
constructor                                        create: - > Priority_Queue;
   create;                                         add: Priority_Queue × Integer
   add (x: Integer)                                   - > Priority_Queue;
transformer                                        delete: Priority_Queue - > Priority_Queue;
   delete                                          empty: Priority_Queue - > Boolean;
observer                                           largest: Priority_Queue - > Integer;
   empty: Boolean;                                 eqn: Priority_Queue × Priority_Queue
   largest: Integer;                                  - > Boolean;
   eqn (B: Priority_Queue): Boolean            declare
var                                                A, B: Priority_Queue;
   A, B: Priority_Queue;                           x, y: Integer;
   x, y: Integer                              semantics
axiom                                              1: empty(create) - > true;
   1: create.empty - > true;                       2: empty(add(A,x)) - > false;
   2: A.add(x).empty - > false;                    3: largest(create) - > - ∞;
   3: create.largest - > - ∞;                      4: largest(add(A,x)) - >
   4: A.add(x).largest - >                             if x > largest(A) then x
      if x > A.largest then x                         else largest(A);
      else A.largest;                              5: delete(create) - > create;
   5: create.delete - > create;                    6: delete(add(A,x)) - >
   6: A.add(x).delete - >                              if x > largest(A) then A
      if x > A.largest then A                         else add(delete(A),x);
      else A.delete.add(x);                        7: eqn(A,B) - >
   7: A.eqn(B) - >                                     if empty(A) and empty(B) then true
      if A.empty and B.empty then true                else if (empty(A) and not empty(B)) or
      else if (A.empty and not B.empty) or                    (not empty(A) and empty(B))
              (not A.empty and B.empty)                   then false
      then false                                      else if largest(A) = largest (B)
      else if A.largest = B.largest                   then eqn(delete(A),delete(B))
      then A.delete.eqn(B.delete)                     else false
      else false                               end
end
```

| (a) Specification in LOBAS | (b) Specification in functional notation |

Fig. 1.   Specifications of the priority queue.

tions. Furthermore, testing each method individually necessitates the construction of complicated drivers and output-checking mechanisms. For example, a test case for the add operation in a priority queue would consist of a priority queue and an item, and the output would be another priority queue. Thus the driver would have to initialize the input priority queue, and checking the output would entail examining the output priority queue to see if it is the correct result. In contrast, our approach to testing classes focuses on the interaction of operations.

In this section, we restrict attention to classes intended to implement ADTs. We require that

(1) operations have no side effects on their parameters,

(2) functions (observers) have no side effects,

(3) functions (observers) can only appear as the last operation of a sequence, and

(4) when a sequence is passed as a parameter to an operation it must *not* contain any functions (observers).

The main reason for placing restrictions 1 and 2 is that we *cannot* specify these kinds of side effects by using either LOBAS or purely algebraic languages. The reason behind restriction 3 is that sequences that mix functions and procedures are not syntactically valid in LOBAS or other algebraic specification languages [Mclean 1984]. Restriction 4 makes it easier to generate test cases using ASTOOT. Note that restriction 4 does not hinder our ability to express test cases involving any parameters to an operation, since when function f has no side effects on its target object (the object to which the message is sent), the target object of a sequence $S.f$ will be observationally equivalent to the target object of S. Techniques for relaxing restrictions 2, 3, and 4 are discussed in Doong [1993].

3.1 Correctness of an ADT Implementation

Consider a class C, intended to implement abstract data type T. Each function in T corresponds to a method of C, and inputting a value of type T to a function corresponds to sending a message to an object of class C. In Eiffel, constructors and transformers are typically coded as procedures; rather than explicitly returning an object of class C, such a procedure "returns" a value by modifying the state of the object to which it has been applied. An observer can be coded as a function which explicitly returns an object of another class. We will refer to the object which a function or procedure message is sent as the *target object* and to the object returned as the *returned object*. For procedures, the target object and the returned object are the same (though typically the *value* of the target object will be changed by the procedure call). Notice that in addition to explicitly returning an object, a function also implicitly "returns" its target object. If the function is side effect free then the value of the target object will be unchanged by the function call.

The syntax of LOBAS, unlike the functional syntax of most algebraic specification languages, allows us to differentiate between the target and returned values. For example, in the sequence create.add(5).add(3).largest the final value of the target is a priority queue whose elements are 5 and 3, and the returned value is 5.

We will say that objects O_1 and O_2 of class C are *observationally equivalent* if and only if:

—C is a built in class, and O_1 and O_2 have identical values; or

—C is a user-defined class, and for any sequence S of operations of C ending in a function returning an object of class C', $O_1.S$ is *observationally equivalent* to $O_2.S$ as objects of class C'.

Thus, O_1 is observationally equivalent to O_2 if and only if it is impossible to distinguish O_1 from O_2 using the operations of C and related classes. Two observationally equivalent objects are in the same "abstract state," even though the details of their representations may be different. For example, consider a circular array implementation of a first-in-first-out (FIFO) queue. Two arrays containing the same elements in the same order would be observationally equivalent (as queues), even though the elements could occupy different portions of the underlying arrays.

We now define the notion of correctness that underlies our approach.

A class C is a *correct* implementation of ADT T, if there is a signature-preserving mapping from operations of T to those of C such that

—for any pair (S_1, S_2) of sequences of operations of T, S_1 is equivalent to S_2 if and only if the corresponding sequences of messages give rise to *observationally equivalent* returned objects.

In other words, there is a one-to-one correspondence between the "abstract states" of T and the "abstract states" of C, which preserves the transitions between abstract states. Note that, based on the definition of *returned object*, our definition of correctness demands that operation sequences consisting entirely of constructors and transformers give rise to observationally equivalent *target* objects and that operation sequences ending in observers return observationally equivalent objects.

Other notions of correctness, some corresponding to other specification methodologies, have also been investigated [Bartussek and Parnas 1986; Gannon et al. 1987; Goguen et al. 1978; Guttag et al. 1978]. Our definition, based on observational equivalence, is similar to that corresponding to trace specifications [Bartussek and Parnas 1986], but is based on the more limited algebraic specification methodology. It is a pragmatic and intuitively appealing one, which lends itself to a convenient testing strategy.

3.2 Test Case Format

This definition of correctness gives rise in a natural way to a framework for testing. If we had an infinite amount of time and a way to check whether two objects were observationally equivalent, we could exhaustively test class C as follows:

—Consider the set $\mathscr{U}$ consisting of all 3-tuples (S_1, S_2, tag), where S_1 and S_2 are sequences of messages, and *tag* is "equivalent" if S_1 is equivalent to S_2 according to the specification, and is "not equivalent," otherwise.
—For each element of $\mathscr{U}$, send message sequences S_1 and S_2 to objects O_1 and O_2 of C, respectively, then check whether the returned object of O_1 is observationally equivalent to the returned object of O_2.
—If all the observational equivalence checks agree with the tags, then the implementation is correct; otherwise it is incorrect.

Unfortunately, we have neither an infinite amount of time for testing, nor a fool-proof way of checking observational equivalence. Nonetheless, this scheme suggests an approach to testing. We demand that C and each class that is returned by a function of C include a method called EQN which approximates an observational equivalence checker, and we select elements of $\mathscr{U}$ as test cases. In addition to shifting the emphasis of testing from functionality of individual methods to the notion of state, this approach to testing facilitates automation of many aspects of the testing process.

Note that the elements of $\mathscr{U}$ can be viewed as "self-checking" test cases. That is, each test case includes information, in the form of the tag, describing the expected result of execution. Furthermore the format of this expected result (a single Boolean) is very concise and is independent of the particular class being tested and of the pair of sequences to be executed. This facilitates automated execution and checking of test cases. Of course, when generating such test cases, it is necessary to consider the specification of the ADT in order to derive the tags. This can either be done semiautomatically by manipulating a formal specification, as described in Section 4, or manually by reasoning about a formal or informal specification.

For example, consider a priority queue of integers, whose functions are described informally as follows:

create—creates an empty priority queue,

add—adds an integer to the priority queue,

delete—removes the largest element of the priority queue,

largest—returns the value of largest element of the priority queue, without modifying the contents of the priority queue, and

empty—determines whether the priority queue is empty.

By reasoning about this informal specification, a person can generate test cases such as,

(1) (create.add(5).add(3).delete, create.add(3), equivalent),

(2) (create.add(5).add(3).delete.largest, create.add(3).largest, equivalent),

(3) (create.add(5).add(3).delete, create.add(5), not-equivalent), and

(4) (create.add(5).add(3), create.add(3).add(5), equivalent).

Test case 1 says that creating an empty priority queue, adding 5 then 3, then applying delete should be the same as creating an empty priority queue and adding 3 to it. Test case 2 says that the objects returned by applying largest to those two priority queues should be equivalent. Test case 3 says that if we create an empty priority queue add 5 and 3, then delete, it should *not* be the same as if we create an empty priority queue and add 5 to it. Test case 4 says that a priority queue obtained by adding 5 then adding 3 should be observationally equivalent to one obtained by adding 3 then adding 5. Unlike the previous three test cases, this test case captures an aspect of the informal specification that is not expressed in the formal specification, and thus it cannot be derived from the formal specification by using term rewriting.[3] This indicates that, even when a formal specification that partially describes the intended semantics of an ADT is available, manual generation of additional test cases may be useful.

We refer to test cases consisting of a pair of sequences along with a tag as *restricted-format* test cases. More general test case formats which are useful for testing classes involving side effects and dynamic binding are introduced in Doong [1993].

3.3 The EQN Method

We now discuss the EQN operation. Ideally, the EQN operation in class C should check whether two objects O_1 and O_2 of class C are observationally

---

[3] If an axiom such as A.add(x).add(y) $\rightarrow$ A.add(y).add(x) were added to the specification, this aspect of the informal specification would be captured. However, the resulting specification would no longer satisfy the finite termination condition.

equivalent; that is, it should check whether any sequence of messages ending in an observer yields the same result when sent to O_1 as when sent to O_2. Since it is clearly impossible to send every such message sequence to the objects, in practice EQN will approximate a check for observational equivalence.

It is often quite easy to produce a recursive version of EQN from the specification of the ADT which C is intended to implement. For example, axiom 7 of Figure 1 specifies such an EQN function based on the priority queue specification. Note that this is actually only an approximation of true observational equivalence because it neglects the possible effects of "building up" the priority queues, then removing elements. Thus, it might say that two objects are equivalent when they are not.[4] Also, since EQN calls largest, and delete, an error in one of these operations may propagate to EQN, causing it to mask out the error. On the other hand, the error propagation can also help in error detection, as demonstrated in Section 5.1.

Another approach to developing the EQN function is to write it at the "implementation level." In this approach, EQN is based on detailed knowledge of how data is represented and manipulated in the class body. For example, knowing that a FIFO queue is represented as a linked list, one can traverse the two lists comparing the elements. In general, if sufficient attention is paid to the details of the representation, EQN can implement observational equivalence exactly. On the other hand, it is possible that the same misconceptions which lead to implementation errors in C's other methods may lead to errors in EQN. Furthermore, for some representations of some data structures, writing an implementation-level EQN operation may be extremely difficult and error prone, even when the other methods are relatively simple.

It is also sometimes possible to use a very coarse approximation of observational equivalence as the EQN function. For example, we might consider two FIFO queues to be equivalent if they have the same number of elements, or if they have the same front element. This version of EQN may consider two inequivalent objects to be equivalent. Naturally, using a coarser approximation of observational equivalence will lead to less accuracy in the test results.

Bernot et al. [1991] discuss a closely related problem and suggest that an "oracle hypothesis" be explicitly stated. In the context of our approach to testing, such a hypothesis would describe the conditions under which the implementation of EQN is equivalent to an actual check for observational equivalence.

4. THE TOOLS

ASTOOT is a set of tools based on the approach described in Section 3. The current prototype, which handles test cases in the restricted format, has

---

[4] For example consider an implementation which completely empties the priority queue whenever the total number of adds performed reaches a particular number $N > 2$. The recursive EQN would consider O1.create.add(1).add(2).delete equivalent to O2.create.add(1), but in fact, performing an additional $N - 2$ adds followed by $N - 2$ deletes on each object would leave O1 empty and leave O2 nonempty.

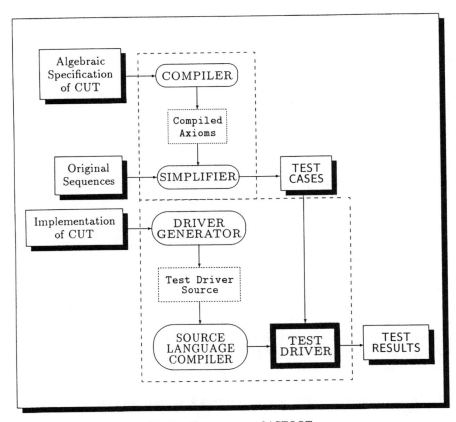

Fig. 2. Components of ASTOOT.

three components: the *driver generator*, the *compiler*, and the *simplifier*. The driver generator takes as input the interface specifications of the class under test (CUT) and of some related classes and outputs a test driver. This test driver, when executed, reads test cases, checks their syntax, executes them, and checks the results. The compiler and simplifier together form an interactive tool for semiautomatically generating test cases from an algebraic specification. Note that when no algebraic specification is available, the drivers produced by the driver generator can be used to execute test cases which have been derived by a person reasoning about an informal specification. The structure of ASTOOT is illustrated in Figure 2, and a screen dump of an ASTOOT session is shown Figure 3.

4.1 The Driver Generator

Our approach to testing leads to relatively simple test drivers, which operate by reading in test cases of the form (S_1, S_2, Tag), one at a time, checking that the sequences are syntactically valid, sending sequences S_1 and S_2 to objects O_1 and O_2 of CUT, comparing the returned objects of S_1 and S_2 with EQN, and checking whether the value returned by EQN agrees with Tag. On the other hand, drivers are complicated enough that writing them manually is a tedious and error-prone task. In particular, checking the syntactic validity of the operation sequences involves complicated parsing and type checking. For example, our driver for the priority queue class has over 400 lines of code (not counting inherited classes), most of which deals with checking the syntax of the operation sequences. Luckily, drivers for testing different classes are very similar to one another in structure. This has allowed us to write a tool, the *driver generator*, which automatically generates test drivers. The driver generator can be viewed as a special-purpose parser generator, which, based on the syntax described in the class interfaces, generates test drivers that parse test cases, as well as executing and checking them.

The driver generator, DG, operates in three phases. The first phase is to collect information about interfaces of the CUT, its ancestors, and all the classes which are parameter types or return types of CUT's operations. DG first checks whether each of these classes has an exported EQN operation.[5] (If, like Eiffel, the implementation language has the facility of selective export then we can let EQN be exported only to the test driver, so the integrity of the implementation can be preserved.) In the second phase, DG builds a test driver, which is a class in the implementation language. The current version of the driver generator is targeted to Eiffel 2.1, but the underlying ideas can be applied to other OO languages. In the third phase, DG compiles and executes the test driver with test cases supplied by the user.

4.2 Test Generation Tools

ASTOOT's test generation component has two parts, the compiler and the simplifier, both of which are based on an internal representation called an *ADT tree*. The compiler reads in a specification written in LOBAS and does some syntactic and semantic checking on the specification[6], then translates each axiom into a pair of ADT trees.

An ADT tree is a tree in which nodes represent operations along with their arguments. Each path from the root to a leaf of an ADT tree represents a possible state of the ADT. The branching of an ADT tree arises from axioms having *IF_THEN_ELSE* expressions on the right-hand side. Each edge of the ADT tree has a Boolean expression, called the *edge condition*, attached to it. The *path condition* of a path from the root to a leaf is the conjunction of all the edge conditions on that path; it indicates the conditions under which the operation sequence on that path is equivalent to the original sequence. The path conditions in a given tree are mutually exclusive. Figure 4 illustrates the ADT tree pair of Axiom 6 in Figure 1. For clarity, the edge conditions are

---

[5] For ASTOOT to access functions that are hidden in the implementation, the CUT should export these functions to the test driver generated by ASTOOT. In Eiffel this can be achieved by "selective export" to the test driver; in C++ this can be achieved by making the test driver a friend class of the CUT.

[6] Because the simplifier and the driver generator operate under the assumption that create is the instantiation operation, the compiler makes sure there is a constructor named create in the specification. Also, the simplifier will insist that the first operation of a sequence is the create operation.

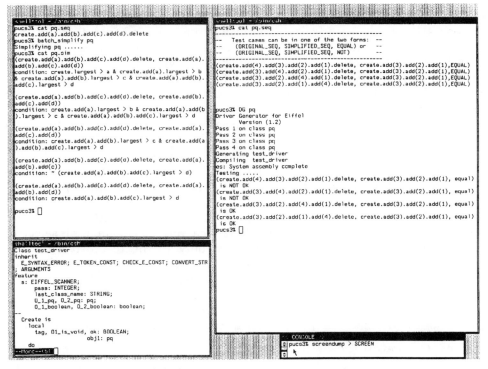

Fig. 3. Screen dump of an ASTOOT session. The upper left window shows the execution of the test generator in batch mode on a priority queue specification. The file pq.seq contains an initial sequence, supplied by the user. The test generator generates five test cases based on this initial sequence and writes them, along with the corresponding constraints on the free variables, to the file pq.sim. The constraint on each test case is obtained by conjoining the condition for that test case with the negations of the conditions on previous test cases. The upper right window shows the four test cases the user has developed by instantiating the free variables with values that satisfy the constraints. (The first of the generated test cases has an unsatisfiable constraint, so it is eliminated by the user). The driver generator is then invoked on an incorrect implementation of the priority queue (described in Section 5.1). It invokes Eiffel to compile the class under test, generates a test driver for the class, compiles it, then executes the given test cases. The first two test cases detect a bug, while the second two do not. The lower left window shows a small portion of the test driver which was automatically generated by the driver generator.

shown in rectangles in the figure; in the implementation, parameters of operations and the operands in the Boolean expressions are, themselves, represented by ADT trees.

The simplifier inputs an operation sequence, supplied by the user, translates it into an ADT tree, and applies the transformations to obtain equivalent operation sequences. The process of simplification is as follows:

(1) Search through the axioms to find an axiom with a left-hand side that matches some partial path of the ADT tree (ignoring the edge conditions).

(2) If an axiom is found, bind all the variables in the axiom to the proper arguments in the partial path of the ADT tree and simplify the argu-

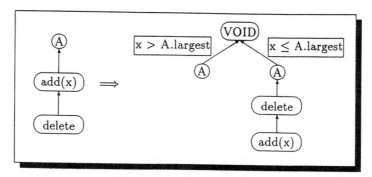

Fig. 4. Axiom 6 of the priority queue in ADT tree form.

ments; then replace the partial branch with the right-hand side of the axiom.

(3) Repeat steps 1 and 2 until there is no matching axiom.

In the worst case, the ADT tree arising from a sequence of ℓ operations may have m^ℓ paths, where m is the maximum number of branches in any axiom. To deal with this complexity, the current prototype can operate either in batch mode, which builds the entire equivalent ADT tree, or in interactive mode, which allows the user to selectively guide the construction of a particular path through the tree.

In order for the simplifier to work properly, the set of axioms in the specification must be *convergent*, i.e., the axioms must have the properties of *finite* and *unique termination* [Musser 1980]. The property of finite termination ensures the process of simplification will not go into infinite loop. The property of unique termination makes sure that any two terminating sequences starting from the same operation sequence have the same results, no matter what choice is made as to which axiom to rewrite or which axiom to apply first.

An example, involving batch-mode simplification of the sequence create.add(x).add(y).delete for the priority queue is shown in Figure 5. The simplifier will generate test cases of the form:

(create.add(x).add(y).delete, create.add(x). equivalent) with the path condition "$y > x$," and

(create.add(x).add(y).delete, create.add(y). equivalent) with the path condition "$y \leq x$."

Note that the simplifier also suggests test cases with not-equivalent tags. For instance, we can exchange the path conditions and the test cases from above to get the following test cases:

(create.add(x).add(y).delete, create.add(x), not-equivalent) with the constraint "$y \leq x$," and

(create.add(x).add(y).delete, create.add(y), not-equivalent) with the constraint "$y > x$."

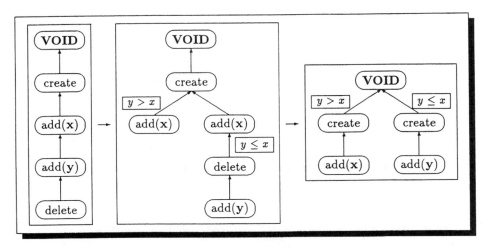

Fig. 5.   Simplification of the sequence create.add(x).add(y).delete.

For an ADT tree with n paths, the simplifier will generate n test cases that have equivalent tags. In principle, the simplifier could also generate $n(n - 1)$ test cases that have not-equivalent tags, where n is $O(m^{\ell})$, ℓ is the length of the original sequence, and m is the maximum number of branches in any axiom. Because there are too many such cases in an ADT tree, the current version of the simplifier leaves selection of such test cases to the user.

Note that the test cases generated by the simplifier contain symbolic values. To make them acceptable to the test driver, the user has to resolve the path conditions (constraints) and instantiate the symbolic values with the corresponding actual values. In principle, this could sometimes be done automatically by a constraint-solving system. In the current prototype, constraint solving is left to the user.

Two important questions remain: how should one select original sequences to input to the simplifier, and how should one select paths through the resulting ADT trees, in order to increase the likelihood of exposing errors?

5. CASE STUDIES

To gain insight into what kind of original sequences the person using the test generation tools should select and what kind of paths through the ADT tree should be generated in interactive mode, we performed two case studies, involving generation of many tests for a buggy priority queue implementation and for a buggy sorted-list implementation. We choose the priority queue ADT because we knew it to be sufficiently complicated to exhibit many interesting phenomena. We purposely introduced the bug, but believe that it is one which could easily occur in practice. The sorted list was based on a 2-3 tree, implemented for a graduate algorithms class. The bug was a slight variation on one which had actually occurred during program development.

We wished to gain insight into the following questions:

(ℓ) How does the length of the original sequence affect the likelihood that a test case will detect an error?

(p) How does the selection of parameters for operations in the original sequence affect the likelihood that a test case will detect an error?

(r) How does the ratio of adds to deletes in the original sequence affect the likelihood that a test case will detect an error?

We addressed these questions by randomly generating and executing several thousand test cases with various original sequence lengths, various ranges in which parameters could lie, and various frequencies of occurrence of different operations. For each original sequence we generated the corresponding simplified sequence, then executed the test case (*original sequence, simplified sequence, equivalent*). Note that it would have been extremely difficult to execute and check so many test cases, had it not been for ASTOOT's "self-checking" test case concept.

5.1 Testing A Buggy Implementation of Priority Queue

In this case study, the CUT was a priority queue, implemented using a *heap* with a bug in the delete operation.[7] Specifically, the *Downheap* (or *sift*) operation performed by delete has an *off-by-one* error which causes it to sometimes fail to swap with the bottom row. The erroneous delete code is shown in the Appendix.

In Figure 6, (a) is the heap resulting from sequence create.add(5). add(4).add(3).add(2).add(1); (b) is the heap resulting from applying a *correct* delete to (a); (c) is the resulting heap when the *incorrect* delete is applied to (a); note that 1 has failed to swap with 2 in the bottom row.

As discussed in Section 3.3, since EQN calls delete, the bug in delete is *propagated* to EQN. Even though the original sequence in test case (create.add(5).add(4).add(3).add(2).add(1).delete, create.add(4).add(3).add(2). add(1), equivalent) produces an incorrect heap (Figure 6(c)), EQN reports that the original sequence and the simplified sequence are equivalent due to the bug in delete. Thus, in this case, the error is *masked* by the propagation of the bug from delete to EQN.

On the other hand, consider the test case (create.add(4).add(3). add(2).add(1).delete, create.add(3).add(2).add(1), equivalent). The original sequence produces a heap with 3 in the root, 1 in the root's left child, and 2 in the root's right child. The simplified sequence produces a heap with 3 in the root, 2 in the root's left child, and 1 in the root's right child. These two heaps are both correct and should be observationally equivalent. However in checking executing EQN to check observational equivalence, we call the erroneous

---

[7]Recall that a heap is a complete binary tree in which each node is greater than or equal to its children; in the heap implementation of a priority queue, the delete operation is performed by removing the root, replacing it by the rightmost leaf, then "sifting" that element down to its proper position.

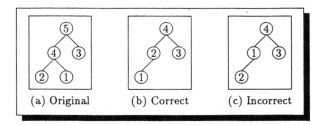

Fig. 6.   Illustration of the buggy priority queue.

delete routine. After the first call to delete the original heap has 2 in the root and 1 in the left child, while the (incorrect) "heap" resulting from the simplified sequence has 1 in the root and 2 in the left child. After one more call to largest, which compares the roots, EQN reports that these two sequences are *not* equivalent, so the bug is detected. Thus, in this case, propagation of the error to EQN helps in error detection.

In order to carry out these case studies, we needed to generate tens of thousands of test cases. In principle, we could have done this using the ASTOOT test case generator by *randomly* generating original sequences with symbolic values as parameters, and sending each original sequence to the simplifier to generate test cases. This would give $O(2^\ell)$ test cases for each original sequence with ℓ operations. Each test case would have symbolic values constrained by the path condition of the corresponding path. To be realistic, we would have to *randomly* choose some test cases and would have to *randomly* instantiate the symbolic values of each test case with actual values that satisfy the constraint of that test case either manually or with the aid of a constraint solver.

Note that the number of test cases needed for these experiments is several orders of magnitude larger than the number of test cases one would typically use in practice to test an implementation of this size. In order to generate this huge number of test cases efficiently and to do a broad range of testing with the three variables, ℓ, p, and r of a test set R, we used a C program to randomly generate test cases with actual values of those three variables, rather than using the ASTOOT test generator. This C program consists of three modules. The first module generates original sequences one at a time according to the three parameters of R, which are

ℓ—the number of operations (excluding create) in an original sequence,

p—the parameter to add is an integer in the range $[1 \ldots p]$, and

r—the ratio of adds to deletes appearing in the original sequences.

Operations of an original sequence are read in by the second module one at a time and applied to a priority queue that is implemented by a list. The third module inspects the contents of the list, generates a simplified sequence, and outputs an appropriate test case. Note that the simplified sequences are the same as if they were generated the test case generator of ASTOOT and instantiated with real values that satisfy the constraints.

246

For each test set we generated 1000 test cases. The average number of adds in simplified sequences is approximately

$$\begin{cases} \dfrac{\ell(r-1)}{r+1} & \text{if } r \geq 1 \\ 0 & 0 \leq r < 1. \end{cases}$$

Results of Priority Queue Case Study

The percentages of test cases that expose the bug in each test set are shown in Figure 7. Inspection of these graphs shows the following:

(ℓ) For large values of p, the parameter range, long original sequences are better than short ones. However, if the parameter range is too small, longer original sequences may do worse than shorter ones. In fact, the results of test sets $R_{(100, 10, 3)}$, $R_{(100, 10, 6)}$, and $R_{(100, 10, 9)}$ are the worst in $r = 3$, $r = 6$, and $r = 9$ respectively, despite the fact that they have long original sequences.

(p) As the parameter range p increases, test cases tend to get better. However, in each case there appears to be a threshold above which the error detection probability levels off.

(r) Likelihood of exposing an error depends somewhat on r.

In this buggy implementation, failure only occurred when it was necessary to swap with the rightmost element in the bottom row of the heap. Apparently, the long sequences were potentially more likely to cause the object to enter such a state, either during application of the original or simplified sequences, or through propogation of the error to the EQN operation. However, simply using a long sequence, without regard to the parameters chosen could lead to objects that never get into these "interesting" states. If the range of parameter values is too small, there will be many duplicates in the heap, so when an item is deleted, it is less likely that the sifted item will be *strictly* smaller than all of the elements it is compared to; thus it is less likely that it was supposed to swap with the bottom row.

5.2 Testing a Buggy Implementation of Sorted List

The second case used an abstract data type, *sorted list of integer*, with six operations, create, add, delete, find, nb_elements, and eqn. The interfaces, preconditions, and informal specification of the sorted list are shown in Figure 8. The EQN operation compared the lengths of the lists, then compared them element by element. Note that we did not use any formal specification for this sorted list. The test cases were generated by using a C program similar to the one in the case study of priority queue.

The sorted list was implemented using a *2-3 tree* (a special case of *B-tree*). The implementation has approximately 1000 lines of Eiffel 2.1 code, and the buggy version was produced by deleting one particular line from the correct

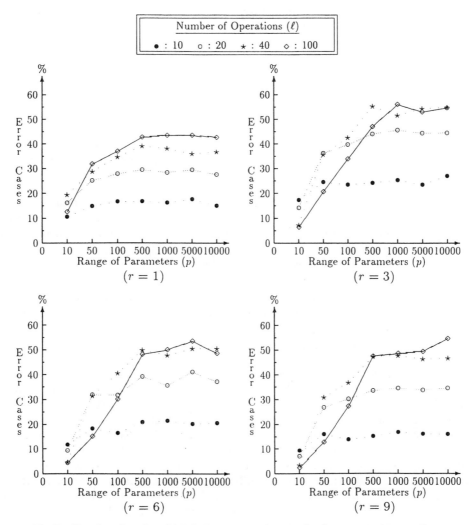

Fig. 7. Results of testing the priority queue using randomly generated test suites.

version of implementation. The absence of this statement affects the state of the 2-3 tree only when the following situation occurs:

(1) A node ((θ) in Figure 9(a)) has three children, such that the first child (α) has three children, and both the second child (β) and the third child (γ) have two children.

(2) One of of γ's children is then deleted.

For example, after deleting 6 of γ from the 2-3 tree in Figure 9(a), the correct procedure is:

(1) copy 5 from β to γ,

(2) delete 5 from β,

```
-- Sorted list without duplicated elements
class SORTED_LIST export
    create, add, delete, nb_elements, find, eqn
constructor
    create;
        -- create an empty list
    add(x: INTEGER)
        -- If x is not in the list
        -- then add x to the list in the proper order
transformer
    delete(i: INTEGER)
        -- If 1 ≤ i ≤ nb_elements then
        -- delete the i-th element
observer
    nb_elements: INTEGER;
        -- Number of elements in the list
    find(i: INTEGER): INTEGER;
        -- Return value of the i-th element
        -- precondition: 1 ≤ i ≤ nb_elements
    eqn (other: SORTED_LIST): BOOLEAN
        -- Is other equivalent to the list?
end
```

Fig. 8. Specification of the sorted list.

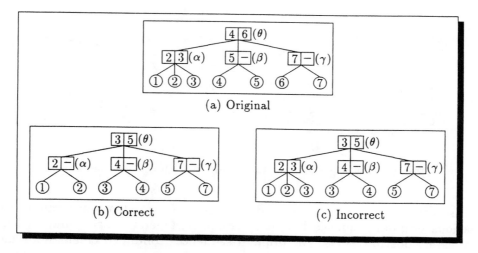

Fig. 9. Illustration of the buggy 2-3 tree.

(3) copy 3 from α to β, and

(4) delete 3 from α.

The line that is missing from the buggy version does step (4) in the above procedure. As illustrated in Figure 9, deleting 6 from (a) will get 2-3 tree (c).

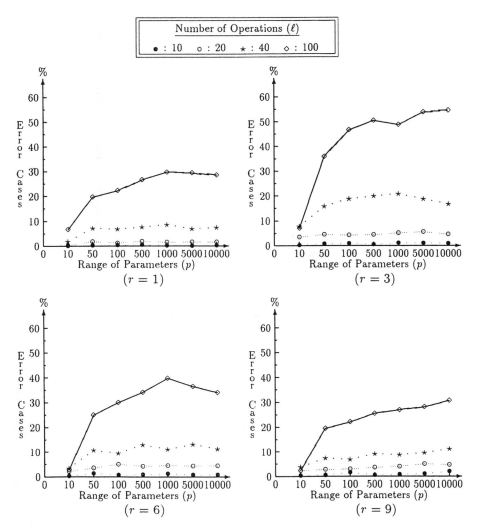

Fig. 10. Resulting of testing 2-3 tree using randomly generated test suites.

As in the priority queue case study, test sets were randomly generated with various original sequence lengths, various parameter ranges, and various ratios of adds to deletes. The original sequences contained create, add, and delete operations, and the simplified sequences contained only create and add operations.

Results of Sorted-List Case Study

The results, shown in Figure 10, exhibit similar phenomena to those discussed for the priority queue example. Since the number of elements in a sorted list is at most equal to the range of parameter values, only long sequences of operations with a large range of parameter values will produce

2-3 trees with a large number of leaves. The error in this program is such that failure only occurs when a deletion is performed on a 2-3 tree in a particular kind of state. Apparently, 2-3 trees with a large number of leaves are more likely to enter such a state.

5.3 Discussion of Case Studies

These case studies were intended to provide insight into the effects of such factors as the length of the original sequence, the relative frequencies of different operations in the original sequence, and the range of parameters to operations. In both of the case studies, the results showed that long original sequences do better than short ones, provided that the range of parameters is large enough to take advantage of the length. Additionally, different ratios of adds to deletes in the original sequence gave different results.

We certainly do not want to overgeneralize from these two small examples. However it seems safe to say that the *potential* that the relative values of the parameters would be important was apparent from the specification. In both of these cases, the specification involved *comparison* of items, using the *less than* operator. It is thus very reasonable to expect that different orderings of the parameters added would lead to different states, some of which might be more likely than others to expose the error. On the other hand, had we been testing a stack or queue ADT, we would not expect that the particular parameters would matter at all, and had we been testing a set ADT, we would expect the number of duplications to be important, but would not necessarily expect the relative order of parameters to be important (unless of course the set was implemented using an ADT based on comparison, such as a 2-3 tree).

Another phenomenon we noticed was that different ratios of adds to deletes led to different probabilities of error detection. When the ratio is one, it is unlikely that the objects will grow very large in the course of testing. In our examples, small objects were apparently not usually complicated enough to excite the failure.

We offer the following tentative guidelines as to how to generate test cases:

—Use (at least some) long original sequences, with a variety of relative frequencies of different constructors and transformers.

—If the specification has conditional axioms (with comparison operators) choose a variety of test cases for each original sequence, with various parameters chosen over a large range. Equivalently, choose a variety of different paths through the ADT tree arising from each original sequence.

While these guidelines might seem obvious, previous research has suggested limiting the complexity of sequences[8] [Choquet 1986; Gaudel and Marre

---

[8]Gaudel's group suggests using relatively simple sequences but including a "regularity hypothesis" asserting that if the simple sequences (such as those with length less than some n) give correct outputs, so will more complex sequences. Our results can be interpreted as saying that such regularity hypotheses do not hold for the ADTs examined for small n. Similar observations lead Gaudel et al. to introduce additional "uniformity hypotheses."

1988] and ignoring the semantics of the specification [Jalote 1989; Jalote and Caballero 1988].

6. RELATED WORK

We now compare our approach to related work on testing data abstractions. Previous systems generally fall into one of two categories—test execution tools and test generation tools. In contrast, our approach gives rise to both test generation and test execution tools.

6.1 Test Execution Tools

One of the first systems to address the question of testing data abstractions was DAISTS (Data Abstraction Implementation Specification and Test System) [Gannon et al. 1981]. DAISTS uses the axioms of an algebraic specification to provide an oracle for testing implementations of the ADT. A test case is a tuple of arguments to the left-hand side of an axiom. DAISTS executes a test case by giving it as input to the left-hand side and right-hand side of an axiom, then checks the output by invoking a user-supplied equality function (similar to our EQN).

Our test execution tool can be considered to be a generalization of DAISTS. For example, recall that Axiom 6 of the priority queue specification shown in Figure 1 says,

$$A.add(x).delete \rightarrow \textbf{if } x > A.largest \textbf{ then } A$$
$$\textbf{else } A.delete.add(x).$$

Executing the DAISTS test case $(A = create.add(1).add(2), x = 3)$ on this axiom is equivalent to our test case $(create.add(1).add(2).add(3).delete, create.add(1).add(2), equivalent)$, in which the second sequence is obtained by using axiom 6 to rewrite the first sequence.

However, DAISTS has no analog of our test cases of the form $(S_1, S_2,$ not-equivalent). This has significant ramifications—even exhaustive testing with DAISTS may fail to detect an error that results in two states being erroneously combined into a single state. As an extreme example, consider an erroneous implementation in which none of the operations changes the state of the object. The two sides of each axiom will return the same state on any input, and thus the error will not be detected.

A second distinction between DAISTS and our approach is that DAISTS requires the availability of a formal specification, while our test *execution* tools, i.e., the drivers produced by the driver generator, can be used when only an informal specification is available, as in our second case study.

Hoffman and Brealey [1989] and Hoffman and Strooper [1991] have developed several test execution tools for abstract data types, based on trace specifications [Bartussek and Parnas 1986]. Their most recent system, *Protest*, consists of two subsystems:

(1) *Protest / 1* tests C implementation using test cases containing the expected output.
(2) *Protest / 2* compares the behavior of a C implementation to that of a user-supplied oracle written in Prolog.

A test case of Protest/1 is a 5-tuple (*trace*, *expexc*, *actual*, *expval*, *type*) where *trace* is a sequence of operations which puts the ADT into some state; *expexc* is the exception raised by the trace; *actual* is an observer; *expval* is the expected value of applying the observer to that state; and *type* is the data type of *actual* and *expval*. In Protest/2 the values *expexc* and *expval* are generated by a Prolog oracle written by the user.

Protest, which is a program written in Prolog, executes test cases by calling the operations in the implementation under test through an interface supplied by the user. For each operation, the interface defines a Prolog predicate which calls the corresponding C function in the implementation. The user also needs to write functions that can be called to construct objects of user-defined classes to be passed as parameters to the operations in the implementation. Like ASTOOT and DAISTS, Protest uses functions supplied by the user to check the equivalence between objects of corresponding ADTs. But, unlike ASTOOT and DAISTS, which use the specification under test to generate expected outputs, Protest/2 uses Prolog oracle to produce expected outputs. This oracle is another program that needs to be tested on its own.

Another distinction between this approach and ours is that by using the EQN function to check outputs, in effect, we combine many Protest test cases into a single test case. On the other hand, Protest's handling of exceptions is certainly an important idea, which we would like to try to incorporate into future versions of ASTOOT.

Antoy and Hamlet [1992] have proposed a system that compares a class implementation to a more abstract representation which is based on term rewriting and is derived directly from the specification. The user supplies an explicit representation function mapping the concrete representation to the abstract representation. The code is instrumented to check that diagrams corresponding to each method commute, i.e., that applying the representation function then the abstract analog of the method gives rise to an abstract state that is equivalent to the one obtained by applying the method then applying the representation function. Such a system would, in some cases, give more accurate checks for correctness than would our approach of using an *approximation* of observational equivalence (the EQN function) to compare concrete representations. However, it imposes on the programmer the highly nontrivial task of writing a correct representation function.

6.2 Test Case Generation

Two previous approaches to generating test cases from algebraic specifications have been reported. Gaudel's research group [Bernot et al. 1991; Choquet 1986; Gaudel and Marre 1988] has developed a general theory of testing based on *testing contexts*, which are triples consisting of a set of hypotheses about the program, a set of test data, and an oracle. This approach has the nice property that if it can be established that the hypotheses hold, and if the test set exposes no errors, then the program is guaranteed to be correct. (But of course, establishing that the hypotheses is a nontrivial task, involving analysis of the program text). Our approach provides test data and oracles; furthermore, the oracles appear in a simple and uniform format. An interesting direction for future research would be to extend our approach to include hypotheses, perhaps by deriving conditions under which one sequence pair can be used to represent a class of sequence pairs and conditions under which one instantiation of parameters can be used to represent a class of instantiations.

Gaudel's group has also built a tool for testing data abstractions based on the theory of testing contexts. The tool inputs a specification written in a dialect of Prolog, and, based on some definition of the complexity of sequences, uses a Prolog interpreter to generate sequences of operations of given complexities, sometimes subject to additional constraints. This approach might provide a useful means to generate interesting original sequences for our simplifier.

Jalote [1989] and Jalote and Caballero [1988] suggest that effective test cases can be generated from the syntactic part of an algebraic specification, without reference to the semantics. Experience with our tools indicates that in fact, it is very important to consider the semantic part as well, since different instantiations of arguments in a sequence, corresponding to different paths through the ADT tree, can lead to profoundly different abstract states of the specification. Thus, it is necessary to select many different paths through the ADT tree arising from a given original sequence, or, equivalently, to choose values of parameters that exhibit different relationships to one another. This phenomenon was demonstrated in our case study of priority queue, where failure only occurred when it was necessary to swap with the bottom row of the heap.

7. CONCLUSION

We have described a new approach to testing classes which places emphasis on the fact that classes are implementations of data abstractions, a set of tools based on this approach, and two case studies. In this approach, each test case consists of a tuple of sequences of messages, along with tags indicating whether these sequences should put objects of the class under test into equivalent states and/or return objects which are in equivalent states. A test case in the restricted format consists of a single pair of sequences with a tag indicating whether the two objects resulting from application of these sequences should be observationally equivalent. Tests are executed by sending the sequences to objects of the class under test, then invoking a user-supplied equivalence-checking mechanism. This approach allows for substantial automation of many aspects of testing, including test case generation, test driver generation, test execution, and test checking.

ASTOOT is a set of tools based on this approach. ASTOOT consists of a tool which automatically generates test drivers from class interface specifications and a tool which semiautomatically generates test cases from an algebraic specification of the class under test. The drivers generated by ASTOOT's driver generator automatically execute and check test cases which have been supplied either by the test generator or by manual generation. Consequently ASTOOT allows for substantial automation of the entire testing process.

We performed two case studies, one using a buggy implementation of a priority queue, and the other using a buggy 2-3 tree implementation of a sorted list. These case studies provided some insight into the effects of such factors as the length of the original sequence, the relative frequencies of different operations in the original sequence, and the range of parameters to operations.

The approach and tools described in this article assume that the specification and implementation satisfy several restrictions which limit the kind of side-effects operations may have. Several extensions to the basic model, intended to make this testing scheme more applicable to "real-world" object-oriented programs, rather than just "pure" abstract data type implementations, are described elsewhere [Doong 1993; Doong and Frankl 1991]. These include a *general format* for test cases, which allows testing of classes whose methods have side effects, and a *dynamic format* that allows testing of virtual classes and some observations on the impact of inheritance on testing.

Directions for future research include the following:

—Interface the test generator with a constraint-solving system in order to decrease the need for manual intervention in test generation.

—Perform additional case studies, including exploration of more complicated ADTs and implementations with a larger variety of errors. While the particular errors in each of these case studies tended to be exposed when the number of duplicate elements in the sequence of insertions was low, it is easy to envision other errors for which the opposite would be true. Much more experience is needed in order to develop better intuition into what kind of test sequences should be generated for arbitrary classes with unknown errors. Ultimately, such intuition can be incorporated into heuristics to guide the selection of initial sequences and paths through the ADT trees, thus enhancing the test generator.

—Explore whether various strategies involving picking "special values" as parameters (such as inserting elements in ascending or descending order) help or hinder.

—Develop specification languages which are better able to express such aspects of object-oriented programming as side-effects, inheritance, and dynamic binding, then building tools based on them.

—Explore the impact of inheritance on testing.

While we have focused so far on unit testing, there are also many interesting questions pertaining to how to system-test object-oriented software. We hope to address these questions in the future, and ultimately, to use the results to expand and improve ASTOOT.

APPENDIX

```
            -- Buggy delete
        delete is
          local
            parent_ptr, child_ptr,
            l_child_ptr, r_child_ptr: INTEGER;
            parent, child: INTEGER;
            stop: BOOLEAN
        do
          if length > 0 then
            -- Move the last element to the first
            array.enter(1, array.entry(length));
            length := length - 1;

            from
              parent_ptr := 1;
              l_child_ptr := 2 * parent_ptr;
              r_child_ptr := 2 * parent_ptr + 1
            until
              stop or l_child_ptr >= length
              -----------------------^------------
              --   The correct statement is      --
              --   stop or l_child_ptr > length  --
              ------------------------------------
            loop
              -- find proper child
              if ((l_child_ptr = length) or
                  (array.entry(l_child_ptr) >
                   (array.entry(r_child_ptr)))) then
                child_ptr := l_child_ptr
              else
                child_ptr := r_child_ptr
              end; -- if

              parent := array.entry(parent_ptr);
              child := array.entry(child_ptr);
              if parent < child then
                -- swap
                array.enter(parent_ptr, child);
                array.enter(child_ptr, parent);
                parent_ptr := child_ptr;
                l_child_ptr := parent_ptr * 2;
                r_child_ptr := l_child_ptr + 1
              else
                stop := true
              end; -- if
            end; -- loop
          end; -- if
        end; -- delete
```

ACKNOWLEDGMENTS

The authors would like to thank Dan Hoffman and the anonymous referees for several useful suggestions.

REFERENCES

ANTOY, S. 1989. Systematic design of algebraic specifications. In *Proceedings of the 5th International Workshop on Software Specification and Design*. ACM, New York, 278–280.

ANTOY, S. AND HAMLET, D. 1992. Automatically checking an implementation against its formal specification. Tech. Rep. TR 91-1, Rev. 1, Portland State Univ., Portland, Ore.

BARTUSSEK, W. AND PARNAS, D. L. 1986. Using assertions about traces to write abstract specifications for software modules. In *Software Specification Techniques*. Addison-Wesley, Reading, Mass., 111–130.

BERNOT, G., GAUDEL, M. C., AND MARRE, B. 1991. Software testing based on formal specifications: A theory and a tool. *Softw. Eng. J. 6*, 6 (Nov.), 387–405.

CHOQUET, N. 1986. Test data generation using a prolog with constraints. In *Proceedings of the Workshop on Software Testing*. IEEE Computer Society, Washington, D.C., 132–141.

DOONG, R.-K. 1993. An approach to testing object-oriented programs. Ph.D. thesis, Polytechnic Univ., Brooklyn, N.Y. Also appeared as Computer Science Dept. Tech. Rep. No. PUCS-110-92.

DOONG, R.-K. AND FRANKL, P. G. 1991. Case studies on testing object-oriented programs. In *Proceedings of the Symposium on Testing, Analysis, and Verification (TAV4)*. ACM, New York, 165–177.

GANNON, J. D., HAMLET, R. G., AND MILLS, H. D. 1987. Theory of modules. *IEEE Trans. Softw. Eng. 13*, 7 (July), 820–829.

GANNON, J. D., McMULLIN, P. R., AND HAMLET, R. 1981. Data-abstraction implementation, specification, and testing. *ACM Trans. Program. Lang. Syst. 3*, 3 (July), 211–223.

GAUDEL, M. AND MARRE, B. 1988. Generation of test data from algebraic specifications. In *Proceedings of the 2nd Workshop on Software Testing, Verification, and Analysis*. IEEE Computer Society, Washington, D.C., 138–139.

GOGUEN, J. A. AND WINKLER, T. 1988. Introducing OBJ3. Tech. Rep. SRI-CSL-88-9, Computer Science Lab., SRI Int., Menlo Park, Calif.

GOGUEN, J. A., THATCHER, J. W., AND WAGNER, E. G. 1978. An initial algebra approach to the specification, correctness, and implementation of abstract data types. *Current Trends Program. Meth. 4*, 80–149.

GOLDBERG, A. AND ROBSON, D. 1983. *Smalltalk-80: The Language and its Implementation*. Addison-Wesley, Reading, Mass.

GUTTAG, J. J. 1980. Notes on type abstraction (version 2). *IEEE Trans. Softw. Eng. 6*, 1 (Jan.), 13–23.

GUTTAG, J. J. 1977. Abstract data types and the development of data structures. *Commun. ACM 20*, 6 (June), 396–404.

GUTTAG, J. J. AND HORNING, J. J. 1978. The algebraic specification of abstract data types. *Acta Inf. 10*, 1, 27–52.

GUTTAG, J. J., HOROWITZ, E., AND MUSSER, D. R. 1978. Abstract data types and software validation. *Commun. ACM 21*, 12 (Dec.), 1048–1064.

GUTTAG, J. J., HOROWITZ, E., AND MUSSER, D. R. 1977. Some extensions to algebraic specifications. In *Proceedings of Language Design for Reliable Software*. ACM, New York, 63–67.

HOFFMAN, D. AND BREALEY, C. 1989. Module test case generation. In *Proceedings of ACM SIGSOFT '89 3rd Symposium on Software Testing, Analysis and Verification*. ACM Press, New York, 97–102.

HOFFMAN, D. AND SNODGRASS, R. 1988. Trace specifications: Methodology and models. *IEEE Trans. Softw. Eng. 14*, 9 (Sept.), 1243–1252.

HOFFMAN, D. M. AND STROOPER, P. 1991. Automated module testing in Prolog. *IEEE Trans. Softw. Eng. 17*, 9 (Sept.), 934–943.

JALOTE, P. 1989. Testing the completeness of specifications. *IEEE Trans. Softw. Eng. 15*, 5 (May), 526–531.

JALOTE, P. AND CABALLERO, M. G. 1988. Automated testcase generation for data abstraction. In *Proceedings of COMPSAC 88*. IEEE Computer Society, Washington, D.C., 205–210.

KNUTH, D. E. AND BENDIX, P. B. 1970. Simple word problems in universal algebras. In *Computational Problems in Abstract Algebra*. Pergamon Press, Elmsford, N.Y., 263–297.

LISKOV, B. H. AND ZILLES, S. N. 1975. Specification techniques for data abstractions. *IEEE Trans. Softw. Eng. 1*, 1 (Mar.), 7–19.

257

MCLEAN, J. M. 1984. A formal method for the abstract specification of software. *J. ACM 31*, 3 (July), 600–627.

MEYER, B. 1988. *Object-Oriented Software Construction.* Prentice-Hall International, New York.

MUSSER, D. R. 1980. Abstract data type specification in the AFFIRM system. *IEEE Trans. Softw. Eng. 6*, 1 (Jan.), 24–32.

STROUSTRUP, B. 1991. *The C++ Programming Language.* 2nd ed. Addison-Wesley, Reading, Mass.

WEYUKER, E. J. 1982. On testing non-testable programs. *Comput. J. 25*, 4, 465–470.

Received December 1991; revised August 1993; accepted December 1993

Robert M. Poston

Automated
Testing
from Object Models

Object-oriented modeling techniques are popular with software developers, because these techniques offer ways to model or specify software systems with pictures. Many developers are delighted to forgo writing specifications in favor of drawing them. A number of commercially available software development tools help developers draw models (i.e., specifications) and capture the models for storage in repositories [9]. Since one of the basic tenets of object-oriented modeling is *reuse,* software practitioners often ask how object models used in analysis and design efforts and stored in repositories can be reused for testing.

Step by step through an example system, this article shows how common object models stored in repositories can be readied and reused for automated testing with a minimum of work and expense. The team that built the example system—a three-person, software testing research team from Interactive Development Environments—used an integrated set of software development tools that included a model-drawing tool called StP/OMT, a test case generator called T, and a test execution tool called XRunner. Long out of research and produced by several industry manufacturers, each of these kinds of tools performs one of the three basic functions that make automated model- or specification-based testing possible. To do such testing, specification information must first be recorded. A modeling tool offers a convenient way to capture the information. Test cases must be created from specification information, and a test case generator provides the only way to create those test cases automatically. Once created, test cases need to be exercised or run, and the most efficient way to do that is to employ an execution or capture-replay tool.

The availability of these already integrated tools enabled the team to measure the costs and benefits of reusing object models for testing with-

slightly familiar with OMT; the other two knew it well. The untrained person made a dedicated effort to learn OMT. Then all the team members reviewed the software life cycle as it is affected by OMT and automated testing tools. The team also reviewed the object, dynamic, and functional models that comprise the composite OMT model. From this joint review the members developed a common understanding of what was going to happen throughout the project and how OMT models would evolve into testing mechanisms. With OMT in mind, the team detailed the tasks that each member would perform at each step of the project.

Figure 1 shows two life cycles. In the OMT life cycle, testing follows implementation. When the OMT life

who had been a tester on numerous projects where various testing tools and manual methods were applied, claimed that at least a test case generator was needed for parallel OMT model and test development.

The tester asserted that if people on the team proceeded without a test case generator, they could lose their work of creating test cases. He explained that when an OMT model changes, test cases must be altered to match the change or be rendered invalid. The team either must throw out manually developed test cases and start from scratch to develop them again in accordance with the changed OMT model or start a painstaking effort to modify the test cases. However, if a test case generator was integrated with their modeling tool,

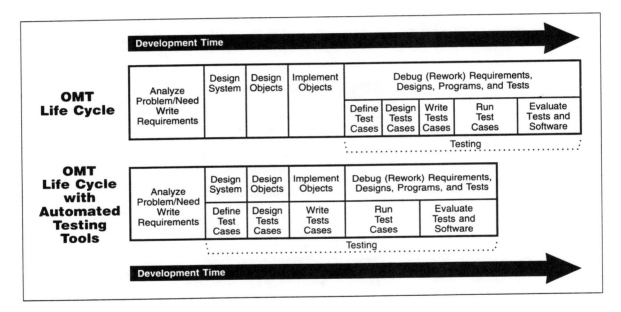

out having to deal with the sometimes confusing cost and productivity factors associated with doing the integration, or building and maintaining tools. For this project the team decided to use an industry-recognized modeling approach called the Object Modeling Technique (OMT) developed by James Rumbaugh and colleagues at General Electric during the early 1980s [11].

Choreographing the Project
One member of the team was only

cycle is supported by automated testing tools, the work of defining, designing, and writing test cases can be performed in parallel with the work of defining, designing, and implementing objects, thus significantly shortening the life cycle. The team's tools are shown in Figure 2 as they apply to the shortened life cycle activities.

One team member argued that test cases could be developed in parallel with the OMT model design without using testing tools. Another member,

Figure 1. Life cycles

any member of the team could change an OMT model, click on a button, and receive quickly new automatically created test cases that would match the OMT model. Since the team had an integrated set of software development and testing tools at its disposal, suggestions of manual testing efforts were dismissed.

The team needed to examine

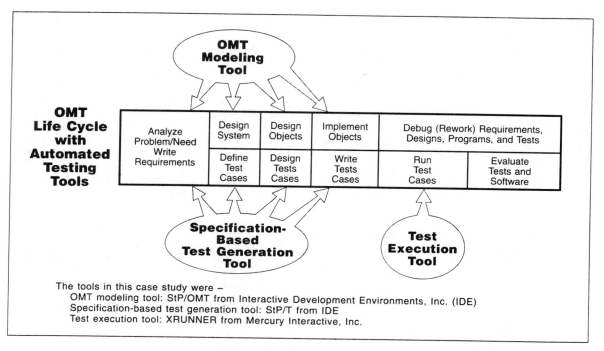

The tools in this case study were –
OMT modeling tool: StP/OMT from Interactive Development Environments, Inc. (IDE)
Specification-based test generation tool: StP/T from IDE
Test execution tool: XRUNNER from Mercury Interactive, Inc.

Figure 2. Life cycle testing tools

OMT models through the eyes of a tester. A tester looks to an OMT model, or to any other kind of model, for defined, detailed information from which to create test cases. A tester consults models to find definitions of actions that the software under test should perform and to discover definitions of data and data relationships that the actions will receive, manipulate, retain, and send. Additionally, a tester wants to find definitions of logic that convey how actions are restricted. Definitions of events and states are also important to a tester. Events signal times when actions or state transitions should take place, and states establish contexts in which actions may be performed. A model is test-ready when a tester can create from it occurrences or instances of data items, events, and states which cause logical conditions to be true and false and actions to be performed.

The people on the team knew that if models were test-ready, testing would be easy and inexpensive. If, however, the models were not test-ready, testing would be difficult and prolonged, because the tester would spend time and effort searching for testing information. The team looked at each of the three models prescribed by OMT to see what testing information the models contained naturally and how missing information could be added. (An earlier study, which is available from the author, examines structured analysis models for testability.)

The object model represents data (i.e., attributes and attribute values), relationships among data (i.e., associations, aggregations, or generalizations), and actions (i.e., operations or methods) on data. Certainly, testers need data from which to produce inputs to software under test. However, definitions of data contained in OMT object models are not complete enough for testing. For example, the object model calls for data to be defined with a name, type, and initial value but does not require data domain definitions. Consequently, a tester working from an object model would not know the range of values that a piece of data could have. A tester would be left asking: What are the high and low boundaries of this piece of data? What set of possible values can this data have? Which values should return a correct result, and which should return an error response?

On further examination of the object model, the team found that a piece of data could not be marked to show that the data might or might not be invalid. Sometimes, input data might be either valid or invalid depending on where the data came from and how well it was verified before its input to software under test. Suppose, for example, that data came from an end user entering a value into the software system for "number of items purchased." The end user could enter the number correctly or incorrectly. A tester must have enough information from which to create test cases for both correct and incorrect possibilities. Now consider a different situation where: 1) the number is coming from another software system, 2) the number has been verified in the other system, and 3) there is no possibility that the number is incorrect. The tester must have enough information to avoid creating unnecessary test cases that probe for incorrect inputs. So the tester wants the model to show a marker or a note that indicates that invalid values are either possible or impossible.

The flexibility of OMT and the team's object modeling tool would let the developers add data domain information to their object models with a simple note for each attribute they modeled [3]. The team members were pleased that they would not need to change OMT graphical notations as they made the models test-ready. They would just need to add new textual notes called testing annotations to their object models.

The team discussed whether or not to define and include such additional data domain information in the object model early on during analysis or later during design. The team decided that information that would be visible to the end user, in such locations as a report or in a window, should be defined at analysis time when the end user still has the opportunity to approve the definition. Information that would be hidden from the end user, such as the minimum size of a queue or a number represented as a long int or a short int, should be defined at design time.

The dynamic model provides graphical notations for events, event traces, states, state transitions, and hierarchies of states. It also allows notations for actions on transitions as well as actions and activities inside a state. Logic in the form of preconditions or guards also may be included in the dynamic model.

From a tester's point of view, the dynamic model is significantly better than the other two OMT models, because it can accommodate most of the behavioral information that a tester needs to create test cases. From a modeler's point of view, though, creating a test-ready dynamic model is challenging and time consuming. To make a dynamic model test-ready, a modeler must define every state and state transition in an object. Since a state is a set of data values (i.e., attribute values), and a state transition is a change in those values, the modeler needs also to define every action that transforms the values. Additionally, since actions can be performed only in a particular state, every action must be defined with a precondition, which is a logical expression that must be true before an action starts.

Fortunately, on this project, the integrated tool set would relieve the modelers of some of the burden of defining states, state transitions, actions, and conditions. The drawing tools would help the modelers produce state transition diagrams, and the annotation tools would help modelers add details to their graphical models. Navigation tools within the modeling tool would enable the modelers to move easily among their drawings, views of their drawings, and annotations.

Verification functions in the modeling and test case generation tools would check that the models conformed to OMT. These tools would check also that every word in every definition on every model had one and only one meaning and that every word was used in one and only one way. Finally, the verification tools would check that every definition was complete enough to enable test case generation. Once checked by these tools, modelers would know that their dynamic models conformed to OMT and that the definitions in the models were unambiguous, consistent, and test-ready.

The team tester pointed out that the OMT dynamic model, even when the modeler makes it tester friendly, does not accommodate temporal logic. Therefore, a requirement, such as event x must occur within 0.5 sec-onds of event y, could not be represented in or tested from an OMT dynamic model. But the tester noted correctly also that temporal logic is only necessary for that small percentage of software products that must operate under very tight timing constraints. Temporal logic was not needed on this project, and this team would consider OMT dynamic models to be test-ready as soon as they were checked by the automated verification tools. (Temporal logic features are planned for upcoming releases of the team's tools.)

The functional model completes the composite OMT model pictured in Figure 3. Since data was defined in the object model, and behavior was defined in the dynamic model, the only things left to be defined in the functional model are actions (i.e., operations, processes, or functions) and constraints on actions. The ac-

Figure 3. OMT model

Figure 4. CSS requirement

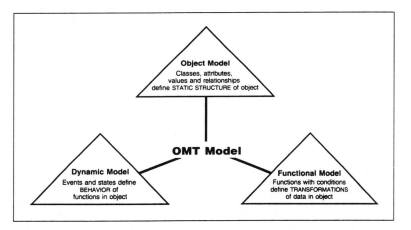

The Customer Service System shall perform the following actions:

Action 1. CSS shall manage a list of currently available products.
Action 2. CSS shall manage a current base price for each available product.
Action 3. CSS shall allow discounts to be applied to any price quote.
Action 4. CSS shall produce price quotes for any quantity of any available product with any valid discount within 0.5 seconds.

tions and constraints to be defined in the functional model must include all the actions and constraints named in the object and dynamic models. Typical functional model actions include data transformations, manipulations, and storage. Typical constraints on actions include preconditions and postconditions.

The OMT functional model will serve this project much the same as an old-fashioned data flow diagram would. It will help the tester identify the inputs to actions, whether the inputs come from the outside world or from retained data stores. Just as a data flow diagram includes a specification for each process, the functional model includes a specification for each action. Pre- and post-conditions should be defined as part of the action, because they represent the logic that controls the processing of an action.

OMT was a carefully developed prescription, that if followed rigorously, would lead to sound models. With minor additions, the OMT

models could be made test-ready. Success now depended on each person performing his development or testing tasks conscientiously.

Each person accepted one or two roles. One person would be the analyst/tester who would create the models and test cases at the system level. The other two people would be developers. Developer 1 would define

the model (i.e., specification) for a graphical user interface (GUI) and then design and code the GUI. Developer 2 would define, design, and write the operational code.

Developing the System

For purposes of its case study the team needed to develop a system large enough to show many testing

---

Figure 5. A sample scenario

Figure 6. CSS object model

```
Start Scenario:
        Caller calls Agent
        Agent asks how the Caller can be helped
        Caller asks how much a selected product costs
        Agent enters into CSS the selected product name
        CSS displays the base price of the selected product
        Agent asks Caller how many copies will be needed
        Caller tells Agent the quantity that will be purchased
        Agent enters into CSS the quantity to be quoted
        CSS displays the total purchase price
        Agent tells Caller the total purchase price
        Agent asks Caller if maintenance should be included
        Caller tells Agent to include maintenance costs
        Agent enters maintenance request into CSS
        CSS displays total cost including maintenance
        Agent tells Caller the total cost including maintenance
        Agent asks Caller for mailing information
        Caller tells Agent mailing information
        Agent enters into CSS the mailing information
        Agent terminates call
        CSS prints Price Quote and a mailing label
        CSS stores the Price Quote for Retention Period
        Agent mails Price Quote
End Scenario
```

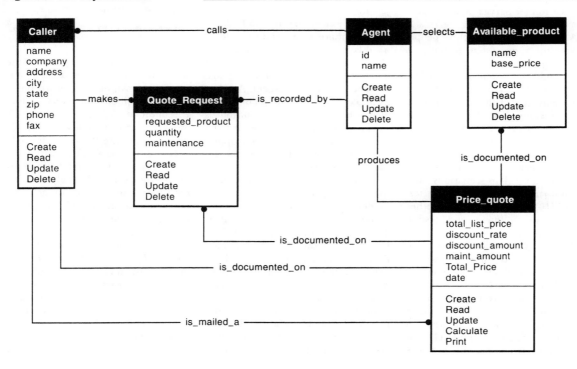

263

problems, yet small enough to be understood from one window. Also, the system had to be complete enough to show how different GUI objects could be modeled and tested and to show most, if not all, aspects of OMT. Developer 1 had heard about the following problem. It met the team's requirements.

An otherwise efficient company could not provide timely price quotes to its customers. Sales agents at the company were taking days or even weeks to calculate price quotes for prospective customers. A formal needs analysis was launched to investigate the problem. Systems analysts determined quantitatively that the company could increase its sales if price quotes could be made promptly. A genuine need for a faster pricing system existed.

Analysts at the company then looked at various ways to satisfy this need. They explored the possibility of adding sales staff, simplifying quote procedures, or using standardized spreadsheets. Finally, the analysts recommended that a centralized software system be built to calculate price quotes automatically.

Adopting this problem for its case study, the team decided to build an automated price-calculating system. The Customer Service System (CSS) was conceived.

A needs analysis helps people choose the right system to build. A precise specification or model helps them build the system right. In Figure 4 is a list of high-level or abstract requirements that the team assumed for this study. This list documents what the team originally agreed that the CSS system should do. In Figure 5 is a scenario that shows how the team thought the system would be used. This scenario is similar to a run [7], use case [4], or test script [10] found in various other software development and testing methodologies.

From Figures 4 and 5 the team analyst identified things or objects that should be modeled for the system. He identified Callers, Products, and Price Quotes as the most important objects to be modeled. After identifying these objects, he went on to define attributes, identify relationships between objects, and organize

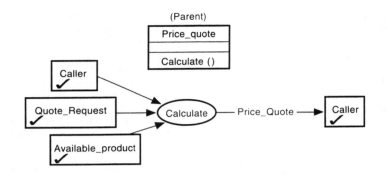

ActsOnlyIf: (Requested_Product as_specified)

This is a restrictive condition. The words "as_specified" mean the values of the attribute "Requested_Product" must be as defined in data domain definitions.

ActsOnlyIf: (Requested_Product == Available_Product)

This is a relative condition. The symbol "==" means the values of the two attributes must be equal. Relative conditions with relative operators such as "greater than", "less than", etc. are allowed also.

ActsOnlyIf: ((Requested_Product as_specified)
&& (Requested_Product == Available_Product))

This is a compound condition. The symbol "&&" means a logical "and". The normal Boolean operators such as "or" and "not" are allowed also.

classes. He worked through this process several times to produce the object model shown in Figure 6. Notice in the object model that both Caller and Agent are a class and that calls is a relationship between the two classes. That relationship can be read left to right as an English language sentence: Caller calls Agent. Another example of an easy-to-follow modeled relationship is Agent produces Price_quote. The tester saw that the information on the model mapped closely to the information in the scenario in Figure 5.

After completing the object model, the analyst produced the behavior model which contained three states: empty or initial, in process or calculating, and cleared or printing. Last he produced the functional model, illustrated in Figure 7. The check marks on the functional model indicate that the checked items are modeled on the object model. The class symbol labeled "(Parent)" on the functional model indicates that the function being modeled, called calculate, is a function from the class

Figure 7. Functional model

Figure 8. Sample preconditions

Price_Quote. While creating the functional model, the analyst was careful to envision and record possible preconditions for every action. Preconditions are called for by OMT and are necessary for testing. Sample preconditions are shown in Figure 8.

Going beyond OMT to bring the models up to the test-ready standard set by the team, the analyst added data domain information to each data item or attribute. Figure 9 shows samples of data domain information that the analyst added to make the object model test-ready. The first two samples in Figure 9 document an enumerated list and a range of values for numerical data types. The second two samples show an enumerated list and a range of values for character or string data types. Figure 10 shows a sample annotation that the analyst added to data definitions in the object model to indicate that invalid values were possible and should be probed.

The test cases. As soon as the OMT model for CSS was completed, the analyst created test cases directly from the model. Usually people in software development first define, then design, and finally code and test their products. However, because the CSS analyst used an integrated set of tools, he was able to generate test cases immediately that would exercise all requirements and probe for Most Probable Errors [9]. The compelling advantage of producing test cases early in the software life cycle is that developers can use those test cases as references against which to create specification-consistent designs and code free of common failures.

To produce test cases for CSS, the analyst clicked on three buttons on his tabletop tool interface: "T Testing," "Extract," and "Generate." These buttons invoked the specification-based, fault-directed test case generator in the tool set. The integration of the modeling tool and the test case generator was so complete that a few menu buttons were all that the analyst saw of the generator. Of course, a great deal was going on behind those buttons.

When the analyst selected "T Testing," the generator's testing menu appeared. When the analyst clicked on "Extract," the modeling tool converted the graphical and textual information captured in the OMT models into a text-only file called a Software Description File (SDF). The SDF, written in accordance with IEEE Std-1175 (see [2]), was a formal-language representation of all the OMT models that the analyst created for the CSS. When the analyst selected "Generate," the test case generator read the SDF and produced test cases.

The generator created test cases by applying a family of six test design techniques [1, 8] to the information in the SDF. Each technique used a particular set of information from the SDF to probe for a certain group of software defects, as illustrated in Figure 11.

The techniques or rules that a tool uses to create *functional test cases* are simple. For every specified action in an OMT model, the tool must create

```
Name: Discount_Type
    Type: real
    Has Values: 5.0, 10.0, 15.0, 20.0, 25.0

Name: Base_price_type
    Type: real
    has resolution: 1.00
    has minimum value: 10000.00
    has maximum value: 100000.00

Name: Person_Name_Type
    Type: string
    has values: //[A-Z][a-z]\{1,20\} [A-Z][a-z]\{1,25\}//

Name: Person_Name_Type2
    Type: string
    has values: "Lee O""", "John Doe",
        "Johnny B. Good", "Lois Lane",
        "Rhoshandiatellyneshiaunneveshenk Williams"
```

```
Name: Person_Name_Type2
    Type: string
    has invalid subdomain: abnormal
```

If the "has invalid subdomain" clause is present, the data item may have invalid values. If it is not present, it may NOT have invalid values.

To reduce the number of possible invalid values the key word "abnormal" may be replaced with any of the following kew words: out_of_type, out_of_bounds, below_bounds, or above_bounds.

Figure 9. Sample data domain definitions

Figure 10. Valid/invalid note

at least one test case. The test case must contain at least one name and one value for every input and the name of at least one expected result.

To a tester, functional testing is so obvious and elementary that it seems trivial. However, a test case generation tool must incorporate the rules of functional testing to guarantee that every function gets exercised at least once. Functional test cases are very good at discovering missing functions. However, as its name implies, functional testing addresses functions only. It provides no guidance for selecting the input values to use. Input value selection is governed by the rules of the test design techniques discussed next.

History shows that most software failures are detected by a tester or an end user applying an input at its first or last or highest or lowest valid values (i.e., boundaries). To detect boundary value failures, the team's test case generator went beyond simple boundary value analysis to create test cases that would probe just above and just below each boundary. These "adjacent" test cases expedited debugging by pinpointing for the tester where a failure occurred.

Every input to software under test has a set of possible values called a domain, which is divided into a valid and invalid subdomain. Sometimes subdomains are further divided into smaller groups called *equivalence classes*. In equivalence class partitioning, the software under test should process every value or member in a class in the same or equivalent manner. Every class is treated a little differently by the code, so each class represents a functional variation. The test case generator produced test cases that would probe every input at least once for every subdomain and every equivalence class specified in the model.

The *cause-effect graphing technique* is more accurately called the logic or condition testing technique. In this technique every condition is probed for a true or false value. Since conditions can have only true and false values, this technique offers an efficient way to test Boolean logic. The test

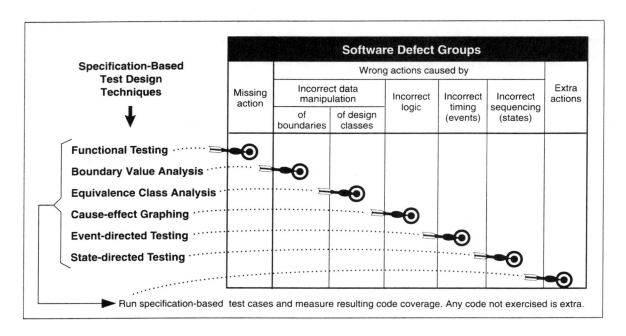

Figure 11. Test design techniques and defect coverage

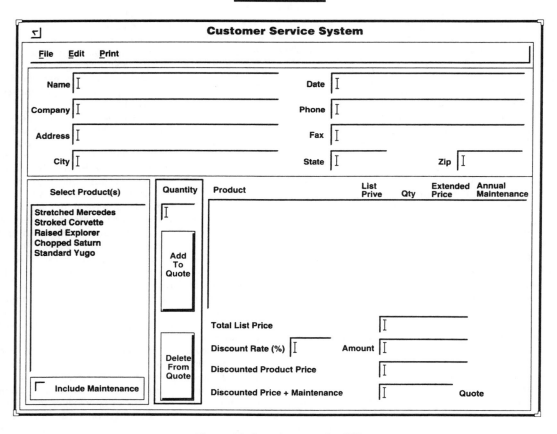

Figure 12. Input screen for CSS

Although most experts would not recommend it,

reference testing is how many testers
derive expected outputs

in the work world.

case generator created test cases for the CSS that probed every condition on every action for true and false values.

An *event* is an occurrence in the outside world that causes an action, such as a state transition, to take place in the software world. A computer operator hits a backup command. That event causes the software to respond by making a backup copy. The test case generator produced test cases that exercised every event at least once.

As discussed earlier, a *state* in OMT is a set of data or attribute values or a logical relationship among the values. A state transition is a change in those values. Therefore, any test cases created to exercise states and state transitions may be redundant with test cases created to exercise functions, data boundaries, data classes, and conditions. The team's test case generator was smart enough to avoid creating unnecessary test cases that would have been produced by the state-directed technique.

The team was able to reuse code from an earlier testing-through-modeling experiment for this study. In the previous experiment, Developer 1 used a GUI-building tool to create a single-window interface for the CSS. Developer 1 modified the interface slightly to make it suitable as shown in Figure 12. Only standard windows objects appear in the window. Most are input objects that allow end users (i.e., sales agents) to enter information into the software. Some fields are edit fields: Name, Phone, Fax, etc. To use an edit field, a user positions the cursor over the field, clicks the left mouse button, and types input values.

The object labeled "Select Product(s)" is a pick list which invites a user to choose one item in the list. The buttons labeled "Add to Quote" and "Delete from Quote" are push buttons; they are self-explanatory. The box to the left of the label "Include Maintenance" is a check or toggle box. A user clicks on this box once to include maintenance, twice to exclude maintenance.

After Developer 1 modified the interface, Developer 2 wrote operational C++ code to perform the price calculations. Since the rest of the code was reused from another project or tool produced, programming progressed quickly.

Figure 13 shows the first test case generated for the CSS. It will be the first test case to run or be executed on the CSS code. Notice that this test case includes a generation date, a unique identifier that names the test case, the name of the action exercised, and the state or window where the action is accessible. The information below the first dashed line is the input information. Each input has a label such as Caller_Name. To run this test case manually, the tester matches a label on the test case to a label on the window. (Some window labels are shortened to save space.) The tester then enters the value from the test case into the corresponding field in the window.

At the bottom of the test case, the test case generator has provided names of expected outputs. However, the generator does not produce expected output values. Most testing experts and researchers believe that a tool that could deliver expected output values is impractical, because then the tool itself could replace code under development [1, p. 458]. Testers must deal with expected output values in one of four ways: range checking, manual projections, simulation, or reference testing.

Range checking amounts to specifying the range of possible values that an expected output can have. When a test case is executed, the actual output is captured and checked to see if it falls within the specified range. Range checking is simple and inexpensive, but it is inaccurate, because it does not verify specific output values.

A manual projection occurs when a tester uses brainpower and paper and pencil to derive a specific output value. Simulation involves development of temporary or substitute code that is equivalent to the software being developed. Such code acts as a simulator that produces explicit expected output values for a given test case. Both manual projection and simulation produce accurate expected output values, but they are expensive undertakings and, probably, are justified only in special circumstances: if human life is affected, for example. However, with the advent of new code generation tools, simulators are becoming more practical to build. Simulation is getting another look from the software-testing industry.

Although most experts would not recommend it, reference testing is how many testers derive expected outputs in the work world. In reference testing, expected outputs are not provided the first time a test case is exercised. Instead, test cases are applied to the software under test, and the actual outputs are captured. The tester then judges that a test case passes or fails. When a test case passes, its actual outputs are recorded and become reference outputs. Every time a test case is run again (regression testing), the reference outputs are used as expected outputs. Reference testing is risky from the technical perspective. But because it is less costly than other alternatives, it is a common way to derive expected output values.

The team tester used manual projections to verify that actual outputs were the same as expected outputs in key test cases that probed for inputs at high and low boundaries and inputs at normal or reference values. The tester used reference testing to derive expected outputs for a few test cases.

Test Case Execution

With test cases, code, and expected outputs prepared, the tester was ready to execute test cases on the code and to compare expected with actual outputs to determine if the CSS software passed or failed its test cases. Once it received test cases from the generator, the test execution tool went to work.

The tester provided two operational descriptions of the test execution tool to help the study team understand how test cases are run automatically. The first described how an execution tool works by itself; the second explained how it works as integrated with the team's test case generator.

"In standalone operation the execution tool works like a VCR or tape recorder," the tester began. To visualize how this tool works, picture information flowing through the CSS. Now imagine a point in that information flow where the tool is inserted, say right behind the computer keyboard-monitor unit. When the tool is in its capture mode, it records all information flowing past that point. When the tool is in the playback mode, it stops incoming information and plays back what has been recorded. A tester inserts the tool into the system, sets the tool to capture mode, and enters test case information manually. When the software produces an actual output value, the execution tool records that value. The tester completes execution of the test case by judging if the system software passed or failed that case. This procedure must be repeated for every test case. Later, if the software changes, the tester may rerun selected test cases to see how changes affect execution. This rerunning is called regression testing and can be performed entirely by the execution tool."

"In integrated operation the first test case is run the same way as in standalone operation. The difference is seen in the execution of all test cases that run after the first one. As the first test case is run, the execu-

tion tool will produce a script or recording of information as if flows past the capture point. By parameterizing that script and adding a simple program loop to encompass all test cases for the CSS, the tester produces a master script which will execute all test cases without further human intervention."

In this study the execution of the first test case took about 30 minutes.

Figure 13. Sample test case

casedate: Wed Dec 22 10:22:58 1993

CASENAME   01000001
EXERCISES   Calculate_A_Price_Quote
IN STATE   Customer Service
            System Window
PURPOSE   all inputs at reference
            values

INPUT DATA
Name – Value

Caller_Name
    – "Lee O"
Caller_Company
    – "Harry's Bar & Grill"
Caller_Phone_Number
    – "012-012-0123"
Caller_Street_Address
    – "456 Main St."
Caller_Fax_Number
    – "012-012-0123"
Caller_City
    – "Little Rock"
Caller_State
    _ "MO"
Caller_Zip
    – "01234"
Requested_Product
    _ "Standard Yugo"
Quantity
    – 5000
Maintenance_Request
    _ "FALSE"
Discount
    – 20.0
Add_Command
    – "Add_To_Quote"
Delete_Command
    – "DoNot_Delete_From_Quote"

OUTPUT DATA
Name – Value

Date – ""
Product – ""
List_Price – ""
Qty – ""
Extended_Price – " "
Annual Maintenance – ""
Total_List_Price – ""
Discount_Amount – " "
Discount_Product_Price – " "
Discount Price + Maintenance – ""

The tester modified the recorded script to produce the master script in less than one hour. After the first test case ran, each of the other CSS test cases ran in less than one minute. Since all the test cases were similar, differing only in values they contained, execution would have taken about 30 minutes per test case without the integrated tools. The team realized a 30:1 reduction in test execution time by having its execution tool integrated with the test case generator.

Evaluating the Project

The team's modeling tool and test case generator were mutually dependent on the information content of the test-ready models. The test execution tool, although it ran the generated test cases efficiently, worked independently from the models. Therefore, for this study, the execution tool was not as significant as the modeling tool and the test case generator.

In less than one day the team analyst created a test-ready OMT model. In less than two minutes the test case generator created 347 test cases, the smallest number of test cases that would exercise every function and every Most Probable Error in the CSS at least once.

In less than five days the two developers assembled, modified, and supplemented the code for the CSS. In less than one day, the test execution tool ran and evaluated all the test cases.

The team debated about the cost it incurred in making OMT models test-ready. One developer insisted there was no real cost for collecting testing information. He maintained that gathering this information is absolutely necessary not only for testing but for development, too. "For example," asked the developer, "how could a programmer code the price_quote calculation reliably if he didn't know the minimum and maximum values that a price could have?" The developer saw the expense of collecting detailed specification information as an unavoidable cost integral to every software development project. Since every project must pay the cost, the only question is: when will it pay?

The team determined that the small labor cost of supplementing the standard OMT models with details did not exceed five percent of the total modeling cost for the CSS. The team spent an eight-hour day modeling, and five percent of that time or 24 minutes went to making the models test-ready.

To measure return on their investment, the team members had to find out what the investment enabled them to save. Because they had made their models test-ready, they were able to press a few buttons and have their test case generator create test cases for them, thereby saving or avoiding the cost of manual test case creation. Capers Jones, well-known industry statistician, gave the team a baseline against which to compare its savings. Without tools, the average tester in the U.S. produces test cases by hand at a rate of about 20 to 300 per month [5]. Therefore, for an investment of 24 minutes of model supplementation, the team saved a month of manual labor during test case creation.

Prior to this study the team tester did a literature search to try to find earlier publications that addressed automated specification-based testing from object models. The only writings uncovered were directed at code-based testing of object-oriented programs, and none addressed automation or related any laboratory or field experience. Recognizing that professional acceptance of technical ideas starts from expert opinion, advances to simulated or laboratory studies, then to field experiments, and finally to comparative analyses, the team saw the importance of offering its work as a simulated case study. While this one small study by itself cannot be statistically relevant, it does open the door to further research as well as to practical implementation.

Acknowledgment

Thanks to the many people at IDE who contributed to this article. Thanks also to Frederick Eddy and James Rumbaugh at GE for sharing their expertise about OMT with me.

References

1. Beizer, B. *Software Testing Techniques.* Second ed., Van Nostrand Reinhold, New York, 1990, p. 458.
2. IEEE. *IEEE/CS Standard 1175, A Framework for Computing System Tool Interconnections.* IEEE, New York, 1991.
3. Interactive Development Environments, Inc. *Software through Pictures/Object Modeling Technique.* IDE, San Francisco, Calif., 1993, p. 10.
4. Jacobson, I., *Object-Oriented Software Engineering: A User Case Driven Approach.* Addison-Wesley, Reading, Mass., 1992.
5. Jones, C. *Applied Software Measurement.* McGraw-Hill, New York, 1991, pp. 158–175.
6. Kramer, M. Large APP development: A job for OO A&D tools. *Software* (Jan. 1994), 39–48.
7. Musa, J., and Ackerman, F. Quantifying software validation: When to stop testing. *IEEE Softw. 6,* 3 (May 1989), 19–27.
8. Myers, G. *The Art of Software Testing.* Wiley & Sons, New York, 1979.
9. Poston, R. Preventing the most probable errors in requirements. *IEEE Softw. 4,* 5 (Sept. 1987), 81–83.
10. Poston, R. A complete toolkit for the software tester. *Am. Program. 4,* 4 (Apr. 1991), 34.
11. Rumbaugh, J. *Object-Oriented Modeling and Design.* Prentice-Hall, Englewood Cliffs, N.J., 1991.